# *Techniques for*
# *Exploring Personal Markets*

# Financial Advisor Series                     *Walt J. Woerheide, Editor*

## *Sales Skills Techniques*

*Techniques for Prospecting: Prospect or Perish*

*Techniques for Exploring Personal Markets*

*Techniques for Meeting Client Needs*

*Ethics for the Financial Services Professional*

## *Product Essentials*

*Essentials of Annuities*

*Essentials of Business Insurance*

*Essentials of Disability Income Insurance*

*Essentials of Life Insurance Products*

*Essentials of Long-term Care Insurance*

*Essentials of Multiline Insurance Products*

## *Planning Foundations*

*Foundations of Estate Planning*

*Foundations of Retirement Planning*

*Foundations of Financial Planning: An Overview*

*Foundations of Financial Planning: The Environment*

*Foundations of Investment Planning*

*Financial Advisor Series: Sales Skills Techniques*

# Techniques for Exploring Personal Markets

Allen C. McLellan
Kirk S. Okumura
Glenn E. Stevick, Jr.

THE AMERICAN COLLEGE PRESS

*©️ 2009 The American College Press*
*270 S. Bryn Mawr Avenue*
*Bryn Mawr, PA 19010*
*(888) AMERCOL (263-7265)*
*www.theamericancollege.edu*

*Library of Congress Control Number*
*ISBN-13: 978-1-932819-77-9*
*ISBN-10: 1-932819-77-0*

*Printed in the United States of America*

# Contents

# *Preface*

The mission of this textbook is to develop your professionalism as a financial advisor marketing financial services and products and prospecting for clients. The purpose of this textbook is to help the financial advisor develop marketing skills to be able to obtain clients and have a successful professional career in the financial services industry. The text is organized around the life cycle of an individual, and discussions are based on the general characteristics and financial needs of individuals in each life-cycle segment. The text will also analyze the technical aspects of different types of financial and insurance products corresponding to these life-cycle segments. It is our objective that this textbook have the right blend of technical knowledge and practical information to accomplish its mission.

While much of the text material will be new to you, some material will, no doubt, refresh previous knowledge. In either case, the text material will be both valuable and necessary if you aspire to be successful in the financial services marketplace. However, the benefits you gain from studying the text material will be directly proportional to the effort you expend. So read each chapter carefully, and answer both the essay and the multiple-choice review questions for each chapter (preferably before looking in the back of the textbook for the answers); to do less would be to deprive yourself of a unique opportunity to become familiar with life insurance and to learn more about selling it.

The textbook includes numerous educational features designed to help you focus your study of life insurance. Each chapter contains

- learning objectives
- examples, figures, and lists
- key terms and concepts
- review questions (essay format)
- self-test questions (multiple-choice format)

The back of the textbook includes a glossary, answers to review and self-test questions, and an index.

Finally all of the individuals noted on the acknowledgments page made this a better textbook, and we are grateful. However, if some errors have eluded us, we are solely responsible, and take full credit for giving those of you who find any errors the exhilarating intellectual experience produced by such discovery.

Allen C. McLellan
Kirk S. Okumura
Glenn E. Stevick, Jr.

# *The American College*

The American College® is an independent, nonprofit, accredited institution founded in 1927 that offers professional certification and graduate-degree distance education to men and women seeking career growth in financial services.

The LUTC program at The American College offers the LUTCF professional designation. Its curriculum is designed to introduce students to the technical side of financial services while at the same time providing them with the requisite sales training skills. Attainment of the LUTCF signifies a commitment to professionalism, continuing education, and excellence in ethical conduct. In addition, it prepares students to undertake more advanced College programs.

In 2003 The College debuted the Financial Advisor Series, self-study courses that provide product knowledge and help professionals develop sales and presentation skills.

The Solomon S. Huebner School® of The American College administers the Chartered Life Underwriter (CLU®); the Chartered Financial Consultant (ChFC®); the Chartered Advisor for Senior Living (CASL™); the Registered Health Underwriter (RHU®); the Registered Employee Benefits Consultant (REBC®); and the Chartered Leadership Fellow® (CLF®) professional designation programs. In addition, the Huebner School also administers The College's CFP Board–registered education program, for those individuals interested in pursuing CFP® certification, the CFP® Certification Curriculum.

Finally, the Richard D. Irwin Graduate School® of The American College offers the master of science in financial services (MSFS) degree, the Graduate Financial Planning Track (another CFP Board-registered education program), and several graduate-level certificates that concentrate on specific subject areas. The National Association of Estate Planners & Councils has named The College as the provider of the education required to earn its prestigious AEP designation.

The American College is accredited by:

The Middle States Commission on Higher Education
3624 Market Street
Philadelphia, PA 19104
267.284.5000

The Middle States Commission on Higher Education is a regional accrediting agency recognized by the U.S. Secretary of Education and the Commission on Recognition of Postsecondary Accreditation. Middle States accreditation is an expression of confidence in an institution's mission and goals, performance, and resources. It attests that in the judgment of the Commission on Higher Education, based on the results of an internal institutional self-study and an evaluation by a team of outside peer

---

Certified Financial Planner Board of Standards, Inc., owns the marks CFP®, CERTIFIED FINANCIAL PLANNER™, and CFP (with flame logo)®, which it awards to individuals who successfully complete initial and ongoing certification requirements.

observers assigned by the Commission, an institution is guided by well-defined and appropriate goals; that it has established conditions and procedures under which its goals can be realized; that it is accomplishing them substantially; that it is so organized, staffed, and supported that it can be expected to continue to do so; and that it meets the standards of the Middle States Association. The American College has been accredited since 1978.

The American College does not discriminate on the basis of race, religion, sex, handicap, or national and ethnic origin in its admissions policies, educational programs and activities, or employment policies.

The American College is located at 270 S. Bryn Mawr Avenue, Bryn Mawr, PA 19010. The toll-free telephone number of the Professional Education Services is (888) AMERCOL (263-7265), the fax number is (610) 526-1300, and www.theamericancollege.edu is the home page address.

# *Acknowledgments*

This textbook was written by Allen C. McLellan, LUTC author/editor and Assistant Professor of Insurance, Kirk Okumura, LUTC author/editor, and Glenn Stevick, Jr., LUTC author/editor and Assistant Professor of Insurance at The American College.

For their valuable contribution to the development of this textbook, appreciation is extended to Patricia Cheers, Permissions Editor and to Jane Hassinger, who provided production assistance.

Special thanks are also extended to Roy M. Lerner, LUTCF, of Walnut Creek, California, a dedicated and experienced LUTC moderator, who offered his editorial comments in many extended phone calls to the authors. Hundreds of dedicated people, such as Roy, make the LUTC program a special and exciting educational experience.

To all of these individuals, without whom this textbook would not have been possible, The College expresses its sincere appreciation and gratitude.

Walter Woerheide, Academic Dean
The American College

# *About the Authors*

**Allen C. McLellan, LUTCF, CLU®, ChFC®, CASL®, CFP®,** is an Assistant Professor of Insurance at The American College. His responsibilities include writing and preparing text materials for LUTC and FSS programs, including *Essentials of Disability Income Insurance* and *Essentials of Annuities,* He is also responsible for *Foundations of Financial Planning: (An Overview), Foundations of Financial Planning: (The Process), and Foundations of Investment Planning.*

Mr. McLellan earned his BS degree from the U.S. Air Force Academy and served for over 21 years as an Air Force officer. He earned his MS in Aeronautical Engineering from the Air Force Institute of Technology. During his military career, Mr. McLellan taught mathematics at the Air Force Academy and served as the Director of Evaluation for the Air Force's Squadron Officer School. After his military retirement, Mr. McLellan worked for nearly 16 years as an insurance agent, registered representative, and financial planner. He is a member of NAIFA (National Association of Insurance and Financial Advisors), the Air Force Association, and the Military Officers Association of America.

**Kirk S. Okumura** is an author/editor at The American College. His responsibilities at The College include writing and preparing text materials for the LUTC and FSS programs. His current course responsibilities include *Techniques for Exploring Personal Markets, Essentials of Multiline Insurance Products, and Foundations of Retirement Planning.* He also is responsible for portions of *Techniques for Prospecting: Prospect or Perish* and has written material for *Essentials of Long-Term Care Insurance, Foundations of Financial Planning: An Overview*, and *Foundations of Financial Planning: The Process.* In addition to his course responsibilities, Mr. Okumura writes articles for *Advisor Today,* the national magazine distributed to members of NAIFA.

Before joining The College, Mr. Okumura worked for State Farm Insurance as a supervisor in a regional life/health office and as a trainer in the Pennsylvania regional office. Mr. Okumura earned a BS degree from The Pennsylvania State University.

**Glenn E. Stevick, Jr., MA, CLU, ChFC, LUTCF** is an author/editor and Assistant Professor of Insurance at The American College. His responsibilities at The College include writing and preparing course materials for the *Techniques for Meeting Client Needs,,Essentials of Life Insurance Products, Foundations of Estate Planning* and *Essentials of Business Insurance* courses. He writes articles for *Advisor Today,* the national magazine distributed to members of NAIFA. He currently teaches insurance courses for The American College in the CLU, ChFC and LUTCF designation programs.

Before joining The College, Mr. Stevick worked for New York Life as a training supervisor for 15 years in its South Jersey office. He previously served as an agent with New York Life for more than two years. In addition to his insurance industry experience, Mr. Stevick has taught psychology at the college level and worked in various educational and mental health programs. Mr. Stevick earned his BA degree from Villanova University and his MA degree from Duquesne University. He holds the CLU and ChFC designations from The American College and the

LUTCF designation from The American College and NAIFA (National Association of Insurance and Financial Advisors).

# Special Notes to Advisors

**Text Materials Disclaimer**

This publication is designed to provide accurate and authoritative information about the subject covered. While every precaution has been taken in the preparation of this material to ensure that it is both accurate and up-to-date, it is still possible that some errors eluded detection. Moreover, some material may become inaccurate and/or outdated either because it is time sensitive or because new legislation will make it so. Still other material may be viewed as inaccurate because your company's products and procedures are different from those described in the textbook. Therefore the authors and The American College assume no liability for damages resulting from the use of the information contained in this textbook. The American College is not engaged in rendering legal, accounting, or other professional advice. If legal or other expert advice is required, the services of an appropriate professional should be sought.

**Caution Regarding Use of Illustrations**

The illustrations, sales ideas, and approaches in this textbook are not to be used with the public unless you have obtained approval from your company. Your company's general support of The American College's programs for training and educational purposes does not constitute blanket approval of the sales ideas and approaches presented in this textbook unless so communicated in writing by your company.

**Use of the Term Financial Advisor or Advisor**

Use of the term *financial advisor* as it appears in this textbook is a generic reference to professional members of our reading audience. It is used interchangeably with the term *advisor* so as to avoid unnecessary redundancy. Financial advisor takes the place of the following terms:

| | |
|---|---|
| account executive | life insurance agent |
| agent | life underwriter |
| associate | planner |
| broker (stock or insurance) | practitioner |
| financial consultant | producer |
| financial planner | property & casualty agent |
| financial planning professional | registered investment advisor |
| financial services professional | registered representative |
| health underwriter | senior advisor |
| insurance professional | |

**Answers to the Questions in the Textbook**

The answers to all essay and multiple-choice questions in this textbook are based on the text materials as written.

# About the Financial Advisor Series

The mission of The American College is to raise the level of professionalism of its students and, by extension, the financial services industry as a whole. As an educational product of The College, the Financial Advisor Series shares in this mission. As knowledge is the key to professionalism, a thorough and comprehensive reading of each textbook in the series will help the practitioner advisor to better service his or her clients. Offering superior service is a task made all the more difficult because the typical client is becoming ever more financially sophisticated with each passing day and demands that his or her financial advisor be knowledgeable about the latest products and planning methodologies. By providing practitioner advisors in the financial services industry with up-to-date, authoritative information about marketing and sales techniques, products, and planning, the textbooks of the Financial Advisor Series will enable many practitioner advisors to develop and maintain a high level of professional competence.

When all textbooks in the Financial Advisor Series are completed, the Series will encompass 15 titles spread across three separate subseries, each with a special focus. The first subseries, *Sales Skills Techniques,* will focus on enhancing the practitioner advisor's marketing and sales skills, but will also cover some product knowledge and planning considerations. The second subseries, *Product Essentials,* will focus on product knowledge, but will also delve into marketing and sales skills as well as planning considerations. The third subseries, *Planning Foundations,* will focus on various planning considerations and processes that form the foundation for a successful career as a financial services professional. When appropriate, product knowledge and sales and marketing skills will also be touched upon.

A full list of current and planned titles can be found in the front pages of this textbook.

# Overview of the Textbook

*Techniques for Exploring Personal Markets* explores how to create a basic marketing plan utilizing target marketing and life-cycle marketing concepts. The core of the textbook is organized around the life cycle of an individual. It examines the common characteristics and major financial product and planning needs of four adult life-cycle market segments.

Chapter 1 introduces the selling/planning process and philosophy that undergirds all of The College's FA courses. It then describes the target marketing process and prospecting methods.

The life-cycle marketing concept and related life-cycle market segments are introduced in Chapter 2. The chapter closes with a look at creating awareness of your personal brand and products and approaching prospects for appointments.

Chapter 3 examines the young-adult market segment. There is also a discussion of universal financial needs, financial planning areas, and the financial planning pyramid. It then reviews disability income insurance, one of the major needs members of this market segment have.

The middle-years adult market segment is described in Chapter 4. The chapter also looks at life insurance, a prominent need of many in this market segment. It closes with an overview of some special markets created by changes in societal norms, demographics, and legislation.

Chapter 5 looks at retirement planning and investments. Chapter 6 resumes the overview of the adult life-cycle market segments with a look at the mature-adult market segment. Medicare supplement and long-term care insurance are also discussed in this chapter.

Chapter 7 discusses policy or contract delivery and how to turn service into a marketing opportunity. The chapter also outlines how to organize ideas discussed in the textbook to formulate a basic marketing plan. It closes with a look at compliance, ethics, and professionalism.

Finally, the textbook concludes with a look at the old-age adult market segment, exploring two planning needs that many members of this segment have: estate planning and distribution planning.

# *Techniques for Exploring Personal Markets*

# *Target Marketing and Prospecting Methods*

---

### Learning Objectives

*An understanding of the material in this chapter should enable you to*

---

1-1. Define the five questions that must be answered when constructing a basic marketing plan.

1-2. Explain the eight steps of the selling/planning process and the client-focused selling philosophy.

1-3. Describe the three steps of the target marketing process.

1-4. Outline common prospecting methods for accessing prospects from the three types of prospecting sources.

## OVERVIEW OF THE TEXTBOOK

An advisor's primary concerns are getting in front of the right people (marketing[1]) and knowing what to say and ask once he or she is before them (selling). This textbook, *Techniques for Exploring Personal Markets*, will address the first concern, building on basic prospecting and selling skills you have mastered already.

The objective of this textbook is to provide information and ideas to help you create, implement, and measure the effectiveness of a basic marketing plan. The elements and procedures for writing the plan are discussed in Chapter 7, "Delivery, Service the Plan, and a Basic Marketing Plan." The rest of the chapters provide the information you will need to answer the five questions that form the basis for constructing and evaluating a basic marketing plan:

(1) What are my objectives?
(2) What am I marketing?
(3) To whom am I marketing?
(4) How will I market to them?

(5) How effective am I?

## What Are My Objectives?

You sell products to earn income. Thus a marketing plan must begin by identifying objectives for income and the activities to attain your income objectives. (We will circle back to this question later when we discuss how to construct a basic marketing plan.)

## What Am I Marketing?

A marketing plan answers the question, "What can my products and services do for people?" The key is to view your products and services as tools that enable people to achieve and/or protect their dreams. For example, a couple may dream of traveling during retirement. Retirement planning and mutual funds (to fund an IRA) are tools that can make that future possible. Likewise, young parents want their children to succeed in life. But if one or both of them die, the success of their children will be impeded by worries about basic necessities and funding for higher education. Life insurance proceeds can fund both of these needs.

Unlike a shiny, new sports car, financial products are intangible. To market them successfully you must connect the results that financial products can produce to the people, plans, and purposes that prospects care about. In the above examples, the advisor could position mutual funds as "a retirement travel fund" and life insurance as "a plan to give your children the opportunity to succeed even if you aren't there."

Take the time to truly understand what your products and services can do for people. In other words, understand what you are marketing.

## To Whom Am I Marketing?

**qualified prospects**

**target market**

Ideally, you will only set appointments with *qualified prospects*: people who need and want your products and services, can afford them, can qualify for them, and can be approached on a favorable basis. Imagine the increased efficiency and effectiveness of your marketing efforts if you could market to a large group of prospects that share common characteristics and needs, and have a communication (networking) system. Such a group of people is known as a *target market*. Not surprisingly, successful advisors typically focus on one or a few target markets. Identifying and selecting target markets are critical aspects of creating a basic marketing plan.

For the purposes of this text, we will focus our marketing efforts on personal markets, meeting the financial needs of individuals and families. Personal markets are in contrast to business markets, which address the financial needs of business owners that result from their owning a business.

## How Will I Market to Them?

Of course, not every member of a target market will be a qualified prospect. It follows that for each target market selected you must choose and apply prospecting methods to access qualified prospects. These prospecting methods should reflect the prospecting source, the most probable financial needs and goals, and the target market's preferences.

In addition, you must identify and implement appropriate ways to position your personal brand and products and create awareness of them. Finally you should find effective methods for approaching prospects and setting appointments. One marketing paradigm, life-cycle marketing, is an effective way for identifying probable needs. It will be one of the core topics discussed in this textbook.

## How Effective Am I?

A basic marketing plan identifies ways to measure and evaluate marketing effectiveness. The most common measures are effectiveness ratios. Analysis of these ratios enables the advisor to identify areas of improvement and make changes to increase productivity. Effectiveness ratios are also the basis for planning in subsequent planning periods (typically annual).

# THE SELLING/PLANNING PROCESS AND PHILOSOPHY

Before delving into matters related to marketing, it is important to understand how marketing integrates with the overall selling/planning process and client-focused selling philosophy.

## Introduction to the Selling/Planning Process

You may be familiar with the 6-step financial planning process advanced by the Certified Financial Planning (CFP®) designation (see Table 1-1). Although most financial services professionals are not financial planners, they still use the financial planning process when working with clients. However, the financial planning process does not reflect the crucial steps of identifying prospects and obtaining an appointment with them. Nor does it reflect the reality that advisors often have to motivate clients to obtain products that will meet their needs. These realities are reflected in the following selling/planning process and in its underlying selling/planning philosophy.

---

**TABLE 1-1**
**The CFP® Model of Financial Planning[2]**

(1) Establishing and defining the client-planner relationship.

(2) Gathering client data, including goals.

(3) Analyzing and evaluating the client's financial status.

(4) Developing and presenting financial planning recommendations and/or alternatives.

(5) Implementing the financial planning recommendations.

(6) Monitoring the financial planning recommendations.

---

### *The Eight-step Selling/Planning Process*

**selling/planning process**

You will notice right away that the *selling/planning process* is simply the six-step financial planning process with two additional steps: identify the prospect and approach the prospect (see Figure 1-1.) These are the steps that will be the predominant focus of this textbook. Let's review briefly all eight steps.

---

**FIGURE 1-1**
**The Selling/Planning Process**

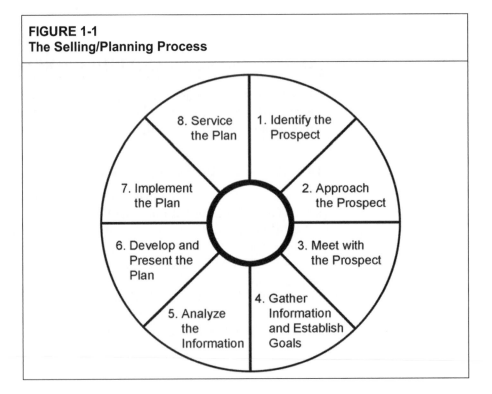

***1. Identify the Prospect.*** Effective selling begins with getting in front of qualified prospects: people who need and want your products, can afford them, can qualify for them, and can be approached on a favorable basis. If possible, you should work with qualified prospects who will value an advisor's guidance and consequently become a source for repeat business and referrals.

Identifying prospects involves target marketing, which operates on the premise that people tend to congregate with people of like values and characteristics. By definition, a target market has a networking system. Thus if you behave professionally and provide valuable products and services, referrals are very likely.

***2. Approach the Prospect.*** In this step, you contact individual prospects with one objective in mind: to set an appointment. The approach is made either on the telephone or face to face. You should base the request for an appointment on a relevant, potential need the prospect may have. This approach will yield more appointments with fewer calls.

**value proposition**

***3. Meet with the Prospect.*** In the initial meeting with a prospect, your objectives are to establish rapport, describe your services and the process involved, ask some thought-provoking questions, and listen attentively. Based on the prospect's responses, you then establish a mutually beneficial reason to do business and describe it in the form of a *value proposition*, which is a clear and compelling reason to conduct business with the advisor. You then see if the prospect wants to proceed to the next step.

***4. Gather Information and Establish Goals.*** Using a company-approved fact finder, ask a lot of questions to gather personal information and qualitative data about the prospect's needs, goals, priorities, and attitudes. You will also collect quantitative data about the prospect's financial situation, often using such documents as a cash-flow statement, personal balance sheet, annual Social Security statement, and so on. You may also gather product design information, especially for insurance plans, to customize the product within a dollar commitment to which the prospect agrees.

***5. Analyze the Information.*** In this step, you analyze the information gathered by creating and/or examining appropriate financial statements; identifying obstacles to desired goals; looking at the prospect's current insurance coverages, savings and investments; analyzing possible alternatives; and so on.

***6. Develop and Present the Plan.*** After analyzing the information, you develop recommendations in the form of a plan. In addition to summarizing the client's situation and the findings of your analysis, the plan should include recommended actions. If alternate solutions are provided, a synopsis of their relevant advantages and disadvantages, and a projection of anticipated costs and outcomes should also be included.

During the presentation you will do the following:

- Confirm the prospect's needs and desires.
- Identify and explain solutions and alternatives that will address the prospect's needs and desires.
- Present recommendations.

***7. Implement the Plan.*** If recommendations are based on the information gathered using a properly completed fact finder, implementing the plan should simply be the logical next step in working together. That does not mean the prospect will not have some concerns or objections. You should be prepared to address them as well as to motivate prospects to take action.

Once the prospect has agreed to the recommendations, help him or her acquire the necessary products and services. For those who sell financial products, implementation includes completing all of the required forms and applications and, in some instances, delivering an insurance policy.

***8. Service the Plan.*** This is the step in which you turn customers into lifetime clients. Service cements the relationship with a customer, giving you the opportunity to make additional sales and obtain referrals.

Some service is reactive—the customer initiates it by requesting a needed change, such as an increase in coverage. In these situations, the customer should expect to receive excellent service.

What can differentiate one advisor from another, however, is the proactive element of his or her service strategy. Many people buy a product and never hear from the advisor again. Proactive servicing strategies, such as monitoring the plan through periodic financial reviews and relationship-building activities, enable an advisor to stay in touch with customers. It is this high-contact service that builds clientele. You need to communicate what reactive and proactive services you will provide and then make them happen!

### Client-Focused Selling/Planning Philosophy

Selling involves communicating, motivating, and persuading. Selling skills are inherently neutral. You can use them to help people implement a plan to achieve their dreams or to manipulate people to buy a product that is

**client**

unsuitable for them. For this reason, the philosophy underlying the selling/planning process is critical.

The selling/planning process described in this textbook is based on a client-focused approach to selling and planning. The objective is to cultivate a mutually beneficial, long-term relationship with a *client*, someone who follows your advice consistently, buys from you again, and refers you to others. (For our purposes, a person who pays an annual retainer, asset management fee, and so on is a repeat buyer.) In other words, the end result is an ongoing relationship that benefits both parties. The initial sale is an intermediate, rather than final, step.

Manipulative, high-pressure strategies are incompatible with the client-focused philosophy, which utilizes consultative and financial planning strategies. Creating solutions that reflect overall client goals, values, and needs requires a careful gathering and analysis of very personal information and feelings. As a result, good communication skills such as asking probing open-ended questions, listening carefully, and confirming your understanding are invaluable. Moreover, motivation and persuasion are employed with the prospect's best interests in mind—not to generate commissions or fees. With the client-focused philosophy everyone benefits. Clients buy valuable products that meet their needs, and advisors receive repeat business and referrals. Consequently the reputation of financial advisors is enhanced in general.

The client-focused philosophy should pervade the entire process, beginning with identifying and approaching prospects.

## TARGET MARKETING

The first two steps of the selling/planning process, identifying prospects and approaching prospects, can be completed in different ways. Over the years, the most successful approach has been target marketing.

**target marketing**

*Target marketing* is a process in which the advisor aims products and services at a target market. A target market is a group of prospects that meets the following criteria:

- The group is large enough to provide a continual flow of prospects.
- Members of the group have common characteristics that distinguish them from nonmembers. At least one common characteristic provides a basis for customized marketing messages and approaches.
- Members of the group have a common need or needs, usually attributed to a common characteristic.
- The group shares information through a formal or informal communication or networking system. This makes it more likely for an advisor to be referred and for the advisor's reputation to precede

him or her. A communication system is the most important criterion in defining a target market.

The reasons for target marketing's popularity are many. Here are a few worthy of mentioning:

- Successful target marketing will result in enhanced referability due to the communication network.
- Concentrating on a few target markets enables the advisor to tailor postsale service strategies to facilitate deeper relationships, which generally translate into increased loyalty.
- Gaining a reputation within a target market for being the expert will discourage other advisors from trying to penetrate the market.
- Target marketing results in higher profits through lower acquisition costs.
- Working with people with whom the advisor has a lot in common will increase the advisor's job satisfaction.

Target marketing can be divided into three major steps:

(1) segmenting your market
(2) targeting a market
(3) positioning your personal brand and products

### Segmenting Your Market

**market segments**

**natural markets**

The first step of the target marketing process is to segment your market into groups of people with common characteristics and common needs, or *market segments*. While market segmentation can be performed on any large group of prospective buyers, such as your general market, the most logical approach is to identify the market segments that comprise your *natural markets*, which are those groups of people with whom you have a natural affinity or access due to similar values, lifestyles, experiences, attitudes, and so on. All things being equal, natural affinity and/or access translates into a higher likelihood of being able to approach prospects on a favorable basis, which is arguably the most difficult part of meeting a qualified prospect.

A very basic and effective approach to segmenting your natural markets is to analyze your personal background and history. Brainstorm to identify the types of people with whom you would like to work (see Figure 1-2). In some cases, you will readily identify groups (markets), while in other cases you will identify personality types for which you will then need to identify where you might find such people. For example, if you are deeply analytical and enjoy working with people who like spreadsheets, you might consider targeting engineers. This analysis will identify initial target markets for you to perform Step 2 and Step 3 of the target marketing process.

A second approach is based on the process used by marketers in other industries. Although it is applied here toward past personal production, it can easily be applied to segment a newly appointed agent's friends, family, and acquaintances list. Furthermore, one could apply it to the undifferentiated, or general, market. This approach involves completing the following:

- Identify your top 20 clients.
- Select relevant segmentation variables.
- Apply the segmentation variables.
- Identify market segments and create profiles.

---

**FIGURE 1-2**
**Natural Markets Checklist**

Your personal background and history have a lot to do with defining your natural markets. Take a few minutes to make a list of the following:

- occupations you have worked well with in the past
- social organizations/associations in which you have been successful
- types of people whose company you enjoy and with whom you enjoy working
- businesses you know fairly well
- organizations, businesses, and associations where you are recognized by most people

---

### *Identify Your Top 20 Clients*

Print or review a list of your current clients and identify the 20 clients with whom you enjoy working the most (out of a suggested minimum of 100 total clients). By enjoyment, we are not talking necessarily about those who generate the highest amount in commissions or fees, but those clients with whom you have the greatest rapport.

### *Select Relevant Market Segmentation Variables*

Next, you will select relevant market segmentation variables, which you will use to divide your natural markets into market segments. A market segment is a potential target market.

*Segmentation Variables.* There are generally four types of segmentation variables that marketing experts use to divide a market: geographic, demographic, psychographic, and behavioristic.[3] The segmentation process utilizes a number of variables from one or more of these four categories.

**geographic variables**

*Geographic Variables. Geographic variables* segment a market by using political divisions such as states, counties, cities, boroughs, and so on, or by territories delineated by neighborhoods, regions, miles, and so on. For most advisors, geography is used to define their territory, mainly because of licensing requirements (advisors must be licensed in each state in which they practice). However, with technological advances, especially cell phones and broadband Internet, more and more advisors are setting up virtual practices that market to a very small high net worth niche market (such as dentists, doctors, or professional athletes) located in several states or even the entire country.

| ***Example:*** | Rachel lives in Burlington County, New Jersey. One of the characteristics of her target market is that many individuals in that market are preretirees. Rachel knows that there are several over-age-55 communities in the county. Geography is a meaningful segmentation variable for her. |
| --- | --- |

**demographic variables**

*Demographic Variables.* Partially because they are easier to measure (through census information or marketing data companies), *demographic variables* are the most commonly used segmentation variable. The differences in prospects' needs and wants are often linked to these variables.[4] For example, interest in Medicare supplement insurance occurs primarily around age 65 because that is when such insurance is an issue for people. Along with age, demographic segmentation includes variables such as gender, education, ethnicity, occupation, income, size of family, marital status, religion, generational cohort (Silent Generation, Baby Boom, Generation X, and so on), and family situation (single, married with kids and a single income, married with no kids and two incomes, single parent, empty nester, divorced, and so on).

**psychographic variables**

*Psychographic Variables.* Advisors use *psychographic variables* to divide a market by lifestyle and attitudes. These variables include leisure activities, values, personality, interests, and hobbies. For example, you may have a few clients who are running enthusiasts, play in a softball league, participate in a bowling league, and so on.

**behavioristic variables**

*Behavioristic Variables. Behavioristic variables* group people by their buying and usage behaviors. This type of segmentation categorizes people according to when they buy (birth of a child, marriage, divorce), type of user (do-it-yourselfer, collaborator, delegator), brand loyalty, benefits sought (convenience, price, quality), buying motivations (for example, motivations for buying long-term care insurance could include not burdening loved ones, ensuring choice of care settings and providers, and/or protecting assets for heirs), and so on. Perhaps you find that upcoming nuptials triggered a few of your best clients to seek your financial advice. It could be a coincidence but, then again, it may be a great target marketing opportunity.

This type of segmentation is quite powerful. Companies are using complex data modeling and computing technologies to harness the marketing potential associated with these types of variables. You can use a low-tech approach by keeping a record of the motivators and reasons for buying for each product sale you make. You can store the information in customizable fields of your contact management system. Do not assume you know; ask clients after they purchase a product, "What do you feel are your main motivations for making this purchase?" and "What do you expect the product to do for you (and your family)?" Then when you are segmenting, you can group clients by motivation and reasons for buying (needs met). Grouping people by their buying behavior may lead you to lucrative target markets for which you will have strategic information with which to build a marketing strategy.

Common segmentation variables used to segment natural markets appear below.

*Example:*          ***Common Market Segmentation Variables Used to Segment Natural Markets***

*Geography:* neighborhood, location of employer

*Demography:* age, income, investable assets, occupation or profession, ethnicity, employer, family situation (married, kids, and so on)

*Psychography:* type of lifestyle (modest, luxurious, and so on), attitudes and values, community interests, social organizations, religious affiliations, clubs, alumni organizations, fraternity, sorority

*Behavior:* financial reasons for buying (income protection, children's education, asset protection, and so on), emotional reasons for buying (desire for security, sense of responsibility, and so on), and referral activity (how many, the quality of referrals, and so on)

*Selection of Relevant Variables.* To select variables, think in terms of the criteria for a qualified prospect and the distinguishing characteristics that identify members of the target market.

You will need to analyze the financial and emotional needs your products and services meet for possible segmentation variables that indicate (1) a need and a desire to meet that need and (2) the ability to afford and qualify for your products (see Figure 1-3). It is assumed that by segmenting your natural markets you can approach prospects on a favorable basis. In many cases, you will probably not be able to find segmentation variables that define *all* the criteria of a qualified prospect.

---

**FIGURE 1-3**
**Possible Segmentation Variables**

|                    | Criteria                                                                                                                                                                                                      |
|--------------------|---------------------------------------------------------------------------------------------------------------------------------------------------------------------------------------------------------------|
| **Need/want/value** | Age<br>Sex<br>Family status<br>Products or services they bought from you<br>Reasons for product purchase<br>Values and attitudes<br>Total commissions, fees, and so on they represent<br>Referrals<br>Occupation or profession |
| **Ability to pay**  | Income<br>Lifestyle<br>Assets                                                                                                                                                                                  |
| **Suitability**     | Income<br>Lifestyle<br>Assets                                                                                                                                                                                  |
| **Approachability** | Occupation or profession<br>Employer<br>Lifestyle<br>Personal traits<br>Ethnicity<br>Social organizations<br>Hobbies<br>Referrals                                                                            |

---

One or more of the variables should reflect possible ways to distinguish members from nonmembers as well as ways to access the potential target market. Such characteristics might include occupation or profession, employer, activities (such as belonging to the same gym or club), neighborhood, and so on. If there are no distinguishing characteristics that enable you to identify and access the market segment, then you do not have a market segment.

### Apply the Segmentation Variables

After you have selected the segmentation variables you will use, begin to segment your market. Make a chart with columns for the client's name and to record information corresponding with each of the demographic variables you chose. Enter the information for each client (see Figure 1-4 for an example of an abbreviated chart).

**FIGURE 1-4**
**Segmentation Chart**

| Client | Product | Financial Need | Inc and Assets | Life | Family Status | Org | Emp |
|--------|---------|----------------|----------------|------|---------------|-----|-----|
| 1 | Term | Inc rep Edu Debt | 70K 100K | Mod | Married 3 children | Kiwanis Ltl league | Fed Ex Elec Bout |
| 2 | Annuity | Ret plan | 150K 500K | Extra | Married | Kiwanis | SMS SMS |
| 3 | Mut Fd | Gen inv | 100K 150K | Mod | Single | GP CPA | KPMG |
| 4 | Term | Inc rep Divorce | 85K 110K | Mod | Divorced 2 children | WRN | Bugs R Us (Self-emp) |
| 5 | Term | Inc rep Debt | 65K 120K | Mod | Married 2 children | Ltl league | EDS |

A spreadsheet application's sort function will help with the analysis. For a more powerful analysis, it is worth considering a database or contact manager (with customizable fields, advanced record filters, and reports).[5]

### Identify Market Segments and Create Profiles

Once you have gathered the information, analyze it for commonalities. If you use a large sample of your client base, you could look strictly for trends (percentages of clients with common characteristics). However, be sure to analyze the data for other relevant information. For example, if Harry Marshwiggle is a CPA and there are no other CPAs on your selected client list, a strict analysis would not identify CPAs as a market segment. However, suppose you are an analytical person who uses a spreadsheet to calculate the optimal time to change the oil in your car. In that case, CPAs should be a market segment to explore further. Here are a few ideas for how to approach your analysis.

***Look for Groups with a Communication Network.*** The communication network is the key to a target market. Examine the segmentation variables that would indicate a client belongs to a group with a system for networking. Groups may be found through such variables as occupation, employer, hobbies or other interests, social or religious organizations, and neighborhood or homeowners' associations. Of course, you need to have gathered and recorded such information in order to analyze it, re-emphasizing the importance of using a contact management system. In the example of Harry Marshwiggle, the CPA market segment would be all the more interesting if Harry were an active member of the Greater Philadelphia CPA chapter (more than 8,700 members) or if he worked at KPMG, a large accounting firm in Philadelphia.

Market segments that lack a communication network typically are not potential target markets. More will be said about such groups a little later.

***Examine Product and Need.*** Look at any commonalities of product (if appropriate), need (for example, if the product were life insurance, a need could be income replacement for dependents), and motivation (if you have determined and recorded that information). Note the common characteristics of clients who bought a product for the same reasons. For example, in Figure 1-4, the clients who have an income replacement need for term life insurance (clients 1, 4, and 5) all have roughly the same income and assets. Two of them are married. Two of them have children and are involved with Little League Baseball; all three have a moderate lifestyle.

***Assess Variables Related to Profit Generation.*** While the level of compensation generated from clients is not the top priority, it is a factor that should be considered. Also consider the quantity and quality of referrals; you will probably have a great deal of referability within a market segment that includes clients who regularly refer good prospects to you.

***Develop Profiles.*** The result will be the identification of market segments that are potential target markets. Develop profiles for the stronger potential target markets, identifying their relevant distinguishing characteristics. Add any missing characteristics that you feel strongly about but for which you may have only anecdotal evidence. For example, you may sense that most clients in the "Little League Baseball parents" market segment are planners because during the interview, they expressed some concrete goals (see Figure 1-5).

---

**FIGURE 1-5**
**Example of Target Market Profiles**

**Little League Baseball Parents**

- Between ages 25 and 40
- Average income: $60,000
- Average investable assets: $50,000
- Children in Little League Baseball
- Looking to insure income at death
- Sensible spenders
- Planners

**Women Business Owners in Chester County**

- Ages 30 to 55
- Average income: $80,000
- Average investable assets: $125,000
- Thinking about retirement
- Looking for tax breaks
- Members of Women's Referral Network or WRN (www.wrnchesco.com)

---

## Targeting a Market

The next step is to narrow your target market options and select one or a few to test and pursue. The following activities are recommended for completing this step:

- Create selection criteria.
- Conduct market research.
- Assess other factors.

### *Create Selection Criteria*

Some market segments make better target markets than others. Take the top five or so market segments you identified and compare and prioritize them using criteria of your choosing. Such criteria will depend largely on your product mix (including services).

Group your criteria into three main categories[6] (you may add your own, of course):

- fit of resources to segment's needs
- level of potential compensation
- level of competitiveness

Assess each market segment and give it a score. You may use a chart like the one in Figure 1-6.

**FIGURE 1-6**
**Selection Criteria**

|  | Market Segment | | | | |
|---|---|---|---|---|---|
|  | 1 | 2 | 3 | 4 | 5 |
| **Fit of resources to segment's needs** | | | | | |
| Products (financial needs I can meet) | | | | | |
| Personal traits | | | | | |
| **Subtotal** | | | | | |
| **Level of potential compensation** | | | | | |
| Potential compensation per client | | | | | |
| Referability | | | | | |
| Size of market segment | | | | | |
| **Subtotal** | | | | | |
| **Level of competitiveness** | | | | | |
| The number of competitors is few | | | | | |
| The competition is not firmly established | | | | | |
| **Subtotal** | | | | | |
| **Total** | | | | | |

**Market Segments**
1—Little League Baseball parents
2—Financially savvy singles from Exton and Downingtown
3—Maxed-out empty nesters who live at Hershey Mills over-55 community
4—Women business owners in Chester County
5—Members of the Kiwanis Club
Score low to high—0 to 5

Consider the details for each of the categories, as explained below.

***Fit of Resources to Segment's Needs.*** Assess how well your resources match your market segment's needs. The best way to do this is to create another chart as illustrated in Figure 1-7. This time, the first column lists the needs your product(s) meet. Create columns for each of the market segments you identified. For each need and feature, rank the relevance to each segment. Factor into your assessment the priority that market segment members would place on meeting that need as well. How high a priority is it in light of other needs, wants, and desires?

**FIGURE 1-7**
**Matching Resources to Needs**

| Life Insurance | Market Segment | | | | |
|---|---|---|---|---|---|
| | **1** | **2** | **3** | **4** | **5** |
| Income replacement | 5 | 1 | 2 | 4 | 1 |
| Education funding | 5 | 0 | 0 | 3 | 0 |
| Debt repayment | 5 | 0 | 2 | 5 | 4 |
| Estate planning | 1 | 1 | 4 | 4 | 4 |
| Philanthropy | 0 | 0 | 0 | 3 | 1 |
| Estate creation | 4 | 1 | 4 | 4 | 1 |
| Maintaining responsibility and preparedness | 5 | 1 | 1 | 4 | 1 |
| **Long-Term Care Insurance** | | | | | |
| Asset protection for heirs | 1 | 1 | 4 | 5 | 1 |
| Preservation of dignity and assurance of choice (avoidance of Medicaid) | 1 | 1 | 5 | 4 | 4 |
| Security that loved ones are not burdened | 4 | 4 | 5 | 5 | 5 |
| Avoidance of Medicaid 5-year lookback period | 1 | 1 | 3 | 3 | 1 |
| Maintaining responsibility and preparedness | 1 | 1 | 4 | 5 | 3 |

**Market Segments**
    1—Little League Baseball parents
    2—Financially savvy singles from Exton and Downingtown
    3—Maxed-out empty nesters who live at Hershey Mills over-55 community
    4—Women business owners in Chester County
    5—Members of the Kiwanis Club
Relevance of need or feature, scored low to high—0 to 5

In addition to the chart, consider your product's affordability. Price your product. For example, if you sell life insurance, calculate the cost of a policy with a typical coverage amount that you expect members of a particular market segment to need. Then compare the cost to the market segment's average income. How reasonable is it?

How well do your personal traits match each market segment? Remember, your personality will have a lot to do with your ability to approach members of the market segment on a favorable basis. If you have created an ideal client profile (see Appendix A for information on how to create an ideal client profile), how closely does the market segment match the profile? (It probably will not be a 100 percent match.) What is your basis for a favorable approach? For example, are members in the market segment your friends? Do they belong to the same country club? How favorable is your basis to approach them relative to other market segments? You could construct a chart similar to the one you made to evaluate the fit of your product.

***Level of Potential Compensation.*** Estimate the possible lifetime profitability that each market segment can produce. Lifetime profitability includes income from product purchases (the initial purchase and repeat purchases of the same or other products) and from referrals. It also accounts for the size of the segment (think in terms of sales volume).

Calculate the price for a likely product purchase, and estimate the income you would receive for all probable purchases over an individual client's lifetime. Do not simply total up the prices for all possible products. Remember the affordability factor. A $1,500 monthly premium for multiple insurance policies for a family with a gross income of $5,000 per month is not reasonable and thus not probable. Estimate a probable average amount and then figure the income that amount produces for you (if you are dealing with a commission). If you have been in the business for a while, you can base these figures on your current clients. Otherwise, ask a more experienced advisor what might be reasonable. This task will require approximating a market segment's average level of income and assets.

How many referrals do you think a client in this market segment will provide if he or she is satisfied with your service? To gauge your referability, determine the formal or informal communication systems that clients in this segment have and how much they use these systems. The presence of a communication system, whether formal (a meeting, a newsletter, and so on) or informal (neighborhood relationships), increases your potential referability. Estimate the income potential from referrals by assuming that a percentage of the referrals will produce the same average income as just calculated above. Multiply the number of referrals by the amount of average income produced. These are estimates, but you only need a general idea.

Demographics are important. How large is the market segment? How fast is it growing? If you are evaluating the market segment of Hispanics in Lehigh County, Pennsylvania, for instance, you would find that the population increased from 31,881 in 2000 to 50,884 in 2007.[7] That is a growing market!

***Level of Competitiveness.*** As sure as a picnic will attract ants, a good target market will attract competition. How competitive are you? To determine your competitiveness you will need to evaluate your competition. Specifically:

- Who are your competitors? How many are there?
- How well are your competitors established in the market?
- How highly rated are your competitors within each market segment?

If the competition already has an established presence within one of your possible target markets, you must evaluate your potential to be a formidable rival or ability to carve out a specialized niche within that segment. Determine whether or not the competition has a good reputation or if there are other unexploited opportunities. If possible, you should choose target markets that are underserved or in which the competition does not yet have a solid presence.

### *Conduct Market Research*

Once you have created selection criteria, you will need to obtain the necessary information to evaluate them. You will need to conduct market research. There are two types of market research: initial research and market surveys. Initial research is less intensive and used as a means to sift the wheat from the chaff. On the other hand, market surveys require more time because they involve talking to people either in the potential target market or who work with its members.

*Initial Research.* A good place to begin your research is on the Internet or at the local library. The Internet is a treasure trove of valuable information. The local chamber of commerce is also an appropriate place to start if you are targeting business owners.

Your main goal is to gather information regarding the selection criteria you previously developed. The information does not have to be precise; a very rough estimate will do fine.

| | |
|---|---|
| ***Example:*** | Cecil wants to target realtors in Chester County, Pennsylvania. Cecil finds the Suburban West REALTORS® Association website located at SuburbanwestRealtors.com. |
| | From the website, Cecil finds that there are more than 5,000 members in the association. Some members are businesspeople who provide products and services related to the real estate industry. |
| | There is also a database of names, phone numbers, and addresses of members that he can use for market research and, ultimately, for prospecting. |

Use your initial research to learn about market segments and to prioritize them. Because of the time commitment required to survey a market segment, you will want to invest that time initially in the top two or three segments. Note that the more information you can gather about any of the market segments you have identified, the fewer questions you will need to ask in your survey. Your initial research can also guide you in developing appropriate questions for the survey.

***Market Survey.*** Select your best potential target markets from the market segments you have chosen, and prepare to conduct a market survey.

Before you construct the survey, you must identify whom you will survey. This will affect what questions you ask. It is important to clearly identify your prospective survey participants.

You will want to survey people from the market segments you identified in the previous step. In particular, you will want to survey current clients who are members of one of the identified market segments, beginning with your best clients. But other professionals who currently target this market segment and potential centers of influence are good people to survey, too. Although this will mean crafting two distinct surveys, it will be worth your time.

Once you know whom you will interview, construct your survey. Keep in mind that the primary purpose is to gather information related to the selection criteria that you were unable to obtain from your initial research efforts. In addition, the market survey can assist you with the following:

- Confirm or discover distinguishing and relevant characteristics common to members of the potential target market.
- Define clearly the most important problems and goals common to most members, especially financial problems and goals.
- Understand how members perceive the financial products and/or services you provide.
- Determine the income potential of the market segment.
- Evaluate the competition's marketing efforts and success within the target market.

Make your survey thorough but concise; you do not want to overwhelm your participants. Keep the number of questions under 10 if you can. Figure 1-8 contains some sample questions from which you can build your own survey.

---

**FIGURE 1-8**
**Market Survey Sample Questions**

**Characteristics**

- What attitudes and interests do you share with others in your group?
- If an outsider went to a convention for [name of market segment], what impressions would he or she get from meeting members?
- Is there something special or interesting that members of your group have in common? Why is this common to your group?

**Fit of Resources to Segment's Needs**

- What are the common problems and concerns people in your situation face? Which are the most important and pressing?
- If you could have a day's fee paid that would allow you to hire a good financial advisor to solve a problem that people like you face, what would you have that person do? Why?
- How do you feel about [the advisor's product or service]? How important do you think it is? Why?
- What determines how you buy [the advisor's product or service]? Price? Quality? Brand name? Customer service? Convenience? Other?
- What do you think is an affordable price for [the advisor's product or service]?
- Where or to whom would you go to find information about [the advisor's product or service]?
- What do you expect from [the advisor's product or service]? What are you looking for in a [the advisor's profession]?

**Level of Potential Compensation**

- What range of income do you estimate people in your group earn?
- What do you feel that people in your group spend money on?
- How would you determine from which company to purchase [the advisor's product or service]?
- What do people in your group read to keep up with the latest information?
- What industries, associations, or clubs support your group?
- How do members of your group network and share information?
- How often do you get together with other people in your group, and what do you do when that happens?
- How often do you consult others in your group for a recommendation of products and services?
- How often do you tell friends, family, business associates, and so on about good products and excellent service?

**Level of Competitiveness**

- Who comes to mind when [name of market segment] think of [the advisor's products and services]?
- How do you know about (name of a competitor)? Does [name of a competitor] send you mail or e-mail? Does [name of a competitor] advertise? Where?
- What reputation does [name of a competitor] have among [name of market segment]?

Ask several members of each potential target market to participate in your survey, assuring them that your purpose is not to sell anything, but to find out more about the potential target market to which they belong. Here are some additional thoughts and tips:

- Be polite and professional. You are probably dealing with a possible prospect and/or center of influence. The survey is an opportunity to create a favorable impression of yourself.
- If you are interviewing a current client or noncompeting professional, consider treating him or her to lunch or a cup of coffee.
- Be observant when interviewing members from your target market. How does the person dress (conservatively, casually, ostentatiously)? What kind of car does the person drive (luxury, minivan, truck, compact)? Where does the person live?
- Listen carefully, especially during small talk. What does the person value? What nonfinancial needs does he or she have? To which organizations does the person belong?

Surveys provide a number of benefits. First, you obtain information about the market segment directly from its members or someone who knows them well. Consequently you are able to make your own judgments rather than relying solely on statistics and data from others. Second, because you develop the questions and possibly interview people yourself, the information you acquire is specific and relevant to your marketing efforts. Moreover, the members of the market segment you interview may notice your efforts, which will let them know you can help solve their problems. This can build your prestige and create awareness of you in your role as an advisor. In fact, it is an excellent first step to prospecting within your target market.

### Assess Other Factors

The market research is complete. The market segments have been evaluated according to the selected criteria. The next phase of the selection process is to assess other factors, including the following.

***Advisors Selling a Single Product.*** Advisors who sell only one product will typically utilize a product specialization strategy in which they market one product to multiple target markets. One best practice is selecting target markets that are related to one another. For example, real estate agents, title insurance agents, home inspectors, and mortgage brokers are related market segments. In fact, if there is a local real estate agents' association, the others may be members. Although the needs and characteristics are different between market segments, there is often a common point of access.

A second strategy, the single-segment concentration, involves marketing one product to a single market segment. This approach is applicable for advisors who are targeting high net worth clients such as dentists, doctors, professional athletes, and so on.

***Advisors Selling Multiple Products.*** Selective specialization is a coverage strategy that involves marketing a few different products to multiple target markets. As with the product specialization approach, it is ideal to target market segments that are related to one another in some way.

The market specialization strategy is like the single-segment concentration strategy in that the advisor specializes in one market's needs. It allows the advisor to devote his or her undivided attention to a particular target market and to become an expert in that market's financial needs. The difference is that the advisor sells multiple products to that market. The advisor should choose a target market that needs and values the products that the advisor sells.

Advisors who sell property and liability insurance along with other insurance and financial products can use an undifferentiated full-market coverage strategy to sell auto and homeowners insurance but then use one of the other coverage strategies, such as selective specialization, for their other products.

***Market Segments without Communication Networks.*** You may identify some market segments that lack a communication network. Most likely, this will happen if you segment by need and motivation. Look a little deeper to see if there is the potential for targeting this market segment within larger undifferentiated groups that do have a communication network (formal or informal). If there is a strong correlation between certain characteristics and buying behaviors, ask: "Where can I find people like this?" The answer may be a common location or within groups that have communication networks.

***Example:*** Eloise notices that a few of her best clients for life insurance were expectant parents. None of them were associated in any way. One day she stopped at a local shopping center. She noticed a boutique that sold maternity and infant clothing. She decides to approach the business owner and see if he would be interested in cosponsoring a 30-minute seminar for first-time parents. The seminar would include a raffle of a few $50 gift certificates to the store, an infant carrier, and anything else the business owner wanted to include.

***Groups Lacking Common Financial Needs.*** As will often be the case, a group may have common characteristics and an excellent communication system but may lack common financial needs. For example, members of a religious group comprised of people of all ages have common characteristics and a communication system. But, their financial needs are different due to their different ages, marital status, and family status. Technically, such groups fail to meet the criteria of a target market. However, because of their common characteristics and strong communication network, these quasi-target markets should be considered target markets.

One approach for working in quasi-target markets is to segment the target market further by life cycle (age) and/or life stage (marital and family status). Then target each resulting market segment according to its members' common financial needs.

---

| | |
|---|---|
| ***Example:*** | Paulo has a client who is on the board of a local gun club. Members of the club are as young as 18 and as old as 70. Paulo believes he could segment the members by life cycle and offer different retirement planning seminars to each age-based market segment. He plans to use metaphors related to hunting in his presentations. |

---

## Positioning Your Personal Brand and Products

**positioning**

According to management expert Philip Kotler, *positioning* is "the act of designing the company's offering and image to occupy a distinctive place in the mind of the target market."[8] The objective of positioning is to create in the minds of your prospects a favorable perception of both your personal brand (image) and your product (offering). Effective positioning results in a value proposition or a compelling reason for prospects to buy financial products and to buy them from you.[9]

### Positioning Your Personal Brand

Your financial plans, insurance policies, and mutual funds cannot set you apart from the competition. If an insurance policy includes a much-coveted feature, you can be sure that other companies will soon offer it to their policyholders. But one thing is virtually impossible for your competitors to copy—you! You and your personal brand are the differentiators. Your personal brand is an amalgamation of the qualities, characteristics, personal experiences, and skills that make you who you are. It is critical to identify the relevant, unique aspects of your personal brand and position them appropriately in your target market. The process includes the following steps:

- Identify a relevant, unique position.
- Put it in writing.
- Test it.
- Establish your position.
- Monitor and protect it.

***Identify a Relevant, Unique Position.*** Your relevant, unique position is determined by analyzing all of the information that you have gathered about your target market to this point. Specifically, organize and analyze the following:

- what the target market needs and values
- your resources, skills, and so on that position you well in the target market
- how your competition is positioned in the target market

Look at the intersection of the characteristics of your personal brand (your life experiences, skills, hobbies, interests, and so on) and what the target market needs and values most. Then examine how your competition is positioned (you may need to conduct more research to understand your competition's position) to address the same intersection of personal characteristics and target market needs. Identify the competition's weak and nonexistent positions, and choose the one you are best suited to address. This is the same process you used to select a target market. In other words, by completing the target marketing process, you will have done most of the work to identify a relevant, unique position.

What remains is to select from the possible positions you have identified the aspects of your personal brand that you will emphasize. There are at least two aspects to which you should give your attention: deliverables and public image.

**deliverables**

*Deliverables* are the ancillary products and service experiences you promise and provide to your prospects and clients. As you carve a position in a target market, look for ways that you can use your skills and background to offer a unique approach to or perspective of the planning process. Consider any ancillary products and services you can provide because of your personal resources and skills.

---

***Example:***    Pat Smith is a former human resources employee of General Motors and he understands the company's employee benefits package. Given the number of GM employees in the area, Pat decides to position himself as a financial advisor who specializes in retirement planning for GM employees.

**public image**

*Public image* is how people—your target market in particular—perceive you. It is composed of all the characteristics that make you recognizable and memorable. As much as you hope it is your financial expertise that causes people to connect with you, more often it is your personal traits and/or the reputation of your character that attracts people to you.

In fact, Peter Montoya and Tim Vandehey contend that you should not market your abilities as a financial advisor as much as you should "market yourself by highlighting a set of characteristics—your military experience, your travels, your family's local history, your previous career racing cars, whatever—that makes you stand out from the crowd, and then hammer those characteristics home over a period of time through consistent marketing efforts."[10]

How much you use your personal traits to position your personal brand will depend on your target market. Some target markets will not respond to such an approach. But others will find personalization of their financial advisor quite appealing.

Regardless of whether you buy into Montoya and Vandehey's idea of personal marketing, an important aspect of your public image is your character. Character qualities such as punctuality, honesty, politeness, and responsiveness should be a part of every advisor's brand. Although your character is not something you can easily advertise and publicize, it is crucial to your long-term success. Guard your character; your reputation is priceless.

***Put It in Writing.*** The culmination of your analysis of personal characteristics and target market needs should result in two written statements: a positioning statement and a value proposition. If you are targeting two or more markets that have very different needs such as parents of young children and seniors (not that such a selection of target markets is recommended), you may have to create positioning statements and value propositions for each.

**positioning statement**

The *positioning statement* consists of one short paragraph. It is a private declaration of how you want your target market to perceive you. The statement should guide all that you do from prospecting methods, advertisements, and planning approaches to postsale service. It is the basis for any value proposition you make to prospects in your target market.

Your positioning statement should answer the following questions:[11]

- Who are you?
- What business are you in?
- For whom?

- What do you do?
- With whom do you compete?
- What will differentiate you from your competition?

---

***Example:***        Pat Smith is a financial advisor who works with General Motors employees to develop and implement retirement plans. Unlike other mutual fund brokers, Pat understands the GM benefits package and can help GM employees structure optimal retirement plans.

---

From your positioning statement, you can create your value proposition. Write it in terms of the tangible results you will deliver to prospects and clients. Unlike the positioning statement, the value proposition is for external communication to your prospects and other interested parties. In addition, it is not aspirational, but based on what you are currently able to deliver.

Ideally, you can boil your value proposition down to a few sentences, articulating the relevant benefits that fall into such categories as

- improving the prospect's financial position through increased income, decreased expenses and taxes, or both
- optimizing the prospect's productivity
- creating emotional satisfaction or relief
- increasing the prospect's competitive advantage (for business owners)

---

***Example:***        Pat has developed his financial planning process to serve the needs of GM employees. His 16 years as a human resources employee at GM give him extensive knowledge of GM's benefits package. Pat can help his clients take full advantage of their employee benefits, and design integrated retirement plans to provide a smoother and more enjoyable ride during the best years of their life.

---

Take time now to define any deliverables (ancillary products and services) you can offer, even though they may not be part of the value proposition. These products and services are the equivalent of the stylish in-store café, spacious aisles, and spotless restrooms that contribute to the distinct shopping experience offered by clothing retailer Nordstrom's. People shop at Nordstrom's to buy clothes, but they choose Nordstrom's because they enhance the shopping experience with these amenities. In the same way, people may buy financial products from you, but why they choose you over your competition can be influenced by deliverables you offer that your competition does not. Again, the focus is on relevance to the target market and differentiation, when possible.

---

***Example:***     Henry is considering offering the following complementary services to his clients and prospects:

- assisting with completion of online student financial aid forms
- sponsoring a website for parents that will provide information about what their children should have mastered at various grade levels, and offer supplemental activities to strengthen their children's abilities
- teaching adult education classes sponsored by the school district that guide parents through the process of preparing their children for postsecondary education and providing strategies for funding it
- offering seminars to high school juniors and seniors on writing essays for college applications
- providing a link with SAT preparation tutors
- sponsoring seminars taught by financial aid officers for parents of middle school and high school students

---

***Test It.*** Before you start pitching your value proposition and any complementary deliverables in earnest, evaluate them. Then ask a few of your best clients and centers of influence from this target market for their feedback. Ask such questions as

- How well does my position reflect the most important needs and values of the target market?
- How meaningful are the differences between the competition's value propositions and mine?
- Will the target market be attracted to my value proposition (position statement plus meaningful differences)?

- Are the elements of any deliverables cost effective in terms of time, energy, and money?
- Most important, can I deliver?

After feedback and evaluation, make any adjustments to your value proposition and ancillary products and services.

***Establish Your Position.*** Establishing your position involves two basic principles: creating awareness of your personal brand and value proposition and delivering on your promises.

Members of your target market need to know who you are and what you do. This is all about creating awareness of your personal brand and thus your value proposition. Some of the more common, basic methods of creating awareness include social mobility, personal brochures, websites, newsletters, and advertising. Start with these foundational methods and innovate. The possibilities are endless, limited only by your creativity (and compliance, of course). In addition, you must make sure selected methods are consistent with your target market's expectations and needs as well as your personal brand.

Above all else, the most important aspect of establishing your position is to deliver what you promised in your value proposition. As the adage goes, "Say what you'll do and do what you say."

| | |
|---|---|
| ***Example:*** | What comes to mind when you think of a Honda? For many car owners, Honda means quality. It is positioned as a reliable, durable, gas-efficient, well-engineered, driving machine.<br><br>It was not always that way. In the 1970s before the gas crisis, Honda was associated with "cheap, low quality, and tinny." This poor reputation existed because of the bad experience American consumers had with other Japanese products. But when the gas crisis hit, the American consumer began to value fuel economy, which was something the Honda Civic offered that American cars did not. People began to buy Hondas, and to their surprise—and much to the chagrin of American automakers—they found the cars to be reliable and well engineered.[12]<br><br>For the past quarter of a century, Honda has forged its hold on a quality position in the automobile industry by delivering consistent reliability, durability, fuel economy, and design as advertised. |

***Monitor and Protect Your Position.*** If you have success in the target market, you will need to monitor and protect your position. Success will attract competitors. Vigilantly monitoring your target market and competition will enable you to make necessary changes to your value proposition, which will keep you in a dominant position.

Keep one eye on your target market. By cultivating relationships in the target market, you will have access to the information you need to make your position more responsive.

Keep your other eye on the competition. Assess their movements within the target market and around it. Although they may not try a head-on attack, they may try to outflank you. It is important to sense your competition's priorities and intentions.

When you have an understanding of any changes in your target market and in your competition, you can make good strategic choices to protect your position. As you develop your strategy, consider the following:

- Keep your name in front of the target market.
- Build a reputation as an expert advisor within your target market.
- Cultivate relationships with key members of your target market.
- Form strategic alliances with other key noncompeting advisors who serve the same target market.
- Look for new, relevant, and meaningful ways to distinguish yourself from the competition.

### Positioning Your Products

Personal branding is not enough. Advisors can stand out from the competition. Their target market may think highly of them. But advisors still need to help prospects see the need for their products and services. Advisors must provide a compelling reason for prospects to choose them as advisors, and a compelling reason for purchasing their products. Why do prospects need a financial plan? Why do they need life insurance? Why do they need mutual funds?

***Logic and Emotion.*** At the heart of positioning is persuasion. Advisors want to persuade people to have a certain perspective—in this case, the need for products or services. According to Aristotle in his classic *The Art of Rhetoric,* there are three elements to a person's argument: ethos, logos, and pathos. Ethos refers to the person's character. Is the person credible? Knowledgeable? Trustworthy? Logos refers to the facts of an argument. Is the argument logical? Pathos refers to the emotional appeal of the argument. How does it make the listener feel? We have already dealt with ethos in explaining personal branding. Let us look at the other two aspects: logic (logos) and emotion (pathos).

To quote the immortal Sergeant Friday, "Just the facts, ma'am." All persuasion must be rooted in the truthful presentation or reflection of the facts. It is important to identify the relevant facts that pertain to the prominent financial needs of the target market and individual prospects. Examine the financial needs you listed in the first step of the target marketing process. What are the facts concerning household income at the death of a wage earner in your target market? What types of current expenditures financed by that income and important to your target market are affected? For example, if you are target marketing parents of children in a private school, the inability to afford tuition could be a relevant logical outcome of the death of a wage earner.

Statistics are often used to present a logical appeal. Be careful, however, in your use of statistics. To safeguard your credibility, use only statistics that have a reliable source. If a book or website quotes a study, it is advisable to find the original source if you can. Also be careful not to overuse statistics. They will detract from your appeal.

Recall that a buyer responds to external stimuli that trigger a sense of need. Triggers are usually based on an emotional response. Therefore the positioning of your products must appeal to your prospects' emotions. In selecting reasons for purchasing the products, advisors need to examine the key emotional reasons that flow from the financial need that the prospect has for the products.

***Creating a Position.*** Once you have identified the key logical and emotional reasons for buying your products and services, you should create a way to communicate them to prospects in the target market. As life insurance great Ben Feldman puts it, "What otherwise would be dull, complex actuarial legalisms are transformed into attractive 'packages of money' that anyone can understand. Packages that solve a problem. Packages that do a specific job; a job that the prospect needs done."[13]

According to Feldman, positioning a product should accomplish at least three objectives:[14]

- First, it should help prospects see their financial needs clearly. This takes a few well-placed facts that will stir up prospects' emotions. Consider creative ways to pique prospects' curiosity. Imagine, for example, that you are a prospect who received a two-foot canoe paddle in the mail from an advisor who has been trying to set an appointment with you. How would you react to the note, "Will your current financial strategies leave you up the creek without one of these?"[15] You might be a little curious!

- Second, prospects should have a general sense of the cost of doing nothing compared to the cost of addressing their financial needs. In other words, you must help them see that "a stitch in time saves nine," meaning it is more costly to do nothing than it is to tackle the problem now.
- Third, the positioning of products should motivate prospects to take action. It should be a trigger to move them from awareness of their need to searching for information and being willing to solve their problems. This is accomplished by statements and questions that cause prospects to evaluate the harsh reality of the status quo.

---

***Example:***    Ben Feldman targeted business owners who had cash flow problems related to their businesses and/or estates. Here is one of the ways he positioned his products:

"You spent 30 years putting this company together. I've never known anybody who had a lease on life; do you? No? Then it's only a question of time until you walk out and Uncle Sam walks in. Know what he wants? Money! And he has a way of getting it. First. Not last. Could you, right now, give me 30 percent of everything you own—in cash—that's the least Uncle Sam will take—without hurting a little bit? Do you think it would affect your credit position? Your working position?"[16]

These are the facts he used to accomplish his objectives: Everyone dies. The federal government assesses an estate tax at a taxpayer's death. The business owner will have to pay an estate tax. The funds for that tax must come from the current cash flow or a liquidation of assets.

Feldman appeals to the emotions of a business owner who has poured his or her life into a company. It would hurt the company if the business owner had to give the federal government 30 percent of what he or she owns. The owner would hate to have the company go under because of his or her death.

---

Granted, you will probably not be able to accomplish all of these objectives in one mailer or advertisement. The important thing at this point is to identify what you must communicate to accomplish your objectives. Remember, too, what works for one advisor and his or her target market may not work for you. As with everything else, your position must reflect facts and feelings that are relevant and important to your target market.

Expect this creative process to take some time. Feldman was known to work for six hours on a 30-second statement.[17]

## SELECTING PROSPECTING METHODS

Whereas target marketing deals more with groups of people, prospecting deals with individuals. The objective of prospecting is to identify individual prospects from the group to preapproach and approach for sales interviews. Prospects will come from one of three sources:

(1) people who know you favorably (friends, family members, clients, and so on)
(2) people recommended by those who know you favorably (referred leads from clients, centers of influence, and so on)
(3) people who do not know you at all

Analyze each target market and estimate the percentages of prospects that come from each of these sources. Then select appropriate prospecting methods based on these percentages and the preferences of the target market(s) involved. What follows is a general discussion regarding prospecting methods that are used when accessing prospects from these three sources.

### People Who Know You Favorably

People who know you favorably are usually the best source of qualified prospects since they are approachable by you on a favorable basis. There are two major groups of people to consider here: clients, and friends and family.

#### *Clients*

Prospecting among your client base is usually applicable when you are cross-selling other products. It is best undertaken using one of three methods: service transactions, financial reviews, and seminars.

***Service Transactions.*** Service transactions are typically initiated by the client (a change to a policy, contribution amount, mutual fund account, and so on). When clients contact an advisor for service, they are thinking about financial matters. Therefore this is a perfect time to see if they need other products or services. This prospecting method works well for advisors who have products, such as property and liability insurance, requiring some amount of servicing.

The prospecting method is simple. Casually ask the client, "What's new?" or "What's going on with you?" These questions not only re-establish rapport, they can gather some important information about changes in the client's financial situation and needs.

In addition, probe to determine the reasons for the requested change. The client's answers may reveal additional financial needs. For example, a client decreasing her IRA contributions may be doing so because she is having a baby, which indicates a need to revisit her life insurance situation. If the situation warrants, ask for an appointment.

**financial review**

***Financial Reviews.*** The purpose of a periodic *financial review* is to monitor the client's progress in meeting financial goals and identify any new financial needs they may have. They are a staple in every advisor's prospecting arsenal, applicable to nearly every financial product or service.

Given their importance, take the time to refine your financial review process to ensure that it provides value to the client because it is one of the best prospecting tools. Furthermore, sell the importance and value of the financial review to clients during the initial sale. This means you need to understand why your clients would value a financial review in the first place.

***Seminars.*** Seminars for clients are better thought of as client education events designed to achieve one or both of the following objectives:

(1) to create client awareness of financial needs and methods for addressing them
(2) to help clients with ancillary aspects of their goal that cannot be addressed with your products and services

The key is to understand your clients' needs on a more holistic basis. It may mean finding other non-competing advisors or service providers to handle aspects of the need you are not qualified to teach.

Relevant client education events will also reinforce your reputation as an advisor who uniquely understands a target market's needs, leading to referrals.

### Friends and Family

Friends and family present an interesting conundrum. They know you favorably, but often advisors are afraid that approaching friends and family may damage relationships. If this is a concern, here are two prospecting methods to consider.

*Introduction of Your Practice.* This method involves meeting with your friends and family and giving a concise 10-minute overview of what you do for a living. The overview should focus on the types of needs someone like them would have, and how your products and services can help address these needs. Clearly state that your intention is to share with them what you do for a living so that if they need help with products and services you provide, they know you are there to help them. That is all.

*Target Market Sounding Board.* A more indirect approach is to use your friends and family as a sounding board for the various target markets they represent. The advisor can ask their friends and family members to answer a market research questionnaire, to respond to particular marketing ideas, to provide feedback on telephone approaches, or to role-play the interview process. This method provides your friends and family insight into what you do. The information you share with them and the questions you ask them will then create awareness of their needs and your ability to help them.

## People Recommended By Those Who Know You Favorably

**referrals or referred leads**

**referrer or nominator**

Very few advisors can survive marketing only among their friends and families. At some point, the advisor will need to gain access to strangers. A prospect who does not know the advisor will be reluctant to meet with him or her. However, the prospect is more likely to meet with the advisor if the advisor has been recommended by someone the prospect knows and trusts. Therefore the best prospecting source that includes strangers are prospects recommended by those who know you favorably. Prospects from this source are known as *referrals or referred leads*. Advisors should handle them with great care since the *referrer or nominator* has put his or her reputation on the line for the advisor.

Referred leads are gained through three different prospecting methods: personal recommendations, centers of influence, and networking. In all three prospecting methods, it is important to have a clear description, such as an ideal client or target market profile, of the type of qualified prospect you are seeking. Outlining characteristics of the prospects you seek will help the referrer provide better qualified leads within the target market.

### *Personal Recommendations*

**personal recommendations**

*Personal recommendations* are the referrals an advisor receives from clients, friends, and family. Personal recommendations are the dominant prospecting method among most advisors. This method is especially important when a target market's communication system is more informal, and interaction between members is in smaller groups, such as a neighborhood community (as opposed to a neighborhood association that has an association newsletter and planned events).

### Centers of Influence

**center of influence (COI)**

A second way to generate referrals is by identifying a *center of influence (COI)* within a desired target market. A COI is an influential person who knows you favorably and agrees to introduce you or refer you to others. Its use is indicated when you can identify a person or persons whom the target market looks to for guidance and leadership. The president of an association is a potential COI, or all of the businesses may use a particular CPA or attorney.

The relationship is a two-way street. Your relationship with the COI should benefit directly him or her, helping the COI achieve personal goals or goals for the members of his or her sphere of influence. Identify what you can bring to the table and make the case for how cooperation will help the COI.

### Networking

**networking**

*Networking* is the process of continually sharing ideas, resources, and prospect names by non-competing businesses that target the same market. It is indicated when there are other professionals and businesses that specialize in working with your target market.

**tips club**

One type of networking, known as a *tips club*, meets solely for the regular exchange of information on prospects. Each member of the tips club shares his or her own expertise, business connections, and social contacts with the group.

Another variation of networking is what authors Bob Littell and Donna Fisher have termed *NetWeaving*: "NetWeaving is all about putting other people together in win/win relationships that will solve problems, satisfy needs, or result in new or expanded business opportunities."[18] In other words, match the person who needs a plumber with the outstanding plumber you know. Or do some pro bono work for someone.

## People Who Do Not Know You at All

The last prospecting source consists of those people who neither know you nor those who know you. Although we will discuss methods for identifying such prospects, keep in mind that these methods should be accompanied by awareness creation strategies relevant toward a particular target market. These strategies should capitalize on a target market's communication network, both formal and informal.

Some target markets naturally lend themselves to these prospecting methods, so consider using them even if you have access to the target market through referrals. If the bulk of the market is not accessible through referrals, these methods will be your only option for effectively penetrating the market.

### *Personal Interaction*

**personal interaction**

*Personal interaction* requires mastering the art of listening and the art of small talk, and showing a genuine interest in others. It also requires an ability to ask meaningful but innocuous questions that help you qualify a prospect. A good interaction is subtle and natural and avoids the appearance of shameless personal marketing. This prospecting method works best at gatherings and events attended by a particular target market, especially if the meetings are informal.

One advisor combines his love for golf and his extroverted personality to prospect on the golf course. He arranges to play golf with complete strangers. After 18 holes, he walks away with contact information that he later parlays into appointments and sales.

One important aspect of using personal interaction as a prospecting method is to have a good response to the question, "What do you do for a living?" One approach is to have a brief commercial tailored, if possible, to the person with whom you are speaking. Here are a few guidelines to help you create and use a ten-second commercial for this purpose:

- Ask strategic, rapport-building questions to gather information that will help you ascertain possible needs the prospect may have.
- Ask a positioning question that is relevant to something the prospect might need. The question positions your response to be a solution to a problem or question they may be asking. It can be based on an analogy as will be demonstrated shortly.
- Follow up with your ten-second commercial, stating your value proposition in terms of the results you achieve for your clients.
- Use some creativity but make sure you do not run afoul of your company's compliance requirements. You may be restricted in the way you can describe your work. Most importantly, don't call yourself a financial planner unless you are properly registered and/or credentialed.
- End with a question that measures interest.
- Always have a business card to hand the prospect.

| | |
|---|---|
| ***Example 1:*** | "Are you familiar with Social Security benefits paid to people who lose an income earner to death or disability?" (Yes or No) |
| | "I help young families like yours create and implement a personal benefits plan using life and disability income insurance. These plans ensure that the dreams young families have will remain achievable should the unexpected happen. Is that something that might interest you? |
| ***Example 1:*** | "Do you know what the U.S. Mint does?" (They make money.) |
| | That's what I do for young families like yours at the time when they need it the most. Through life insurance, I help them ensure that their basic needs are met if something should happen to a parent. Is that something you have thought about? |

Another way to use the personal interaction method is through popular social networking websites such as Facebook and LinkedIn (if your compliance department approves). Online networking will work when your local target market participates in an online community or would be interested in one that you intend to start. Groups dominated by younger members have a higher likelihood of responding to these methods.

### Public Events

Another prospecting method is to sponsor or establish a formal presence at a public event that appeals to your target market. You could sponsor a child safety fair at a local school, coordinating your efforts with the local police department. Your booth, if you are a life insurance agent, could promote life insurance as a means for a parent to protect their children's financial future. Although the main purpose of using public events is to create awareness, there are opportunities to gather names and contact information of people who may want more information about life insurance and other financial needs.

---

## Prospecting with a Fishbowl

All of us have dropped one of our business cards in a fishbowl so our names could be drawn for a prize. Do you ever wonder what happens to all those cards with names and addresses? It's a great way to prospect. You might start with a restaurant that you like. It should be a spot where you eat on a fairly regular basis so that the host or owner recognizes you. Set up the drawing for your winning names so that each contest lasts for a week or a month. Two free lunches would satisfy the customer and make the restaurant happy too. Be sure you pay for them ahead of time. You will keep the waiter happy if you leave an extra tip for the unusual circumstances.

You can follow-up by phone or mail to announce the winners, and offer everyone else the second prize. It could be a free financial checkup or something else that will promote your business. A successful agency in the South uses a variation of this by placing a fishbowl next to the cash register in a busy baby furniture and clothing store. Their monthly winners receive a copy of a book listing names for newborns. Everyone else is eligible for a discussion on juvenile insurance and a planning session on college costs.

One advisor used this idea in a maternity clothing store. With a $50 gift certificate for first prize, she made five sales from the other names in the fishbowl in less than a month. Pick a targeted prospect group and think about how you can approach them by offering a prize they will enjoy. You can use a garden shop, a drycleaner, a school supply store, a sports store, the county fair, a golf show, a mall fair, and so on. Study the stores and events in your area. Be sure that the customers include those with whom you can work and that the main prize will satisfy both the storeowner and the prospects.

---

### *Group Presentations*

**group presentations**

Once you have established a good reputation, you will have the opportunity in some target markets to conduct *group presentations* to educate target market constituents about a topic on which you are an expert. It is different than a seminar in that, in most cases, it is not appropriate to give a sales pitch. Group presentations are more of a method for creating awareness than selling a product.

Group presentations would be appropriate only if the advisor is comfortable speaking in front of a group. Like the personal interaction method, the group presentation method is excellent for target markets that have regular meetings. Often, such groups are looking for speakers to talk about meaningful and important topics.

---

***Example:***          Hunter Jones is a life insurance agent whose target market is members of the West Brandywine Gun Club (WBGC). Many of the members are young parents. Hunter works with the WBGC to host an educational event discussing the financial needs of young parents. An estate attorney will discuss the basics about wills and guardianships. Hunter will discuss the state inheritance tax and life insurance.

### *Direct Response*

**direct response**

Another prospecting method is *direct response*, which involves sending letters with reply cards that prospects can return if they are interested in an appointment or more information. Sometimes, the letter will offer a small gift, such as a road atlas or a free booklet, to prospects who respond to the direct mail letter and agree to a free consultation with the advisor. An alternative is to use e-mail, if e-mail addresses are available. If prospects are not on a do-not-call list, advisors may follow up with a phone call to set an appointment.

The direct response method is only viable if you have names and appropriate contact information. Of all the methods, it is probably the least effective because of the federal and state do-not-call laws. It is more viable if the advisor is using information he or she personally gathered from the prospects themselves using one of the other methods discussed earlier. For example, if Mary Hart has a booth at the Philadelphia Home Show for which she gathers e-mail addresses, she could send a follow-up e-mail with information and an offer for a free consultation or perhaps a seminar on a relevant topic.

## NOTES

1. Marketing, as defined by the American Marketing Association is, "the activity, set of institutions, and processes for creating, communicating, delivering, and exchanging offerings that have value for customers, clients, partners, and society at large." Thus marketing includes selling and is not distinct from it.
2. Certified Financial Planner Board of Standards, Inc., "The Financial Planning Process," http://www.cfp.net/learn/knowledgebase.asp?id=2 (accessed January 22, 2009).
3. Marian Burk Wood, *The Marketing Plan: A Handbook* (Upper Saddle River, NJ: Pearson Education, Inc., 2003), 57.
4. Philip Kotler, *Marketing Management*, 11th ed. (Upper Saddle River, NJ: Prentice Hall, 2003), 287.
5. OpenOffice is an open source office suite that includes a word processor, spreadsheet, database, and presentation applications. As of this writing, it can be downloaded free. Visit OpenOffice.org for information.
6. Marian Burk Wood, *The Marketing Plan: A Handbook* (Upper Saddle River, NJ: Pearson Education, Inc., 2003), 64.

7.  Pew Hispanic Center, "Lehigh County, Pennsylvania," pewhispanic.org/states/ ?countyid=42077 (accessed May 1, 2009).
8.  Philip Kotler, *Marketing Management*, 11th ed. (Upper Saddle River, NJ: Prentice Hall, 2003), 308.
9.  Philip Kotler, *Marketing Management*, 11th ed. (Upper Saddle River, NJ: Prentice Hall, 2003), 308.
10. Peter Montoya and Tim Vandehey, *The Brand Called You: Personal Marketing for Financial Advisors* (Costa Mesa, CA: Millennium Advertising, 1999), 30.
11. Harry Beckwith, *Selling the Invisible* (New York, NY: Warner Books, Inc. 1997), 113–114. This is an adaptation of questions Beckwith recommends.
12. Edmunds.com, "Manufacturers Histories: Honda," www.edmunds.com/reviews/ histories/articles/65329/article.html (accessed September 28, 2006).
13. Andrew H. Thompson with Lee Rosler, *The Feldman Method* (Chicago, IL: Dearborn Financial, 1989), 30.
14. Andrew H. Thompson with Lee Rosler, *The Feldman Method* (Chicago, IL: Dearborn Financial, 1989), 32.
15. Pamela Yellen, "Web Site Exclusive: Secrets of Successful Prospecting," *The Advisor Today*, August 2001, www.advisortoday.com/archives/2001_august_ web.html (accessed October 5, 2006).
16. Andrew H. Thompson with Lee Rosler, *The Feldman Method* (Chicago, IL: Dearborn Financial, 1989), 50.
17. Andrew H. Thompson with Lee Rosler, *The Feldman Method* (Chicago, IL: Dearborn Financial, 1989), 31.
18. Robert Littell and Donna Fisher, *Power NetWeaving: 10 Secrets to Successful Relationship Marketing* (Cincinnati: The National Underwriter Company, 2001), 5.

## CHAPTER ONE REVIEW

*Key terms and concepts are explained in the Glossary. Answers to the review and self-test questions are found in the back of the textbook in the Answers to Questions section.*

### Key Terms and Concepts

| | |
|---|---|
| qualified prospects | deliverables |
| target market | public image |
| selling/planning process | positioning statement |
| value proposition | financial review |
| client | referrals or referred leads |
| target marketing | referrer or nominator |
| natural markets | personal recommendations |
| market segment | center of influence |
| geographic variables | networking |
| demographic variables | tips club |

| | |
|---|---|
| psychographic variables | personal interaction |
| behavioristic variables | group presentation |
| positioning | direct response |

## Review Questions

1-1. List and explain the five questions that must be answered when constructing a basic marketing plan.

1-2. List and describe the eight steps of the selling/planning process.

1-3. Describe the client-focused selling philosophy.

1-4. Define target marketing and list its advantages.

1-5. Outline the segmenting step of the target marketing process.

1-6. Explain the second step of the target marketing process: targeting a market.

1-7. Describe how to position your personal brand and products.

1-8. List and describe methods for identifying prospects that know you favorably?

1-9. List and describe methods for identifying prospects recommended by those who know you favorably.

1-10. List and describe methods for identifying prospects who do not know you at all.

## Self-test Questions

*Instructions: Read Chapter 1 and then answer the following questions to test your knowledge. There are 10 questions. Choose one answer for each question, and then check your answers with the answer key in the back of the textbook.*

1-1. Identifying target markets of qualified prospects is associated with which of the following questions used to construct a basic marketing plan?

    (A)    What am I marketing?
    (B)    To whom am I marketing?
    (C)    How will I market to them?
    (D)    How effective am I?

1-2.   In which step of the selling/planning process does the advisor establish rapport, explain his or her business purpose, and ask thought-provoking questions?

(A)   Approach the prospect
(B)   Meet with the prospect
(C)   Gather information and establish goals
(D)   Service the plan


1-3.   Which of the following questions would best help determine the level of competitiveness an advisor may have in a particular target market?

(A)   How much networking occurs within the market segment?
(B)   What level of income could be expected from the market segment?
(C)   How many referrals do you think a client in this market segment would provide you?
(D)   How well are your competitors established in the market?


1-4.   Which of the following statements regarding positioning your personal brand and products is correct?

(A)   A positioning statement is designed to be used with your prospects.
(B)   A value proposition defines the value of a target market to an agent in dollars and cents.
(C)   Public image is composed of all the characteristics that make an advisor recognizable and memorable.
(D)   Preapproach involves creating awareness of your personal brand.


1-5.   Which of the following statements regarding important factors to be assessed when selecting a market to target is (are) correct?

   I.   Groups with a communication network but lacking common needs should be avoided.
   II.   A product specialization strategy is perfect for multiline insurance agents.

(A)   I only
(B)   II only
(C)   Both I and II
(D)   Neither I nor II

1-6.  Positioning a product should accomplish which of the following objectives?

   I.   It should help prospects see their financial needs clearly.
   II.  It should provide a general sense of the cost of doing nothing compared to the cost of addressing one's needs.

   (A)  I only
   (B)  II only
   (C)  Both I and II
   (D)  Neither I nor II

1-7.  Which of the following prospecting sources uses centers of influence (COIs) to identify prospects?

   I.   people who know you favorably
   II.  people recommended by those who know you favorably

   (A)  I only
   (B)  II only
   (C)  Both I and II
   (D)  Neither I nor II

1-8.  All of the following statements regarding identifying market segments and creating profiles are correct EXCEPT

   (A)  Examine the segmentation variables that would indicate that a client belongs to a group with a networking system.
   (B)  It is important to consider the quantity and quality of referrals.
   (C)  Note the common characteristics of clients who bought a product for the same reasons.
   (D)  The level of compensation from clients is the only factor that should be considered when evaluating the ability to generate profits.

1-9.  All of the following prospecting methods are typically associated with identifying prospects among people who do not know you EXCEPT

   (A)  financial reviews
   (B)  personal interaction
   (C)  public events
   (D)  group presentations

1-10.   All of the following are advantages of target marketing EXCEPT

(A)   It enables the advisor to work with a wide variety of needs.
(B)   The advisor can tailor postsale service strategies to facilitate deeper relationships
(C)   It enhances an advisor's referability due to the communication network.
(D)   The advisor gains a reputation within a target market for being an expert.

# *Life-Cycle Marketing, Awareness, and Approaches*

---

**Learning Objectives**

*An understanding of the material in this chapter should enable you to*

---

2-1. Explain how life events and the five life-cycle market segments are used to implement life-cycle marketing.

2-2. Describe five common methods for building prestige and creating awareness of your personal brand.

2-3. Describe two common preapproach methods used to create awareness and interest in your products and services.

2-4. Outline four major elements for approaching the prospect effectively.

---

This chapter introduces life-cycle marketing, a strategy many successful advisors use to penetrate target markets for which the common needs are not well defined. Next, the chapter examines ways to create awareness of one's personal brand and products; this typically precedes approaching individual prospects to set appointments. Finally, we will cover how to approach a prospect for an appointment. This section will examine how to: write a script, follow do-not-call laws, handle voice mail, and project a professional phone image.

## LIFE-CYCLE MARKETING

A target market's common characteristics are useful for creating a position and awareness of the advisor's personal brand. If the advisor is working with a target market whose members have common needs, then creating awareness of products and approaching prospects to set appointments can be based on these needs as well. Often, this is not the case. However, the advisor can use the life-cycle marketing strategy to accomplish these two tasks instead.

**life-cycle marketing**

**life-cycle market segments**

*Life-cycle marketing* is a strategy that operates on two generalizations:

(1) From birth to death, people experience common life events that affect their insurance and other financial needs.
(2) These life events tend to occur among people in certain age ranges, or *life-cycle market segments*.

By knowing a prospect's age, the advisor can create awareness of products and approach a prospect for an appointment based on probable needs. With additional demographic information, such as marital status and number of dependents, the advisor can execute these two tasks with even greater precision and achieve better results.

This section begins by examining life events and the financial needs they indicate. Then it provides an overview of the life-cycle market, segments which will be covered in more detail throughout the rest of this textbook.

## Life Events

**life events**

*Life events* are important occurrences, such as graduating from college or getting married, that often result in substantial changes in peoples' lives. They are important to marketing financial products and services for at least two reasons.

First, many life events inherently create or increase a prospect's need and/or ability to pay for financial products.[1] For example, when a prospect graduates from college and begins earning income, different financial needs are created, including a need to save for a down payment on a house or for retirement, and a need to protect savings from the effects of a long-term disability. (See the table that follows for a list of life events and potential corresponding needs.) Furthermore, because the prospect has earned income, he or she has a greater ability to pay for needed products and services.

**trigger**

Second, a life event often serves as a *trigger* that raises a prospect's awareness of financial needs or increases his or her interest in meeting them.[2] Sometimes a life event will cause the prospect to begin looking for information and solutions, much as you would look in the yellow pages for a plumber when you discover your sewer line is clogged. With some target markets, there may be an opportunity to establish a presence with the resources to which members of a target market turn. This is especially true if members of a target market rely on one another or a center of influence, such as an attorney or CPA, for recommendations of service providers.

| Life Event | Potential Financial Needs |
|---|---|
| Graduating from high school | • Health insurance<br>• Renters insurance (off campus)<br>• Checking, savings, and/or money market account<br>• Credit card |
| Graduating from college | • Short-term health insurance<br>• Auto insurance (own policy) |
| Obtaining first job | • Disability income insurance<br>• Emergency fund<br>• Life insurance (pay for final expenses)<br>• IRA or Roth IRA<br>• Individual health insurance<br>• Mutual funds |
| Moving out of parents' home | • Renters insurance<br>• Saving for a down payment on a house |
| Buying a home | • Home mortgage<br>• Homeowners insurance<br>• Mortgage disability income insurance |
| Getting married | • Life insurance<br>• Spousal IRA or Roth IRA<br>• Personal articles floater |
| Having a baby | • Life insurance (on parents and/or baby)<br>• 529 plan and/or Coverdell education savings account<br>• Mutual funds (save for child's wedding) |
| Changing jobs | • Life insurance (replace group term)<br>• Disability income insurance<br>• Rollover of qualified plan to IRA |
| Getting a divorce | • Life insurance<br>• Individual health insurance<br>• Checking, savings, and/or money market account<br>• Rollover from a qualified plan to IRA (due to a QDRO)<br>• Mutual funds (invest divorce settlement) |
| Starting a business | • Home equity line of credit<br>• Small business retirement plan<br>• Business insurance products<br>• Group insurance products<br>• Personal umbrella liability policy |

| Life Event | Potential Financial Needs |
|---|---|
| Attending to aging parents | • Long-term care insurance<br>• Life insurance<br>• Annuities |
| Inheriting money | • Mutual funds<br>• Personal umbrella liability policy |
| Last child leaving the house | • IRA or Roth IRA<br>• Annuities<br>• Long-term care insurance<br>• Mutual funds (retirement investments) |
| Retiring | • Annuities (especially immediate annuities)<br>• Life insurance<br>• Long-term care insurance<br>• Medicare supplement |
| Having a grandchild | • 529 plan or Coverdell education savings account<br>• Life insurance (on child or grandchild) |

Very often, life events are partial triggers that require some advisor-initiated contact to raise awareness of the resulting financial need and/or opportunity. For example, a couple having a baby has an increased need for life insurance. The couple may be motivated to buy life insurance if they are made aware of this important need. An advisor can utilize a preconditioning strategy by raising awareness of the need prior to, or at the time of, the life event. Most often, however, an advisor will implement awareness strategies after the life event.

### Life-Cycle Market Segments

In the past, life events occurred in a fairly predictable pattern over a person's life. The evolution of societal norms has changed the order and timing of some of these events. For example, people are marrying later in life. Despite these changes, the life-cycle paradigm is viable because life events continue to occur within certain age ranges. For example,

- People tend to graduate from college in their twenties.
- First marriages usually occur while men and women are in their (late) 20's.
- A woman's childbearing years generally end around age 40.

Consequently without specific information about a prospect's personal and financial situation, the advisor can use the prospect's life-cycle market segment to create initial awareness strategies. In addition, the advisor can incorporate the dominant needs of the prospect's life-cycle market segment in his or her approach for an appointment.

With that in mind, here is an overview of the life-cycle market segments. There are a few different ones used in the industry. This textbook uses five segments:

- Youth—Ages 0 to 19
- Young Adulthood—Ages 20 to 37
- Middle-Years Adult – Ages 38 to 58
- Mature Adulthood—Ages 59 to 75
- Old Age—Ages 76 and older

### *Youth—Ages 0 to 19*

These are the growing and learning years marked by dependency on adults. Youth is characterized by physical, emotional, and intellectual development. This is the stage of life when people are most impressionable. Toward the end of this phase, the teenage years involve a search for identity. There is also a tendency to believe in one's indestructibility that translates into taking more risks. This mindset carries over into the Young Adulthood phase. It is notable that members of the Youth life-cycle market segment typically neither make their own financial decisions nor have the ability to pay for products. Therefore their needs are usually identified and addressed through their parents.

### *Young Adulthood—Ages 20 to 37*

The early part of this phase involves transitioning from depending on parents to becoming independent and establishing one's own identity. It is often a time for making commitments to work, marriage, and family. Toward the middle of the phase, one tends to reexamine commitments made to career, marriage, assumed roles and lifestyles. Thus job changes are fairly common as are divorces. Major emphases throughout this phase are typically one's career, achievements, status, power, money, and acceptance of financial responsibility.

### *Middle-Years Adulthood—Ages 38 to 58*

In the earlier years of this phase, many people begin searching for real meaning to life and/or attempt to hold onto lost youth. Some may experience a mid-life crisis as dreams and reality are reconciled. Toward the middle of the phase, the realities of life have been generally accepted. For most, the importance of one's career often increases with the decreasing responsibilities as a parent. Toward the end of this phase, some may be in the position of retiring. Those who are not are making preparations for retirement. If there have been children in the household, this is when they are moving out, creating an empty nest feeling. In some cases, the void created by the departing children is replaced by assuming the care and support of an elderly parent.

| TABLE 2-1 Median Income and Assets by Age of Householder (2007) | | | |
|---|---|---|---|
| Age of House-holder | Number of Households[3] (Thousands) | Median Income[4] | Median Assets[5] |
| Less than 35 | 25,779 | $37,400 | $11,800 |
| 35-44 | 22,448 | 56,600 | 86,600 |
| 45-54 | 24,536 | 64,200 | 182,500 |
| 55-64 | 19,909 | 54,600 | 253,700 |
| 65-74 | 12,284 | 39,000 | 239,400 |
| 75 or more | 11,829 | 22,800 | 213,500 |

### Mature Adulthood—Ages 59 to 75

These are the fulfillment and yearning years. Many people achieve some self-actualization during these years. It is common for a renewed focus on the spiritual dimension to emerge. The early part of this phase is usually when people are preparing for retirement or retiring. Wealth accumulation is important early on; toward the end of this phase more attention is placed on seeking new achievements and education, working in the service of others, and enjoying leisure time and accumulated wealth. This phase is also when the loss of a spouse and other family members frequently occurs, and when health problems become more common for many.

### Old Age—Ages 76 and up

With the increased life expectancies achieved in the last century, many changes have occurred in the lifestyles of our oldest citizens. Many seniors in the 70's, 80's, and even 90's remain active in their jobs, volunteer activities, and religious and social groups. However, for most Americans, old age is when a person becomes a seasoned citizen. It is the wise and more fragile phase of life, a time to remember and recall the past. This phase encompasses the consumption and distribution of wealth. Long-term care is a key issue and often a major concern. Demographically, there will be three times as many women as men.

# CREATING AWARENESS

It is critical for the advisor to plan and implement strategies to create awareness of his or her personal brand through prestige-building activities. In addition, the advisor must educate and motivate prospects regarding the financial and emotional needs the advisor's products can satisfy. The advisor can educate and motivate through preapproach activities, which the advisor can use with all prospects, not just for complete strangers.

This section will discuss prestige-building and preapproach techniques. Although discussed as two distinct marketing activities, there is overlap between them. In addition, the advisor looks to create strategies for increasing awareness of his or her products and the need members in the target market have for them.

## Prestige Building

prestige building

*Prestige building* is your public relations campaign to position your personal brand favorably in your target markets. The limit to prestige-building activities is your imagination. Which methods to use will depend on your personal traits and strengths as well as the target market's receptiveness to various methods. If possible, you should use a method that maximizes the effectiveness of the target market's communication network.

This section will examine several techniques: social mobility, personal brochures, Internet websites, newsletters, and advertising. Use them as a starting point and innovate based on your strengths and personal characteristics.

### *Social Mobility*

social mobility

Usually the most effective way to promote your personal brand to your target market is by increasing your *social mobility*. From a socioeconomic standpoint, social mobility is "the ability of individuals or groups to move within a social hierarchy with changes in income, education, occupation, etc."[6] We will follow the concept of movement from this definition. Thus social mobility in this textbook refers to a person's movement within and impact on a community. The result of social mobility is a reputation within the community. This makes it the most appropriate tool for creating awareness of your personal brand.

There are a variety of ways to create social mobility. All of them allow prospects in the target market to see you active in their community. What follows are some of the more common ways to increase social mobility.

***Community Involvement.*** The first method to think about is *community involvement*. If the target market coincides with a social, civic, business, charitable, or religious organization, this is usually the preferred method for creating awareness of who you are and what you do.

Keep in view a few guiding principles if this is an organization with which you are not currently involved. First, get involved with organizations and causes that you personally support. Second, determine a realistic view of your capacity for involvement to help you make decisions regarding your level of commitment. Finally, aim for visibility and not shameless self-promotion. People have negative impressions of those who like to tell everyone how good they are and what good they are doing.

There are four levels of involvement to consider. The easiest level of involvement in terms of time and energy is sponsorship and giving. If your target market is parents with children and you love baseball, sponsor a Little League Baseball team. Donate money to the league for new equipment. There are endless opportunities for giving. Again, do not worry about getting credit. Word gets out.

The second level of involvement is volunteering. As a volunteer, your commitment level is minimal (although you should follow through on any commitments you make). Yet volunteering is an effective way to build relationships with people. Your involvement with an organization bonds you to other members or volunteers. By working together to reach a common goal, you build relationships spontaneously and naturally. Volunteering is a way for you to do some common good, as well as to get to know the heart and soul of an organization before you go to the next level: joining.

A third level of involvement, and one that requires more commitment, is joining. Remember to assess the time commitment and your ability to support the charter and goals of the organization. If you have the opportunity to interact with members regularly, which membership (and volunteering) allows, you will become better acquainted. People will discover your talents, your values, and your character.

The fourth level of involvement, requiring the greatest level of time and energy, is leading. Members in organizations have opportunities to lead by holding an office or chairing various initiatives the organization sponsors. This level of involvement offers the greatest visibility and thus requires a great deal of time and attention. The benefits, however, can be far reaching. First, it is an opportunity to showcase your talents and abilities without uttering one word of self-promotion. Second, the leaders of these organizations are usually the more successful and influential people in your community. And, depending on the purpose of the group, they have learned that success involves contributing to the good of the community. In other words, they are most likely good centers of influence.

*Writing.* If you can write short articles and your target market has a newsletter or reads certain publications, then write an article and have it approved by your compliance department. Writing an article or a book positions you as an expert and enables you to demonstrate your knowledge of your target market's needs and your ability to help. In addition, print publications of all sizes are seeking quality content that serves the interests of their readers. Their need is your opportunity to get your name and company in front of a large number of prospects in a highly cost-effective manner.

If you do write articles, make sure you properly cite all sources. Borrowing ideas without attributing credit is the same as stealing. It would be an excellent idea to review with a professional writer the basics of dealing with intellectual property to avoid problems down the road.

*Speaking to Groups.* Some organizations will offer their members free educational seminars about pertinent topics. If this opportunity is available and you are comfortable speaking to groups, let the appropriate persons in the organization know your availability and the topics you would be willing to address.

The primary goal of speaking engagements is to establish your reputation as an expert. Thus focus on educating and motivating your audience. Outline the problems clearly, but create a sense of curiosity and a need to seek solutions.

Keep promotional information to a minimum. It should be brief and presented at the end of your presentation. If people want more information, they can contact you.

Having said that, members of the audience should take with them—at a minimum—your business card and/or personal brochure (discussed later). Ideally, they should also take something else, such as a Q & A brochure, a handout with your presentation slides on them, or some other handout that will remind them of your message points. Your contact information should appear on everything you distribute.

*Other Media Opportunities.* There are other media opportunities, including local radio and television. There are many financial advisors who host their own 1-hour radio or television show on local public access channels. Others find their way on to local radio talk shows and local television news, and into newspaper articles as financial experts. Let local media know you are available, and inform them of the topics on which you can provide expert opinion. If they call you, the exposure is free and will help establish you as an expert in your field.

### Personal Brochure

**personal brochure**

A second important method for creating awareness of your personal brand is a *personal brochure* (for some captive agents, this may not be allowed). You may have seen these brochures from other successful professionals or advisors, or from the service providers who create them. The personal brochure is typically a one-page (usually front and back) document or tri-fold that introduces the advisor. Treat it as the prospect's first impression of you. It should impress, inform, and create interest. Here are a few aspects to keep in mind:

***Value Proposition.*** Design your personal brochure so that it appeals to your target market or target markets. Specifically, design the brochure around your value proposition, using supporting information and images that communicate the logical and emotional benefits you promise to provide.

***Standard Information.*** A personal brochure should include the following standard business information:

- company name
- company address
- company phone number
- e-mail address
- web address
- products and services offered

***Personal Information.*** The amount of personalization is up to you. Some advisors subscribe more to a résumé approach, listing their professional accomplishments and credentials with little personal information. Other advisors include more personal information, communicating both their credentials and their personality. How much personalization you use will depend on your target market. It is important that you know what information members in your market want to know about their financial advisor.

Personal information that many advisors share in their brochures, includes the following:

- photographs of the advisor and/or family
- pictures of the advisor taking part in his or her hobbies and interests
- list of causes and organizations the advisor supports
- description of values and convictions relevant to the target market

***Credentials, Experience, and Accomplishments.*** Remember to design your brochure from the perspective of what members in your target market want to know. Include accomplishments and credentials that they feel are important. If you went to a cardiac specialist, how would you feel if her résumé indicated that she was the highest paid doctor on the East Coast? You might care; however, you would definitely care that she was recognized as one of the top 10 cardiac surgeons in the country.

| | |
|---|---|
| ***Example:*** | You qualified for Million Dollar Round Table (MDRT) honors. Do you include this in your personal brochure? Ask yourself, "Is it important to members of my target markets? Will it attract them?" If you are working with high-net-worth markets, this information will probably be important (successful people want to work with successful people). But it might repel target markets in the middle class because the connotation might be that you made a lot of money at their expense. |

Most importantly, present your experience and credentials in a way that emphasizes the benefits to the prospect. Prospects may not care that you have earned your LUTCF or ChFC unless you can tell them how it benefits them. It is impressive that you have been working with business owners for 10 years, but what does that mean to the prospect?

Compare the statements in the following examples:

| | |
|---|---|
| ***Example:*** | Sue has been working with small business owners for 10 years. |
| | Sue's 10 years of working with small business owners means she has the experience to identify and address financial problems that often are overlooked. |

Avoid the clichés regarding your outstanding service and expertise. Everyone is "top rated," provides "exceptional service," has "integrity," and is "uniquely qualified." Reading personal brochures that many advisors use could make you wonder if they all live in Lake Wobegon, Garrison Keillor's fictional Minnesota town, "where the women are strong, the men are good looking and all of the children are above average." Instead of meaningless accolades, communicate your service and expertise in terms of the results you have achieved for your clients.

---

***Example:***           Kelly has helped many of her clients save a minimum
                         of $100 per month for their children's college edu-
                         cation. The benefit? Their children graduate with a
                         lower student loan balance and, consequently a better
                         starting financial position in adult life.

---

***Layout and Printing.*** A promotional brochure is the first impression many prospects will have of you. Unless you have a graphic design background, you should strongly consider leaving the layout and design to a professional. It will cost, but it will be worth it. Spend a little money here and put your best foot forward.

***Compliance.*** As with other materials, your brochure must meet your company's compliance standards. Make sure you engage your compliance department early in the process.

***Uses for Your Personal Brochure.*** The personal brochure is a tool that you can use in different situations that support the main purpose of the brochure, which is to introduce you to the prospect. Here is a quick list of ways to use the personal brochure:

- Send it along with a cover letter as a preapproach.
- Use it as one of your handouts at a seminar or public speaking engagement.
- Give a few copies to centers of influence to pass on to potential prospects.
- Gain permission to place it in strategic locations frequented by your target market (chamber of commerce, doctor's office, book store, senior center, and so on).
- Pass copies out at a trade show or an event you sponsor.

### Internet Presence

According to an April 2006 report by The Pew Internet & American Life Project, 73 percent of all adults in the United States use the Internet (the Internet means, among other things, surfing the World Wide Web and/or corresponding via e-mail) and 42 percent of all households access the Internet through broadband connections (DSL, cable, and so on).[7] With the ability to connect to the Internet through cell phones and other wireless devices, having an online presence is important for advisors.

Although online buying of financial products is still evolving, one thing is certain: people who visit a financial services website want to obtain information. This is especially true of younger consumers. According to a LIMRA study, 69 percent of Generation X and 67 percent of Generation Y use the Internet to research information for insurance, annuities, and investments.[8] Thus the pages on your website devoted to education are critical. Here are a few suggestions of what to include:

- *articles about financial topics* about which your target market wants information. Your company may have some articles, or website developers who work only with financial advisors can provide content for you. The best option, if you can write and have time to do so, is to write articles yourself, as you will know what specific topics to address.
- *financial calculators, worksheets, and spreadsheets* that will help members of your target market make financial decisions
- *links to other websites* (Bankrate.com, Kiplinger.com, Money.com, MorningStar.com, MotleyFool.com, SavingforCollege.com, and so on). You should obtain permission to link to a home page (the page that comes up when you put in www.sitename.com). Permission is required for links to any pages other than the site's home page.

Again, make sure all materials on your website are approved by your compliance department.

Presumably, you have much in common with members of your target market. Therefore you do not have to do a lot of extra work to discover and understand them, and you can consider additional issues that affect your target market. For example, if many people in your target market own or will purchase a home in the near future, information and links about buying a home and home ownership might be an added value. Similarly, if your target market is within a fixed locale, you might include community information and local merchants.

**weblog (blog)**　　Some advisors have gone so far as to create their own *weblog*, or blog for short. A blog is an online journal that allows for interaction between you and your web audience. Advisors who blog typically will post an article from a financial publication or online news source and give their opinion. Readers can then ask questions and make comments (if the advisor selects this option). Postings need to be frequent; weekly is a good goal. This strategy is more appropriate if you are dealing with a target market that is regional or national, and one that is interested in blogs.

***Creating a Website.*** Now that you have some background information, let us talk about what you need to do to create a website.

First, talk to members in your target market. Find out the following:

- Where (books, websites, magazines, radio, television, and so on) do they go to obtain information (about your products and services)?
- What websites do they visit to gain information (about your products and services)?
- What information would they like to see?
- Have they ever used online financial calculators? Which ones? How did they like them?

Second, identify the different areas you want to include on your website. Think about how much time it will take to update your site. A site that doesn't change may not be effective for some target markets. Here are a few areas you might want to include:

- home page
- index
- site map
- About Us page
- company/carriers
- glossary of financial terms
- search engine (to search the site)
- articles and information
- stock quotes
- financial calculators
- event calendar (for seminars and other events)
- driving directions
- referrals to other advisors

Third, look for a professional website developer. If you do not know one, consider a company that specializes in developing websites for financial advisors. Some of these companies provide articles and financial calculators for additional cost. Unless you are planning to offer portfolio tracking, insurance quoting, and so on, the cost for developing the website will be fairly reasonable. You will not need to spend thousands of dollars.

Fourth, do not use third-party information without securing permission. As already mentioned, it is a good practice to obtain permission simply to link to another website. In addition, observe the copyright laws. Give attribution when someone else's material is used. As always, run all of your content through your compliance department.

Fifth, when the website is finished, put the web address on everything that goes out of your office. Publicize it on your newsletters, business cards, advertisements, and personal brochure.

Finally, track whether or not prospects and clients have been to your website, and obtain feedback for suggested improvements.

### *Newsletters*

Newsletters are another way to build prestige and create interest in your products. Although traditionally geared to relationship building and marketing to current clients, newsletters can be used with prospects as well.

One cost-effective method is to send your newsletters to selected prospects who have indicated an interest in them. If you are writing some of the articles, this will be an opportunity to demonstrate your expertise.

The same holds true if you send out your newsletters via e-mail and/or post them to your website. The added bonus here is that an electronic newsletter is typically less expensive to produce than a printed one. If you do send your newsletter electronically, put a link on your website that allows people to sign up for it online.

You can send a prospect a newsletter that addresses a topic or need in which he or she has expressed an interest or concern. You could send a newsletter with a note such as, "It was nice to meet you. I thought you might be interested in this." Even if you have not written any of the articles, this method demonstrates that you listen to people. Furthermore, the relevant article(s) may make the prospect more aware of a need and more open to meeting with you.

### *Advertising*

**advertising**　　*Advertising* is the use of persuasive messages communicated through the mass media. The ultimate goal of advertising is to create new clients. For the purposes of financial products, advertising seems best suited to create awareness of an advisor's personal brand rather than to induce prospects to purchase specific products.

The premise for using advertising is that prospects typically want to work with advisors with whom they have some level of comfort and trust. All things being equal, they will want to work with an advisor they have at least heard of rather than a total stranger. Advertising promotes in a prospect a level of familiarity with the advisor. It may predispose the prospect to a favorable response when the advisor approaches him or her.

You should realize the case for advertising is not universally accepted by successful advisors. Judging from arguments on both sides, advertising effectiveness largely depends on the target market and its interaction with various advertising media.

***How Your Target Market Identifies Potential Advisors.*** Determine how members in your target market find advisors like you. Do they use the phone book, or do they use referrals? The type of products you sell could influence this. For example, homeowners and auto insurance are products for which prospects will shop for the lowest price, using online rate quotes and/or a telephone directory. Advertising in a telephone directory (paper or online) would make sense for these types of products. The bottom line is that if your target market turns to a particular source for financial advisors' contact information, that is a good place to advertise.

***Where Your Target Market Frequents.*** Consider advertising any places where a high concentration of your target market frequents. By places, we mean physical locations as well as radio shows, radio stations, websites, and so on. For instance, one very successful life insurance agent began advertising on a radio show geared toward the traditional senior market. Eventually, she gained an endorsement from the show's host, and her annuity sales skyrocketed.

***What Connects with Your Target Market.*** Select advertisements that are appropriate to your target market. If you are unable to create your own marketing messages, consider retaining the services of an advertising firm for assistance. As always, check with your compliance department for approval and guidance.

***The Effectiveness of Your Advertising Efforts.*** It is important to track and assess the effectiveness of your advertising efforts. Ask prospects (regardless of the source) if they have seen any of your advertisements. Some advisors ask for this information using a form much like the one you complete when you go to a doctor's office for the first time (see Figure 2-1 for some sample questions).

---

**FIGURE 2-1**
**Sample Questions from a Prospect Information Form**

How did you hear about us? Please check <u>all</u> that apply.

❏ Yellow Pages                               ❏ _____ told me about you

❏ Heard your ad on radio station          ❏ Your company's website
_____

❏ Saw your ad in _____            ❏ Saw your billboard at _____

❏ Phone directory on the Internet          ❏ Link from website _____

❏ Received your letter or postcard          ❏ Other_____

---

## Preapproaches

**preapproach**

Although there is overlap between prestige building and preapproaches, we delineate between the two. Whereas prestige building deals mainly with creating an awareness of who you are and what you do, a *preapproach* focuses more on heightening a prospect's interest in your products and services. Thus a preapproach is any method used to stimulate the prospect's interest and precondition him or her to agree to meet with you about potential financial needs. Two of the more common preapproaches are seminars and preapproach letters.

### *Seminars*

**seminar**

A *seminar* is a prospecting method in which you, alone or as a part of a team of professional advisors, conduct an educational and motivational meeting for a group of people. Seminars are distinct from speaking to groups in that a seminar's objective typically is to produce appointments. Thus there is a predetermined method for asking for appointments after the seminar has concluded. Sometimes, however, seminars are designed with prestige-building objectives in mind.

Seminars can be expensive, and they require a lot of time to plan and execute. There are many variables to consider and manage. In spite of these disadvantages, seminars provide some distinct advantages and should be considered as a marketing tool. These advantages include the following:

- Prospects who agree to a follow-up appointment are really coming to a fact-finding interview because they already have an understanding of their potential need and how the product can help them. In other words, a seminar is like conducting an initial interview for several prospects at one time, which is a tremendous time saver.
- Assuming that you and other presenters give educational and motivational presentations, seminars build your credibility as an expert.
- Seminars allow you to maximize your public speaking skills.
- The natural next step of a seminar is either asking for an appointment or setting the expectation that you will be calling for one.

Using seminars as a preapproach is indicated when your target market is responsive to them and you have access to appropriate seminar material relevant to the target market's needs. Seminars have been successful with seniors because they have time to attend and often want more information about relevant financial products and services. Another potential group may be employees of a small business (although this would be less of a preapproach and more of a prestige-building use of seminars). The best way to find out if seminars will be successful is to attempt a few seminars after researching some of the points discussed below.

It is helpful to have a written game plan—a step-by-step description of what you need to do and when you need to do it. A checklist, such as the one provided in Figure 2-2, lets you see at a glance where you are and what remains to do.

***Define Your Objective.*** The first step in planning a seminar is to establish your objective. Ask yourself what the seminar should accomplish. Your goal must be specific, attainable, and measurable. For example, you may set a goal of making 10 appointments with seminar attendees. Or your goal may be to provide an informational seminar for 15 of your best clients. The goal you set is important because it will affect other decisions regarding the seminar details.

***Set a Budget.*** It is especially helpful to establish a budget and work to stay within this constraint. Food is generally not served, but if you wish to provide refreshments, keep them simple and inexpensive. If you are using a hotel or restaurant, you may need to resist the pressures to serve lavish meals. Remember you are selling your knowledge and expertise—not giving away food.

***Determine the Invitees.*** Determine how many people to invite. Begin by setting a goal for the number of attendees you wish to have. This will depend on the purpose of your seminar. Keep in mind that it takes roughly 15 to 20 attendees to justify the expense of holding a seminar, depending on the selection of facilities and other frills. You will learn from experience how many people to invite to have the desired number of attendees. One rule of thumb is to invite 10 people for each desired attendee. The ratio of invitees to attendees will improve as your seminars become better known.

Once you have determined how many people to invite, create a list of names. Derive your list using prospects obtained from the prospecting methods you have previously identified for your target market. One of the more popular sources is a list directory from a third-party vendor.

**FIGURE 2-2**
**Seminar Checklist**

### Arranging for a Meeting Room

- Has the meeting been confirmed?
- Who's your contact?
- Have you met this person?
- Have you seen the facility?
- Have you done a walk-through to see what it will be like when prospects arrive and go to the meeting room?

### Guest List

- Do you know who will attend?
- Will anyone from your company be there?
- How many prospects will your budget cover?

### Seminar Promotion

- Have you arranged a schedule for printing promotional and other material to be distributed during the seminar? Does the schedule include time to proofread printed material to avoid potentially embarrassing errors? Does it allow for delays at the print shop?
- Have letters or formal invitations been sent at least four weeks prior to the seminar?
- Have the invitees been called during the week just prior to the seminar to confirm their attendance?
- Have announcements been sent to local newspapers, radio stations, and other media outlets?

### Getting There

- Do prospects know the date and precise time of the seminar?
- Do they have directions to the meeting rooms?
- Will they have to use a special entrance?
- Have you asked the hotel or office complex for signs with directions?
- Will you have a check-in desk?
- How will early arrivals be handled?
- What are the provisions for parking?
- Will your prospects need a means of identification such as name badges?
- Who will look after late arrivals?
- Will you need a message board?

### Meeting Facilities

- How will the room be arranged?
- Do you want chairs only or chairs and tables?
- Will you need signs for reserved seats?
- Are you supplying paper, pens, and pencils?
- Will you need a microphone? If so, do you have an extra one in case one cannot be located at the meeting facility?
- Will you need a lectern?
- Will the speakers need help with any equipment during the presentation?
- Is the lighting adequate?
- Will there be a projection system?
- Will there be a screen?
- Will you have spare projector bulbs?
- Will you need a flip chart, writing pad, or magic markers?
- When the projector is on, do the main room lights need to be turned off? If so, who will do this?
- Have you supplied water and glasses for the speakers?
- Who will make the introductions?
- Will there be a coffee break?

### Seminar Content/Speakers

- What topics will be covered?
- Who are the best speakers to address each area?
- How long should each person speak?
- What is the most appropriate format for the presentation (for example, lecture, round table discussion)?
- How much compensation (if any) should the speakers be offered?

### Problems

- Whom do you contact if there is a problem?
- Will the house audio/visual technician be available?
- What do you do if someone becomes ill?
- Where are the fire escapes located?
- Are there any security measures required?
- How will people make outgoing telephone calls?
- Who will handle the incoming calls?
- How will you deal with cell phones ringing in the middle of the presentation?
- Do you have a reliable assistant to help you run the meeting?
- Have you thought of everything that could possibly go wrong?

***Choose the Content.*** The content of your seminar should be a blend of technical information and motivational material about a topic that is most relevant to your target market's needs. How much of each depends on the needs of the prospects you invite. Remember, you want them to understand their financial needs and motivate them to meet with you. Avoid giving them so much information that they do not need to make an appointment with you. Remember, the program should be compliance-approved. For some advisors, this means using only those presentations approved by their company.

***Select the Presenter(s).*** If you are not a good public speaker, you can utilize another speaker, such as a company expert, to present the bulk of the material.

One of the most effective ways to develop and present a seminar is to use a team approach (per your compliance area). For example, for an estate planning seminar, the team could consist of a life insurance agent, an estate planning attorney, and/or an accountant versed in estate planning issues. In effect, prospects are offered a complete package of services. This also provides an opportunity to split the costs of sponsoring the seminar.

***Choose a Date and Time.*** This may seem unimportant, but choosing a date and time is critical. Avoid holidays and dates that coincide with important local or national events that interest your target market. Also consider how the time of day may affect your target market's willingness or ability to attend. For example, evening seminars may not be appropriate for seniors.

***Select a Convenient Location.*** The site you select should be convenient for the members of your targeted group. Parking may be a prime consideration in urban and suburban areas. The location should also be neutral. It is generally recommended that you do not use your office. The fear here is that invitees may see your office as a high-pressure environment and therefore fail to attend. An outside space creates an environment of neutrality and objectivity. The site of the group's regular meetings would be an excellent suggestion, provided it is conducive to a seminar

***Announce the Seminar.*** The invitation should clearly inform the prospect that the seminar will be educational in nature. It should provide the topic, date, time, and length of each seminar session as well as any fees to be paid. The seminar title should be clear and relate to the perceived needs of the targeted audience. If your seminar will include workbooks or data forms, the invitation should highlight the benefits of these materials to the prospect. You may wish to plant a seed for follow-up by informing the prospect that each attendee will be entitled to a personalized complimentary analysis of his or her situation. If an expert will be featured, note this on the seminar invitation together with the expert's credentials and accomplishments.

In addition to the invitation itself, your letter should contain a response mechanism (a telephone number, e-mail address, or a stamped, self-addressed postcard) for more information. Some financial advisors send a second (reminder) mailing. For best results, follow up replies with calls confirming attendance a day or two prior to the presentation.

It is important to monitor both the mailing of the invitations and the response rate. Careful monitoring will allow time for you to make adjustments. The mailing itself should usually begin at least four weeks prior to the seminar date. When you are sending large numbers of invitations, seed the mailing with your name and those of a few trusted friends or colleagues. This gives you a mechanism to determine whether or not invitations have reached their intended destinations.

*Check the Facilities.* Checking and rechecking the facilities you have chosen will help your meeting run smoothly. Try to visit the facility while another meeting is in progress. This will give you the opportunity to evaluate the lighting, the sound system, and the visibility of any screens you will use with a projector. You can assess how well everyone in the room can see the speaker and judge whether the ambiance of the room reflects the feeling you wish to convey to your audience. Consider what audiovisual equipment or visual aids, such as an easel or whiteboard, you will need before you begin calling facilities.

*Prepare a Feedback Mechanism.* Plan to use a feedback mechanism. Some seminar presenters ask attendees to sign in and give their names, addresses, and phone numbers. Others design an evaluation form that asks the attendees for this information, as well as for feedback on the quality and usefulness of the presentation. See Figure 2-3 for a sample post-seminar questionnaire.

*Address Miscellaneous Details.* It is important to pay attention to details, as they send your prospect a message about yourself. Remember to bring nametags, pens, paper, and handouts. Do not skimp on quality. For example, handouts of the highest quality that include your name and address convey the message that you are professional and that you are willing to put your name on the work you do. Having paper and pens available sends the message that what you say is important enough to write down.

**FIGURE 2-3**
**Post-seminar Questionnaire (Long-Term Care Seminar)**

We would greatly appreciate your help by answering the following questions. Your responses will guide us in improving future seminars and determining if our organization may be of assistance to you in the future.

1.  Which speaker did you find the most helpful?

    _____

2.  Which subject(s) covered during the seminar was (were) of most interest to you?

    _____

    _____

3.  Briefly list any subject areas that were not covered in the seminar that you think should have been covered.

    _____

    _____

    _____

4.  You may have some questions that you did not have an opportunity to raise during the question-and-answer session. Please briefly list these questions below. We will make every effort to answer these questions for you or to find experts who can provide responses.

    _____

    _____

    _____

| For the following statements, circle the response that best describes how you feel. | Strongly Disagree | | Agree | | Strongly Agree |
|---|---|---|---|---|---|
| I fear depending on family or friends for my care as I get older. | 1 | 2 | 3 | 4 | 5 |
| If I ever need long-term care, I want the freedom to decide what type of care I will receive and where I will receive it. | 1 | 2 | 3 | 4 | 5 |
| I am afraid I may not qualify for long-term care insurance if I wait too long. | 1 | 2 | 3 | 4 | 5 |
| I want to protect my assets from the potentially high costs of long-term care. | 1 | 2 | 3 | 4 | 5 |
| I am concerned about taking care of my parents or another relative should they need long-term care. | 1 | 2 | 3 | 4 | 5 |

**Name:** _____    **Address:** _____

**Phone:** _____    _____

**Fax:** _____    **E-mail:** _____

***Conduct an Effective Follow-up Campaign.*** Seminars present you as a knowledgeable professional to a group of potential prospects. Most effective seminars are low-key and avoid overt attempts to sell products or specific services. Any one-on-one selling typically occurs after the seminar. For this reason, the follow-up phase of the seminar takes on real significance. Many advisors end their presentation by telling their audience that the advisor will contact each attendee to answer any questions that might result from the seminar. Others bring their appointment book to the seminar and schedule appointments on the spot. The post-seminar questionnaire is an invaluable tool for understanding each prospect's interest as well as for collecting contact information.

### Preapproach Letters

preapproach letter

A *preapproach letter* is a letter or postcard mailed (or e-mailed) to a prospect with the goal of introducing the advisor and arousing the prospect's interest in meeting with the advisor. Properly used, preapproach letters can be a powerful aid to your approach.

One of the advantages of the preapproach letter is that it creates a sense of familiarity. The very fact that you can start by saying, "I wrote to you last week, mentioning that I would call on you," gives you a basis for contacting the prospect. In addition to preparing prospects to receive your call, effective use of preapproach letters can result in other advantages to your prospecting efforts as follows:

- They make prospects more receptive because they create an awareness of possible financial needs and problems that prospects should address.
- They help develop good work habits. By sending a definite number of letters on a regular basis, you commit yourself to calling on prospects every week. This gives you a measure of outside discipline—discipline that requires a regular schedule of prompt follow-up calls. When you use direct mail regularly, you let the law of averages work in your favor.
- They relieve some of the pressure of the first call. The prospect has seen your name at least once.
- They improve the ratio of interviews to calls. All things being equal, a previous contact with the prospect, however slight it was, means you have a better chance of obtaining a fact-finding interview than if you made a completely cold call.

Consider the impact of the following preapproach letter.

***Example:***        ***Preapproach Letter for Life Insurance***

Dear (Prospect),

The events of Hurricane Katrina have demonstrated that a lack of planning can make a difficult situation worse. The same holds true in the case of the death of a parent. Financial difficulties will only intensify the emotional pain that the surviving loved ones feel.

However, proper planning now will mean an easier adjustment period and greater financial security for those left behind.

I help families like yours design an emergency plan using life insurance and other planning techniques. Several families I have worked with will attest that planning made all the difference for them.

If you are interested in meeting with me, please return the postage-paid reply card and I will contact you promptly. I look forward to meeting with you soon.

Sincerely,

Mercedes Hightower, CLU, FSS

***Choosing Effective Preapproach Letters.*** Keep in mind the following guidelines when you are choosing from among your company's inventory of standardized mailings:

- Select letters that reflect your target market's needs.
- Generally the shorter the better.
- Postcards are often more effective than letters because there is no envelope to open.

If you feel your company's standard letters are not adequate, obtain company approval to draft your own. Your three main objectives in writing a preapproach letter are to

- trigger your prospect's interest by briefly highlighting a problem that needs to be solved
- communicate the relevant parts of your value proposition related to meeting that need
- prepare the prospect for your call or request his or her response (if the prospect is on a do-not-call list)

Letter writing is an art. Expect an effective letter to take a fair amount of time to compose. Before you write your letter, review how to position your products. Here are a few additional guidelines to consider:

- Aim to write something that grabs the prospect's attention.
- Establish a basis for your contact by referring to how you have heard of the prospect.
- Describe the most probable and acute financial need that the prospect faces and that you can address.
- Link that financial need to an appropriate emotional need.
- Do not overstate the need; that is manipulative.
- In communicating your value proposition, keep it to one or two sentences. Avoid platitudes and clichés.
- Confirm the credibility of any statistics you use, and use them responsibly and appropriately (do not overuse them).
- Pay strict attention to wording, grammar, spelling, and punctuation.
- Ensure that the letter conveys an image of professionalism by using quality stationery and typeface.
- Ask a current client from your target market to review the letter's message and appearance.

Figure 2-4 is a guide to help you draft your own preapproach letters.

***Preapproach Letter Logistics.*** Think about the logistics related to mailing preapproach letters. Sometimes the little things can make a big difference. Evaluate and try some of the following:

- No letter is good enough to do a selling job by itself. An efficient and effective follow-up system is crucial to the success of any direct mail program. Do not send letters to more prospects than you can follow up with during the next week.
- Consider addressing letters by hand. Some advisors have found that handwritten addresses increase the probability that prospects will open the letters.
- Affix postage with an individual stamp rather than a postage meter. Some advisors highly recommend the use of commemorative stamps.
- Consider including an attention-getter in the envelope. One advisor includes a dollar bill to pay the prospect for reading the letter. Another advisor includes a Band-Aid with a health insurance preapproach letter.
- E-mail is another way to send a preapproach letter. If you are dealing with a technically savvy target market, e-mail may be more effective than regular mail.

**FIGURE 2-4**
**Writing a Preapproach Letter**

### Template for Drafting Letter

| | |
|---|---|
| **Basis for contact (if applicable)** | Met the prospect at a fund raiser for leukemia |
| **Financial need/ problem** | To pay for children's college tuition and other expenses |
| **Corresponding emotional need** | A desire for children's financial security and success |
| **Problem definition** | College tuition and expenses are costly now. What will they be in 10 or 15 years? How much debt will your children have to incur to pay for college? |
| **Value proposition** | I can help you find money today to save for tomorrow's education, thus minimizing debt and giving your children the opportunity to get started in their adult life on a more solid financial footing. |
| **Closing** | I will be calling in the next week to see if I can help you. |

### Letter to Prospect

Dear (Prospect),

It was a pleasure to meet you last week at the Chester County "Find the Cure" fundraiser.

You mentioned you had three young children. You probably have considered the importance of their college education. Indeed, over a lifetime, the earnings for a person with a bachelor's degree is estimated to be more than $1,000,000 above those of an employee with only a high school education. (Source: U.S. Census Bureau statistics).

But consider that one year of college costs an average of over $14,000 for a public college (in-state) and over $34,000 for a private college in 2008-09.* What will the cost be in 10 or 15 years? How much debt will burden your children after they graduate?

I help families like yours find money today to save for tomorrow's education costs. By planning today, you can minimize your children's student loan debt, enabling them to get started in their adult life on a more solid and secure financial footing.

I will be calling in the next week to see how I might be able to help you.

Sincerely,

Winston Dunn, ChFC, FSS

* Source: College Board's Trends in College Pricing 2008

**third-party influence piece**

***Third-Party Influence Piece.*** A variation of the preapproach letter is the *third-party influence piece.* Many advisors have found that marketing material from their own companies or commercial services can be valuable in creating awareness. Various publishing houses have available such items as a series of tax letters, legal bulletins, and other mailing pieces that are of interest and value to business owners and executives. It would help to establish your prestige if you send prospects such publications. You could also enclose articles of this kind with a preapproach letter.

Prospects who receive third-party material from an advisor will probably recognize that the advisor has an appreciation of financial matters. They may remember the advisor's name, especially if they receive material from the advisor on a regular basis (every month or every quarter, for example). Thus they are more likely to be willing to listen to what the advisor has to say.

## APPROACHING THE PROSPECT

**approaching the prospect**

The next step in the selling/planning process is *approaching the prospect.* This is the process of obtaining the prospect's consent to see you, and setting the date, time, and place of the appointment. This section will discuss some telephone strategies you can use to approach prospects. Following these proven methods will enable you to approach prospects with confidence. You can also apply some of these principles to face-to-face approaches.

### Write Telephone Scripts

Appointment setting is arguably the most difficult aspect of selling financial products. Yet without appointments the selling/planning process grinds to a halt. Given that appointment setting is such a critical aspect of the selling/planning process, it makes sense to plan what you will say and how you will say it. In addition, writing, scripting, and practicing a telephone script has the following advantages:

- You sound professional and natural because you know what you will say. A rehearsed script will help reduce the "ums," "you knows," "I means," and "uhs," and give you confidence. If you sound confident in yourself, you give the prospect reason to have confidence in you.
- Practicing a script helps you refine your statements and questions to ensure they are clear. You can also eliminate the telemarketing trademark—sounding like you're reading from a script, which is deadly.

- A script ensures consistency, which helps you duplicate success and troubleshoot failure. If you are not consistent, how will you know something does not work or how will you repeat your success?
- When you know what you are going to say, you can concentrate more on the prospect's reaction, listen carefully, and respond in a meaningful way. As you become familiar with typical responses and objections, you will feel more natural and confident in your conversations with prospects.

With these benefits in mind we will discuss how to write a script. Keep in mind that there are no magic scripts, but there are some that work better than others. A good telephone script has only one objective: get the appointment. Some advisors prequalify, too. This is recommended, but the overwhelming objective remains to secure the appointment.

Before we begin writing scripts, we should state upfront that what you say will greatly depend on whom you are approaching. For example, you may find that you can be more direct with friends and family than with a cold call or a referred lead. We suggest that you have scripts for each of the following sources:

- family/friend
- someone you met
- referral or center of influence
- seminar
- cold call
- existing client
- direct mail follow-up

### Greeting

In the greeting, you will introduce yourself and confirm that the prospect is willing to talk to you. This is your opportunity to make a good first impression. Here are a few tips for what to include in your greeting.

- Open your conversation with "Good morning" or "Good afternoon." It is more upbeat than "Hello." Also it gives the prospect a little extra time to settle and begin to listen to you.
- Identify who you are and what company you represent. If you are calling someone who knows you, don't assume they recognize your voice. Identify yourself.
- As a matter of courtesy, ask the prospect if he or she has time to talk. Pushing your agenda on the prospect may turn a "not right now" into "not ever." You can do this simply by asking, "Have I caught you at

a good time?" If the prospect indicates he or she has the time, communicate your respect for their time. For example, you could say, "I will only take a moment of your time."

---

***Example:***          "Good morning, this is Kelly Martin from ABC Financial Services. May I speak to Juanita?" (Wait for a response.)

"Have I caught you at a good time?" (Wait for response.)

"Great. I will take only a few minutes."

---

### Creating Interest

In this step, you will explain why you are calling and implement a method designed to pique the prospect's interest so he or she will agree to meet with you.

Typically, the reason for your call is to follow up on a preapproach letter or article you sent, a comment card from a seminar, or a referral of that person by a friend. (Using a preapproach helps reduce the awkwardness of calling in that it provides a legitimate reason for contacting the prospect.)

There are at least two different methods used to create interest. Some advisors take a direct approach and simply address the prospect's most probable financial needs as indicated by his or her life-cycle market segment.

---

***Example:***          "The reason I am calling is to follow up on the letter I sent you a few weeks ago about making sure your and your family's needs are taken care of even in the most challenging life situations. Most people do not understand the limitations of Social Security benefits and the pitfalls of depending on them."

---

This approach is appropriate if the advisor has a narrow product base and/or has already determined the prospect's need. For example, if you are selling Medicare supplement plans or long-term care insurance to a senior market, such an approach may be very effective. The weakness of this approach is that it does not allow you to gauge the prospect's interest or touch on other needs you do not mention.

A second method for achieving this objective is to ask an open-ended question that allows you to uncover potential needs the prospect has. The advisor can provide a list of the most probable needs, applying the life-cycle marketing strategy, and asking the prospect which of these needs he or she considers most pressing.

Depending on the prospect's answer to the question, you can follow up with questions designed to uncover a logical basis for the appointment. In other words, you are looking for a good logical foundation upon which to position your request for an appointment.

---

***Example:***     "I'm calling to follow up on the article I sent you about common needs young families have. Did you have a chance to read it?

If yes: "What did you think?"

If no: "Which do you feel is your greatest need: to provide monies to help a surviving spouse pay for final expenses and eliminate debt; to start saving for retirement; or some other financial goal or need?"

Possible follow-up questions:

- "What are your goals regarding [financial goal or need]?"
- "What are your concerns related to addressing [financial goal or need]?"
- "What have you done to address your situation?"
- "How do you feel about the planning you've done so far?"

---

### Asking for the Appointment

This is the reason you are calling. In asking for the appointment, you are going to first offer a value proposition, a clear and compelling reason why the prospect should meet with you based on the prospect's most probable need. This may be your value proposition for your practice or one for the product you are selling. Either way, the statement should capture the essence of the results you create for people like the prospect (the target market). Personalize the results if you can.

Second, ask for the appointment, but do not refer to it as an appointment. People associate appointments with doctors and dentists—places they go because they have to go. Some alternatives are "meet," "see," or "get together."

---

***Example:*** "Many parents I talk to at the karate club feel the same way. My practice is focused on helping parents like you apply, what I like to call, financial self-defense strategies to protect their families from the unexpected. I would like to meet with you to see if some of these strategies might help you. Would you have some time to come to my office either next Wednesday in the evening or Thursday morning? It should take about one hour."

---

### *Prequalifying*

**prequalifying**

For those advisors who believe in *prequalifying*, this would be an appropriate time to do so. Prequalifying involves asking the prospect a few questions to ensure the meeting will not waste the prospect's and the advisor's time. The questions are related to underwriting issues (for insurance) and/or suitability issues. Some advisors ask a question to identify any third party who may influence the prospect's decision, such as a CPA or an adult child.

Whether or not you prequalify prospects depends on your type of practice and personal views. If you have other products or services to offer someone who does not qualify for a particular product, prequalifying is not necessary. On the other hand, if you are not able to help those prospects who fail to meet underwriting and/or suitability requirements, you risk angering them for wasting their time.

If you decide to prequalify, incorporate that into your script. You will need to transition from setting the appointment to the prequalifying questions. One commonly used transition is, "I know your time is valuable. So to make our time together as productive as possible, it would help for me to know some basic information about you." Then pause and ask three to five brief and simple questions.

You will need to script how you will respond if a prospect is not qualified for the product you are selling. Knowing what you will say will help you move past this potentially awkward moment.

| *Example:* | "Ms. Jones, I am really sorry but it looks like from the health information you gave me, we will not be able to help you at this time. I highly recommend that you establish an emergency fund of 6 to 12 months of income to replace lost income if you are unable to work. If I can be of any assistance to you in other ways, please do not hesitate to call." |
|---|---|

### Ending the Call

Ending the call is the last step of the telephone approach script. This step is when you confirm the appointment and affirm your desire to meet the prospect. Depending on where you meet, you may either have to give or obtain directions.

| *Example:* | "Great! I will see you Thursday at 7:15 in the evening here in my office. I am really looking forward to getting to know you." |
|---|---|

### Handling Objections

Unfortunately, prospects often have objections to meeting with you. You will find that they will usually fall into one of four categories:

- no hurry
- no money
- no need
- no trust

Sometimes an objection may fall into two categories. For example one common objection is, "I have an advisor already," which could be placed in the no need or no trust categories.

Rather than be caught off guard and have no idea how to handle objections, write a script for each of the more common ones you face. Even if you do not use the script, having written it will ensure you have given some thought as to the issues underlying the prospect's objections and strategies for helping the prospect work through them. As a result, you will have confidence as you address the prospect's objections. The perception of confidence will have as much of an impact as the actual approach you use to address their resistance.

A common strategy for handling objections is to use the "Feel, Felt, Found" technique. This technique works well for objections that the advisor feels need no further clarification and are simple to handle.

---

*Example:*          "Juanita, what you feel is normal. In fact, some of my clients originally felt the same way as you. But after they met with me they found that there was more to insuring their future than what they originally anticipated. I was able to help them achieve financial peace of mind, and I would like to meet to see if you feel I can help you, too. Is that fair enough?" (Wait for an answer.)

Would next Wednesday morning or Thursday afternoon work for you?"

---

The "Acknowledge, Clarify, Resolve" technique works for all objections. The steps are as follows.

***Acknowledge the Objection.*** In most cases the prospect's objection is common and understandable. Express that to the prospect:

---

*Example:*          "You feel like you do not have enough money. I hear what you are saying. No one likes to spend money unnecessarily."

---

***Clarify the Objection.*** In some cases, you need more information about the prospect's objection before you respond. For example, you may need to determine what is causing the prospect to feel the way he or she feels, or even whether or not the stated objection is the real objection. A few carefully chosen questions can unlock the prospect's feelings.

---

*Example:*          "Have you gotten quotes from other insurance companies? If so, what is the price and for how much insurance?" (Wait for answer.)

---

***Resolve the Objection.*** Once you feel you understand the prospect's objection, restate it, if necessary, to confirm your understanding. Then apply the appropriate strategy for resolving it and ask for the appointment again.

*Example:*    "Many of my clients who felt like you were surprised at how reasonable the cost is, especially when compared to the amount of coverage they received. Wouldn't it make sense to explore what you need and see if we can find a way to fit your budget?" (Wait for answer.)

"If Yes: "Then would next Wednesday morning or Thursday afternoon work for you?"

**escape close**

***Use an Escape Close.*** Sometimes the prospect's resistance remains after your best attempt to overcome it. In these situations, you need an *escape close*, which is a way to end the conversation that leaves the door open. You should not try to debate someone into accepting an appointment. If you detect a prospect has no interest after you have attempted twice to schedule an appointment, have an escape close ready to end the conversation.

One method for keeping the door open is to ask the prospect if he or she would be interested in receiving mail. Most importantly, remind the prospect to contact you if he or she should have a change of mind. Thank the prospect for his or her time and close.

*Example:*    "Okay. I understand. Would you like to receive information periodically about insurance and other financial products?" (Wait for answer.)

"If you change your mind or know of anyone like yourself who needs help understanding how to protect his or her financial future, give me a call. I am in the phone book under Kelly Martin Insurance. Thanks for your time. Have a good evening."

### Follow Do-Not-Call Laws

**do-not-call laws**

The Federal Communications Commission (FCC) and the Federal Trade Commission (FTC) have created *do-not-call laws*, which are designed to protect consumers from telemarketing abuses. In addition, some states have enacted state regulations. Make sure you know the ones for your state.

### The Do-Not-Call Laws

The do-not-call laws are designed to eliminate unsolicited telemarketing calls without the consumer's prior consent. One of the major provisions of the regulations is the creation of a national Do-Not-Call (DNC) list. Calling a person on the DNC list may result in a fine of $10,000 or more per violation. In addition, the regulations place limitations on telemarketers. Some of the important ones include the following:[9]

- Sales calls to persons who have placed their residential or mobile phone numbers on federal or state DNC lists are prohibited.
- Calls cannot be made before 8 a.m. or after 9 p.m.
- Sellers must maintain an in-house DNC list of existing customers who do not want to receive sales calls.
- Sales callers must, at the beginning of every sales call, identify themselves, the company they represent, and the purpose of the call.
- Telemarketers may not intentionally block consumers' use of caller identification.
- Stiff penalties are placed on violators.

There are four exceptions to the national DNC list. If a consumer meets one of these four exceptions, and has not placed their name and number on your company's DNC list, the advisor can call that person. The exceptions are the following:[10]

- *Established business relationship.* A business relationship exists in which a product or service is in place, and for 18 months after that product or service is no longer in effect or active. Several states have stricter requirements. If a consumer contacts an advisor, whether by phone, mail, e-mail, or in person, to inquire about a product or service, an existing business relationship exists for three months after that inquiry.
- *Business-to-business.* The DNC regulations do not apply to business-to-business calls.
- *Prior written permission.* Advisors may make calls to persons on the DNC lists if they have a signed, written agreement from the consumer in which he or she agrees to be contacted by telephone at a specified telephone number. An e-mail from the prospect that clearly grants permission and identifies a number to call should suffice. Advisors may not call persons on the DNC list to ask for written permission to be called.

- *Personal relationship.* Calls may be made to people with whom an advisor has a personal relationship, including family members, friends, and acquaintances.

### Working within the Rules

These laws make contacting prospects for appointments more challenging. Even referrals are affected. Advisors cannot contact prospects who are referred leads unless they receive written permission from the prospects to do so. Here are a few ideas to address these challenges.

***Ask for Personal Introductions.*** An arranged meeting over lunch, a cup of coffee, a round of golf, and so on would be ideal. This would give you a little more time to build rapport and probe for needs.

***Ask for an E-mail Recommendation.*** The best method for using e-mail is to have the referrer write an e-mail recommending you to the prospect and letting the prospect know that you will be in contact with him or her. The referrer should carbon copy (Cc) you so that you have the prospect's e-mail. Then you may send an introductory e-mail along with a request for permission, a phone number, and a best time to call. Have your e-mail approved by your compliance department, if necessary.

***Send a Direct Mailer with Response Cards.*** If the prospect does not have an e-mail address or the referrer is reluctant to give it out, consider sending a prospecting letter with a compliance-approved response card. The card should request a signature and a phone number to call.

***Invite the Prospect to a Seminar.*** Ask the referrer to jot a recommendation on a 3 x 5 index card. For example, "Lance really helped me make some important financial decisions." Mail the recommendation along with an invitation to a seminar you are holding. If the prospect comes to the seminar, you will have an opportunity to gain permission to call face to face.

### Implement a Strategy for Caller Identification and Voice Mail

Caller identification and voice mail have made it more difficult to reach prospects by phone. The only way to work with caller identification is to avoid cold calls!

To work with voice mail, you will need to be creative. One approach is to use a 15- to 30-second commercial, or elevator speech, that advertises the results you help your clients achieve. The purpose of this short sound bite should introduce who you are, explain what you do, and communicate your value proposition. Another alternative is to use the statement you normally use to create interest in meeting with you. For example, you could leave a message like this:

| | |
|---|---|
| ***Example:*** | "Good evening, Juanita. This is Kelly Martin. I met you at karate class. Listen, I represent ABC Insurance Company. My practice is focused on helping parents like you apply, what I like to call, financial self-defense strategies to protect their families from the unexpected. I would love to get together with you to see if some of these strategies might help you. I will give you a callback sometime next week." |

Many advisors will not leave a callback number with a request for the prospect to return the call. These advisors feel initiating the contact gives them more confidence by knowing exactly what they will say. If the prospect initiates the call, the advisor may not remember where the lead came from or may have to ad-lib, rather than follow a script.

---

### How to Write an Elevator Speech

First, write down the deliverables—the services or features that you provide. Then think in terms of the benefits that your clients or employer could derive from these services. You could use several successful client outcomes.

Create an opening sentence that will grab the listener's attention. The best openers leave the listener wanting more information. And you do not have to include your title, especially if you think it has a negative connotation (an IRS agent, for example).

Finally, your elevator speech must roll off your tongue with ease. Practice your speech in front of the mirror and with friends. Record it on your answering machine, and listen to it. Do you sound confident? Sincere? Is it engaging? Tweak accordingly. Then take it on the road!

*Copyright © 2002 Dale R. Kurow. Reprinted with permission. Dale Kurow is a career and executive coach in private practice. She helps individuals find success and personal enrichment in their vocations, and she works with corporations to maximize the potential of valuable employees. Contact Dale by e-mail at dkurow@nyc.rr.com or by telephone at (212) 787-6097.*

---

### Practice, Practice, Practice.

Once you have written your scripts, it is time to practice them. Read them to other advisors and get their feedback. You can also record yourself and see what you sound like. Does it sound natural or scripted?

## Project a Professional Phone Image

When you meet the public, it is easy to think about creating an image. We dress a certain way, are well groomed, and put on our best smile. Whether you meet the public in person or by phone, the goal is the same: you want to create a picture of a confident professional. In creating a relationship with someone, these first impressions are important in the establishment of trust and rapport. The prospect is judging whether you sound like a knowledgeable and trustworthy advisor on the telephone. When you call someone, they cannot see you. Instead they must draw a mental picture of you from what you say and how you say it. We have already looked at what you say; now we will examine how you say it.

### *Attitude*

It all begins with your attitude. Listen to how you sound. Would you buy from you? Here are few reminders about projecting a professional attitude:

- Be cheerful and smile. Your smile can be heard over the telephone.
- Wear proper business attire to help you feel more professional; it will show in your voice.
- Stay low-key, relaxed, and do not press too hard.
- Stay healthy. Illness and fatigue will affect how you sound. Many advisors stand up to aid both their energy level and breathing.
- A good way to start a telephoning session is to stand up and stretch, especially your stomach muscles to relax your diaphragm.
- Breathe from your stomach, not your lungs, to relax your voice and give it more presence.
- Be courteous. Listen to the prospect and do not interrupt.
- Pay attention to what is said, think about it, and then respond. Pausing to think about what your prospect has said does not show weakness; it shows consideration. One advisor says he often closes his eyes when he is listening to the prospect. He says he can hear a variety of things this way. Try it.
- Approach every call like it's the only one you will make that day. Act as if that person is the most important person in the world. Keep in mind that you are calling people, not numbers or names on a list. People like to feel as if they are the only person you are calling, not one of the masses from a list of compiled names.
- Speak conversationally. You are prepared and you have practiced the script, but it should be so well prepared and practiced that it sounds spontaneous.

- Practice your telephone approach until you know it by memory, but keep it in front of you when you make your calls. Its presence will give you extra self-confidence. Your opening and voice-mail message should be totally scripted, word-for-word.
- Keep your conversation brief.
- Use the prospect's name once or twice, avoid overusing it like telemarketers do. Remember, though, that no one is flattered if you mispronounce it.
- If you are calling with a referral or a reference of any kind, use it. It will help establish you as a person to be taken seriously. It will give the prospect something to remember you by.
- Always watch your use of words. Speak carefully using proper grammar. Don't stammer. Try to eliminate non-words (like "um" or "er") completely. Your prospects want to work with decisive and skilled people. Be sure you sound the way you wish to be remembered.

### *Voice*

Studies show that people depend more on how they see you than what you say or even how you say it. Since you are not seen on the telephone, you lose more than half of your message. Your voice becomes what they see.

- Speak in your natural voice. You should sound relaxed and sincere. Try to make every call sound as if you are calling a good friend.
- Speak clearly. It takes the listener a few seconds to get used to a new voice, so your first few sentences are critical.
- Keep a good posture. Sit up straight or stand up to get the most out of your voice.
- Listen to what others give as feedback. If you are often asked to repeat yourself, you may need to improve your enunciation.
- Speak distinctly. If this means slowing down, then slow down. Your message is worth it.

## Keep Good Records

Setting appointments is a critical task. Therefore it is important to have a good idea of how the activities involved with appointment setting are working. The best way to do this is to track daily prospecting and selling activity and results. Some agents use simple tally sheets to track their prospecting activity (see Appendix A for samples). Others use reports generated by a contact management system. Whatever means you use, you will want to track for each target market and source of lead such items as

- number of contacts attempted
- number of contacts made (spoke to the prospect)
- number of appointments made
- number of initial meetings or interviews
- number of fact finders conducted
- number of closing interviews
- number of sales made
- number of hours spent setting appointments
- amount of commission and/or fees

Keeping accurate records of your daily prospecting and selling activities enables you to generate effectiveness ratios for setting appointments and making sales. These ratios will provide valuable data you can use to make decisions about target markets, approach scripts, and interviewing techniques. For example, from the above activities and results, you can calculate how many appointments it takes to generate one initial interview. A high no-show or cancellation rate indicates a different target market or a different approach script may be necessary.

# NOTES

1. Gordon D. Hawkins, *Prospecting Systems for Success*, (Indianapolis: The Research & Review Service of America Inc., 1981), 41.
2. Gordon D. Hawkins, *Prospecting Systems for Success*, (Indianapolis: The Research & Review Service of America Inc., 1981), 41.
3. U.S. Census Bureau, "Table HINC-01. Selected Characteristics of Households, by Total Money Income in 2007," http://pubdb3.census.gov/macro/032008/hhinc/new01_001.htm (accessed February 27, 2009).
4. Brian K. Bucks, Arthur B. Kennickell, Traci L. Mach, and Kevin B. Moore, *Changes in U.S. Family Finances from 2004 to 2007: Evidence from the Survey of Consumer Finances*, The Federal Reserve Board's Division of Research and Statistics, 2009, A5, http://www.federalreserve.gov/pubs/bulletin/2009/pdf/scf09.pdf (accessed February 27, 2009).
5. Brian K. Bucks, Arthur B. Kennickell, Traci L. Mach, and Kevin B. Moore, *Changes in U.S. Family Finances from 2004 to 2007: Evidence from the Survey of Consumer Finances*, The Federal Reserve Board's Division of Research and Statistics, 2009, A11, http://www.federalreserve.gov/pubs/bulletin/2009/pdf/scf09.pdf (accessed February 27, 2009).
6. Social mobility. Dictionary.com. Dictionary.com Unabridged (v 1.0.1). Based on the *Random House Unabridged Dictionary*, Random House, Inc. 2006, http://dictionary.reference.com/browse/social mobility (accessed October 24, 2006).

7.  Mary Madden, "Internet Penetration and Impact April 2006," Pew Internet & American Life Project, http://www.pewinternet.org/pdfs/PIP_Internet_Impact.pdf (accessed October 27, 2006).

8.  Mary M. Art, "Generations X and Y Online: The Wired Generations," LIMRA Intl. (Windsor, CT: 2003), 24.

9.  Federal Communications Commission, "Consumer Factsheets on FCC Do-Not-Call Rules," http://www.fcc.gov/cgb/donotcall/#relatedrules (accessed March 2, 2009).

10. Federal Trade Commission, "Information for Businesses," National Do Not Call Registry, https://www.donotcall.gov/faq/faqbusiness.aspx (accessed March 2, 2009).

## CHAPTER TWO REVIEW

*Key terms and concepts are explained in the Glossary. Answers to the review and self-test questions are found in the back of the textbook in the Answers to Questions section.*

### Key Terms and Concepts

| | |
|---|---|
| life-cycle marketing | advertising |
| life-cycle market segments | preapproach |
| life events | seminar |
| trigger | preapproach letter |
| prestige building | third-party influence piece |
| social mobility | approaching the prospect |
| community involvement | prequalifying |
| personal brochure | escape close |
| weblog (blog) | do-not-call laws |

### Review Questions

2-1.  Life-cycle marketing operates on two generalizations. What are they? Explain each of them.

2-2.  Define prestige building and describe five methods of prestige building.

2-3.  What is a preapproach?

2-4.  Briefly describe the advantages of seminars and some of the important steps for conducting them effectively.

2-5.  Describe how to choose effective preapproach letters.

2-6.  Describe the objectives in writing a preapproach letter and list the guidelines for doing so.

2-7.  Outline the logistics for using preapproach letters.

2-8.   Discuss the steps for creating an effective telephone approach script.

2-9.   Explain the limitations set by the do-not-call laws and methods for working within these rules.

2-10.  List and describe two components for projecting a professional phone image.

2-11.  What are some of the activities you will want to track? Why?

## Self-test Questions

*Instructions: Read Chapter 2 and then answer the following questions to test your knowledge. There are 10 questions. Choose one answer for each question, and then check your answers with the answer key in the back of the textbook.*

2-1.   Which of the following life-cycle market segments would be most likely to have members who experience the empty nest feeling as children leave their home?

   (A)   Young adulthood
   (B)   Middle-years adulthood
   (C)   Mature adulthood
   (D)   Old age

2-2.   Which of the following is generally considered a preapproach?

   (A)   billboard advertising
   (B)   seminar
   (C)   Internet website
   (D)   listing in the phone book

2-3.   Which of the following advisors is following the do-not-call rules correctly?

   (A)   Mary contacts all of her referrals after the referrer has contacted them.
   (B)   Harry calls prospects on Saturdays at 7:30 a.m.
   (C)   Jerry calls his friends without receiving their written permission to do so.
   (D)   Kari blocks the use of caller identification.

2-4.   Which of the following statements regarding writing a preapproach letter is (are) correct?

    I.    Aim to write something that grabs the prospect's attention.

    II.   Your letters should be filled with statistics to enhance your credibility.

    (A)   I only
    (B)   II only
    (C)   Both I and II
    (D)   Neither I nor II

2-5.   Which of the following would be appropriate for the greeting of your telephone approach?

    I.    Open your conversation with "Good morning," or "Good afternoon."

    II.   As a matter of courtesy, ask the prospect if he or she has time to talk.

    (A)   I only
    (B)   II only
    (C)   Both I and II
    (D)   Neither I nor II

2-6.   Which of the following statements regarding how to handle caller identification and voice mail is (are) correct?

    I.    Never leave a message on a prospect's voice mail; keep calling until you are able to speak to him or her.

    II.   The only solution for handling caller identification is to avoid cold calls.

    (A)   I only
    (B)   II only
    (C)   Both I and II
    (D)   Neither I nor II

2-7. Which of the following statements regarding projecting a professional phone image is (are) correct?

    I.   What you wear when you make your telephone calls does not matter.

    II.  Use non-words like "um" to create an informal, conversational tone.

    (A)  I only
    (B)  II only
    (C)  Both I and II
    (D)  Neither I nor II

2-8. All of the following statements regarding life events are correct EXCEPT:

    (A)  Life events are often useful as triggers that raise awareness of resulting financial needs.
    (B)  Life events are important occurrences in people's lives that often result in substantial changes in their lives.
    (C)  Many life events inherently create or increase a prospect's need and/or ability to pay for financial products.
    (D)  Life events have not been affected by changes in society and will always occur in the same order and timing as they have in the past.

2-9. All of the following statements regarding community involvement are correct EXCEPT:

    (A)  The easiest level of involvement in terms of time and energy is sponsorship and giving.
    (B)  Volunteering requires a tremendous amount of time and should be undertaken with great caution.
    (C)  Joining an organization allows people in the organization to discover your talents, your values, and your character.
    (D)  Leading is an opportunity to showcase your talents and abilities without uttering one word of self-promotion.

2-10. All of the following statements regarding seminars are correct EXCEPT:

    (A)    The date and time are critical.

    (B)    The site you select should be convenient for the members of your target market.

    (C)    If you are not a good public speaker, seminars should be avoided.

    (D)    Plan to use a feedback mechanism.

# *Financial Needs, Young Adults, and Disability Income*

| Learning Objectives |
|---|
| *An understanding of the material in this chapter should enable you to* |

3-1.  Discuss the typical financial needs of individuals and families that should be considered in developing a financial plan.

3-2.  Explain the budgeting process and how it can be used with a client.

3-3.  Describe the distinguishing characteristics and needs of the four subsegments of the young adults segment.

3-4.  Explain the importance of having disability income insurance.

3-5.  Describe the policy features and riders common to disability income policies.

This chapter focuses on the common financial needs most people face. It then provides an overview of the young adult life-cycle segment. The chapter closes with a discussion of disability income planning, examining the disability income need and the corresponding insurance products available to satisfy this need.

## FINANCIAL NEEDS

For most people, income and assets are limited. A dollar of life insurance premium is a dollar that cannot be spent meeting other financial needs. That is, there is a high level of integration and dependency within a prospect's overall financial situation. It is important to consider the prospect's overall financial picture to ensure that recommendations to address one need do not supersede or conflict with a more important one. To help understand this integrated approach, financial planning has been divided into different areas, including the following:

- general principles of financial planning, including budget planning
- retirement planning
- estate planning
- investment planning
- employee benefits planning
- income tax planning
- insurance planning and risk management

**integrated planning approach**

Those advisors who do not conduct comprehensive financial planning still have an obligation to propose recommendations regarding their products within the context of the prospect's overall financial situation and needs. For example, a life insurance agent should not recommend utilizing all of a prospect's disposable income to buy permanent insurance if the prospect has other financial needs, such as disability income insurance and retirement savings. This is an *integrated planning approach*.

For those areas that you lack expertise, consider referring prospects to non-competing advisors who can assist them. You may even form a team of specialists and serve as its manager, coordinating the team's efforts as well as contributing your expertise in your field of specialization.

Financial planning is a process that determines an individual's financial problems and/or financial goals, and develops a plan to solve the individual's problems and/or achieve his or her goals. In most cases, you will be addressing only one or a few of the most important financial needs for the client at your initial and subsequent meetings. Although some clients could benefit from comprehensive financial planning, they are unwilling typically to invest the time and money that it requires. In fact, except for the wealthy, most clients cannot afford or need to have a comprehensive plan. Many people find it difficult to deal with the totality of their financial problems and/or goals all at once. Instead, they prefer the single-purpose or multiple-purpose approach to financial planning because they have to concentrate on the most pressing of their problems. If these clients participate in several multiple-purpose planning meetings over a period of years, they will eventually have a comprehensive plan in place.

This planning approach might be called sequential financial planning. It encompasses a series of multiple-purpose planning sessions that generally take place over a period of months or years as the client progresses through his or her financial life cycle. Whatever approach is used in planning, it must follow the selling/planning process or financial planning process: develop a client-advisor relationship, determine goals and needs based on fact finding, analyze the information, and develop a plan that fits the client's circumstances and goals. In the following section, we will review some of the needs and processes covered in the financial planning process.

## Budget Planning

budget planning

There is no exact method for determining what someone can afford, but you should offer solutions that will not require clients to forego other needs that are at the same level of priority. This is the purpose of *budget planning.* You may address the budgeting planning process directly with a prospect, or make recommendations based on your knowledge of this process and the prospect's financial situation. In many cases, a lack of good budgeting habits leads people to financial problems. This section will take you through the budgeting process as it fits with the insurance and financial products you sell.

### The Budget

Budgeting and cash flow management are the most basic tools of financial planning. Clients often resist the cash flow management process even though it is critical to reaching a goal. Communicating the importance of these processes and helping clients use them can be among the advisor's most valuable services. These processes are always useful and especially beneficial when the client needs to accomplish specific financial objectives.

***The Benefits.*** Proper budgeting can help the client obtain adequate insurance protection, savings, or retirement funds. Although you may not be involved in implementing all of these solutions, financial products are not sold in a vacuum. Doing what is best for the prospect or client will ensure the type of relationship that will provide future sales and referrals.

Budgeting is the means not the ends. Most people do not like budgeting because it often is not linked to financial goals they are trying to achieve. When meeting with prospects, you will often get a sense of their goals and objectives, their needs, and their attitudes and values. If not, you can ask.

***Personal Goal Planning.*** Start by understanding the clients' goals and vision of the future. Goals can be wants, needs, desires, and objectives. Clients should set short-term, intermediate, and long-term goals, prioritize them, evaluate alternatives, and decide upon a plan of action to reach them. They must then take action to accomplish their plans. Without these steps, goals are nothing more than wishes. Goals must be realistic, be as concrete and specific as possible, and yet allow for flexibility. In your role as a financial advisor, you can provide valuable assistance in helping clients and prospects through this process.

Consider long-term goals first. These are 5-10 years and longer. They set the course and determine other goals. Intermediate goals are those for more

# Cash Flow Worksheet

## INCOME

| | |
|---|---|
| Your salary | _____ |
| Your spouse's salary | _____ |
| Commissions | _____ |
| Tips | _____ |
| Bonuses | _____ |
| Interest | _____ |
| Dividends | _____ |
| Rental property | _____ |
| Royalties | _____ |
| Social Security | _____ |
| Pension benefits | _____ |
| Profit sharing | _____ |
| Annuities | _____ |
| Life insurance benefits | _____ |
| Other | _____ |
| **Total Income** | $ _____ |

## EXPENSES

| | |
|---|---|
| Fixed | |
| Housing | _____ |
|     (rent, mortgage payments) | _____ |
|     Household maintenance | |
|     (fuel, utilities, and so on) | _____ |
| Food | _____ |
| Clothing | _____ |
| Transportation | _____ |
| Medical/dental care | _____ |
| Insurance premiums | |
|     Life | _____ |
|     Health, DI, LTCI | _____ |
|     Homeowners | _____ |
|     Automobile | _____ |
| Taxes | _____ |
|     Income | _____ |
| Property | _____ |
| Business (use Schedule C form) | _____ |
| Variable | _____ |
| Entertainment/recreation | _____ |
| Restaurant | _____ |
| Charitable giving | _____ |
| Personal/miscellaneous | _____ |
| **Total Expenses** | $ _____ |
| **Difference** | $ _____ |

(Total Income minus Total Expenses)

than a year but less than the long-term goals. Short-term goals are those for this week, month, or year.

As your prospects or clients set goals, they also have to prioritize them. Then you must help them estimate the dollar value of each goal. How much will it cost? Some family concerns are universal and provide the basis for specific goals. Typical concerns include the following:

- the necessities of life
- a comfortable standard of living
- a nice home
- a good education for the children
- a family vacation every year
- a secure retirement income

***Universal Needs.*** Universal needs are the basic needs that determine a family's goals. Some family goals will create a need to save. If a family has a goal to buy a vacation home, it would require them to accumulate funds to make a down payment. Other goals will create a need for insurance. For example, a young family should insure the income earners' lives to protect the survivors' desired standard of living. Some goals create a need for accumulation and insurance. For instance, clients may really want their children to attend college and feel strongly enough to save for the associated costs. They also may feel it is important enough to purchase insurance, ensuring that a college savings fund is created even if they die or become disabled. In general, universal needs in this case deal with risk management, and most of them are found in the foundation of the financial planning pyramid. They include the following:

- protection against loss in the event of dying too soon
- protection against the long-term costs of living too long
- protection against the loss of income in the event of disability
- protection against personal property loss and liability claims
- protection against health or hospitalization expenses
- funds to cover unexpected emergencies
- funds to take advantage of opportunities

Each of the family's goals should be prioritized. When a family identifies any of the listed financial needs, it creates powerful planning possibilities. Many of these financial needs can be satisfied through life insurance or related products and services.

---

### Budget Guidelines

- Creates awareness of total income and anticipated expenditures.
- Provides an accurate picture of where your money goes.
- Allows you to decide what you can or cannot afford.
- Provides a sense of control and promotes real economic freedom.
- Discourages buying on impulse and spending on things you do not need.
- Facilitates saving to attain goals.
- Allows you to decide how best to protect against adverse financial consequences.
- Encourages peace of mind, thus reducing stress and conflict.
- Develops opportunities to make investments.

---

### The Budget Process

Now the family is ready to create a budget. The sample "Household Budget Summary" sheet will help illustrate this process.

*Estimating Income.* First, the family should estimate total income. Look at all sources; consider earned income, unearned income (interest, dividends, and so on), and other income potential. It is better to underestimate than overestimate if earnings are irregular.

*Estimating Expenses.* Next, the family should estimate expenses. Determine where money will likely go based on past experience.

**fixed expenses**

*Fixed Expenses.* Start by listing all *fixed expenses*. These expenses are recurring and unavoidable. Some are regular and are the same amount each month, such as rent, mortgage payments, taxes, and regular installment payments. Others are recurring but variable. Examples include items such as food, clothing, utilities, and transportation.

**discretionary expenses**

*Discretionary Expenses.* Once fixed expenses have been determined, the prospect should budget for *discretionary expenses* (expenses that can be prevented or timed through proper budgeting). An expense like dining out can be decreased, and a purchase of a new car can be timed.

**special consideration expenses**

*Special Consideration Expenses.* Also think about *special consideration expenses* such as seasonal spending, private education needs, special medical needs, and emergency funds. Consider money being set aside for intermediate and long-range goals. Finally review the household budget summary and family financial needs checklist shown below. These tools can be used in various ways to stimulate discussion about expense levels and priorities. This checklist has frequently been used as a preliminary fact-gathering device.

---

## Household Budget Summary

**INCOME:**

Personal Income Expected                                        $ _____

Spouse Income Expected                                          $ _____

Total Other Income Expected (list)

   1. _____          $ _____

   2. _____          $ _____

   3. _____          $ _____

**Total Expected Income**                                      $ _____

**EXPENSES:**

**Fixed:**

  1.  Food                                            $ _____

  2.  Home (mortgage, rent, taxes, repairs, utilities)      $ _____

  3.  Taxes (excluding taxes on principal home)            $ _____

  4.  Medical expenses (doctor, dentist, prescriptions)    $ _____

  5.  Clothing and cleaning (total of family)             $ _____

  6.  Transportation (gas, parking, maintenance, public transit, and so on)    $ _____

  7.  Debts (budgeted debt liquidation, credit card payments)    $ _____

  8.  Property and liability insurance (auto, homeowners, and so on) $    _____

  9.  Life and individual health insurance (disability, long-term care,
     and so on)                                       $ _____

 10.  Current education and childcare expenses            $ _____

**Discretionary:**

 11.  Vacations                                        $ _____

 12.  Home improvement and furnishings                 $ _____

 13.  Entertainment and recreation                     $ _____

 14.  Charity and gifts (church, donations, holidays, birthdays, and so on)    $ _____

 15.  Savings                                          $ _____

 16.  Investments                                      $ _____

 17.  Education fund                                   $ _____

 18.  Miscellaneous (list)

   1. _____          $ _____

   2. _____          $ _____

   3. _____          $ _____

**Total for Household Expenses**                               $ _____

**ANTICIPATED NET PROFIT (LOSS)**                              $ _____

| Family Financial Needs Checklist | | |
|---|---|---|
| | **Consider (Y/N)** | **Amount** |
| Final Expenses: | | |
|    Medical expenses | _____ | _____ |
|    Outstanding bills | _____ | _____ |
|    Unpaid taxes | _____ | _____ |
|    Legal and probate fees | _____ | _____ |
|    Federal and state estate taxes | _____ | _____ |
| Income for the Family: | | |
|    Dependency period income | _____ | _____ |
|    Surviving spouse income | _____ | _____ |
| Mortgage redemption | _____ | _____ |
| Education Expenses: | | |
|    Children | _____ | _____ |
|    Spouse | _____ | _____ |
| Special Needs: | | |
|    Special-needs child(ren) | _____ | _____ |
|    Dependent parents/others | _____ | _____ |
| Needs of Other Family Members: | | |
|    Spouse | _____ | _____ |
|    Children | _____ | _____ |
|    Others | _____ | _____ |
| Charitable Bequests: | | |
|    Church | _____ | _____ |
|    School | _____ | _____ |
|    Charity | _____ | _____ |
|    Others | _____ | _____ |
| Emergency fund | _____ | _____ |
| Opportunity funds/savings | _____ | _____ |
| Education needs | _____ | _____ |
| Retirement Needs: | | |
|    Income | _____ | _____ |
|    Travel | _____ | _____ |
|    Long-Term Care | _____ | _____ |
|    Other | _____ | _____ |
| Disability Income: | | |
|    Husband | _____ | _____ |
|    Wife | _____ | _____ |

In compiling lists of fixed, discretionary, and special consideration expenses, your prospects or clients should look at their past records, receipts and canceled checks to make estimates based upon experience. They should then consider what may be cut or what may be increased in the future. If they don't have records, they should track expenses for three to six months to provide accurate estimates for budgeting.

Major expenditures are usually best handled if anticipated and saved for in advance. This avoids mounting debt and unnecessary loans. The critical difference is interest—the cost of money. Do they want to earn interest or pay interest? This major philosophical decision is more important in budgeting than any other single factor.

It is normally advisable to clear debts, pay off bills, and get spending under control before embarking on intermediate or longer-range accumulation goals. An exception is participating in a qualified retirement plan where employers match some percentage of employee contributions. Clients should also set up a cushion for emergencies. Planning for the unexpected will take a lot of stress out of life and prevent setbacks to their budget from emergency expenses.

---

### Budget Guidelines

- Spend less than you make.
- Make a commitment to be a saver and pay yourself first.
- Limit the use of credit.
- Shop around for the best price on big-ticket items.
- Keep good, complete, accurate records.
- Review your budget regularly.

---

***Putting It All Together.*** Once they have listed and prioritized expenses, the family can balance their income and expenses to properly allocate funds among various needs and goals. This balancing act requires commitment and willpower.

Look for ways to trim the largest fixed expenses first, and then see where discretionary expenses can be cut. Try not to assume obligations or acquire a more expensive lifestyle than income allows. The key to sound financial management is living within one's means. This means cutting expenses to less than income or increasing income to cover all expenses with some surplus.

The budgeting process is the key to marketing needs. By discussing a prospect or client's financial goals, you begin to uncover the need for insurance and other financial products. The budget also helps you determine how serious prospects are about addressing their insurance and other financial needs. Budgeting is a valuable tool to help your clients and prospects attain and maintain their financial dreams.

## Retirement Planning

Clients should clarify how they want to live during retirement and what financial resources will be available to support the desired lifestyle. Like budgeting, retirement planning is largely developing a plan based on anticipated income and expenses, and reconciling and balancing them. Retirement is ideally the achievement of economic independence. It is a threshold that clients often cross with a changed outlook on life, certain post-retirement lifestyle assumptions, and modified financial planning objectives. How much money will your client want or need during retirement? The answer to this question varies with your clients and depends on the following factors and assumptions:

- your client's target retirement age
- the number of years your client will spend in retirement
- a target income based on your client's lifestyle expectations for retirement
- an assumed inflation rate
- the total financial resources available to the client
- the amount of interest earnings on savings and assets earmarked for retirement
- your client's projected amount of savings by his or her retirement age
- how long your client will live

## Estate Planning

Estate planning involves both conservation planning and distribution planning. This entails structuring the assets in the client's estate for lifetime and testamentary transfers of property to best achieve the client's overall estate distribution objectives.

## Investment Planning

Investment goals should be identified and prioritized. All securities in your client's investment portfolio should be listed. The portfolio should then be analyzed with respect to its marketability, liquidity, diversification, and overall performance. The suitability of the investments in relation to your client's goals, financial ability to sustain a loss (risk tolerance), and personal management capabilities must be addressed.

## Employee Benefit Planning

The plan should review the current status, use, and cost of your client's employee benefits. It should address the likelihood that these benefits will be modified or terminated in the future. Also, the plan should analyze the types of benefits available and their relationship to other plan components such as insurance coverages, retirement planning, and estate planning.

## Income Tax Planning

Income tax planning includes an analysis of your client's income tax returns for the current year and for recent past years. It should also include projections for several years into the future. Projections should show the nature of the income and deductions in sufficient detail to permit calculation of the tax liability. The analysis should identify the marginal tax rate for each year and any special situations, such as the alternative minimum tax, passive loss limitations, and other issues that may affect your client's tax liability.

## Education Planning

The plan should analyze any future capital needs that your client might have for special purposes such as funding college educations for children. The analysis should include a projection of resources expected to meet these needs and the time horizon required for funding each goal.

## Insurance Planning

Insurance planning involves risk management, accumulation, maintenance, and protection of financial assets. Insurance planning is a part of the overall financial plan, regardless of whether your client or prospect has a formal plan. While you must not call yourself a financial planner until you have the proper authority and permission from your company, it is important to know where insurance planning fits into this bigger picture. This will help you position your products and services more effectively and see opportunities should you decide to specialize in a specific planning area or market.

Peace of mind and love are examples of motives to purchase insurance products. Financial needs are the logical expression of a prospect's emotional desire to protect his or her family. What are these financial needs?

### *Insurance and Accumulation Needs*

There are seven common insurance and accumulation needs described below. They determine how much money a person will have available to spend on life insurance products you sell. For example, by law everyone is required to carry auto insurance. Mortgage companies require fire or homeowners insurance. What is left over in the person's insurance budget purchases health, life, long-term care, disability, and other insurance products.

| Insurance or Accumulation Need | Appropriate Product |
|---|---|
| Protection against personal property loss and personal liability claims | Auto, Fire, Personal Liability, Umbrella, Personal Article, and so on |
| Protection against health or hospitalization expenses | Health |
| Protection against loss in the event of premature death | Life |
| Protection against the long-term costs of living too long | Long-Term Care, Annuities, Mutual Funds |
| Protection against the loss of income in the event of disability | Disability Income |
| Funds to cover unexpected emergencies | CDs, Money Market, and so on |
| Funds to take advantage of investment opportunities | Mutual Funds, Stocks, Bonds, and so on |

*Life Insurance.* As a financial advisor, you have the ability to create solutions that can mean the difference between a family having to struggle to make ends meet and having a solid financial foundation upon which to pursue their dreams. While many occupations have a significant impact upon a family's financial security, few have the ability to deliver more at the time of need.

After a loved one dies, those left behind can face many financial problems such as

- paying for final expenses resulting from death
- maintaining a desired standard of living
- replacing the missing income
- paying on or liquidating the mortgage
- paying for education costs
- paying estate and other taxes
- ensuring the continuity and security of business interests

Life insurance can help to solve all of these problems. Through the products you sell, you create money in situations where money did not previously exist or would not otherwise have existed. You create an immediate estate, or money when it is needed the most. Insurance provides time for people to recover emotionally from a tragedy without the need to cope with a financial burden as well.

Understanding these needs makes it easy to understand why life insurance is an emotional purchase. Probably the most common reason for buying it is the love someone has for those who may survive him or her. Insurance provides the money so heirs can maintain a lifestyle to which they have grown accustomed. Insurance provides income after death to keep people from suffering the loss of a loved one compounded by an unnecessary loss of income.

Unlike property insurance, life insurance does not replace what it insures. A human life is irreplaceable. Instead, it replaces what the insured would have been able to provide had his or her life continued. It is the creation of capital by installments. No matter what happens, as long as the installments (i.e., premiums) are made, the capital is guaranteed. It is more than insurance—it is comfort, lifestyle, education, peace of mind, assurance that life for a person's loved ones can continue successfully after the insured's death.

There is an old expression in the life insurance industry: "Life insurance is not bought—it is sold." This does not imply that high-pressure sales tactics are ever appropriate. However, while people can generally sense a need for life insurance, they seldom think about it without your help, and they often underestimate their need. While we must not coerce people into buying life insurance, the advisor's job is to help people identify and understand their needs and motivate them to take action. For customers who decide to address their needs, your job is to implement and monitor an appropriate insurance plan.

*Income Replacement.* When a wage earner dies, the family will usually need to replace the lost income to meet continuing and future financial needs. This is the most common purpose for the purchase of life insurance.

Every person has an economic value in life, much of it associated with potential income. Each income source should be considered, and any shortfall at death properly insured when someone depends on that income for financial security. Note that most life insurance companies will normally insure a healthy applicant for up to 20 times his or her income. Thus someone earning $50,000 per year can qualify for $1,000,000 of death benefit. Certainly, most of your prospects are seriously underinsured!

Do not overlook the need to insure a homemaker. Although he or she does not earn an income, there is definite value to the work that he or she does. Without the homemaker, would there be a need for domestic services such as a maid? Would daycare costs cause financial stress on the surviving spouse?

---

***Example:***         Barbara is a physician, while her husband Phillip is a stay-at-home dad for their two small children. Barbara recognizes that if Phillip died, she would need to continue working, and she would need domestic help and extensive daycare for the children. Based on her objectives and costs in their area, Barbara and Phillip decide to apply for a $250,000 20-Year Level Term life insurance policy on Phillip.

---

*Final Expenses.* There are always expenses related to dying. Some examples of final expenses are costs related to burial, medical bills, probate costs, and estate taxes. Life insurance is an excellent way to pay these expenses when no other capital is available or when the prospect desires to allocate existing assets for family income.

*Emergency Fund.* If there was not one prior to death, an insured may want to provide a death benefit to create a fund for unexpected expenses. One common rule of thumb is to set aside three to six months of normal household expenses.

*Adjustment Income.* Prospects may desire to provide money that enables survivors to adjust to the death of a parent or spouse. Life insurance can establish a cushion to keep a newly single parent at home for a few months to care for children, consider career alternatives, or reduce the pressure to make quick decisions.

*Mortgage Liquidation or Payment.* A prospect may want to use life insurance to liquidate a mortgage or establish a fund for future mortgage payments. Families who rent may consider establishing a fund for future rent payments. Doing so ensures housing for survivors or, in the case of homeowners, prevents the need to sell quickly and below fair market value.

*Debt Repayment.* Most of us do not hesitate to use credit because we are confident that we can repay our debts from future earnings. Short-term debt, such as credit cards and auto loans that can be paid off in a relatively short time, should be paid when the insured dies.

*Education Fund.* A common concern for families is their children's post-secondary education. For most families, these costs rank second only to the mortgage on their home. Parents who want to provide college or other post-secondary education for their children must plan carefully for these costs.

Life insurance cash values can assist with future bills, and the death benefit guarantees the money to fund the education if the insured parent dies.

*Bequests.* Religious bequests and charitable gifts to special organizations or causes are as common in estates as philanthropy is during a benefactor's lifetime. Advisors can assist with planning gifts to charities, but you will usually recommend that other financial needs and obligations—especially to the family—be met first. Many individuals wish to leave money or property to family members, and life insurance can provide the funding or replace those funds directed elsewhere.

*Estate Taxes.* Sizable estates will have taxes to pay, and taxes cannot be postponed. Regardless of the circumstances, estate and final income taxes must be paid before other creditors and survivors get their shares. Estate taxes under current law affects only approximately one percent of estates, but other estate expenses affect a much larger segment of the population.

For example, if the family's only asset were their farm, insurance proceeds could help pay taxes and protect the land and equipment from being sold to raise necessary cash. Assets such as stocks, bonds, vacation homes, or even the family's primary residence are also protected from forced sale, perhaps below their full market value, by the use of life insurance in estate conservation planning. When there is sufficient liquidity in an estate to pay taxes without insurance, a prospect can use life insurance to keep the estate whole.

*Business Continuity.* Business interests may be significantly devalued at the death of an owner. The deceased's family may assume it can rely on the business to help financially. The business, however, will have its own problems coping with the loss of an owner. Life insurance can provide the cash needed to preserve the business whether it is retained for the family, run by a hired manager, or sold. Life insurance can ensure that both the heirs and any surviving owners receive full value for their interests in the business.

*Supplemental Retirement Income.* Permanent life insurance plans can offer the added living benefit of supplementing retirement income. Although not a primary source for income, the cash value can assist with unforeseen expenses or increases in standard of living during retirement.

*Connecting the Financial and Emotional.* A person must have financial needs in order to buy life insurance. However, many people have financial needs and still do not buy life insurance. The emotional bond between family members opens the doors for life sales. The primary motive for most purchases of life insurance is love. You may hear an experienced advisor say, "Insurance is not bought unless somebody loves someone."

*Ask and Listen.* Find out your prospect's goals for him- or herself and for their family. Many times the conversation can be as simple as asking, "What are your dreams? What do you wish to see happen with your family in thirty years?" Find out what is truly important to them by asking something like, "Which of these would you like to see happen even if you were not alive?" Determine how they envision that their dreams will still happen by asking, "How do you feel you can make that happen?" In the event that they do not have a viable solution, insurance is there.

*Medical Expense (Health) Insurance.* Medical expense insurance used to pay medical bills as a result of accidents or illness is arguably the most important type of insurance protection to most Americans, and the one that causes the most anxiety if lost or unaffordable. It is an expensive form of insurance if the client must purchase it, but many people have medical expense insurance as an employee benefit, where the employer pays some or all of the cost. It is important for an advisor to help a client determine if their coverage is adequate, and if not, assist them in obtaining full medical or supplemental coverage.

*Disability Insurance.* While the need for life insurance receives a great amount of attention, the need for disability insurance is often ignored and rarely discussed. Studies show that

- a 30-year-old has a 24 percent chance of being disabled for at least 90 days before reaching age 65
- at age 45, the chance of suffering a disability is only reduced to 21 percent
- a person disabled for 90 days will probably remain disabled for at least four years

Despite these statistics, very few people have adequate protection against long-term disability. The public may purchase life insurance for their family's protection but they have largely neglected their own income protection, even though the odds are far greater for a working-age person to become disabled than to die. Disability income insurance is discussed later in this chapter.

*Long-term Care Insurance.* Long-term care has become an important consideration in risk management planning, and this topic will be discussed in detail in Chapter 6. The likelihood that a person will need to enter a nursing home increases with age. The out-of-pocket payments for long-term care by individuals who must use personal resources can be astronomical. Today, average nursing home costs are over \$75,000 for private accommodations. It is becoming more difficult for families to provide long-term care, and most private medical expense policies and Medicare exclude convalescent, custodial, or rest care.

***Property and Liability Insurance.*** A financial plan that does not include property/liability insurance and risk management potentially leaves a client's entire asset base at risk. Failure to carry appropriate and adequate property and liability coverage can result in a severe uninsured loss that can ruin an otherwise sound plan for capital appreciation and preservation. Property and liability insurance is complicated, and exposures and policies must be thoroughly analyzed to determine if the client is adequately protected. If you do not provide this type of service, it is essential that your client consult with someone who does.

## The Financial Planning Pyramid

**financial planning pyramid**

**building-block approach**

One method for organizing all of these financial needs is the *financial planning pyramid*. The financial planning pyramid uses four levels: wealth foundation, wealth accumulation, wealth preservation, and wealth distribution. The pyramid in its entirety represents an integrated and comprehensive financial plan. The individual blocks illustrate how most people feel comfortable building their financial plans—one or a few blocks at a time. The term *building-block approach* is used to describe this incremental approach. Some pieces, like auto and homeowners insurance, are easy to change and can be put in place without too much integration with other blocks. However, other blocks, such as life insurance, are more difficult to change because they require new evidence of insurability (the client's insurability could change) and may result in higher premiums (due to increased age). Such products require more understanding of other current and potential needs the client may have concurrently or in the future.

Although each person sets financial goals throughout his or her life cycle, most people need to address five basic financial objectives:

- Protect against risk.
- Provide for financial security.
- Develop a comfortable life style.
- Provide for a comfortable retirement.
- Plan for the distribution of assets.

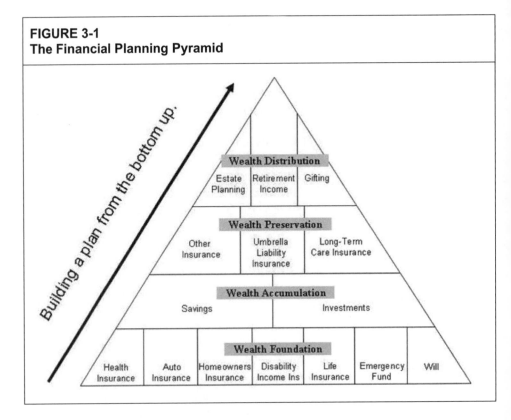

**FIGURE 3-1**
**The Financial Planning Pyramid**

The various levels provide some guidance as to a general order in which to address financial needs. The first level represents the foundation, the basic needs that should receive primary attention as they apply. Failure to address these needs leaves any savings and investments vulnerable if an uncovered loss occurs. Thus basic insurance products, a simple will, and an emergency fund form a wealth foundation.

Once the foundation is in place, a person can begin buying products in the wealth accumulation level such as CDs, stocks, bonds, mutual funds, real estate, and so on. Once assets are acquired, wealth preservation tools are needed. When the accrual of assets reaches a threshold, a person will need to consider products such as umbrella liability and long-term care insurance to preserve assets from lawsuits or the potential need for long-term care. Most likely, with increased wealth will come additional property needing to be insured, such as a summer home, a boat, a jet ski, and so on. At the wealth distribution level, products are needed to manage retirement income to ensure it will last. In addition, estate planning tools are used to conserve the estate for heirs, provide for an orderly distribution of wealth, and provide for charitable causes.

Once products are in place at a lower level, it does not mean they can be forgotten. Financial and life situations and goals change over time. It is important to review them periodically and make any necessary adjustments. For example, a divorce will mean that assets are divided and a new will is necessary.

# LIFE CYCLE: YOUNG ADULTS

**young-adult market segment**

This section will look at the *young-adult market segment*, which includes men and women who fall into the group between the ages of 20 and 37. Obviously there is a lot of variation between characteristics and needs in a segment this broad. Therefore we will examine this segment by grouping them into the following subsegments:

- single—individual with no partner and no kids
- dual income with kids—individual with a partner and kids
- dual income with no kids—individual with a partner and no kids (referred to as DINKs)
- single income with kids—individual with a partner and kids where the partner is not employed outside of the home. Also included in this grouping are single parents.

## Young Adults in General

Before looking at the nuances found in each subsegment, we will review the young-adult market segment in general.

### *Common Characteristics*

This segment will experience many firsts: first car, first house, first marriage, first child, first divorce, and so on. More life events create more financial and insurance needs. Life changes and milestones typically are times when life insurance needs become prominent. Because of the variety of situations you will find in this segment, we will discuss common characteristics of all the groupings as we examine each one.

### *Common Needs*

As we look at the subsegments, you will see more differentiated needs. The following are some needs common to young adults.

***Final Expenses.*** This is a need in every market. Final expenses cover burial, probate and estate administration costs, any state inheritance or federal estate taxes that are due, and any medical costs associated with the death.

***Emergency Fund.*** This is the recommended three to six months of living expenses needed to keep a person financially solvent in the event of losing a job, being disabled, or facing a financial emergency. For a single person, three months would be adequate while six months would be more appropriate for those individuals with children. The stability and reliability of continued income would also be a consideration in the size of the emergency fund. The amount should be at least enough to get a person through the elimination period on a disability income policy.

***Debt Liquidation.*** Often, credit card debt begins to mount during this phase. It begins early because most young adults have not been educated on how to use a credit card responsibly. You could provide some wise counsel regarding the advantages of paying off these balances and providing for their liquidation at death. Vehicle or personal loans also fall under this category. Generally budget planning is a need for members of the young-adult market segment.

***Disability Income.*** Protection against loss of income due to disability should be addressed as soon as a person begins earning an income. For young adults, it now becomes a pressing need.

***Retirement.*** It's never too early to begin saving for retirement. Many people make retirement a low priority until it is too late. Systematic saving over a working lifetime is a key to supplementing other retirement programs. The old rule of thumb is still valid when it comes to saving: if you tuck away 10 percent of annual income, financial independence can be attained. Young families with even modest incomes should start with something, even if they cannot make a total commitment to this 10 percent guideline at first. This is more important if any kind of employer-match on retirement savings is available.

***Will.*** This is the point in life when most people should have a will drawn. The financial advisor can help the new career person plan the financial aspects of his or her will.

## Singles

### *Common Characteristics*

People in this stage of life are typically young, healthy, and energetic. They are in a position to have more freedom and more cash. They have a zest for life. We find most entering this phase of life have carefree attitudes carrying forward from the family home. This is when new responsibilities are undertaken and maturity begins to replace irresponsible actions of youth. It can be a major transition in a young person's lifestyle.

*No Constraints.* Singles may have a problem facing new responsibilities and challenges. While they need sound advice and counsel, they are often not receptive to new ideas. Some young adults view new responsibilities as threatening because they feel constraints are being imposed on them and that their new freedoms may be restricted. Even though they often have discretionary income, they probably have not established savings plans or cash reserve funds for an emergency.

*Time Is on My Side.* A feeling of indestructibility and immortality is characteristic of those in their early 20s. The prevailing thought is, "Time is on my side," which is true if young people plan properly. Unfortunately, young singles tend to make poor choices regarding their financial needs. They may be used to putting off decisions. Consequently it may be difficult to convince them to begin planning for their future.

*High Debts.* Single young adults are likely to be concerned with debts and paying obligations such as student loans acquired in the process of getting to this life stage. One of the other causes of debt is the misuse of credit cards. Unfortunately, we find this a characteristic in all segments.

### Common Needs More Unique to Singles

In addition to the needs common to the entire segment of young adults, the following needs are more common to singles.

*Savings.* There may be an increased need for life insurance at this life stage, however the need to save money is more pressing. Saving has typically been ignored up to this point, as education costs or excessive spending have prevented it.

*Debt Liquidation.* The debts caused by credit cards, car loans, and school loans will be a priority for many in this segment. You can approach them by educating young clients about the financial burden their death could have on parents or others who may have cosigned a loan for them. You can also assist them in budgeting to pay off debts and teach them how to build a financial future.

*Disability Income.* Members of the single/never married life stage are among the best prospects for DI coverage. Without dependents, disability will generally affect the single person and his or her family (parents and siblings) financially more than death. It is far more likely that younger workers will become disabled than die during their working years. Disability income insurance will partially replace income when an insured worker is ill or injured and unable to work.

*Future Insurability.* For those who have no debt and no other immediate insurance need, ask about their future. Do they expect to find a partner or have children? If so, you can discuss a life insurance program that will protect their future insurability with guaranteed purchase options.

### Marketing Approaches

Your greatest challenges in working with single adults will be their sense of living in the present and lack of concern about the future. The good news is that the spotlight on Social Security solvency has made young adults more aware of a need for retirement planning, which will help you talk to them about insurance planning. Point out to the single adults that if something were to happen to them, someone else might have to settle their bills, debts, and final expenses.

---

**The Advantages of Starting a Life Insurance Program Early**

1. Provide for guaranteed, immediate financial security now.
2. Lock in lower premiums available at a younger age.
3. Qualify for lifelong protection while you are insurable regardless of later conditions of health, avocations, or occupations.
4. Begin building cash reserves for emergencies and for new opportunities.
5. Allow compound interest to work over a longer period of time with greater rewards.
6. Enable more choices and greater flexibility later, when status changes.
7. Funds become immediately available to pay off debts and honor bequests in the event of early death.
8. Larger cash values at retirement are available if a plan is started at a younger age.
9. Secure the qualification for additional coverage and additional benefits at the most favorable rates in the future with guaranteed purchase options.
10. Enjoy great pride, satisfaction, peace of mind, and a feeling of well being for taking positive actions now.

---

*Illustrating the Cost of Waiting.* In presenting solutions to single, young adults, it is important to stress the advantages of wise planning, saving money on a systematic basis, and beginning immediately. Successful advisors use a concept known as *the cost of waiting* to overcome apathy and procrastination in prospects. The cost of waiting concept compares a life insurance or retirement plan started immediately and one started three to five years in the future. For example, an illustration can show the large difference in accumulated savings in 25 years for someone starting immediately, compared to the amount 25 years in the future for someone who waits another five years to start saving. Although the idea is straightforward and logical, most people fail to recognize the enormous increase in value for those who begin to save early in life.

For life insurance, some advisors find it effective to go back in age, to a point three to five years earlier, showing what the cost of waiting has already done to premiums or savings. By waiting, the premium will be higher, the cash value growth over the prospect's life will be smaller, they will be without the protection, and they could lose their insurability in the interim. These are all good reasons to buy life insurance today.

## Dual Income No Kids (DINKs)

### Common Characteristics

It often takes longer than the traditional four years for many young adults to complete college. In addition, many careers are open only to those with graduate degrees or advanced educational experience. The pursuit of a master's degree or doctorate often leads to delays in marriage, children, and the formation of a family. There are many cases in which both spouses work, and they delay having children or do not plan to have any.

***Higher Household Discretionary Income.*** Without children, DINKs will have higher discretionary incomes because no money is being diverted to daycare, food, diapers, and other expenses created by children. They should have more money to invest and purchase necessary insurance and other financial products.

***No Budget or Plan.*** While they make more money, DINKS also tend to spend more freely. Without the constraints created by dependents, they tend not to have a budget. Spending without planning and failing to prioritize needs often put this segment into a vulnerable position, and they find themselves in debt with little savings.

***Possibly a Temporary Situation.*** For many couples, this life-cycle status is a transition between being single and having children. For those in transition, anticipating the needs that will arise when they do have children should be a top priority. This includes deciding whether both parents will continue working, estimating costs associated with daycare, and assessing the cutback in income should one or both parents alter their work.

### Common Needs Unique to DINKs

*Income Adjustment.* Survivors may need a sum of money to help them adjust to the death of their partner. These funds can provide a temporary cushion to give the survivor time to adjust to his or her new situation, to consider career alternatives, and make informed, rational decisions. Additional death benefits earmarked for this purpose should be considered.

*Future Insurability.* Like their single counterparts, DINKs may not have a large, immediate insurance need. Ask them about their expectations for the future. Do they expect to have children or take care of an elderly parent? If so, you can offer a life insurance program that will protect their future insurability.

### Marketing Approaches

Seminars and workshops on money management, insurance planning, or other specific financial topics can be successful with members of this life-cycle market segment. There are substantial quality business opportunities with dual income no kid families. Consider their situation as a precursor to either accruing a lot of wealth or having children, either of which increases the need for insurance.

## Dual Income Young Families

### Common Characteristics

Over 50 percent of the families in the United States have two or more income producers. The majority of households earning over $40,000 annually are two-income families.

*High Desired Standard of Living.* The trend towards dual-income families is partly due to the increase in a family's desired standard of living. Combined incomes are essential to develop and maintain the financial security and lifestyle these families want. The loss of either income would jeopardize the family's financial well being.

*Shared Roles and Responsibilities.* The roles and responsibilities of husbands and wives are similar. In two-income families, there is more sharing of household chores. Both marriage partners must balance the needs of work and home, so sharing becomes necessary.

***Hard to Save.*** Even with two incomes, couples still find it hard to save. The dual income family is a financially complex situation. They often pool resources to enhance their standard of living and to achieve financial independence. The desire for a wealthy lifestyle brings with it increased taxes and can create a very challenging situation. While spending and savings patterns vary considerably, families with two incomes tend to save less. Two-income families may view that second income as insurance against loss of the first income, creating a false sense of security.

---

**Human Life Value**

"(Prospect), if you had an incredible money-making machine that could make hundreds of thousand of dollars over the next 40 years, and you knew that it could be lost, stolen, destroyed by fire or other hazards, but you could insure it against loss, would you insure it?"

"For how much?"

"Have you considered the amount of money you will earn in your lifetime?"

"Shouldn't you insure the risk of losing this incredible money-making machine?"

"Let me show you how."

---

### Common Needs

***Income Replacement.*** For a family with dependent children the first priority is adequate protection against losing the income of a wage earner through premature death.

***Mortgage.*** The desire to provide funds for liquidation or payment of a mortgage is another significant goal of many young families. A mortgage is the largest obligation most families face. Leaving a mortgage-free home (or money to pay the mortgage) is fundamental to maintaining a desired standard of living and preventing additional disruption to the family unit.

***Education.*** Another priority for young families is to build adequate funds for college. The need for education is clear. College graduates earn more money, enjoy better lifestyles, and generally have more rewarding careers than people without a college education.

The cost of tuition is increasing at a rate far exceeding increases in the general cost of living. It is essential that every young couple desiring to send their children to college start a substantial savings plan as early as possible. Giving compound interest an opportunity to work is crucial to the success of any long-term savings plan. Saving in a tax-favored vehicle is also a major consideration in today's tax climate.

Additional education to acquire new or better skills is often a consideration of one or both partners in a young family. The death of one spouse can increase the need of additional education for the surviving spouse. Again, life insurance can provide funds to obtain an education, leading to a job, which a surviving spouse can use to maintain the family's lifestyle.

*Accumulation.* Most young families will also have a need to accumulate funds for future purchases such as a vehicle or down payment on a home. They should be encouraged to accumulate at least three to six months of living expenses as an emergency fund.

*Retirement and Savings.* There is a temptation to delay or downgrade savings for retirement to fund children's education needs. This is generally a bad decision. As a minimum, each spouse should contribute to an employee-sponsored retirement plan, to the extent of any employer match. Many young couples can also benefit from a Roth IRA. In addition, there should be at all times an adequate emergency and savings fund available to take care of unexpected needs for funds, as well as needs that have been planned, such as replacing a vehicle or repair bills. Having adequate savings can eliminate or minimize stress and the need to go into debt for these expenses.

## Single Income Young Families

### Common Characteristics

It appeared in the 1990s that the single income with kids segment would disappear. However, in the late 1990s many young professionals began to re-evaluate their situation. For a variety of reasons, more families today are deciding to keep one parent at home, at least for the first few years after children arrive. Families often find that the money from the second income is negligible after paying child-care and other work-related costs. This is especially true when one parent has a low-paying job.

*Greater Dependence on One Income.* The most obvious financial challenge is a greater reliance upon one income. This forces single-income families to live more frugally than their dual-income counterparts because they have less discretionary income. This may also increase the exposure of the family in the event of disability or death.

*Stay at Home Dads.* The greatest change in this market is the number of men who have become the homemaker in the family. We may see this trend increase as many women now earn more money than their husbands. From a financial perspective, this makes a father staying at home with the children a more logical choice.

***Temporary Situation.*** In many cases, families plan to have the spouse re-enter the workforce to provide extra income. This will usually occur at one of three junctures: when the youngest child enters grade school, when the youngest child enters high school, or when the youngest child graduates from high school. At this point, these families will have more discretionary income.

***Single Parents.*** Some young families have one income because only one wage earner is available. The majority of single parents are female, and their need is more acute than their two-parent family counterparts. In addition, their ability to pay is often further limited by lower income and the additional expense of childcare that the two-parent single income family does not have.

### Common Needs More Unique to Single Income Families

***Income Replacement.*** As with their dual-income counterparts, the first priority is adequate protection against losing the income of the primary wage earner through premature death or disability. One asset and insurable risk that is commonly overlooked in this scenario is the value of the homemaker. While no outside income is earned, family expenditures for daycare and housecleaning are reduced or eliminated. It's good to point this out.

***Mortgage.*** This is the same need as described for the dual-income family.

***Education.*** This is the same need as described for the dual-income family.

As you can see, the Young Adult segment is diverse. Breaking it into subsegments enhances your ability to customize your approach, as each subsegment has some distinguishing characteristics and needs.

As a whole, you will find this to be a market with which you can grow. Remember, many life events increase one's insurance and financial needs. The longer a person is your client, the more opportunities you will have to assist him or her through life events as their insurance planner.

## DISABILITY INCOME INSURANCE

In this section, we will review the needs, the available products, and the markets for disability income (DI) insurance. We will end with a discussion on approaches. We will also discuss how to position disability income with life insurance so they support each other.

## The Need for Disability Income Insurance

We have seen that insurance protects against financial catastrophe from many different perils. Life insurance helps replace the income generated by the efforts of the deceased insured. Liability insurance protects the insured's income from being subjected to a liability judgment. Medical expense insurance protects the insured's earnings from the high costs of medical care. Long-term care insurance protects assets from depletion in the event that people will require chronic care in the end stage of their lives.

Obviously income that is the primary source of a family's financial security also needs protection. Disability can put an end to a person's ability to earn an income, and disability is far more likely to occur than death during a worker's earning years. Even if a disability is relatively short, the loss of income puts most people in a financial crisis that affects their lifestyle for a long time.

Disability income insurance cannot protect people from having heart attacks and car accidents. It cannot prevent disabilities. What it can do, however, is provide financial support to replace income lost as the result of an accident or illness. It can also help keep financial worries from adding to the hundreds of concerns that a disabled person must face.

### Establishing the Need for DI Insurance

The art of establishing the need involves some basic principles. The first is to focus approaches and discussions on relevant needs. Then in a non-manipulative manner, help the prospect or client weigh the costs of doing nothing against the cost of acting immediately to secure the protection and benefits provided by the products you are selling.

### Using Life Stages to Identify Potential Needs

One of the underlying themes in this textbook is that of using life-cycle segmentation to help identify potential needs. Life-cycle segmentation can provide a starting point to guide your marketing and selling efforts with regard to the DI insurance need.

***Singles.*** Members of the single/young adult market segment are among the best prospects for DI coverage, and they are often the easiest to sell. Without dependents, disability will generally affect the single person and his or her family (parents and siblings) financially more than death. Even if a young person were disabled and qualified for Social Security Disability

Insurance, he or she would likely need additional help to maintain even a modest standard of living. Parents may be a potential source of financial support in the event of a disability, if they are able and willing to help. Many of them are not able, however, and often singles have little desire to burden their parents with a request for financial support. The hot button for most singles/young adults will be either an unwillingness to be an emotional and financial burden on their family or the desire to preserve their independence. Thus DI insurance will typically be a higher priority than life insurance.

Established singles (ages 30 to 49), especially those who want to remain as such, are the ones who need this coverage the most and should have the easiest time affording and qualifying for it.

*Marrieds.* Most members in the young adult married market segment do not yet have dependent children, and both spouses usually work outside the home. Initially, with two incomes, that may seem to lessen their need for DI insurance. However, a couple's lifestyle usually rises to its level of income. The advisor should do an analysis to compare current income to projected income if one spouse becomes disabled. Often couples need both incomes to cover all of their obligations such as a mortgage, any other long-term debts, car payments, credit card repayments, and utilities. It should also be noted that the disabled spouse's condition could curtail the other spouse's income-producing activity. A good way to begin the conversation is to ask, "If one of you could not work for the next year, could you still pay all your bills?

*Families.* The majority of families are dual-income families. Unlike their childless counterparts from the young adult married market segment, they have dependents that create expenses but typically no income. In general, children create markedly higher financial obligations while the family earns less income (in many dual-income families, the second wage earner may work part-time). Thus a disability would wreak a greater amount of havoc on the dual-income family than the childless couple.

For single-income families, the need for DI insurance on the wage earner is still crucial. While the non-working spouse may eventually find employment, it may be difficult in a tight job market.

DI coverage for single parents is essential. A sole income that supports a household must be protected. The economic disruptions caused by a single parent's disability can result in disaster because there is no spouse's income to rely on. It is likely that there is no one to care for the single parent or to help care for the children in the event of disability. Sufficient DI insurance is needed to make sure his or her financial future will not be threatened. Of course, the challenge is finding the funds to pay the premium.

### Explaining the Need for DI Insurance

Once you determine that DI insurance is the prominent need, you must help the prospect consider the financial problems and emotional aspects associated with becoming disabled. Then examine the adequacy of personal financing alternatives and government programs, and demonstrate how DI insurance is the best solution for this potentially devastating financial problem.

***Discuss the Risk of Disability.*** If prospects have not experienced disability, they may not feel that they need DI coverage. There is a common tendency to think that accidents or illness always happen to someone else. Using some of the disability statistics available may help point out to prospects that income interruption by disability is a real possibility for everyone.

Out of 1,000 people, the number who may become disabled before age 65 is substantial (see Table 3-1).

| TABLE 3-1 Probability of Becoming Disabled Before Age 65 | |
| --- | --- |
| **At Age** | **Probability of Disability** |
| 25 | 40 percent |
| 30 | 39 percent |
| 35 | 37 percent |
| 40 | 34 percent |
| 45 | 31 percent |
| 50 | 26 percent |
| 55 | 20 percent |
| Source: Commissioner's Individual Disability Table A. | |

In addition, while the probability of becoming disabled before age 65 decreases as you age, the average duration of disability increases (see Table 3-2).

**TABLE 3-2**
**Average Duration of Disability That Lasts Over 90 Days**

| At Age | Average Duration |
|--------|------------------|
| 25 | 2 years, 2 months |
| 30 | 2 years, 8 months |
| 35 | 3 years, 1 month |
| 40 | 3 years, 6 months |
| 45 | 3 years, 11 months |
| 50 | 4 years, 2 months |
| 55 | 4 years, 11 months |

Source: Commissioner's Individual Disability Table A.

Statistics indicate that the odds of death during an individual's working years are much less that the odds of a significant long-term disability (one lasting more than 90 days).

***The Need for Income.*** Even after talking about the strong statistical possibilities of disability, some people may feel that they have enough DI coverage with Social Security, workers' compensation, and/or by self-funding using personal financial resources.

You must show prospects that an insurable need to continue income during a disability may still exist for them. It is only after a prospect acknowledges everyone has a potential need for DI that you can concentrate on the specific amount of income he or she will need. Prospects may consider the shock that an illness or injury might cause, but fail to understand that it could lead to an ongoing crisis made worse by financial chaos. Disability can cause unimaginable change in a family's lifestyle.

***Financing Alternatives to DI Insurance***

***How to Pay Monthly Expenses During a Disability.*** A helpful technique for selling DI insurance is to ask, "How would you pay your bills if you were disabled?" Many prospects will exhibit a total lack of knowledge concerning this topic. There are many misunderstandings and myths regarding DI and the resources available for financing a period of disability. As a financial advisor, you need to educate your prospects on the shortcomings of the various personal financing alternatives to DI insurance and any applicable government programs, such as Social Security.

*Personal Financing Alternatives.* Using personal savings, taking loans, converting assets to cash, and even Social Security DI payments are usually incomplete solutions to the need for disability income.

*Savings.* The first place most people would look to replace income if they became disabled would be savings. The savings put away for the rainy day could help temporarily to replace lost earnings, but most people do not have significant savings. Even if they have saved money, a family's savings earmarked for other specific uses such as children's educations or retirement would cause those financial goals to be put in jeopardy.

*Loans.* Loans from family and friends can be considered charity—especially if the disability is permanent or lengthy. The lenders could not expect the loan to be repaid if the disability drags on and on. For the same reason, no financial institution is likely to loan money to a disabled person who has no current income or the prospect of any income in the foreseeable future. Borrowing to get through a period of disability can be virtually impossible.

*Converting Assets to Cash.* People may rely on expensive homes and cars, vacation homes, and collections of art, jewelry, or other valuable objects to get through a period of earnings losses from disability. This tangible property would have to be converted to cash, likely on short notice, to replace lost income. Few types of property can yield their full value if they must be sold in a hurry to raise cash. Not only would these people be giving up the property itself in order to get by, but also would likely suffer a loss on the sale.

*Social Security.* The prospect may believe that Social Security DI payments would be sufficient to cover a period of disability. You can help your prospects define what they need by showing them the approximate Social Security Disability Income Insurance (SSDI) dollar amount they can expect to collect if they qualify for benefits. These figures are available on the prospect's own annual Social Security benefits statement. This may convince the prospect just how inadequate SSDI benefits will probably be for him or her.

Remember, a disability must be total and permanent before a person can qualify for Social Security benefits. Fewer than half of those who apply for benefits are accepted initially. Furthermore, nearly one-third of approved applicants were denied benefits initially and then appealed the decision (a process that can take a year or more to complete). Social Security benefits should be considered when analyzing DI coverage, but the prospect needs to know that Social Security is not a basis for a secure DI plan. Rules for eligibility are strict, getting approval may require lengthy (and costly) legal actions, and benefits may be inadequate for higher income earners.

***Workers' Compensation.*** People may confuse workers' compensation plans with disability protection. Workers' compensation plans, which fall under the regulation of individual states, pay monthly benefits to workers who are disabled by on-the-job or job-related injuries or sickness. The amount received is a percentage of wages up to a maximum monthly benefit set by the state.

Workers' compensation pays no benefit for injuries or sickness not related to the job. A disability arising from a sports injury on a weekend outing would not be covered. Further, the maximum amount paid under a valid workers' compensation claim may be less than the amount required to meet the individual's needs.

### *The Logical Solution: DI Insurance*

This leaves DI insurance as the most viable option for most prospects. The only sensible answer to financing the expenses associated with disability is to transfer the risk to an insurance company. This solution provides many advantages:

- A reasonable investment of present income can be budgeted for DI insurance premiums to ensure the continuation of that income during a disability from an illness or injury.
- DI insurance reduces the burden of constant worry about money to pay bills without borrowing, depleting savings, or selling assets.
- DI insurance protects personal assets from the ravages of a long-term disability, and avoids forced liquidations.
- Living standards can be maintained for all family members.
- An insurance company offers freedom in choosing DI insurance options.
- Wealth that has accumulated is preserved for the benefit of a spouse, children, charity, or other purposes.

## The Disability Income Insurance Product

**disability income (DI) insurance**

*Disability income (DI) insurance* is a financial product that indemnifies its owner for the lost capacity to earn income resulting from an impairment caused by either accident or illness. In other words, DI insurance replaces lost earned income that results from the insured's becoming disabled.

### Defining Total Disability

A DI policy's definition of disability is central to DI insurance. It provides the basis for determining whether benefits will be paid. For life insurance benefits, death is a fact that can be verified. The disabling nature of an illness or injury to trigger the payment of DI benefits is open to a variety of interpretations. Furthermore, there are several levels of disability—total disability, presumptive disability, partial disability, and residual disability. All of these can be either short- or long-term in duration. As the definition of disability determines when coverage is triggered, it is very important to understand your DI insurer's definitions. Compare your DI insurer's definitions with the descriptions that follow.

**total disability**

The *total disability* concept generally refers to the inability to do the duties of one's job. We will examine total disability definitions and then consider other definitions that developed in response to the limitations of the total disability definition.

**any-occupation definition of disability**

***Any-Occupation Definition of Disability.*** The most narrow and strict definition of total disability is the *any-occupation definition of disability* which is "the inability to perform the duties of any occupation." Defining total disability in this way means that a person capable of doing anything at all, even selling magazine subscriptions, would not be considered disabled. Obviously a definition like this severely limits the number of people who would qualify for benefits. Fortunately, private DI insurance carriers no longer use such a narrow and restrictive definition of disability.

**unrestricted own-occupation definition of disability**

***Unrestricted Own-Occupation Definition of Disability.*** Some insurance companies use an *unrestricted own-occupation definition of disability* (also known as own-occ). An insured is considered totally disabled if that individual is unable to perform the substantial and material duties of his or her regular occupation, that is, the occupation at the time of disability. Even if the insured returns to work in another job while remaining unable to perform his or her own regular occupation at the time the disability occurred, the person is still considered totally disabled for benefit purposes. In-force policies containing this liberal provision are common, but the current trend is toward a more restrictive definition of disability provisions.

**dual or split definition of disability**

***Dual or Split Definition of Disability.*** The d*ual or split definition of disability* restricts the own-occ provision to a specific time limit (typically two years). During the first 24 months of a total disability, benefits would be paid if the insured is unable to perform the material and substantial duties of his or her occupation. After the first 24 months, benefits would continue only if the person continues to be unable to work in any occupation for which he or she is reasonably suited by education, training, or experience.

**partial disability**

***Partial Disability.*** *Partial disability* can be defined as the inability to do some of the specific duties relating to a job or profession. Its original purpose was to pay limited benefits to an insured who was attempting to return to full-time work after a period of total disability. It could be defined in terms of the number of hours that can be worked. It typically requires a period of total disability prior to receiving partial disability benefits.

**residual disability**

***Residual Disability.*** Residual benefits in disability policies represent a further refinement in the partial disability definitions. Under *residual disability* coverage, benefits are proportionate and based on a percentage of lost income. If needed, they are usually payable for the contract's entire benefit period instead of the limited time available under a partial disability definition. Thus the residual benefit encourages the disabled to return to work. The definitions are numerous, some even incorporating various qualification periods as trigger dates to enact benefits. Study these details to fully understand the policies you sell, or are selling against.

**presumptive disability provisions**

***Presumptive Disability Provisions.*** DI insurance policies typically include provisions setting forth specific losses that qualify for permanent total disability status. They are referred to as *presumptive disability provisions* because the individual is presumed to be totally disabled even if he or she is able to return to work or gain employment in a new occupation.

Presumptive disability provisions generally include loss of sight, loss of speech, loss of hearing, or the total loss of use or severance of both hands, both feet, or one hand and one foot. As with other DI insurance coverage, the presumptive disability benefits cease if the insured individual recovers to an extent that he or she no longer qualifies for the presumptive disability. However, under the presumptive disability clause, contract benefits will last for the length of the policy's basic benefit period, regardless of whether the person is working or earning an income, as long as the disabling condition endures.

Presumptive disability provisions typically will waive the regular elimination period required, and pay basic policy benefits as of the first day presumptive disability requirements are met.

### *Policy Definitions*

It is important that you know precisely how the terms of your DI insurer's policies are defined. Here is a brief list of some of the more important definitions:

- sickness
- injury
- capital sum

- earnings and prior earnings
- premiums
- recurrent disability
- concurrent disability

### *Exclusions*

Normally, exclusions are found only in a section clearly labeled as "exclusions" or "limitations of coverage." Frequently, policies will exclude preexisting conditions for some period (for example, 12 months). Other common exclusions include disabilities resulting from war, self-inflicted injuries, illegal substance abuse, acting as a pilot or aircraft crewmember, or driving under the influence of alcohol or other controlled substance.

### *Policy Features and Riders*

**noncancelable**

*Renewability.* The ability to renew the policy is one of the most important features of the product. The most favorable renewability option is the *noncancelable* policy. As long as the policyowner pays the guaranteed premium specified in the contract, the policy cannot be cancelled or changed in any way. Noncancelable policies are available to the best risk occupational classifications.

**guaranteed renewable**

A *guaranteed renewable* policy will be renewed as long as premiums are paid. Premiums are not guaranteed and can be raised, but not selectively on individual policies. The premium may be raised, with approval of state insurance authorities, for all insureds who own a particular class of policy or who are in a specific underwriting class. A noncancelable policy will cost more than a similar guaranteed renewable policy, as the noncancelable policy is more advantageous for the insured.

**elimination period**

*Elimination Periods.* The period the insured must be disabled before benefits are payable is called the *elimination period* (or waiting period). This may range from 30 days to one year (although 30- 60- and 90-day elimination periods are common). The elimination period reduces the cost of a DI policy by requiring the insured to self-insure during the period before DI payments begin. The longer the waiting period for benefits, the lower the premium will be.

**benefit period**

*Benefit Period.* The length of time the company will pay benefits under the contract is known as the *benefit period.* Some policies distinguish between illness and accidents while others do not. Plans are available that pay benefits for one year, two years, five years, or to age 65 or later.

***Level of Benefits Payable.*** All DI insurance policies specify the amount of monthly benefits payable during periods of total disability after the elimination period has been satisfied. The amount of benefit issued is determined by three factors: the company's issue limit, the insured's income, and other disability coverage in force. The larger the benefit is, the higher the premium. Companies limit maximum benefit amounts because they may be received tax-free and are worth more to the insured than pretax income. Further, giving a disabled employee an income comparable to his regular earnings encourages absenteeism and diminishes the incentive to return to work. Thus a person with a $5,000 monthly income may only qualify for a $3,000 monthly benefit.

**cost-of-living adjustment rider**

***Cost-of-Living Adjustment Rider (COLA).*** The benefit provided by *cost-of-living adjustment rider* attempts to adjust the base amount of coverage to reflect cost-of-living changes due to inflation. The insured usually must be disabled for at least 12 months before the COLA is applied to the benefits. Some companies offer a flat percentage of the base amount while others tie the payment to the Consumer Price Index. The cost-of-living rider is used only at claim time. When the insured recovers, benefits return to the original level unless a special rider is provided, at extra cost, to maintain the increased level of benefit.

**future increase option (FIO)**

***Future Increase Option.*** The *future increase option (FIO)* rider in DI contracts provides guaranteed physical insurability. Coverage can be increased to the limits provided in the option without future evidence of medical or occupational insurability. The insured must still show that his or her earned income qualifies for the increased protection.

**social insurance offset (SIO) rider**

***Social Insurance Offset (SIO) Rider.*** Many insurance companies offer an optional provision in the form of a *social insurance offset (SIO) rider*. It requires an extra premium to cover additional benefits that are payable when the insured is disabled under the base policy and does not initially qualify, or only partially qualifies, for social insurance benefits. These social insurance benefits could be Social Security disability income, workers' compensation, state temporary disability benefits, and so on. The supplemental benefit from the SIO rider is paid in addition to the base DI benefit of the policy, but will not exceed the insurance carrier's issue and participation limits.

**waiver of premium**

***Waiver of Premium.*** Most DI policies automatically include a *waiver-of-premium* provision as part of the base policy. For other policies, it is an optional rider for which the insured pays an extra premium. Most companies waive premiums after 90 days of disability, while other companies waive premiums after 60 days. Some policies waive only those premiums after the waiver-of-premium elimination period has been satisfied. Other policies retroactively waive prior premium payments made after the onset of disability but before the waiver-of-premium eligibility requirements have been met.

Once the insured recovers and DI benefits stop, the insured must resume making premium payments. Premium waivers generally do not continue beyond age 65 even in policies which provide benefits to a greater age.

### Taxation of Individual DI Insurance

The tax implications of individual DI insurance coverage are relatively simple and are different from the taxation of employer-provided coverage. The insured cannot deduct from income the premiums paid for personal DI policies, and benefits received from them are not taxable income to the insured (IRC Section 104). This tax treatment is another powerful argument for using DI insurance coverage to provide funds when earnings are lost through disability. Your prospects will see that personally owned DI insurance protection is a bargain. The premiums for the coverage are minor compared with the amount required to accumulate a sinking fund for protection against loss of income. Additionally, even if the prospect could eventually accumulate the needed amount of savings, he or she would risk having a disability before the fund is fully established. Only DI insurance can provide coverage when it is needed, promptly, reliably, and economically.

### Designing the Plan

Your objective is to help the prospect get the best value for his or her money through an effective plan design. Plan design is a balancing act between the prioritized coverage needs of the prospect and his or her premium commitment.

The steps involved in designing the plan include the following:

- Identify goals.
- Gather quantitative information.
- Quantify needs.

#### *Identify Goals*

If you are conducting a financial and insurance planning interview, you should have identified some, if not all, of the prospect's goals. Even so, there may be some specific goals related uniquely to disability income planning. Thus it is a good idea to ask the prospect, "If you experience a long-term disability, what do you want for yourself and your family (if applicable)?" Here are some possible responses:

- I want my family to retain roughly the same lifestyle as before my disability.
- I want to keep my home.
- I do not want to burden my family with having to take care of me. (This could show an interest in long-term care insurance.)

If you do not know the prospect's other financial goals, ask about them as well. For example, the prospect may want his or her children to go to college, and would like to save for it even if disabled. The point here is not whether all of the prospect's goals will be achieved. Some may not be feasible. Your role should be to help the prospect prioritize and focus on meeting the most important, achievable goals.

### *Gather Quantitative Information*

Advisors typically use a compliance-approved fact finder (see an example below) that helps organize the process and ensure that recommendations appropriately reflect the prospect's financial situation and goals. In addition, a fact finder can help you reinforce the need for DI insurance and begin collecting data to complete the application. You will need to determine the following:

- current expenses
- current household income
- estimated market value of assets

Using these figures for the client's situation, the "Estimate of Financial Need during Disability" worksheet will help you calculate the coverage required in a DI policy.

The amount of the policy's parameters (elimination period, monthly benefit amount, and so on) will obviously affect the cost of the policy. You must determine the precise amount of these benefits that match the client's individual needs. To determine a starting point from which to develop an individual DI insurance policy, ask the client to prioritize the available benefits (a shorter elimination period, larger monthly benefit, longer benefit period, and so on). Later, as you fine-tune the plan to fit his or her budget, you can adjust the parameters accordingly.

| Estimate of Financial Need during Disability | |
|---|---|
| How much money will be needed each month to pay expenses while you are disabled? | While disabled, guaranteed income will be received each month from the following sources: |
| <u>Regular Continuing Expenses Each Month</u> | <u>Guaranteed Income Sources to Pay Monthly Expense</u> |
| Mortgage/rent payment......................$_____ | ..........................................  $_____ |
| Food...................................................$_____ | |
| Utilities .............................................$_____ | ..........................................  $_____ |
| Clothing.............................................$_____ | |
| Required installment payments...........$_____ | ..........................................  $_____ |
| Car payment .....................................$_____ | |
| Gas, oil, and car maintenance ...........$_____ | ..........................................  $_____ |
| Taxes................................................$_____ | |
| Children's school expenses ...............$_____ | ..........................................  $_____ |
| Insurance premiums .........................$_____ | |
| Other expenses ................................$_____ | ..........................................  $_____ |
| ..........................................................$_____ | |
| ..........................................................$_____ | ..........................................  $_____ |
| ..........................................................$_____ | |
| Total Income Needed Each Month ......$_____ | ..........................................  $_____ |
| Less Guaranteed Income Sources (from next column) ......................$_____ | Total Income Guaranteed Each Month............................  $_____ |
| Net Additional Monthly Income Needed ..................................$_____ | |

### Obtain a Premium Commitment

Obtain a commitment from the client concerning the amount that he or she can afford to spend on DI insurance premiums. It does not have to be a dollar figure. It may be best to get a range of affordability in terms of monthly or annual cost. In any event, you will want to make sure that the premium commitment does not strain the client's budget. While all the financial information is still fresh in everyone's mind, you may want to say something like this to the client:

> "Mr. or Ms. Client, as you agree you have a need for $_____ of monthly income in the event of a disability, and you want DI coverage, how much could you comfortably afford per month to address that need? I don't expect you to have an exact dollar figure in mind, but if you can give me a good idea of what you can afford, I will customize a DI insurance plan that fits your budget. Does this make sense to you?"

Advisors who are relatively new to selling DI insurance should strongly consider setting up another meeting to present the plan. This approach will enable the advisor to get help from a mentor or a home office person to analyze the client's information and develop a viable plan. As advisors gain more experience in conducting analysis and developing plans, they may forego the follow-up appointment.

## Preapproach and Approach Strategies to Market DI Insurance

Once you have identified a few target markets or market segments, the next step is to select some general preapproach strategies to identify yourself to prospects and precondition them so you can approach them about DI insurance. This section discusses the use of these preapproach and approach strategies for prospects within several segments of the DI insurance market.

### *Preapproaches*

The purpose of a preapproach is to create awareness of who you are and to generate an initial interest in your products and services. You need to precondition your prospects to agree to meet with you when you call them. They will be less likely to meet with you if they do not know you or have no idea what you can do for them.

Using the preapproach to make your prospect curious and more receptive to listening to your subsequent approach can be done in several different ways. We will discuss some direct-mail preapproaches. The ones you use will depend on your target market, your prospecting methods, and your creativity.

Direct mail is one of the most common preapproaches because it is an easy and relatively inexpensive way to precondition prospects. It allows people to see your message who otherwise might not look in the telephone book or your website. Furthermore, direct mail can customize your message to your target markets, such as two-income families, single parents, and so on.

The preapproach is an important part of the selling/planning process. In DI insurance coverage, prospects must be aware of their risk from disabilities before their interest in the product is aroused. The entire process will go more smoothly if your prospects have already thought about the financial problems associated with disability and if they know who you are.

### Approaches

Generally advisors use the telephone to approach prospects for sales appointments. This section will review some of the basics of effective telephone, pivoting, and face-to-face approaches to prospect for DI insurance.

***Telephone Approach.*** Using the telephone effectively remains a key to success for financial advisors. You must learn to make telephone appointments with prospects who are not on the national do-not-call registry or who have requested information and consented to your contacting them. Phone scripts help you feel more comfortable and enable you to project a more confident phone personality. They free you to focus on the prospect and listen for clues to his or her level of interest. Scripts also help you repeat success and diagnose failure. A good script is short and creates interest. You must practice it until it sounds very natural and unscripted.

Below is an example of a follow-up to a preapproach mailing.

---

**Follow-up to a Mailing to Single Prospects**

"Hello, this is John Gray from XYZ Insurance Company. I recently sent you some information on how DI insurance can keep you financially independent if an illness or injury prevents you from earning a living.

"As a DI insurance specialist, I would like to meet with you and explain how this product can support your financial security and guarantee your lifestyle if you can't work. People in situations similar to yours have found it useful to learn how DI insurance can protect you.

"Are evenings good for you, or do afternoons work better?"

---

**pivoting approach**

***Pivoting Between DI Insurance and Other Financial Products.*** An effective approach is to pivot or transition from one product to another using previously shared information to ask a question relevant to another product. The *pivoting approach* can be used with almost any type of other financial product sale to pivot to DI products.

How and when to pivot are going to depend on factors such as what type of product the prospect purchased from you (or did not purchase), the client's level of satisfaction, and so on

For example, life insurance and DI insurance are closely related. Both protect financial security by providing funds if the ability to earn is interrupted. Both are an essential part of comprehensive financial plans. The progression from one subject to another is logical in a sales situation. Many prospects purchase life insurance to assure that premature death does not destroy their financial plan. This objective also indicates the need for good DI insurance coverage. Here is a sample pivot:

---

***Example:***            "(Prospect), you've purchased life insurance to be sure that even your death will not destroy the financial security you want for your family. However, there is another threat to that financial security that could be even more devastating than your death.

"What would happen if you are too ill or injured to work and your income stops? That situation could destroy your financial security even more surely than death. Fortunately, there is an easy way to make sure that will not happen. Can we get together next week or another time convenient for you to discuss how?"

---

***Face-to-Face DI Insurance Approach Talk.*** An effective opening or pivoting presentation contains a series of good sales ideas that lead the prospect to a positive decision. Below is an example of a quick, thought-provoking approach to get prospects thinking about the financial impact that a disability can create. It should take no longer than five minutes to present.

## Rich Enough

"(Prospect), would you say you are rich? Except for rich people, most of us have a financial picture that looks like this:

*(At this point, draw two horizontal lines—not too far apart. Label the top line "normal income" and the lower line "normal expenses." See illustration below.)*

"Most of us manage to keep a little of what we earn after expenses are paid. The difference between income and expenses—savings—may not be much. But as long as the income line is above the expense line, we'll be all right. Do we agree so far?

"Now, suppose something comes along to change the directions of these lines. One something that will surely do this is a disability. Notice how the income line heads south and the expense line goes up, like this:

*(Draw income line down toward bottom of page, expense line up.)*

"Savings are eaten up in a hurry—not just by excess medical bills, but by routine living costs. The difference between income and expenses now is not savings, but debt.

"What do you do? There is a limit to what people will lend to someone totally disabled and out of work. Relatives and friends would help some, but they have their own problems, and wouldn't they rightfully expect you to use up your own financial resources before they begin contributing theirs?

"You could possibly sell your car or even your home, but I'm sure you wouldn't want to do that. Banks won't loan you money if you have no income. Fortunately, there is a better way to solve the problem.

"In a manner of speaking, the better way is to be rich enough—not rich in the usual sense, but in the sense of having an extra source of money when earnings stop, a source of money to mitigate the disability problem. Let me show you how easily it can be arranged."

# CHAPTER THREE REVIEW

*Key terms and concepts are explained in the Glossary. Answers to the review and self-test questions are found in the back of the textbook in the Answers to Questions section.*

## Key Terms and Concepts

| | |
|---|---|
| integrated planning approach | residual disability |
| budgeting planning | presumptive disability |
| fixed expenses | provisions |
| discretionary expenses | noncancelable |
| special consideration expenses | guaranteed renewable |
| financial planning pyramid | elimination period |
| building-block approach | benefit period |
| young-adult market segment | cost-of-living adjustment rider |
| disability income (DI) insurance | future increase option (FIO) |
| total disability | social insurance offset (SIO) |
| any-occupation definition | rider |
| unrestricted own-occupation | waiver of premium |
| definition | pivoting approach |
| dual or split definition | guaranteed renewable |
| partial disability | noncancelable |

## Review Questions

3-1. Describe the integrated planning approach and identify the major planning areas for which this planning approach accounts.

3-2. Explain the budgeting process and how it can be used with a client.

3-3. Discuss the financial planning pyramid and how it can be used with a client.

3-4. Describe the characteristics and needs of the four subsegments of the young-adult market segment.

3-5. Discuss the need for disability income insurance.

3-6. Define the following terms in a disability income insurance policy:
- total disability
- elimination period
- residual disability
- cost-of-living adjustment rider (COLA)
- future increase option

## Self-test Questions

*Instructions: Read Chapter 3 and then answer the following questions to test your knowledge. There are 10 questions. Choose one answer for each question, and then check your answers with the answer key in the back of the textbook.*

3-1.     Which of the following definitions of disability applies when an individual is paid disability benefits based on a percentage of lost income?

      (A)    residual disability
      (B)    presumptive disability
      (C)    partial disability
      (D)    total disability

3-2.     An emergency fund is normally recommended to cover what period of living expenses?

      (A)    1-2 months
      (B)    3-6 months
      (C)    6-12 months
      (D)    1-2 years

3-3.     Which of the following is the first step in establishing a budget?

      (A)    Estimate anticipated total income.
      (B)    Estimate discretionary expenses.
      (C)    Consider money being set aside for intermediate and long-range goals.
      (D)    Consider what might be cut or what may need to be increased in the future.

3-4.     Which of the following best describes the unrestricted own-occupation definition of disability?

      (A)    the inability to perform the duties of any occupation
      (B)    the inability to perform the substantial and material duties of one's regular occupation
      (C)    unable to work in any occupation for which one is reasonably suited by education, training or experience
      (D)    inability to do some of the specific duties relating to a job or profession

3-5.   Which of the following statements concerning personal financing alternatives when a worker becomes disabled is (are) correct?

      I.   Most workers will be able to use their emergency funds (savings) to get through a period of disability.

     II.   For most workers, Social Security DI payments will be enough to cover a period of disability.

(A)   I only
(B)   II only
(C)   Both I and II
(D)   Neither I nor II


3.6.   Which of the following statements about life insurance planning is (are) correct?

      I.   Life insurance can help solve most of the financial problems facing the  survivors of a deceased insured.

     II.   The most common reason for buying life insurance is the love a person has for his or her survivors.

(A)   I only
(B)   II only
(C)   Both I and II
(D)   Neither I nor II


3-7.   Which of the following statements concerning disability income insurance is (are) correct?

      I.   The definition of disability changes according to each disability.

     II.   The definition of disability can vary greatly from one policy to another.

(A)   I only
(B)   II only
(C)   Both I and II
(D)   Neither I nor II

3-8.    All of the following statements regarding a noncancelable disability policy are correct EXCEPT

(A)    Coverage cannot be cancelled if the premiums are paid as due.
(B)    Premiums can be increased if claims exceed expected levels.
(C)    Benefits cannot be modified by the company based on employment or income.
(D)    Premiums are guaranteed not to increase until the end of the policy period.

3-9.    All of the following are advantages of starting a life insurance program early EXCEPT

(A)    lock in lower premiums at a younger age
(B)    qualify for lifelong protection while you are insurable
(C)    larger cash values are available at retirement if a plan is started at a younger age
(D)    cash values are immediately available to pay off debts and use for investment

3-10.    All of the following statements concerning Dual Income Young Families are correct EXCEPT

(A)    The majority of families in the United States have two or more income producers.
(B)    The loss of either income will usually jeopardize the family's financial strength.
(C)    With two incomes, families find it easier to save money to meet financial goals.
(D)    While they make more, two-income families tend not to have a budget.

*4*

# *Middle-Years Adults, Life Insurance, and Special Markets*

---

## Learning Objectives

*An understanding of the material in this chapter should enable you to*

---

4-1.    Discuss the common characteristics and needs of the middle-years adult segment.

4-2.    Compare and contrast the types and features of life insurance products.

4-3.    Explain the income tax consequences of life insurance premiums, death benefits,  and living benefits.

4-4.    Describe marketing opportunities caused by socio-economic, legislative, and demographic changes.

4-5.    Describe the opportunities, challenges, and strategies for marketing to women and non-traditional families and couples.

4-6.    Describe the opportunities, challenges, and strategies for marketing in an ethnically and culturally diverse market.

4-7.    Explain the tax implications of life insurance in divorce situations.

---

This chapter focuses on the middle-years adult segment, their insurance and financial needs, and the products appropriate for them. It also discusses the types, features and tax treatment of life insurance. The chapter also discusses the financial impact of divorce and the new marketing possibilities created by this change of family status. Additionally, the chapter looks at emerging and ethnic markets, and the marketing impact of socio-economic, legislative, and demographic changes.

# LIFE CYCLE: MIDDLE-YEARS ADULTS

The more carefree days of young adulthood for most people eventually give way to a more serious outlook on life. Somewhere during the young adulthood phase, some people have begun new careers. Others have found a partner and some have had children. Toward the end of the young adult phase, people have begun to establish themselves, as they transition into the middle years of adulthood.

**middle-years adult market segment**

For some members of *the middle-years adult market segment*, the middle years (between roughly age 38 and 58) are a period of emotional turmoil known as the mid-life crisis. Sensing their youth is fading away, the mid-life crisis causes people to do things that will help them retain the image of their youth. Eventually, there is an acceptance of fading youth and a forward focus on building for retirement. Of course, not everyone has this experience.

This section begins with a discussion of the common characteristics and needs for people in the middle years. We will also explore the Baby Boomers, a generation that currently makes up the majority of the middle-years market.

## Common Characteristics

While we will attempt to define some common characteristics and needs for the middle-years adult segment, these can only serve as general guidelines. People in our society move through this life stage with an increasing variety of living arrangements and family situations. For example, more and more couples are choosing to have children later in life, even in their 40s and beyond. Factors such as advances in medicine, delaying marriage to advance one's career, and divorce and remarriage result in many people having children later in life. Thus some in this segment will have more in common with the previous life-cycle segment, young adults with children.

### *Established Career*

In the middle years, people tend to be established in their careers. They may change jobs or employers, but typically not what they do for a living. Tenure in their field means they are moving toward the peak of their earning potential, and as they approach the middle of the segment, they are more aware of their need to prepare for retirement. Also contributing to their increased saving potential (for those with children) is the lessening of parental responsibilities as children grow up and leave the home.

### Empty Nest

Toward the late part of this phase, around their 50s, many parents experience an empty nest as their children move out and become independent. The empty nest requires an emotional adjustment as parents face the reality that they no longer have day-to-day responsibilities for their children. For many, this experience is exhilarating and reintroduces many freedoms to middle-years parents who now have more disposable income and more time. For others, it may be a sad time that calls for reflection and a reordering of priorities as their children leave home to venture out on their own.

Inevitably, empty nesters will begin to look more closely at their retirement situation. With more disposable income, they will have the means to save more. For some, retirement may occur toward the end of the middle-years phase when they are in their mid- to late-50s. The majority, however, will still need to be working and saving for retirement.

### Aging Parents

In this segment, many people are caring for aging parents and/or another elderly relative. Women tend to be the primary caregiver more often than men. For convenience, they may move the elderly person into their own home and care for them as long as possible.

**sandwich generation**

For a growing minority of people providing eldercare, the middle-years group is adding this responsibility to the responsibility of raising their children. Demographers have named people with multi-generational responsibilities the *sandwich generation*. People in this situation must plan their retirement, manage their aging parents' needs and finances, and save money to pay for their children's college education and/or wedding. In some ethnic groups, sandwich generations are much more common.

### Inheritance

For some, this phase of the life cycle means  receiving gifts from living parents or inheritances from deceased parents or relatives.

### Common Mistakes

This segment of the life cycle covers a broad spectrum of diverse subgroups. Because of this diversity, there are many approaches to meeting the challenges facing those in the middle-years stage. It is easy for financial mistakes and errors to be made by this group, and some of these mistakes can affect one's financial standing for many years. Here are some of the most common mistakes:

- procrastination in saving for future needs. This is probably the greatest single failure because the benefit of compound interest is lost forever.
- failure to provide adequate protection for major risks
- overuse of credit, especially for non-essential consumer items
- over-acceptance of strategies introduced in financial periodicals
- neglect in keeping property coverages and protection up-to-date
- unrealistic, low estimates of future needs for children's education
- too much reliance on company-sponsored benefits
- inadequate safeguards against the eroding effect of inflation on purchasing power
- untimely and inadequate provisions for retirement
- excessive risks with investments
- failure to seek competent, professional counsel from qualified financial advisors
- failure to provide for sufficient income in the event of disability

## Common Needs

Common needs in the middle-years adult segment include those discussed below. Obviously, factors such as marital status, and presence and ages of children will create a variety of different profiles of needs.

### Emergency Funds

Middle-years adults need emergency funds to protect against the loss of a job and/or to facilitate a career change. Some might call this a walk away fund because it gives an experienced person the option of walking away from a job to pursue another that fits better with their needs and goals.

### Mortgage Payment Protection

The need to protect a mortgage is still a top priority in the middle years. If you find a couple agreeing on the need to protect the mortgage at this stage, you may also find an opportunity for long-term care insurance to protect all family assets.

### Final Expenses

Planning for final expenses is universal for all segments.

### Income Replacement

The need for income replacement will vary, manifesting itself differently in this stage of life. For some, the traditional need to provide for survivors will still be important, especially considering that 21 percent of parents between the ages of 40 and 45 have a child under the age of six, according to the U.S. Census Bureau. Additionally, the growing number of family eldercare situations may require income for continued care of an elderly or disabled relative upon death of a provider.

### Education

The traditional need to provide for a child or spouse's education will still apply to many households in this life-cycle phase.

### Debt Liquidation

Unfortunately, debt is not limited to one generation. People are always buying cars, consumer items, and overusing their credit cards.

### Disability

Disability protection is necessary as long as one works. In this stage, because retirement is approaching, disability insurance could be promoted to ensure that one's retirement plan stays on track.

### Retirement

It is never too early to start, but the middle years are when people tend to take retirement planning more seriously. With more disposable income, people are able to make decisions for which they may not have previously had the money. Where retirement income for a surviving partner will not be enough, life insurance can address the need.

### Will

Many in this segment may still not have a will—especially those who are not married or couples without children. An advisor can help them understand the importance of a will to carry out their desires after death.

### Long-Term Care

In the early parts of this life-cycle segment, people are open to discussing the long-term care needs of their parents. Once they hit 50, they are more open to talking about purchasing long-term care coverage for themselves.

This is especially true for those who have assisted with or observed the long-term care situations of parents or other family members.

### Estate Planning

Especially toward the end of this phase, many clients have a better grasp on what retirement income they can expect. They will need estate planning to avoid or greatly diminish the erosion of their assets caused by estate and inheritance taxes, and estate administration expenses.

## The Baby Boomers

The baby boomers are comprised of those born between 1946 and 1964. Some 77 million people, or almost one-third of the United States population, fall into this category. The baby boom has been divided into two waves. The first wave is comprised of babies born in the late-1940s, following World War II, until the peak of the baby boom years in 1957. Those born after the peak until the mid-1960s are known as second wave baby boomers. The majority of the baby boomer population is currently in the middle-years stage. The earliest boomers reached the mature adult phase in 2004 and are now eligible for early Social Security retirement benefits at age 62 or later.

### Characteristics of Baby Boomers

*Income Trends.* The first wave boomer prospects are primarily homeowners. They bought their homes when prices were much lower than current prices. The second wave homeowners have had to contend with a considerable increase in national home values and prices. The homes they purchased cost much more than the homes of the first wave group, so they spend a much higher percentage of their income on housing.

With higher incomes and lower mortgage payments, the first-wave boomers have more discretionary income on average than the younger boomers. The personal disposable income of early boomers has increased substantially over the years and has outpaced the rate of growth in the Gross National Product (GNP).

*Education.* A major factor in identifying market potential in the middle years is the level of education. Half of all baby boomers are college educated. The more educated your prospects are, the more likely they will understand the value of financial planning and the role of financial products and services.

*Family.* Baby boomers generally have married later, have delayed having children, and have had fewer children than previous generations.

While the previous generation became empty nesters by age 45 or 50, baby boomers experience an empty nest in their mid-50s. In many cases, they must finance their children's education and their retirement program simultaneously.

*Constant Change.* In past generations, people in their middle years were predictable. The traditional man reaching age 50 was married to his first wife, with grown children who were on their own, and he was looking forward to retirement with a company he had worked for most of his life.

Today, the middle years for many people are quite different. Some are in a second or third marriage and have started a new family. Changing jobs and moving often is a way of life for this group. They have many more options today. You must be prepared to provide individualized approaches and tailor-made presentations, rather than cookie-cutter solutions for these prospects. Clear, careful, and detailed fact and feeling data gathering is important to determine needs and personalize your recommendations.

*Divorce.* Divorce has become more common and the number of divorces, along with divorce rates, has more than doubled in the past two decades. Many middle-years prospects, having been through at least one divorce, may want individual investment and insurance programs for each spouse.

The dependence upon alimony payments is a major concern of many divorced individuals and represents a significant sales opportunity. Many recipients of alimony need guaranteed income upon the payor's death. Frequently, courts are mandating life insurance on the payor as part of divorce agreements. We will discuss this in more detail later in this chapter.

*Retirement Planning.* Over the next 20 years, a huge wave of the baby boom generation will be retiring, living their senior years, and shaping the nation's future public policy. Second-wave boomers are entering their most productive work years, and they will dominate the workplace for the next decade or so. They will see their children grow up while their parents age. With demographic and economic power, they will influence government policy on education, employment, family issues, retirement programs, health care, and long-term care.

Boomers will surely raise important questions about generational fairness and financial equity, especially regarding health services and long-term care public policy. Understanding their attitudes, problems, and needs can help you succeed with this huge market segment.

During the middle years, your prospects face the challenges and rewards of career development, forming a family, raising children, acquiring assets, and retirement planning. Many will need professional assistance addressing their insurance and other financial needs. This is an opportunity for you to help them obtain their goals with products to create and protect their financial security.

# LIFE INSURANCE PRODUCTS

We begin with a review of life insurance products, and how they provide solutions to individual and family needs.

## General Characteristics

All life insurance products are based upon the interaction of mortality, interest, and the expenses associated with creating, distributing, and servicing these products. Every insurance company adds its own variables and assumptions to reach a final premium for their policies. These variables result in life insurance products with significantly different premiums, even though they may appear identical in value to you or your prospect. These variations in price are affected by operational efficiencies, investment performance, mortality assumptions, underwriting practices, profit objectives, and commissions paid to the field force.

### *Understanding Mortality Tables*

**2001 CSO Mortality Tables**

About every 20 years, new mortality tables are developed for individual life insurance products by the National Association of Insurance Commissioners (NAIC). In December 2002, the NAIC adopted the *2001 CSO (Commissioners Standard Ordinary) Mortality Tables*, to replace the 1980 CSO Mortality Tables used in insurance reserve valuations.

*2001 CSO Mortality Tables.* There have been significant improvements in mortality in the two decades since the introduction of the 1980 CSO Mortality Tables. Thus the 2001 tables should reduce reserve requirements (the amount of money states require an insurer to maintain for its in-force life insurance policies).

One significant change in the new mortality tables is the increase in the maximum age to attained age 120 (compared with age 100 with the 1980 CSO). These changes will affect newly issued policies only, as in-force policies will continue under their prior mortality and expense criteria. The 2001 CSO mortality tables take full effect in 2009, and most companies have developed products using these mortality tables.

## Types of Traditional Life Insurance Products

The function of life insurance is to create a principal sum of money, either through the death of the insured or through the accumulation of cash value (for permanent plans). We will review the principal types of life insurance products on the market today.

### Term Life Insurance

Term life insurance provides pure and temporary protection. Since it has no cash value savings element, term will initially cost much less than other types of life insurance, particularly for most adults under age 40. Term insurance offers the maximum coverage at minimum cost at the time it is purchased.

Term insurance is suitable when the need for protection is temporary, or when the need for protection is permanent but the insured cannot afford to pay the higher premiums for permanent life insurance. Among the many temporary needs suitable for term protection are the following:

- cash to pay an outstanding mortgage at the insured's death
- collateral to obtain a loan to protect the lender should the owner die before repayment is completed
- replacement funds for income should the insured die during his or her working years
- coverage for working parents who may likely need more insurance than they can afford while children are dependent
- riders to increase coverage on the insured's life and for other family members
- many business situations

**Features.** The marketability of term life insurance contracts is greatly enhanced by two important features available in most plans: renewability and convertibility. Because these two provisions put a company at a slightly higher risk of adverse selection, they will generally increase policy premiums. Normally, the extra benefits and flexibility these provisions provide are well worth the small extra cost to the policyowner.

**renewability provision**

**Renewability Provision.** The *renewability provision* allows the policy owner to extend the contract beyond the original period of insurance without new evidence of insurability. It guarantees the insured the right to continued protection in the insurance plan. Each renewed period of insurance is usually for the same duration as the original contract period (for example, 5, 10, or 15 years). The premium at renewal will increase based on the insured's attained age.

**convertibility**
**provision**

***Convertibility Provision.*** The *convertibility provision* guarantees the policy owner the future right to exchange the term contract for a permanent life insurance contract. This allows buyers to postpone the higher premium associated with permanent insurance until they can afford it or decide which type of permanent insurance to buy. He or she can buy the term insurance protection today with a convertibility feature and make a decision about conversion later.

The conversion is made to a permanent plan without additional underwriting. Thus an insured could be gravely ill and still have the guaranteed privilege of converting the term policy to permanent coverage. Advisors should always consider a term policy's convertibility feature when making recommendations to a client.

Some companies allow policies to be converted retroactively, at the original policy date, within the first few years after issue. In that case, the premium for the permanent contract is the same as if the insured had originally purchased the permanent contract instead of the term. The insured is required to pay the difference in premium between the two plans, which could be a considerable amount of money. There are several methods used to achieve this; you should check to determine the practice of your company.

***Re-entry Term.*** Companies use re-entry term as another method to develop rates that are more competitive. Also known as select and ultimate term, re-entry term is based on two types of mortality tables: select and ultimate tables. A select table reflects the insurer's mortality experience of newly insured lives only. As this group was recently approved for life insurance, their mortality is somewhat better than others of the same age and gender. The insurance company can more accurately predict this group's mortality results during the select period, which usually extends from 5 to 15 years.

**ultimate mortality**

Over the years, people have changes in health, lifestyle, habits, and occupations, and their mortality rates worsen. A second mortality table, called *ultimate mortality*, applies to people who have been insured for some years and have higher mortality rates because time has passed since the initial company underwriting.

**re-entry term**

The name *re-entry term insurance* comes from the fact that the insured may re-enter the select group periodically by submitting to new underwriting requirements and demonstrating satisfactory insurability. If this is not done, or the insured fails to satisfy the underwriting standards to re-enter with select rates, the policy premium jumps to the higher ultimate rates for the duration of the contract.

***Waiver of Premium.*** Waiver of premium is available to both term and permanent insurance policies. The waiver of premium rider, available to policyowners for a small cost, offers added value if an insured becomes disabled. This rider will waive the premiums of the policy if the insured becomes totally disabled, usually after an elimination period of six months.

### Term Insurance Plans

Term life policies usually provide either a level or decreasing death benefit. A few term riders provide an increasing death benefit.

*Level Face Amount Term Life Policies.* Most term life insurance sold today provides a level death benefit over a specific period. The premiums on these policies normally increase with age at renewal or may remain level at younger ages.

*Increasing Premium Contracts.* Many term policies have increasing premiums with level death benefits and are renewable. They include products like the annual renewable term (ART), 5- or 10-year renewable term, and re-entry term.

The ART may be referred to as yearly renewable term (YRT) by your company. The premiums increase each year for the length of the renewal duration, which may be one, 5, 10, 20, 30 years, or to age 70. Some plans extend to age 100 and have a large number of rate bands for sums ranging from $100,000 to $1 million. Many offer different premium categories based on underwriting qualifications such as standard/preferred, tobacco user/nonuser, and various combinations of these.

*Decreasing (Face Amount) Term Life Policies.* Some term insurance products have face amounts that decrease over time. Decreasing term policies are commonly used to pay off loans at death. When used as a mortgage protection policy, decreasing term can be designed to reduce at the same rate the home mortgage reduces.

In decreasing term, the premium remains fixed for the length of the contract, while the face amount gradually decreases. Decreasing term premium may be significantly higher than for the same initial amount of level term. Advisors should be aware of this difference and recommend level term if appropriate for the clients.

*Term Riders.* Most companies allow policyowners to add term riders to either a term or permanent policy. The convenience of term insurance as a rider, and the advantages of combining different types of protection under one contract, have earned term riders a lasting place in your portfolio. Because a policy fee is charged for the contract as a whole, the term rider will save the cost of an additional policy fee for most company plans.

A level term rider can provide temporary additional term protection for a specific number of years. For example, income earners may need extra income protection during their peak earning years. A 10-, 15-, or 20-year level term rider on a basic policy would meet this objective.

Level term riders are also used to insure other family members. The spouse and children of the primary insured may be covered individually under a spouse or children's rider or collectively under a family term rider.

### Endowment Life Insurance

While term policies pay the full policy amount only at death, endowment policies provide for a death benefit or payment of the total face amount on the endowment date. The endowment policy is said to mature or endow, and the full face value is payable to the policy owner. For many years, people purchased these policies to provide life insurance during their working years, and the cash value at retirement. Favorable tax advantages for withdrawals of the cash values made them very attractive.

Tax law changes in 1984 (TAMRA) extended the tax benefits available under most other forms of cash value life insurance, but not to endowment plans sold since January 1, 1985. While sales of this contract in the United States have ceased, TAMRA grandfathered endowment policies sold before 1985 and retained their tax preferences. You may find examples of these among your clients' old insurance contracts.

### Whole Life

**whole life**

**ordinary life**

**limited-pay life**

*Whole life*, a traditional permanent life insurance product, is designed to stay in force for the insured's whole life. This is in contrast to term life insurance, which only pays a death benefit if the insured dies during the specified term. Whole life's name refers only to the duration of the protection and not to how premiums are to be paid. If premiums are paid throughout the insured's lifetime, the policy is called *ordinary life*. If premiums are paid only during a specified period of years or to a certain attained age, the policy is called *limited-pay life.*

***Ordinary Life Insurance.*** Ordinary life premiums are paid during the entire life of the insured. Sometimes dividends in participating policies are used to offset premium payments and may even replace the need for continued payment out of pocket. Ordinary life provides the lowest recurring premium for permanent life insurance and is the most basic form of permanent life insurance.

At the maximum age of a company's mortality table used in its design, the plan will mature. A cash value, equal to the face amount of the policy, is paid to the policyowner if the insured is alive. This will be at age 100 under policies issued under 1980 CSO tables, and age 120 under CSO 2001 tables.

In this way, ordinary (whole) life is similar to endowment life insurance with an endowment age of 100 (or 120).

**net amount at risk**

Ordinary life insurance includes a pure insurance element and a cash value element. As the cash value increases, the pure insurance decreases. The life insurance component at any time is the difference between the face amount and the cash value, and is known as the *net amount at risk*. The costs of underwriting, issue, sales commissions, and other expenses are subtracted from the premiums paid over the first few years leaving little cash value buildup before the third or fourth year for most contracts.

The policyowner may surrender the policy for the cash value at any time. Surrendering the policy automatically cancels the contract and ends the life insurance protection. Surrender of a policy within the first 5 to 10 years will result in a considerable loss to the policyowner because the surrender values reflect the company's recovery of initial policy acquisition costs. Policyowners should intend to keep the ordinary life policy for at least 20 years.

The policyowner may borrow against the cash value at an interest rate detailed in the policy. Borrowing against the cash value does not cancel the contract unless the policy loan amounts with accumulated interest exceed the cash value. If the insured dies while there is a policy loan, the beneficiary receives the face value less any loan and accumulated interest. Therefore borrowing against the cash value reduces the death benefit.

**nonforfeiture options**

The *nonforfeiture options* of an ordinary life policy include surrendering the contract as discussed above. A second option is to take a reduced amount of paid-up permanent insurance payable on the same conditions as the original contract. This option uses the net cash value of the policy as a single premium to purchase the reduced paid-up policy. The actual amount of the reduced paid-up insurance depends on the attained age of the insured.

The third nonforfeiture option is extended term insurance. This is paid-up term insurance in an amount equal to the original face amount of the policy, increased by accumulated dividends and reduced by policy indebtedness. The length of the term of the full face value of insurance under this option depends on the insured's attained age and the amount of cash value available. This will determine the period, or term, over which the extended term coverage will remain in force. At the end of the term, the coverage expires.

Despite the popularity of newer life insurance products, ordinary life insurance continues to be in demand. The primary appeal is the guaranteed lifetime death benefit for a guaranteed level cost. With these guarantees, ordinary life can provide coverage for final expenses, family expenses and income, estate conservation, and many insurance applications in the business market.

Another use for whole life is taking distributions from the cash value or dividends to supplement retirement income from Social Security, pension plans, and personal savings. Whole life is also a good option for younger people, who can take advantage of the low premium schedules.

| **Life Insurance Product Lines** <br> **Annualized Premium Market Share** | | |
|---|---|---|
| | **2003** | **2007** |
| Universal Life | 35% | 42% |
| Variable Life | 1 | + |
| Variable Universal Life | 15 | 16 |
| Term | 22 | 21 |
| Whole Life | 27 | 21 |
| + Less than one-half of one percent. <br><br> *Source: U.S. Individual Life Sales, 2008, by LIMRA International, Windsor, CT. Reprinted with permission.* | | |

***Limited-Pay Whole Life Insurance.*** With limited-pay whole life insurance, the face value of the policy is payable at death, but premiums are paid for a limited number of years, after which the policy becomes paid-up. Limited-pay policies are ideal for clients who want a policy paid-up by a specific age (for example, 65), or in a specific number of years from the issue date.

Premium payments must be larger than for policies that extend premiums over an entire lifetime, such as ordinary life. The shorter the premium payment period, the higher the premium and the faster the cash value accumulation. The premiums payable under a limited-pay policy are actuarially equivalent to the premiums payable for the insured's entire lifetime under an ordinary (whole life) policy. The ultimate limited-pay plan is a single premium policy in which the policyowner pays the full amount of premiums due on the contract in one payment.

An advantage of the accelerated cash value buildup in a limited-pay policy is that the sum available to borrow, or to surrender, will be greater than in ordinary life. This will be useful in times of financial emergency, retirement planning, or other cash accumulation needs.

There is an important difference between a limited-pay policy and the alternate-premium, or vanishing premium, paying approach. Limited-pay plans guarantee a paid-up policy at the end of the accelerated premium-paying period. Alternate-premium payments use policy dividends to pay all of the premiums if dividends are adequate to do so. Remember that dividends are never guaranteed, and make sure your client understands that. While dividends may increase in the future, recent economic difficulties have caused some insurers to decrease or even eliminate dividends. A policy whose premiums had vanished could suddenly have premiums reappear. The policyowner would have to resume partial or full premium payments or surrender the policy.

| **Life Insurance Product Lines**<br>**Individual Life Insurance In-Force Policies** | |
| --- | --- |
| | **2007** |
| Universal Life | 15% |
| Variable Life | + |
| Variable Universal Life | 5 |
| Whole Life | 51 |
| *Total Permanent* | 72 |
| | |
| *Total Term Insurance* | 28 |
| + Less than one-half of one percent. | |
| *Source: Annual Individual Life Insurance Sales and In-Force Survey, 2007, by LIMRA International, Windsor, CT. Reprinted with permission.* | |

Limited-pay plans are attractive to upper-income individuals who want faster cash accumulation in addition to a death benefit. Limited-pay plans build cash values sooner to use for needs such as a down payment on a home, college tuition, retirement planning, emergencies, or business opportunities. They also appeal to parents, grandparents, or other relatives who want to purchase life insurance as a gift for a child without the child having to pay the premium later in life.

**modified whole life insurance**

***Modified Whole Life Insurance.*** Another variation of whole life is *modified whole life insurance*. This product offers a lower premium for a period of time (such as three to five years) and a level face amount. After a premium increase, the premium stays level for the rest of the life of the contract. This product is used for clients who may not have the money to purchase level premium whole life now, but expect to be able to afford the premiums in a few years. Examples include a young family or a medical intern or doctor just starting out in a practice.

### Comparing Term and Permanent Insurance

Both term and permanent plans provide protection that once purchased can be canceled only by the policyowner. Permanent insurance is designed to provide protection for life, or at least a long term, typically 20 years or more. Otherwise, term may be a better purchase. Term insurance is designed for special purposes or for specific lengths of time. Permanent insurance builds equity through cash value accumulations and other nonforfeiture benefits which provide ownership rights in the policy.

Cash value life insurance is often the best solution for many people because it provides lifelong protection. With few exceptions, once you have been approved for the coverage, your policy cannot be canceled by the insurer. Regardless of your health, or any other insurability issues, the insurance will remain in force. This eliminates the problem of future insurability with term insurance after the coverage period expires.

Permanent life insurance builds cash value. This amount, part of which is guaranteed under many policies, can be used for anything the policyowner may want. For example, it can provide supplemental retirement income, pay for education, or make a down payment on a home.

Term insurance does not provide cash value buildup or other guaranteed benefits. The insured buys the term death benefit to last the period of time the policy is designed to cover. Term insurance is often called pure insurance protection because cash values are not part of the design and only a pure death benefit is purchased.

Term insurance does have drawbacks. Term insurance provides a death benefit only for a specific period. When the coverage ends, so does the protection. For example, suppose you own a $250,000 term policy. You keep the coverage in force for 10 years and the policy expires at midnight on December 31. If you die at 11:59 p.m. on New Year's Eve, the policy pays the full benefit. If you die at 12:01 a.m. on New Year's Day, no payments are made under the policy because the contract has expired.

Buying term versus whole life is often compared to renting versus purchasing a home. Term insurance, like renting, provides no permanence or equity. When you rent, you get full and immediate use of the house, but only for as long as pay the rent. As soon as your lease expires, you must leave. Even if you rented the house for 30 years, you have no equity or value that belongs to you. Whole life, on the other hand, provides permanence and equity build-up similar to owning a home where the value of the home, in excess of any indebtedness, belongs to the homeowner.

Premiums for permanent insurance products are initially higher for any age than for a term insurance product of the same face amount. However, permanent premiums usually remain level while term premiums increase as the insured grows older. The net premium charged for term insurance is determined by the death rate for people with the same attained age as the insured. At later ages of a term insurance contract, the premiums for the same amount of insurance will be higher in the term contract than in a permanent plan of the same duration. The reason term premiums are so low initially is that most term contracts do not cover the years when death is most likely to occur. This makes the cost of insurance very high at those older ages. Even after age 40, most term contracts experience a sharp premium increase. Eventually people drop the policy because they no longer need or want the coverage, or they cannot afford it.

There is a real danger of becoming uninsurable when the term coverage expires. While many term policies are convertible to permanent coverage, others are not. Even if coverage is convertible, there are time limits for the conversion. If the term policy expires, you may be required to reapply. If you are uninsurable at that time, you could be left with no coverage at a critical time in your life.

---

### Buy Term and Invest the Difference?

It's been debated for generations. Term insurance versus permanent insurance—which one is better? Many argue that rather than buy permanent life insurance you should purchase a lower-cost term insurance policy and invest the difference, usually in mutual funds.

Before one can answer this question, several questions need to be considered. How long do you need life insurance coverage? Which type of coverage can provide financial security for an entire lifetime? Do you prefer renting or owning? Where should you invest the difference? What investment and other risk exposures will the strategy present? What interest assumptions are required? What are the differences in taxes under each approach? Will you be able to invest regularly? Pay yourself first is a great strategy, but do you have the discipline to carry this out? How have you done so far?

---

## Interest-Sensitive Life Insurance Products

**interest-sensitive life insurance**

High inflation in the 1970's influenced consumers to demand insurance products that could provide higher returns to outpace inflation. To stay competitive, life insurance companies developed *interest-sensitive life insurance* products that used current assumptions, rather than long-term assumptions, for mortality, interest, and expenses, which are the foundation of traditional whole life products.

By current assumptions, we mean using current, or recent actual company experience, mortality, expenses, and interest rates to price policy values. This creates a policy that is more flexible and can adjust to changing conditions. If mortality improves, companies can expect to pay fewer claims in the earlier years of a group of policies, resulting in the ability to lower the mortality costs. Likewise, as companies develop more cost-efficient means of doing business, the expenses estimated on newer policies are much less than those written years ago. The newer policies can adjust to changes in the company's investment experience so that permanent life insurance can reflect periods of sustained investment growth.

### Universal Life

universal life (UL)

*Universal Life (UL)* brought many innovations to the life insurance marketplace. Along with providing interest rates that reflect current market conditions, the universal life policy also features flexibility. It allows policyowners to adjust coverage amounts and premiums (within limits) as their needs change or as inflation creates a need for more protection.

unbundling

***Unbundled.*** One aspect of universal life that boosted its popularity is that the component parts of earnings, mortality costs, and expenses are separately identified to the policyowner. This is referred to as *unbundling* the insurance components.

Universal life combines the features of renewable term insurance with a tax deferred cash value account that earns competitive market interest. Policyowners may pay premiums on a flexible, nonscheduled basis. The policyowner can increase or decrease the amount of death benefit protection of the policy at any time within company and IRS (IRC Section 7702) rules for life insurance.

Universal life policies have either front-end or back-end loading (expense charges). With a front-end load, the company's expenses are deducted before the premiums are added to the cash value account. With back-end loading, expenses are recovered from surrender charges, which reduce the account value at policy surrender. Surrender charges typically apply for a limited number of years, usually between 10 or 25, grading down to zero over the period. UL policies normally assess a premium expense charge, which is an administrative expense for each premium paid.

***Flexible Premiums.*** The policyowner selects an initial amount of life insurance protection, the face amount, and must pay a premium that is at least a minimum contractual amount. The premium, reduced by premium expense charges, is put into the cash value account. Each month the cost of term insurance and monthly administrative charges are deducted. Current interest is then credited to the remaining cash account. Current interest consists of a minimum interest rate (for example, 3 or 4 percent) plus an excess interest rate declared annually by the insurer that reflects the insurer's experience, or profitability.

After the initial contract year, policyowners can determine when to make premium payments and how much to pay within preset guidelines. The policy cash value depends on the amount and frequency of the premiums paid, interest earned, and which death benefit option is chosen. The one constraint regarding premium payments is that the aggregate premiums paid, regardless of their timing, must be adequate to cover the costs of maintaining the policy. Consider the analogy of an auto's gas tank, where premium payments are like filling the tank. Premium payments (tank refills) can be made frequently to keep the tank nearly full at all times. With that approach, the auto is likely never to run out of gas. The same auto, however, can operate on a just-in-time philosophy, where additional fuel (premium payments) of minimal amounts are made only as frequently as necessary to keep the car (the policy) from running out of gas.

Under a universal life insurance policy, if the policy's cash value is inadequate to cover the next 60 days of expense and mortality charges and any surrender charge, the policy will lapse. If an additional premium payment is made soon enough, the policy may be restarted without a formal reinstatement process. However, if the additional premium comes after the end of the grace period, the insurance company may require the policyowner to apply for reinstatement of the policy. The reinstatement may require proof of insurability by the insured.

***Flexible Death Benefit Amount.*** Subject to meeting underwriting requirements, company limits, and possible IRS limits, the policyowner may increase or decrease the death benefit amount. For example, if a policyowner has a $100,000 universal life policy and needs an additional $50,000 in life insurance, he can request a face amount increase, subject to underwriting approval. The advantage of this is that a policyowner can have one policy for life and pay only one policy fee.

**death benefit options**   ***Flexible Death Benefit Option.*** Two *death benefit options* are available with universal life: a level death benefit and an increasing death benefit. Diagrams of each are presented below.

*Level Death Benefit Option (Option 1).* The Level Death Benefit Option emphasizes cash accumulation and is much like the traditional whole life design. The amount of the term protection, or net amount at risk, decreases as the cash value account increases. To comply with the definition of life insurance stipulated in the Tax Equity and Fiscal Responsibility Act of 1982 (TEFRA), the ratio between the net amount at risk and the cash value cannot exceed IRS Guidelines (IRC Section 7702). Stated another way, the IRS requires the insurer to carry a certain level of net risk in the policy, at least until the insured's age 95.

When the cash value approaches the minimum face amount, an additional amount of insurance, called a corridor, is automatically added and maintained. This may happen in the later years of the policy. The corridor keeps the policy from endowing and retains the associated tax benefits of its status as a life insurance contract. (See Figure 4-1.)

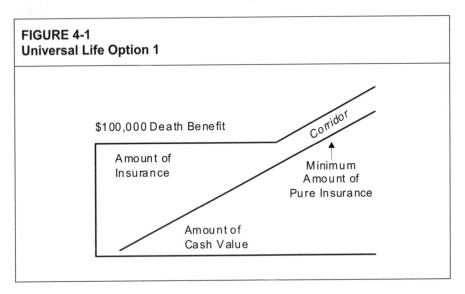

**FIGURE 4-1**
**Universal Life Option 1**

*Increasing Death Benefit (Option 2).* The Increasing Death Benefit Option emphasizes insurance protection. The amount of term insurance protection, or net amount at risk, remains level with the increasing cash value account used to increase the death benefit. This design pays the policy's stated face amount plus its cash value at the insured's death. Universal life policies with Option 2 overcome the criticism of whole life policies where the death benefit consists partly of the whole life contract's cash value. Option 2 is diagrammed in Figure 4-2.

How does the policyowner choose? The choice of death benefit depends on the policyowner's situation and objectives, and can be changed at least once per policy year. Changing from the level death benefit option to the increasing option may require underwriting.

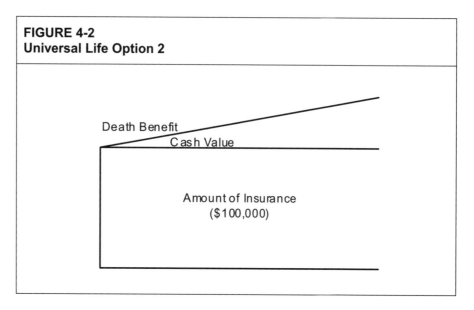

**FIGURE 4-2**
**Universal Life Option 2**

***Withdrawals and Surrenders.*** Universal life cash or account values can often be partially surrendered (also known as a withdrawal) for part of the total cash value. The only limitation is that the amount left in the account must be enough to keep the policy in force.

Total surrender of a contract for cash can occur at any time as with other forms of permanent life insurance. A surrender charge may be imposed if the contract is within the surrender period. Any policy gain resulting from the surrender may be subject to income taxation.

***Benefits and Riders.*** Most universal life policies offer the full range of additional benefit riders available with other personal permanent policies. A monthly deduction from the cash value is made to pay for this additional protection.

***Suitability.*** Universal life is a flexible policy that will meet the needs of many of your prospects. The reasons given above contribute to its popularity, but UL is not for everyone. The term insurance costs within the policy increase with age. This increases the policy's monthly deductions for the cost of insurance each year, making it more expensive as the insured grows older.

It requires self-discipline to make sufficient payments to a universal life contract to keep the policy in force. It should be overfunded; the policyowner must avoid the temptation to minimally fund the policy because he or she could lose the insurance protection.

UL shifts investment and insurance risks from the insurer to the policyowner, although newer secondary guarantees overcome the problem of the policy lapsing as the insured gets older. Not everyone is comfortable with fewer guarantees. The risk tolerance of some prospects, especially in light of recent economic and stock market turmoil, may call for more conservative products that offer more guarantees.

*Market Applications.* Universal life's flexibility can be shown in a typical family situation with children. Changed to Option Two, the policy can provide the extra income protection families with children must have. When riders are added, these policies can include term coverage for family members. When family needs require it, UL premiums can decrease or even stop for a period. This is possible as long as the account values are adequate to carry the policy. When the family needs change again, premiums can be increased or reestablished.

As the insured's income grows, the life insurance protection and cash accumulation in the policy can track with career success. When the children are ready for college, premiums may be temporarily discontinued and funds can be withdrawn or borrowed from the cash value account to pay college costs.

After graduation, the premium payments may be resumed as the parents begin preparing for retirement. Premium payments may be increased to make the most of the tax-deferred cash buildup in the policy, within policy limitations.

In the mortgage market, universal life has proven to be a particularly versatile policy. A policyowner could increase the face value of an in-force policy to meet an additional need for mortgage insurance. Cash accumulations may help pay off the mortgage at an early date.

### Other Non-Variable, Interest-Sensitive Products

Two other non-variable, interest-sensitive products include current assumption whole life and interest sensitive whole life.

**current assumption whole life**

***Current Assumption Whole Life.*** *Current assumption whole life* (CAWL) is a variation of whole life that uses current mortality charges and interest earnings that are based on current yields rather than overall general account yields. It does not offer the premium flexibility of universal life.

Sometimes it is described as universal life with fixed premiums. Despite this oversimplification, as the premiums may be restructured at specified anniversary years, it describes how CAWL differs from a traditional policy. If premiums are paid on schedule, CAWL guarantees a death benefit and a minimum guaranteed interest rate to be credited on cash values.

**interest-sensitive
whole life**

***Interest-Sensitive Whole Life.*** Some companies guarantee the mortality charge and the expense charges in current assumption plans. When the mortality and expense charges are guaranteed, the policy is often referred to as an *interest-sensitive whole life* policy because interest credited to the cash value becomes the only element not guaranteed in the contract.

### Variable Life Insurance (VLI)

**variable life
insurance (VLI)**

*Variable life insurance* was the first life insurance policy designed to shift the entire investment risk to policyowners. It is an interest-sensitive or interest-credited product offering a combination of permanent life insurance protection and the growth potential of variable fund investments.

***Unique Feature.*** Its unique feature is that the policy's cash value is invested in an account made up of one or more funds of equities, money market accounts, or bonds. The policyowner decides where to invest the money and, periodically and within contract limits, may transfer funds from one fund account to another.

If the designated premiums are paid on time, the policy guarantees a minimum death benefit, but the actual death benefit will vary according to investment performance. The cash value also varies with investment performance.

There is more risk associated with VLI because the cash values are not guaranteed, and investment risk is transferred to the policyowner. If the investments to which the cash values are allocated perform poorly, the variable life cash values may grow at a lower rate than in traditional products. Of course, there is a potential for the investments to grow at significantly higher rates than traditional fixed-interest products.

***Policy Features.*** The premium is level for the duration of the policy. There are no flexible premium payments with this product as there are with universal life. The fixed guaranteed premium must be paid as scheduled. This policy guarantees a minimum death benefit regardless of investment performance. If all of the required premiums are paid, the insurance company guarantees that the death benefit will be paid even if the investment funds are otherwise inadequate to support the policy.

Variable life is classified as both a life insurance and an equity product. Life insurance advisors who sell variable products must be life licensed and registered with the Financial Industry Regulatory Authority (FINRA) and state securities regulators. Variable life is regulated by both state law, where applicable, and by the federal Securities and Exchange Commission (SEC). Companies that sell variable life must provide a prospectus to prospects prior to or during the sales interview.

***Market Applications.*** The market for variable life is with mid- to upper-income prospects who need permanent life insurance protection, have a basic understanding of investments, and believe they can make good investment decisions. They must have a relatively high-risk tolerance. If the sometimes uncertain, non-guaranteed nature of VLI makes an individual uncomfortable, this is not the product to buy. It can be an attractive product for almost any age group, but advisors must determine the prospect's risk tolerance and suitability before recommending VLI.

### Variable Universal Life

**variable universal life (VUL)**

*Variable Universal Life (VUL)* combines features of variable and universal life insurance. It offers policyowners the flexibility of universal life with the investment growth of variable, without the fixed premium aspects of variable life.

***Comparison with Variable Life.*** With VUL, the policyowner selects an initial insurance amount and premium level. Premium dollars can be directed to one or more investment funds and switched from one fund to another, as with variable life.

VUL policies offer the policyowner choices among several separate investments accounts, known as subaccounts. VUL is classified as a security, and the same registration with FINRA and licensing are required to sell it. Because VUL is a registered product, it also requires delivery of a prospectus to the prospect.

***Comparison with Universal Life.*** Policyowners can decide how much premium to pay into the policy and when to pay it, just like UL. As with UL, the VUL cash account must always be large enough to pay the monthly cost of the term insurance element and administrative expenses. Within certain limits, policyowners can make larger or smaller premium payments. VUL shares the flexibility of UL; it offers the same death benefit options, the ability to change options, and other features discussed with the UL product.

VUL is attractive to some buyers because it offers greater investment potential and tax deferred cash accumulation. This is more control for the policyowner than that offered by a UL policy because the policyowner can select and change separate account investments within the policy. VUL should always be sold as life insurance first based on the need for coverage and second as an investment opportunity.

***Market Applications.*** This product can be very useful in personal and business insurance situations as described earlier, but the buyer must first understand and accept the risks of owning VUL. The speculative nature of the investment accounts should be stressed. If they perform poorly, the policy performs poorly. Buyers must understand that these contracts may present future risk to their coverage or changes in their non-guaranteed elements such as premium charges.

## Income Taxation of Life Insurance

Life insurance is beneficial to the public because of its contribution to the financial preservation of families and decreased pressure on the nation's social programs. Because of this, both the federal and state governments provide favorable tax benefits for life insurance products to encourage their use. In most cases, clients should not purchase life insurance contracts only because of the tax advantages. Nevertheless, the tax benefits combined with its other advantages make the life policy worth considering for many people.

Some prospects will have questions about the taxation of personal life insurance policies, such as the tax treatment of premiums, death benefits, dividends, and cash surrenders. To help answer these questions, this discussion summarizes the main points of taxation of premiums, death proceeds, and the living benefits of a life insurance contract.

### *Income Taxation of Life Insurance Premiums*

Premiums paid for individual life insurance policies are considered a personal expense and are not deductible for income tax purposes. In the few exceptions to this general rule, life insurance premiums are deductible because they also qualify as some other type of deductible expense, not because they are life insurance premiums. For example, premiums paid for life insurance in an alimony agreement may be deductible as alimony payments. Premiums paid for life insurance owned by and paid to a charity as beneficiary may be deductible as a charitable contribution. The premium is deductible because it is treated as a charitable contribution, not because it is a life insurance premium. Similarly, in business situations, employers can deduct premiums for life insurance as a business expense if they are paid as a bonus (compensation) to the employee. If life insurance is part of a pension plan, the premiums are deductible as an employer contribution to a tax-qualified plan. The deduction for premiums is because the IRS treats them as contributions to a tax-qualified retirement plan, rather than life insurance premiums.

### *Income Taxation of Death Benefits*

The tax-free death benefit is one of the most outstanding advantages of life insurance. However, there are a few situations, discussed below, where income taxes are a consideration.

---

| **Taxation of Death Benefits** |
| :--- |
| **Federal Estate Tax**—There are possible federal estate taxes if the deceased had incidents of ownership. |
| **Income Tax**—The amount of death benefit is not generally taxable, but any interest earned on it is taxable. |
| **State Death and Inheritance Taxes**—There are possible state death or inheritance taxes depending on your state. |

*Lump Sum Payment.* Generally death proceeds from a life insurance policy are exempt from income taxation when paid in a lump sum. Congress recognizes that life insurance ownership provides a significant social benefit, and should be encouraged.

*Accelerated Death Benefits.* These are amounts received under a life insurance contract covering the life of an insured who is terminally or chronically ill. The payments are excludible from income as a portion of the death benefit if certain conditions are met. A physician must certify the insured's terminal illness, and the condition must typically be expected to result in death within 24 months of the certification.

*Settlement Options.* Death proceeds distributed as a series of payments under a life insurance settlement option generally include earned interest, which is taxable. However, the portion of a settlement option payment that represents principal (the policy's face amount) is non-taxable.

*Interest Option.* When life insurance proceeds are placed under the interest option, all interest paid or accrued is fully taxable. When the principal (face amount) is paid later, it will be non-taxable.

*Fixed Options.* When life insurance proceeds are placed under the fixed-period or fixed-amount option, the monthly installments are taxed under a special rule. First, the total amount of guaranteed payments is computed. From this figure, the amount of insurance proceeds is deducted. The difference is divided by the number of years for which benefits are guaranteed. The resulting amount is reported by the insurer as taxable income each year.

*Life Income No Refund.* If a beneficiary selects the life income no refund option, the proceeds are taxed in a manner similar to that used for the fixed-period option. However, because we do not know how long the beneficiary will live, we do not know how long the guaranteed payments will continue. Thus the Internal Revenue Service provides a life expectancy table that serves as the basis for computing the tax. The IRS life expectancy of the beneficiary is assumed to be the period for which payments are paid.

To determine the annual taxable portion of the income, first multiply the monthly income times 12, and then multiply by the beneficiary's life expectancy (in years) at the time the option is selected. This is the total expected return. From this figure, subtract the amount of proceeds from the life insurance that is placed under the option. The difference is then divided by the beneficiary's life expectancy when the option is selected.

***Life Income Period Certain.*** Under this option, proceeds of the policy will be paid out (or refunded) over a specified (certain) period, even if the initial beneficiary dies before the end of that period. The life income period certain option requires an additional calculation to determine the taxable portion of each payment. The present value of the refund feature must be calculated using IRS tables and is subtracted from the excludible amount to be prorated. The insurer is responsible for making all the annuity calculations and issuing Forms 1099 to the beneficiary for tax purposes.

### Income Taxation of Living Benefits

living benefits    The term *living benefits* describes the use of cash values and dividends of a permanent life insurance policy while the insured is alive. As you know, the cash value of life insurance currently receives favorable tax treatment and grows tax deferred. If a policy earns dividends, the dividends may or may not receive favorable tax treatment. There are several ways to tap into these living benefits including the following:

- loan
- partial surrender or withdrawal (for universal life policies)
- dividend withdrawal (for participating policies)
- cash surrender

Depending on the situation, there may be taxable consequences. Any taxable proceeds are taxed as ordinary income and not capital gains. In this way, life insurance is treated differently from an investment such as stocks or real estate that are taxed as capital gains (or losses).

The income tax effect of these transactions depends on the policyowner's tax basis in the policy. The tax basis is initially calculated by adding the total premiums paid into the policy and subtracting any dividends paid by the insurer. If nontaxable withdrawals have previously been made from the policy, those amounts reduce the policyowner's basis.

***Loans.*** One living benefit offered in most permanent policies is the loan provision. This gives the policyowner a right to borrow a percentage of the cash value in the policy. The policyowner is charged interest on the borrowed amount, and the interest is not tax deductible. If the policyowner does not pay the loan interest, it is added to the loaned amount. Unless a policy is a modified endowment contract (MEC), policy loans are non-taxable providing the policy remains in force. We will talk about MECs shortly.

If a policy is surrendered with a loan outstanding, the loan amount is added to the cash surrender value. If that amount exceeds the cost basis, as discussed above, there will be a taxable gain. If there is no loan outstanding and the surrender value exceeds the cost basis, then the difference represents gain and is taxable.

***UL and VUL Partial Surrenders (Withdrawals).*** UL and VUL policies offer the ability to withdraw cash value from the policy, known as a withdrawal, a partial withdrawal, or a partial surrender. The death benefit and cash value are reduced dollar for dollar by the amount of the partial surrender.

Partial surrenders are taxable when the total amount of all withdrawals exceeds the cost basis of the policy. The exception is when the policy is a MEC; in that situation, harsher tax rules apply. In some cases, surrender charges may apply as well.

**dividends**

**participating policies**

***Dividends.*** Mutual insurance companies pass along favorable experience in mortality, interest, and expenses through a return of premium called *dividends*. Policies eligible for dividends are called *participating policies*. In most cases, mutual insurance companies that provide participating insurance plans build a margin into their premium for contingencies. Dividends are not taxable unless the total amount of all dividends paid exceeds the total premium paid. Because policy dividends are a nontaxable return of premium, they reduce the policyowner's basis. If total dividends paid exceed total premiums, additional dividends are taxable.

Dividends are paid annually and can be paid in five ways:

(1) *Cash.* A check is sent to the policyowner.
(2) *Reduced premium.* The dividend is applied to the next premium due and a bill is sent for any balance.
(3) *Accumulation at interest.* Dividends are left with the company in the equivalent of a savings account and earn a variable interest rate. The interest earned is taxable and reported on a Form 1099-R. They can be withdrawn later or used in other dividend options.
(4) *Paid-up additions.* Dividends purchase paid-up insurance based on specific rates for the insured's gender and attained age. The dividends serve as a single-premium to purchase small amounts of

additional whole life insurance, requiring no future premiums. These paid-up additions generate their own cash value, are eligible for dividends, and grow tax-deferred.

(5) *One-year term insurance.* Some insurers allow dividends to purchase an amount of one-year term insurance equal to the current cash value. Any leftover dividends accumulate at interest or purchase paid-up additions. For some insurers, the entire dividend is used to buy one-year term insurance. In either case, the cost of the insurance depends on the insured's gender and attained age, and underwriting may be required for this option.

***Cash Surrenders.*** Income tax is payable on the surrender of a non-MEC policy for cash (or the maturity of an endowment) if the amount received over the life of the contract exceeds the net premiums paid. Net premiums paid determine the cost basis and equals the gross premium less any dividends received. If the amount the policyowner receives upon surrender exceeds the net premiums paid (cost basis), then the excess is fully reportable as a taxable gain in the year received. An exception to this rule would be for certain government policies or GI insurance. Any gains realized with these types of policies are tax exempt.

Premiums paid for supplementary benefits such as waiver of premium or accidental death riders are not included in the cost basis. Policy loans and cash value withdrawals, prior to full surrender, reduce the cost basis.

**Section 1035 policy exchange**

***Section 1035 Policy Exchanges.*** A special situation arises when a policyowner exchanges an existing policy for a new one in accordance with the Internal Revenue Code Section 1035. In a properly executed *Section 1035 policy exchange*, no taxable gain is realized on the exchange. The adjusted cost basis of the old policy is carried over to the new one.

The purpose of Section 1035 is to allow taxpayers to exchange a life insurance (or annuity) contract that no longer serves the taxpayer's best interest with a contract better suited to his or her needs. This may occur, for example, when the investment risks of an old policy no longer suit the policyowner's preferences, or where a more modern, less expensive, or more flexible policy is available.

To qualify for a Section 1035 exchange of life insurance, the insured (or annuitant on annuities) must be the same on both the old and new contracts. Section 1035 allows tax-free exchanges on exchanges between two life insurance policies, life insurance to annuity exchanges, and exchanges of annuities. Section 1035 does not allow tax-free exchanges from an annuity to a life insurance contract.

**Modified Endowment Contract (MEC)**

***Modified Endowment Contract.*** The *modified endowment contract (MEC)*, was created by the 1988 amendment to the tax code (Technical and Miscellaneous Revenue Act, or TAMRA, IRC Section 72 and the added Section 7702A). Prior to this time, some people used life insurance as a tax-deferred investment vehicle and put large amounts of money into life insurance to accumulate the money on a tax-deferred basis. While it was legal, this went against the basis premise of income tax law that life insurance was given tax benefits to provide a death benefit.

TAMRA applied a 7-pay test to determine if a policy is classified as a MEC. The 7-pay test imposes MEC status on policies that take in too much premium during the first seven policy years, or in the seven years after a material policy change. If the policy is overfunded, it becomes a MEC and distributions (loans or withdrawals) from the policy are subject to different taxation rules than non-MEC policies.

If a material change occurs to a policy once it is in force, the 7-pay test period is reset. Examples of material changes include an increase or decrease in coverage, or an added rider or benefit. Your home office will specify whether a policy would be classified as a MEC.

If a policy becomes a MEC, it is treated the same as any other life insurance policy with one exception—some distributions from a MEC are taxed on a LIFO (last-in-first-out) basis on any gains in the policy. Distributions from a MEC include policy loans (including automatic premium loans), cash surrenders, cash dividends, partial surrenders or withdrawals, and policy lapse. Therefore the first cash withdrawals or a loan will be taxable if the cash values exceed the cost basis of the policy. In addition, the taxable gain is subject to a 10 percent penalty tax unless the distribution occurs after the policyowner is aged 59½, or if death, disability, or annuitization occurs.

Once a policy is classified as a MEC, it always remains a MEC. This classification carries over to any policy that is issued in exchange for a MEC even if the new contract normally would not be classified as a MEC. This means that care must be taken with making a Section 1035 exchange.

A Section 1035 exchange is a material change for purposes of the MEC rules. According to IRS rulings, the policy received in exchange is treated as a newly issued policy with a new seven-year period beginning on the date of exchange and must be tested under the special 7-pay test. If the policy fails the test, it is classified as a MEC. Once again, your home office will provide guidance on these situations.

If a policy is a MEC, it is treated the same as any other life insurance policy for tax purposes unless certain distributions are made from it. These distributions include dividends received as cash or paid-up additions surrendered for cash. When dividends or excess interest are used to pay premiums internally, to buy paid-up additions, or to buy one-year term insurance they are not considered a MEC distribution.

# SPECIAL MARKETS

The only constant is change, but change paralyzes some people. For an entrepreneur, it should represent opportunity. In this section, we will discuss the role change plays in special markets, or markets that are discovered or created by change. We will cover three different types of changes that affect the insurance and financial services arena and a marketing strategy to take advantage of special markets.

## Types of Change

Change comes in many different ways. In this section are examples of how these changes create marketing opportunities. Listing all of the types of change would be impossible, but here are a few examples.

### *Legislative*

Tax laws change frequently and some will hinder the way we do business. For example, the Technical and Miscellaneous Revenue Act (TAMRA) effectively reduced the tax deferral privileges of overfunded life insurance products like the single premium life. Others, like the creation of the Roth IRA under the Taxpayer Relief Act of 1997 (TRA97) and the increase in contribution limits for retirement plans, provided new marketing opportunities for those who sell mutual funds and variable annuities.

Another example of the impact legislation has on the insurance and financial services industry is the Economic Growth and Tax Relief and Reconciliation Act (EGTRRA) of 2001. This law made many changes including increasing IRA contribution limits, increasing the applicable credit amount for federal estate tax purposes, and increasing contribution limits to the Coverdell Education Savings Account (formerly the Education IRA).

### *Socio-Economic*

The financial services industry must constantly adapt to changes in societal values and conditions. The family unit continues to change in its definition and composition. Divorce rates are still high, and women exert increasing influence in the marketplace. For example, not only are women a major force in the small business market, they make up over 50 percent of current college undergraduates.

Nontraditional, same-sex marriages, and life partnerships between same-sex couples have raised many questions related to group employer-sponsored benefits, beneficiary arrangements, and the benefits and rights that were traditionally restricted to heterosexual marriages. Advisors will need to stay current on new regulations in this area and on how new rules differ from state to state.

---

### Implications of Alternative Living Arrangements

A major social change in the last few decades is the increasing number of alternative living arrangements, in which two unrelated adults live together but are not married. These situations present some unique planning implications.

In most states, a surviving spouse automatically inherits all or a portion of the estate. Cohabitants typically do not have this protection. All individually titled property, such as real estate, furniture, and autos, is transferred to those named in a will or the next of kin (if there is no will).

Disability is complicated because of uncertainty regarding assets and personal responsibilities for household debts or other obligations.

You can assist clients in these alternative living arrangements by

- encouraging them to create a will or trust to handle the transfer of property at death
- helping them understand the impact of a disability on the use of their collective assets
- discussing their financial goals and helping them make decisions about the insurance needed to protect them
- referring them to a few attorneys who can help them understand the legal ramifications of their situation

---

### *Demographic*

Demographics, such as age or ethnic background, can have a huge impact on your marketing opportunities. We are seeing significant demographic changes with increases in minority populations and the growth in the number of people over 50. We will explore some marketing opportunities created by the growth of minority populations.

## The Impact of Socio-Economic Change

We live in a time full of change. Experts who study social and organizational structures know that when pressure produces societal change, the smallest social units, the individual and the family, are the first to respond.

The growth of two-income families shows how the family unit reacted to the need for more income in times of high inflation. Inflation also put competitive pressures on the life insurance industry as well, and it responded with new products to address needs in a new economy. This demonstrates how societal change affected the family, and the positive way the insurance industry responded to the new opportunities created by economic change.

To capitalize on sales opportunities created by change requires the advisor to recognize when change is taking place, understand how it affects financial needs, and know how available products and services meet the new needs. Because there is a universal need for life insurance, and you can offer a variety of insurance and financial products, you can adapt to almost any kind of change. To illustrate, we will consider some situations that have involved significant social or economic change. Note the marketing implications they offer in prospecting and working with client needs. The list includes the following:

- the increasing economic force of women in society
- the trend toward fewer traditional families
- the trend toward marriages later in life
- growing numbers of divorced couples
- growing numbers of single heads of households
- the impact of dual income families
- new types of home buying patterns
- the increase in the number of small business start-ups
- the aging of the population
- consumer awareness of the need for financial planning

## The Economic Force of Women

Why do women represent an important market segment? First, consider that women control many of the financial decisions in the household. Although women have traditionally been less active than males in the financial services arena, they now have much more economic clout and are more interested in insurance and financial products. As you will see, buying behaviors of today's women indicate that in general they will be the kind of clients you will want in your business.

### *Common Characteristics*

Women now represent over 50 percent of all college undergraduates. This translates into a well-educated and well-informed market segment. More women are waiting longer to marry in order to focus on their careers. Both of these trends mean women will have more assets, and they will have more insurance and financial needs.

One significant mark women are making on the business world results from the increasing number of women who start new businesses. Current estimates say women already make up almost 40 percent of all business owners, and this percentage will probably increase. The greatest motivation for this trend is that women want more flexibility. They are still the primary caregivers for their children, grandchildren, and elderly relatives, and they are squeezed by multiple responsibilities. If a career cannot offer the flexibility they need, many women will start their own business.

### Common Buying Behaviors

Studies show that women, on average, have a longer buying cycle than males. They do more research before making a purchase and seek more advice. Women typically focus on security and on making good decisions. The reality of the careful female value shopper has replaced the stereotypical female bargain shopper. Today's women want the best value their money can buy. They understand the benefits of long-term relationships, appreciate competent advice, and want a collaborative selling process. When they are satisfied with their advisor, women are loyal clients and readily give referrals.

### Common Needs

The increased earning power of women has resulted in more disposable income for dual-income families. These families have a greater need for financial products and can better afford them. Generally you will find the following common needs:

- With families so dependent on two incomes, the loss of either spouse could mean economic hardship. Interestingly, LIMRA studies show that working wives often have no individual life insurance to protect their incomes. If wives do have coverage, they tend to be underinsured. Generally males are insured more frequently and for larger amounts than females, although these gaps are decreasing (Individual Life Buyers in the United States, 2007, LIMRA International Inc.).

- Because of the family's dependence on dual incomes, it is advisable to insure both incomes against disability as well.

- Women outlive men on average, and therefore have a greater need for supplemental retirement income. This makes women good candidates for retirement plans (for example, IRAs or Roth IRAs). It also means they are good candidates for non-tax qualified products such as annuities or mutual funds. Women business owners will often want a SIMPLE plan or SEP/IRA for themselves or employees.

- Women are more likely than men to require long-term care and, on average, require the care for longer periods than men. This makes long-term care insurance a more acute need for women in general.

- Women, more often than men, are the primary caregivers for elderly relatives, especially their own parents and their spouse's parents. Many women will want long-term care insurance protection for those who may depend on them.

### Communication System

Women network more than men. They generally are more open to sharing their experiences (good or bad) with other women. They are more likely to refer you to others in their circle of friends and family members.

### Marketing Strategy

The keys to any marketing strategy are listening and being a learner. Ask questions and find out both what to do to appeal to a market and why. Here are some things you can do to access the women's market.

*Target Market.* The women's segment is too large and diverse for you to efficiently market. Identify a smaller more homogeneous segment within the women's market such as women business owners in your area. In many metropolitan locations a Women's Business Association can provide a ready-made communication system.

*Access.* Your initial goal should be to gain access. For example, if you decide to target women small business owners, get a list of them from your chamber of commerce. Learn which groups dedicated to women business owners meet in your area, and contact them for information. Many such groups will welcome you as a speaker at their regular meetings. If you decide to market to working mothers, visit daycare facilities in your area to discover marketing opportunities. If gaining access is too difficult, the market segment may not be a good match for you. If you decide to target a market segment, try to find centers of influence in that segment.

*Market Research.* Talk to women in your target market to identify their needs and what they want in a financial advisor. Find out whom these women seek for financial advice. Conduct your own market research as discussed earlier in this textbook.

*Preapproach.* Find out the best point of entry and access. For example, a local daycare center may hold special seminars for parents on timely topics, such as parenting skills. The daycare center may allow you to give a seminar on a topic such as budgeting or education planning. Remember, women want to develop long-term relationships and want education to make informed decisions. Your preapproach strategies should incorporate these common characteristics.

## Planning for Nontraditional Couples and Families

Today, the traditional nuclear family of husband, wife, and children is a minority living arrangement. Only about 24 percent of all U.S. households consist of married couples with children. That figure includes households with remarried parents and blended children, so the percentage of single-marriage traditional households is even smaller. The modern American families reflect a wide variety of households: divorced parents raising children alone, stepparents sharing blended families, singles, widows and widowers, adoptive parents, same-sex partners with or without children, grandparents caring for grandchildren, and adult children caring for aging parents. As nontraditional living arrangements are becoming more common, it is important to review the unique financial aspects of these relationships.

### *Laws Favor Traditional Families*

Many aspects of financial planning are affected by laws largely created with the traditional nuclear family in mind. Today more than ever, planning methods and software programs modeled on a traditional household do not apply. There are nearly 1,400 rights and benefits of marriage at the federal and state levels, many affecting financial matters, which do not help individuals in nontraditional families. Federal benefits related to income tax, gifting, estate taxes, Social Security benefits, IRAs, and retirement plans governed by ERISA are still out of reach, because under the Federal Defense of Marriage Act (1996) non-married persons often have the legal status of strangers.

### *Unmarried Couples*

Unmarried couples face many legal difficulties, starting with the home in which they live. For example, if one partner owns the home and wants to share ownership with his or her partner, the donor may be subject to gift taxes. If the house was worth $200,000 and the unmarried partner was named a joint owner on the title, there would be a gift tax imposed on $100,000 minus the amount of the annual gift tax exclusion ($13,000 in 2009, indexed annually). Married couples, on the other hand, have an unlimited right to transfer property from one spouse to the other with no gift taxes.

Estate tax laws also favor married couples. First, there is the unlimited marital deduction, which allows unlimited gifts between spouses, thereby negating estate as well as gift taxes at the death of a spouse. There may also be state inheritance taxes imposed on money passed from one unmarried partner to the other. Advisors should stay current on state laws and encourage clients to obtain the proper legal instruments; otherwise, under most state intestacy laws, the unmarried partner receives nothing. In most states, if there is no legal spouse or heirs of a deceased person who dies intestate, or with no valid will, the state will distribute the assets to the closest relatives. The unmarried partner receives nothing unless a will specifies the distribution of assets to that person. Additionally, unmarried partners should have a durable power of attorney and advanced health care directives. Life insurance needs will be similar and just as important as for traditional relationships.

Retirement planning should normally be done separately for unmarried partners. Remember that ERISA rules protecting spousal rights to many retirement plans currently do not apply to unmarried partners. Thus if the relationship ends, an ex-partner may have to go to court to lay claim to retirement benefits of his or her former partner. Nontraditional couples also cannot draw Social Security benefits based on an unmarried partner's work history and usually will not benefit from a partner's pension.

### *Psychological Factors*

There are important psychological factors affecting nontraditional relationships to which the advisor should be sensitive. For example, other family members may be unhappy with the nontraditional relationship, and that may affect gifting or estate issues. Single or widowed persons may feel isolated, vulnerable, and fearful of becoming dependent on children or other family members as they get older. Divorced persons may have conflicts and other negative emotions in dealing with a former spouse, especially when children are involved. Unmarried partners may struggle with their individual financial commitments to the relationship. Some may pool their money in a joint bank account to cover household expenses, while others choose to maintain completely separate assets. As nontraditional family arrangements proliferate, and state and federal laws regarding them change, advisors must be aware of the issues that affect these relationships.

## Ethnically and Culturally Diverse Markets

The face of America continues to change with dramatic ethnic population shifts in many states and large cities across the nation. By 2050, Hispanics are projected to make up 24 percent of the U.S. population, and all minorities together will compose 47 percent of Americans. The rapid growth of ethnic and cultural groups is creating tremendous marketing advantages for insurance and financial advisors.

In this section, we will first discuss some opportunities found in the ethnic market. We will then identify some common characteristics and strategies in the Hispanic and Asian markets. We will profile these markets because they are the two fastest growing minorities in the United States. By 2050, both Asian and Hispanic populations are projected to double their current percentages. As you read these profiles, you will understand what makes them great target markets. However, you must decide if it makes business sense for you to approach these markets. Investigate thoroughly before you make a decision.

### Why Consider These Markets?

*Demographics*. Ethnic minorities are the fastest-growing segment of the population due to several factors. First, immigration from Latin America (Mexico and Central America) and Asia (Philippines, South Korea, and Southeast Asia) has increased since U.S. immigration laws were liberalized in 1965. Second, birthrates among ethnic minorities are higher than within the white majority. If current trends continue, minorities will make up almost 50 percent of the U.S. population by 2050. In some cities and states, these demographics are even more pronounced. For example, the states showing the greatest Hispanic population growth are California, Florida, Texas, New Jersey, and New York. In California, Hispanics already comprise over 30 percent of the population.

*First to Market Strategy.* In evaluating any market, you should project how your services and products will benefit those in that market and how receptive the market will be. One opportunity with emerging markets is the first-to-market strategy in which you approach a market in which a particular product or service has little or no exposure. The goal is to make inroads, create loyalty, and grow with the market. Loyalty is high in these situations and that is the key to the success of this strategy.

A good non-insurance example of this strategy is the success that former basketball star Magic Johnson had with inner city businesses in the early 2000's. Johnson developed movie theaters, gourmet burger restaurants, and upscale coffee shops in inner cities—products not normally associated with this market. When other businesses tried to penetrate the market, Johnson and his partners had the advantage of being there first. The advantage of being first helps to cement customer loyalty. That is the goal of the first-to-market strategy, and it can work in any emerging market.

*Excellent Target Market.* Ethnic and cultural groups create excellent target markets. Their members share many common characteristics in language, culture, and lifestyle. They have common needs because of their culture and because they are separated from their natural support system of relatives and friends. Most importantly from a target marketing perspective, they have a communication system that can create a perpetual flow of prospects.

Communication systems in ethnic markets are both formal and informal. Formal systems include newspapers in their language and various organizations. Informal systems are based on a natural tendency to gain information from people you know and trust. For example, many ethnic minorities congregate in a specific area of a city. This is especially true for those who speak their native language at home. The formal and informal networks within ethnic groups allow a more targeted presentation for the advisor's products and services.

*Misconceptions.* Two serious misconceptions are that an advisor must be of the same ethnicity or speak the same language to sell in these markets. Undoubtedly possessing one or both of these characteristics can help, but you can be very successful in ethnic markets without either characteristic. The key for success in marketing insurance and financial products is trust. Regardless of ethnicity or language barriers, people will buy from you if they trust you. In the strategies section, we will discuss ways to overcome barriers in the ethnic markets.

### Asian Market Profile

*Common Characteristics.* Most Asian Americans emphasize education and are three times more likely to get a college degree than the average American. Asian Americans have the highest median household income of all ethnic groups. According to the 2000 U.S. census, their median income is 32 percent above the median income of the general population. There are many entrepreneurs among Asia Americans, and many are self-employed or own a family business.

Asian Americans are a diverse group. Korean and Vietnamese languages are completely different. Korean Americans and Vietnamese Americans may have little in common other than having roots in the same continent.

While we must always be cautious about stereotyping any ethnic group, some generalizations are accurate, and an understanding of them will assist the advisor. For example, honor, or saving face, are extremely important values within Asian American communities. This sense of honor creates a strong feeling of obligation and responsibility to the family. Traditional Asian cultures promote ancestral worship, and that culture has fostered a high regard for one's parents and elders in general. This may affect an Asian American's views towards products such as long-term care insurance.

*Common Buying Behaviors.* Marketing research shows that cultural differences among Asian groups influence the products they buy. For example, both Chinese and Korean Americans place importance on protecting their families, education, saving, and investing. Many of them invest in small family-run businesses. Whole life insurance with its cash value buildup and guarantees is attractive to Chinese Americans. Korean Americans, on the other hand, tend to buy more universal life policies. They purchase life insurance more for its protection than for the cash values. Business insurance has appeal to both groups because one-fifth of all minority businesses are Asian.

***Common Needs.*** While many Asian Americans come from a background where insurance systems are not sound, most realize the importance of insurance in the United States. Traditionally, parents, children, and cousins— the entire extended family—helped one another in times of need. In the old country, the elderly relied on their children during retirement. The new immigrants can no longer depend as much on their extended family. In America, families are busy trying to establish their own businesses, earn good incomes, and educate their children. Today's Asian Americans will need most of the same products and services that other Americans require, including protection and investment products.

### Hispanic Market Profile

***Common Characteristics.*** In addition to its size, several other factors make the Hispanic market attractive to the financial industry. Market research shows that Hispanics tend to buy all their insurance products from one company. If you sell a Hispanic client one insurance product, making additional sales to that person is likely to be easier.

Hispanic Americans are generally very traditional and family-oriented. This can be an important piece of cultural information for the financial advisor working with Hispanics. For example, in first generation Hispanic families, it may be interpreted as disrespectful if you speak to the wife by herself, or direct your questions to her instead of the husband. While this may sound old-fashioned, remember it is a different culture than what you may have known. However, it may produce a desired situation for you, an interview with both spouses present.

Many Hispanic Americans prefer to deal face-to-face in business situations. For this reason, you may be more successful with door-to-door canvassing in the evenings than by making the initial approach by telephone. Do not to try to sell anything on the initial contact. Use the door-to-door strategy only as a means of approaching the prospect.

Speaking Spanish does not mean that all Hispanics are similar in other characteristics. It is important to know a prospect's country of origin and how long he or she has been in the United States. An early Cuban immigrant in Miami or a Mexican-American in San Antonio may prefer information in English more than a recent Hispanic immigrant might.

***Common Buying Behaviors.*** Although Hispanics, on average, do not have the high-income levels of Asian Americans, Hispanics also prefer whole life insurance, which accounts for a majority of sales to this market. One major life insurance company reports that almost 90 percent of their life insurance sales to Hispanics are whole life policies.

***Common Needs.*** Life insurance to meet final expenses is frequently a dominant need. Some cultures place a high importance on being buried in their homeland, and that cost can place a burden on surviving family members. A second dominant need crosses all ethnic groups: the education and welfare of children. Asking your Hispanic prospects what they hope for their children can open the way to discovering needs for income replacement and education.

***Communication System.*** Word of mouth communication is integral within the Hispanic community and other communities where English is a second language. When you provide great service and impress a few clients in this community, they are loyal and they will readily tell others. Many Hispanic communities have newspapers printed in their home languages. Advertising in these can be effective, but make sure your advertisement says what you intend to say—in their language!

### Marketing Strategy

From these two examples, we can draw some general conclusions.

***Access.*** Look for opportunities you may already have to access an ethnic market. Do you currently have a client who is a member of that market? Do you know a businessperson who is a member of that market or does business in that market? If you do not speak the language, you will probably need a center of influence to help you gain access to the market.

***Overcoming the Language Barrier.*** In considering language barriers within ethnic markets, remember that several Asian countries either commonly use English or teach it as a second language in their schools. For example, Indians, Pakistanis, Malaysians, and Filipinos all learn English as a second language. Filipinos make up over 20 percent of the Asian-American population and outnumber Chinese, Korean, Vietnamese, and Japanese in the United States.

If there is a language barrier, you have a few options. You could attempt to create a strategic relationship with a business professional from the ethnic community. For example, you may work with an attorney or an accountant who speaks the language. It may be possible to access ethnic families through their children, as churches and social workers have successfully done for years. If affordable, you might sponsor children's events around holidays or summer breaks. Advisors who have office staff can hire a person from that particular community and mentor them.

*Market Research.* As with any potential target market, you should do your research. The U.S. Census information (available through the Internet) will help you determine the size of an ethnic population in your city, county, and state.

Next, you should learn as much as possible about the ethnic community's culture and values. Culture plays a huge role in how you interact with the community. It largely determines how the members view insurance and financial products. You must learn what is important to them for you to reach them on a favorable basis. Knowing that many Chinese believe that discussions about death are a bad omen will make you more careful in how you address life insurance.

*Preapproach.* The best way to generate trust as you prepare to work in a new community is to find some professionals within the target community and ask them to help you. Doctors, attorneys, accountants, or non-competing insurance advisors are good choices as centers of influence. Look at the recurring advertisements in local newspapers directed to this market for possible centers of influence, especially among community leaders. These leaders generally understand the importance of networking, community responsibility, and ethnic pride. They also want to help their ethnic communities. If the leaders see you as trustworthy and able to provide solid financial solutions, they should be inclined to help you. Be prepared to demonstrate how you can solve financial problems in their community, and ask for their recommendations. Help your centers of influence see the benefits of your services and products to their community.

Children are the universal bridge into any community. Making a difference in the lives of their children will demonstrate that you care and can be trusted. Here are some ideas:

- Volunteer at the local school (grade school or secondary). Some companies have public affairs kits that you can use in a classroom. If not, Junior Achievement is an organization that produces curriculum you can use. (See www.ja.org.)
- Offer to teach basic financial planning (budgeting, use of credit, and so on) for high-school students.
- Donate equipment to a class in the school.
- Volunteer at a youth athletic club serving this community.

If you are able, volunteer to teach English as a second language or adult literacy classes at a community center. As always, you should enjoy these activities to make them a useful part of your strategy.

Many companies have excellent marketing and sales brochures addressed to the larger ethnic groups. Make good use of these materials. Remember, the key is building trust regardless of the market you are approaching. Take your time and develop the relationship. The best approach is to go into the situation as a learner. If you genuinely desire to learn about the ethnic community's way of life, you will enjoy great success.

## Divorce

According to the U.S. Census Bureau, over one-half of the marriages in our country end in divorce. Although divorce rates have decreased slightly in recent decades, it is almost a certainty that some of your clients will be among the divorced population. In fact, for the middle-years segment, it is statistically more likely for a married client to divorce in the next five years than to die. The subject of this section is the long-term impact of divorce on the insurance and financial needs of spouses and their children.

We will first discuss the advisor's role in what is often a very sensitive situation. Then using a case study format, we will look briefly at divorce tax law and planning alternatives related to permanent and term life insurance. We will close with some thoughts on selling challenges you may face in divorce situations.

### *Financial Considerations in Divorce*

Marriage typically involves the joining of many financial arrangements. In divorce, these arrangements must be untangled, thus a major part of a divorce or separation is transferring property from one spouse to the other. Shared and individual properties must be separated according to state laws or court orders. Other financial issues must also be rearranged often at considerable expense of time and money.

During divorce proceedings, legal instruments such as wills and trusts must be reviewed and modified based on changes caused by the divorce. The unlimited federal estate tax marital deduction will no longer be available to a divorced taxpayer. Divorced persons may need to change estate representatives (administrator or executor) and legal guardians for minor children. Divorced spouses may need new or revised estate planning instruments such as trusts and powers-of-attorney. Property, such as a home, investments, real estate, and other assets may need to be split or re-titled. Beneficiary designations on life insurance, annuities, and retirement plans should be reviewed and changed as necessary.

**qualified domestic
relations order
(QDRO)**

Divorce may leave one or both partners with little or no pension benefits or other private sources of retirement income. If the marriage lasted at least 10 years, a divorced person may be eligible for Social Security retirement and survivor benefits based on their former spouse's earnings record. A divorced person could be entitled to part of the former spouse's qualified retirement plan benefits if the divorce decree includes a *qualified domestic relations order (QDRO)*. QDROs are decrees issued by state courts that allow an employee's qualified retirement plan assets to be used to satisfy marital property rights, child support, or alimony payments to a former spouse or dependent.

Divorce may change the family relationship, but both spouses will continue to have insurance needs. The plans established during the marriage to provide protection for children may be even more important after divorce than before. Life, health, property, and other forms of insurance will need to be continued and possibly revised. For example, a divorced person who had dependent health coverage through a spouse's company health plan may be eligible for up to 36 months of continued coverage under COBRA rules after the divorce.

### *Your Role*

On a list of major life events that trigger the need for financial planning, divorce is near the top. While many money issues have emotional as well as financial components, few cause such intense and conflicting feelings as those related to the breakup of a marriage.

Divorce often leads to a financial settlement that creates a radically different financial status for at least one spouse. How the settlement is structured and managed after the divorce will have a significant long-term impact on a divorced person's life.

When you work with a client involved in a divorce, he or she will likely experience anger, fear, loss, and a desire to either prolong the proceedings or end them quickly. Your first challenge is to recognize those feelings and consider how they might influence the person's decision-making. In many cases it will be hard for the client to imagine—let alone plan for—their future after a divorce.

Each divorce or separation case will present a unique set of challenges. You must deal with them in a sensitive but straightforward manner. Your response will normally be shaped by four factors:

- the personal terms under which the spouses are parting
- the legal conditions of the separation or divorce set down by the court
- the number and ages of the children involved

- the wishes of the couple

There are several ways that you may learn your clients are getting divorced. Your initial response upon hearing about the divorce will depend on your relationship with the couple. In general, you should express your regret and tell both clients you are willing to help them any way you can. Let them know there are considerations for both their present insurance and any new coverage resulting from the settlement.

Meeting jointly with both spouses is usually better than trying to act as a go-between unless it is simply not practical for the two spouses to meet together. Try to determine if the divorce is amicable, as financial adjustments can be much easier in amicable divorces or separations.

***Two Levels of Service.*** You can provide two levels of service to your clients in divorce situations.

*First Level.* Make sure that no necessary coverage is inadvertently lost because of the divorce or separation. Both spouses and children will continue to have insurance and other financial needs.

Typically, if life insurance proceeds are re-directed toward the benefit of the children after a divorce or separation, the insurance is more likely to remain in force than if the former spouse remains beneficiary of the policy. An exception to this is any coverage for a spouse's benefit that is required by the divorce court as part of the settlement. In many cases, life insurance is kept in force if it is to benefit the children. However, in hostile situations a divorced policyowner may try to get revenge on the former spouse by using the children as a tool and threatening to cancel insurance coverage. If that is the case, any hope of continuing an existing program may be lost.

Review with your clients their plans to keep current life insurance protection in force after divorce. Try to ensure the clients are not so distracted by their situation that they fail to pay their current life insurance premiums. Discuss any changes of beneficiary designations that may be necessary.

*Second Level.* Life insurance is valuable property and now figures prominently in many court judgments. In these situations, you should be the professional advisor who recommends the most beneficial approach for both parties and facilitates the various policy arrangements and adjustments.

To understand better the role that life insurance plays in a divorce or separation let us look at a couple, Bart and Cynthia Smith, currently in the process of divorce.

## CASE STUDY: BART AND CYNTHIA

Bart has been married for five years to Cynthia. They have one child, Eric, who is three years old. Bart has asked you to discuss the impact of his impending divorce on his life insurance program. Bart is an engineer and hopes to establish his own computer consulting business.

Bart became a client of yours just before his marriage. At that time, Bart purchased a $100,000 whole life policy on himself. Cynthia is currently the beneficiary of this policy. Bart also owns a $250,000 term insurance policy on his life.

Bart is very concerned about his son, and he will pay both alimony and child support to Cynthia. Cynthia's attorney wants life insurance on Bart to secure both alimony and child support payments.

Cynthia's attorney has said he would agree with the transfer of the $100,000 whole life policy and the $250,000 term policy as security for the alimony. The attorney estimates child support will total about $250,000 from now until Eric reaches majority at age 18. The attorney has said that additional insurance on Bart's life is necessary to protect the child support in case Bart dies before Eric reaches legal age.

Bart is not sure whether he should apply for new life insurance or simply transfer the two old policies to Cynthia to secure the alimony. He is not sure who should be the owner or beneficiary of any new policies taken out to secure the child support payments. Bart wants to look also beyond Eric's 18th birthday and make sure there will be funds to pay for his college.

### Divorce Tax Law

***Alimony and Child Support Payments.*** There are two general tax rules to keep in mind when dealing with divorce:

- Alimony payments are tax deductible for the payor.
- Child support payments are not tax deductible for the payor.

These tax rules are reversed for the recipient:

- Alimony payments are taxable income to the recipient.
- Child support payments are nontaxable to the recipient.

Different tax rules also apply to life insurance in divorce situations. Whether premiums are deductible depends upon the premium payor, the owner, the beneficiary, and the purpose of the insurance in the divorce. Similar factors will determine whether premiums are income to an ex-spouse.

***Permanent Life Insurance Divorce Tax Rules.*** If Bart transfers his whole life insurance policy to Cynthia to secure alimony payments, the following tax results occur:

*Deductible Premiums.* If Bart is required by the settlement to continue paying premiums on the policy, the premiums are deductible by Bart as alimony if Cynthia is named as policyowner with the right to name the beneficiary. In other words, control over the policy and its proceeds must be shifted to Cynthia.

*Premiums as Income.* Premiums which are deductible by Bart are taxable for Cynthia as alimony income.

*Cash Values.* Cash values in a life insurance policy transferred by Bart to Cynthia are not alimony. Rather, they represent a nontaxable transfer of property pursuant to the divorce.

*Basis.* Cynthia will assume Bart's cost basis in the policy for calculation of gain or loss. If she surrenders the policy, any gain or loss will depend upon what Bart has paid into the contract before the transfer of ownership plus any subsequent payments put into the contract while Cynthia was the owner.

*Proceeds.* The proceeds payable at Bart's death under the policy will be income tax free.

***Term Insurance in Divorce.*** Term insurance follows whole life tax rules in divorce situations.

***Role of Negotiations.*** Divorce decrees are subject to negotiations and many variables may enter into the picture. For example, Cynthia's attorney may wish to minimize her taxable income.

The terms of a separation agreement or divorce decree are important. There are often substantial negotiations over the exact terms and wording of the agreement. All parties involved, especially the couple and their attorneys, should exercise caution in the proceedings.

In our case study, Cynthia's attorney may wish to keep her reportable income low while retaining the benefits of the life insurance. For example, the divorce decree could state that Bart is to retain ownership of the policy and that Cynthia

- is to be given physical possession of the policy
- is to be named as an irrevocable beneficiary
- shall have power over Bart's right to surrender the policy

- shall have power over Bart's right to take out policy loans
- shall receive proof of premium payments

Despite these important benefits to Cynthia, the premiums will not be deductible as alimony payments for Bart because the decree provides that he is to remain the owner of the policy.

### Planning Alternatives

There are several choices open to Bart in providing for Cynthia and Eric under the divorce.

***Decreasing Term Insurance.*** Bart could purchase a new decreasing term policy to secure the alimony. Bart's alimony obligation is expected to last for five years, and should decrease month by month. Each time he makes a payment, Bart's remaining liability toward Cynthia should be less.

This same rationale applies to the child support for Eric. The closer Eric gets to age 18, the fewer payments remain during which child support will be due.

With this in mind, the parties may agree that a decreasing term insurance policy on Bart will be adequate to secure what should be his decreasing liabilities for alimony and child support. Decreasing term offers coverage at a very reasonable cost.

On the other hand, Cynthia's attorney may be concerned that the ultimate liabilities will not actually decrease over time. Additional court action, for example, may be necessary to raise the child support as its purchasing power decreases or if Eric has special needs such as private schooling.

Decreasing term also offers no cash values from which to borrow. In the future, Bart could experience a financial setback, making payments difficult. Policy loans could help him continue paying for the policy. A permanent policy may be a better solution.

***An Insurance Trust for Both Alimony and Child Support.*** A planning alternative that both parties may accept is the establishment of an insurance trust. Here a policy (or a group of policies) is placed in one trust established for the benefit of both the ex-spouse and child (Cynthia and Eric). As always, a qualified attorney should handle all trust arrangements.

This alternative offers several non-tax advantages to Bart. If he died, the death proceeds ensuring the child support payments will be paid to the trust and used for the benefit of his son. This reduces the chances that Cynthia would control the proceeds and use them for herself or for a second spouse should she remarry.

***New Policy Purchase Versus Old Policy Transfer.*** Bart should consider whether he wishes to transfer his current insurance as part of the divorce. He may wish to maintain his current coverage as a foundation of an insurance program for a second family if he remarries. New policies, such as a decreasing term, can be tailored to fit the exact needs and amounts dictated by the divorce situation.

On the other hand, Cynthia's attorney may insist on receiving the older cash value policy to make certain a reserve is available to meet premium obligations and keep the insurance in force. The final decision will be based on each side's analysis of the situation and the result of negotiation.

### Selling in the Divorce Atmosphere

A divorce situation presents special challenges to the advisor. Dealing with divorcing clients requires patience and sensitivity. These individuals are going through an emotionally painful experience in which their lives are turned upside down. Divorcing clients' finances are often in disarray, and they frequently need a trusted advisor. A divorce situation may offer a variety of sales opportunities, including a need for life insurance (for alimony and child support agreements), disability income insurance to avoid interrupted premium payments, and retirement income planning.

The divorce situation can present complex situations related to retirement planning. When a divorce occurs, a spouse may be entitled to pension benefits or other employee benefits provided by his or her former spouse's employer. When IRAs, 401(k)s, and other individual retirement assets are split between a divorced couple, one or both spouses may accept your assistance to roll over funds into a proper accumulation vehicle. You may also be able to offer individual health insurance to a spouse who loses coverage after a divorce.

***Impact of Divorce on Financial Plans for the Extended Family.*** Divorce has a significant impact on the couple involved and frequently on their parents as well both on emotional and financial planning levels.

In our case study, Bart's divorce may affect how his parents wish to leave property to Bart or his family in the future. The parents may fear that Bart will fall into a pattern of divorce-remarriage-divorce. This could allow Bart's inherited property to fall into the hands of hostile ex-relatives and strangers. In most states, assets acquired during a marriage such as retirement savings, a home, and investments are considered marital assets subject to equal division upon a divorce. Inherited properties are generally excluded from this equal split. However, with multiple marriages, Bart could gradually convert the inherited property into joint property while married, and it would lose the legal protection upon a subsequent divorce.

## CHAPTER FOUR REVIEW

*Key terms and concepts are explained in the Glossary. Answers to the review and self-test questions are found in the back of the textbook in the Answers to Questions section.*

### Key Terms and Concepts

middle-years adult segment
sandwich generation
2001 CSO Mortality Tables
renewability provision
convertibility provision
ultimate mortality
re-entry term
whole life
ordinary life
limited-pay life
net amount at risk
nonforfeiture options
modified whole life insurance
interest sensitive life insurance

universal life (UL)
unbundling
death benefit options
current assumption whole life
interest-sensitive whole life
variable life insurance (VLI)
variable universal life (VUL)
living benefits
dividends
participating policies
Section 1035 policy exchange
Modified Endowment Contract (MEC)
qualified domestic relations order (QDRO)

### Review Questions

4-1. Discuss common characteristics and needs of the middle-years segment.

4-2. Describe the main features and types of term insurance.

4-3. Summarize the variations of whole life insurance.

4-4. Summarize the key features of universal life insurance.

4-5. Describe two other types of interest-sensitive products that do not require registration with FINRA to sell: current assumption whole life and interest-sensitive whole life.

4-6. Explain the key differences of variable life and variable universal life from their fixed versions.

4-7. Explain the situations when life insurance premiums may be tax deductible.

4-8. Describe the various living benefits associated with life insurance policies and their tax treatment, assuming they are not modified endowment contracts (MECs).

4-9. Define modified endowment contract (MEC) and explain the tax consequences that may occur upon its surrender.

4-10. Discuss the considerations and skills needed to work in emerging, ethnic, and culturally diverse markets.

4-11. Discuss your role as an advisor when clients are separating or divorcing.

4-12. What are the financial considerations in a divorce situation?

4-13. Explain the tax rules for the payer and recipient of alimony and child support..

## Self-test Questions

*Instructions: Read Chapter 4 and then answer the following questions to test your knowledge. There are 10 questions. Choose one answer for each question, and then check your answers with the answer key in the back of the textbook.*

4-1.   A man purchased a $100,000 whole life policy. Many years later, he surrendered the policy for its cash value of $50,000. At that time, he had paid $45,000 of premiums and received dividends of $10,000. What were the income tax consequences upon receipt of the cash surrender value?

(A)   He received the entire $50,000 tax-free.
(B)   He received $45,000 tax-free and $5,000 as ordinary income.
(C)   He received $35,000 tax-free and $15,000 as ordinary income.
(D)   He received $15,000 tax-free and $35,000 as ordinary income.

4-2.   The greater the number of premium payments in a limited-pay permanent life insurance plan, the more closely it will resemble

(A)   variable life
(B)   ordinary life
(C)   universal life
(D)   single premium life

4.3.   The *sandwich generation* refers to middle-years adults who are

(A)   planning for their own higher education as well as that of their children
(B)   managing their aging parents' and their children's needs and finances
(C)   in need of long-term care services as are their own parents
(D)   balancing home and career duties and obligations

4-4.   The latest mortality tables introduced by the NAIC are called the

(A)   1980 CSO Tables
(B)   1990 CSO Tables
(C)   2001 CSO Tables
(D)   2009 CSO Tables

4-5.   Which of the following is (are) characteristic of universal life insurance?

I.   Face amounts of this plan can be increased with additional underwriting approval.
II.   Premiums are fixed and inflexible except by formal adjustments between the policyowner and company.

(A)   I only
(B)   II only
(C)   Both I and II
(D)   Neither I nor II

4-6.   Which of the following statements regarding variable life is (are) correct?

I.   An advisor must have a FINRA (securities) registration before selling variable life insurance.
II.   A prospectus must be delivered to a prospect prior to or during the sales interview.

(A)   I only
(B)   II only
(C)   Both I and II
(D)   Neither I nor II

4-7.  Which of the following statements regarding the income tax consequences of divorce situations is (are) correct?

  I.   Alimony payments are tax deductible for the payor.
  II.  Child support payments are not tax deductible for the payor.

  (A)  I only
  (B)  II only
  (C)  Both I and II
  (D)  Neither I nor II

4-8.  Premiums are deductible in all of the following situations EXCEPT

  (A)  a policy paid by the insured where a charity is the owner and beneficiary
  (B)  a policy that an uncle takes out on his niece
  (C)  a policy that is a part of a qualified retirement plan
  (D)  a policy that is part of alimony in a divorce decree

4-9.  All of the following are common characteristics of the middle-years adult segment EXCEPT

  (A)  many have aging parents
  (B)  some will experience an empty nest
  (C)  most have no concern about retirement
  (D)  most are established in their careers

4-10.  All of the following are typical characteristics of female buyers EXCEPT

  (A)  Women usually have a longer buying cycle.
  (B)  Women do more research and seek out more advice.
  (C)  The female value shopper has replaced the stereotypical female bargain shopper.
  (D)  Women rarely choose to work with a financial advisor.

# 5

# *Retirement Planning and Investments*

| Learning Objectives |
|---|
| *An understanding of the material in this chapter should enable you to* |

5-1.  Describe the retirement planning process.

5-2.  Describe four characteristics of an annuity.

5-3.  Identify and describe three types of annuities.

5-4.  Compare various investments in terms of risk, liquidity, and rate of return.

In this chapter, we examine retirement planning, which nearly every prospect will need. We will also look at different investment choices used to accomplish personal financial objectives.

## RETIREMENT PLANNING

Almost every prospect you meet will need retirement planning. Retirement needs provide market opportunities for such products as life insurance, disability income insurance, mutual funds, annuities, and long-term care insurance. If you understand your prospects' retirement goals, you can help coordinate their long-term needs with their short-term ones. Insurance planning and retirement planning are pieces of the larger financial planning puzzle. Because the products you sell affect retirement income, you must understand the basics of retirement planning.

We will first look at why retirement planning is important. Next, we will give a broad overview of the retirement planning process, and products available to your clients. Finally, we will discuss several marketing opportunities in retirement planning.

### An Opportunity

Few people want to talk about dying. Most would rather talk about how they can enjoy their lives and their money. If you can help them create a budget and a plan, you will usually uncover related insurance and financial needs. Your prospects are likely to be concerned about their retirement.

Regardless of whether you make an immediate sale, your simple and valuable advice will demonstrate a sincerity and desire to help, and not a wish to sell a product the prospect may neither need nor want.

| **Do You Know People Who Are Retired?** |
|---|
| How do the retired people you know live? Do they live well? Do they take pride in their situations? You likely know some people who have retired successfully and others who are not as comfortable as they would wish. When you discuss retirement with your prospects, ask them these same questions. See if they can describe the difference between successful retirement and a less satisfying one. Ask them how they wish to live when they stop working. How will they plan for it? How much income will they need? What are the sources of income? The discussion may open their eyes. |

### Why Retirement Planning Is Necessary

Few people would feel confident relying only on Social Security benefits for retirement income even if they were to reduce their personal expenses. Social Security has major problems resulting from the demographics of the U.S. population. Birthrates in the 1970s and 1980s were much lower than the high rates between 1946 and 1964, which created the baby boomers. Today we have an aging population of baby boomers and fewer workers paying Social Security and federal income taxes that support social programs. To worsen the problem, advances in medicine and life expectancies indicate that baby boomers will live significantly longer than previous generations.

To meet huge increases in costs of Social Security benefits, Medicare, and Medicaid, we can expect the government to reduce benefits, increase taxes, and/or increase the age of eligibility for benefits. Many surveys show that Americans are largely unprepared financially to meet the challenges of retirement. Most Americans begin their savings with employer-sponsored retirement plans, and they make payments into Social Security and Medicare throughout their working years. However, most people do not look seriously at individual retirement issues until they reach their 40s.

While it is never too late to start planning for retirement, younger people benefit from more time to save for their retirement years and to enjoy the power of compounding interest. Let us consider the powerful way that money can work for us over time.

**cost of waiting**

**time value of money**

***The Cost of Waiting and the Time Value of Money.*** The chart that follows shows how starting to save early in life pays off. The age a person begins saving for retirement makes a substantial difference in the dollars invested and the ultimate value of the fund. The nearby chart illustrates two

### Starting Early Pays Off

This chart illustrates two investment programs with annual investments of $2,000. One individual starts at age 22 and stops investing at age 30, and the second individual starts investing at age 31. Compare the values of their investments at age 65 to see the power of compounding returns.

| AGE | INVESTMENT MADE EARLY | AGE | INVESTMENT MADE LATE |
|---|---|---|---|
| 22 | $2,000 | 22 | $0 |
| 23 | 2,000 | 23 | 0 |
| 24 | 2,000 | 24 | 0 |
| 25 | 2,000 | 25 | 0 |
| 26 | 2,000 | 26 | 0 |
| 27 | 2,000 | 27 | 0 |
| 28 | 2,000 | 28 | 0 |
| 29 | 2,000 | 29 | 0 |
| 30 | 2,000 | 30 | 0 |
| 31 | 0 | 31 | 2,000 |
| 32 | 0 | 32 | 2,000 |
| 33 | 0 | 33 | 2,000 |
| 34 | 0 | 34 | 2,000 |
| 35 | 0 | 35 | 2,000 |
| 36 | 0 | 36 | 2,000 |
| 37 | 0 | 37 | 2,000 |
| 38 | 0 | 38 | 2,000 |
| 39 | 0 | 39 | 2,000 |
| 40 | 0 | 40 | 2,000 |
| 41 | 0 | 41 | 2,000 |
| 42 | 0 | 42 | 2,000 |
| 43 | 0 | 43 | 2,000 |
| 44 | 0 | 44 | 2,000 |
| 45 | 0 | 45 | 2,000 |
| 46 | 0 | 46 | 2,000 |
| 47 | 0 | 47 | 2,000 |
| 48 | 0 | 48 | 2,000 |
| 49 | 0 | 49 | 2,000 |
| 50 | 0 | 50 | 2,000 |
| 51 | 0 | 51 | 2,000 |
| 52 | 0 | 52 | 2,000 |
| 53 | 0 | 53 | 2,000 |
| 54 | 0 | 54 | 2,000 |
| 55 | 0 | 55 | 2,000 |
| 56 | 0 | 56 | 2,000 |
| 57 | 0 | 57 | 2,000 |
| 58 | 0 | 58 | 2,000 |
| 59 | 0 | 59 | 2,000 |
| 60 | 0 | 60 | 2,000 |
| 61 | 0 | 61 | 2,000 |
| 62 | 0 | 62 | 2,000 |
| 63 | 0 | 63 | 2,000 |
| 64 | 0 | 64 | 2,000 |
| 65 | 0 | 65 | 2,000 |
| **Total Invested** | $18,000 | | $70,000 |
| **Amount Available at 65** | $398,807 | | $372,204 |

The numbers prove a point. If you start investing early, you invest less and accumulate more. These figures are based on a hypothetical annual rate of return of eight percent. Of course, not everyone can invest $2,000 each year beginning at age 22. However, any amount invested at an early age will make a dramatic difference later. The longer your dollars are allowed to grow and compound, the more you will accumulate. The message here is to put time on your side.

important concepts of retirement planning: the *cost of waiting* and the *time value of money*. The cost of waiting concept demonstrates that the earlier a person starts saving, the fewer invested dollars are needed to meet a retirement goal. The time value of money means that the interest earned inside the investment compounds over time. Consequently, a person can save fewer dollars over a longer period, and still accumulate a lot of money through the power of compound interest. It is perhaps the most important lesson we can learn about planning future money needs. The problem is that many younger people simply do not understand these concepts; too many live for the present and give little thought for tomorrow.

Many people dislike planning and budgeting because they realize they lack knowledge and understanding of those topics. Most young people do not know the limitations of Social Security and how, even with full Social Security benefits, other assets will be required for a comfortable retired life. They do not understand the time value of money or know how compound interest can benefit them. You can educate these people and help them prepare for the future by stressing that retirement planning is both necessary and possible.

### *Sources of Retirement Income*

We will now examine the sources of retirement income. Broadly speaking, there are only three sources of income available in retirement:

- people at work
- money at work
- charity

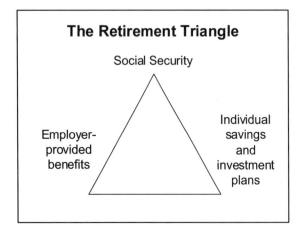

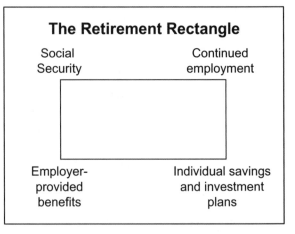

***People at Work.*** If your clients carefully plan for retirement, most will not have to continue working during their retirement years. They may choose to work to stay active and involved, but will not need to in order to pay the bills. The financial need to continue working in retirement is sometimes created by misfortune, but the need most often reflects a failure to plan and implement that plan during one's most productive earning years.

Advisors traditionally have used a retirement triangle to illustrate three sources of retirement income: Social Security, employer-provided benefits, and individual savings and investments. In 2009, after a decade of poor investment returns, many now use a rectangle because more people must continue working after retirement to reach desired income levels.

***Money at Work.*** A second source of income for retirement is money working for you. In this textbook, we will study government-sponsored, employer-sponsored, and personal retirement savings programs. We will discuss different asset classes, investment risks, and advantages and disadvantages of common investments. We also will cover tax rules that apply to typical savings and investment accounts, such as 401(k) plans and IRAs.

***Charity.*** Realistically, not every person can continue to work throughout retirement. If a retiree cannot work, has no savings, and social programs do not provide enough income, only charity can make up the shortfall. Most of your prospects would not want to depend on charity, either from their children or from government welfare programs. This fact makes retirement planning a serious subject, indeed!

---

**Basic Steps of Pre-Retirement Planning**

- Help establish retirement goals.
- Gather all relevant facts.
- Assess risk tolerance and suitability factors.
- Develop a plan to achieve client goals.
- Discuss available products and techniques, and select alternatives that offer the most promise of success.
- Implement the plan.
- Periodically meet to review progress and adjust the plan if necessary.

---

## Retirement Planning Process

It is difficult to plan for retirement because it requires several key assumptions about the future. To project retirement benefits, you must estimate future inflation, wage scales, probable promotions during one's working years, investment returns, life expectancies, and so on. The analysis is very dependent on your planning assumptions in two areas: inflation and investment returns. It is prudent for the advisor to be conservative in both of these assumptions. Retirement planning is easier and improved when you consistently follow the basic steps described below.

### Setting a Goal

The starting point in retirement planning is identifying the prospect's financial goal for retirement income. How much money does the client need to live comfortably when he or she stops earning income? You can estimate income goals for retirement by using the prospect's preretirement living standard. As many retirees will reduce their expenses in retirement, a familiar rule of thumb states that all sources of retirement income should generate about 60 to 80 percent of preretirement income. For example, taxes will be lower because of lower income, work-related expenses will be less or eliminated, and contributions to retirement plans will stop. A more accurate approach to estimating the retirement income goal is to do a thorough cash flow analysis and precisely identify which preretirement expenses will decrease or go away when the client retires. The cash flow analysis may show a need for more than the 60 to 80 percent estimated by the rule of thumb approach. For some retirees, their standard of living may remain the same or even be higher because they want to take more trips and enjoy their increased leisure time after they retire.

| **Reduction in Expenses** |
| --- |
| **Reductions in Taxation**—Social Security taxes, increased standard deduction for those over 65, only a percentage of Social Security benefits are subject to taxes, retirees often have a lower tax bracket |
| **Reductions in Living Expenses**—no work-related expenses (clothing, meals, and so on), mortgage may be fully paid, no dependent children, senior citizen discounts, no longer saving for retirement |

### Forecasting Needs

**current retirement gap**

After a prospect decides on a retirement income goal, and you identify all income sources, you can apply the formula to calculate the *current retirement gap*. This is a simple calculation that assumes your prospect will retire tomorrow.

*Determine their current expenses.* Include housing, personal expenses, recreation, and planned spending (for example, gifts, vacations, or auto purchases)

*Calculate existing resources.* Determine the current resources available to meet expenses. Existing resources include estimated Social Security and employer-sponsored retirement benefits, cash values from existing permanent life insurance, rental income, savings, and other long-term investments intended for retirement.

*Retirement income need = percentage of current income.* For most people, a figure of 60 to 80 percent of preretirement expenses is realistic. Your prospects may choose a higher percentage to use in the calculations, especially if they are younger retirees who intend to remain active. Remember, the client sets the goal, so use his or her amount as the starting point in the formula.

*Retirement income need – existing resources = current retirement gap.* The difference between retirement needs and today's resources is the current retirement gap. The result is in today's dollars and does not account for the time value of money or effects of inflation. Current income requirements will almost certainly change in the future with changes in the economy and individual needs.

The current retirement gap will normally increase each year, as current income needs increase. In addition, as retirement needs grow, some existing resources (Social Security, 401(k) assets, cash values in life insurance, and personal investments and savings) may also increase, but they may not keep up with inflation in the income need.

***Keeping the Gap Closed.*** Your goal in retirement planning is to close the current retirement gap and keep it closed. This means you must closely monitor your client's plans through service work and annual reviews. You must make periodic adjustments to a client's retirement plan as events unfold, such as poor investment results, higher inflation, unexpected expenses, divorce, or health problems. Some clients may even have to un-retire and go back to work when the income gap becomes too large. You will be a valued resource to your clients who have to make such adjustments in their plan. They will appreciate your services and be willing to refer you to others.

Active retirement is a significant life-cycle segment in our American culture. More Americans are reaching retirement age than ever before, and they are living longer in retirement. These numbers will continue to increase as the aging baby boomers reach retirement age in great numbers for years to come. Just a few decades ago, the life expectancy of Americans age 65 was about 10 years. Today, half of all Americans age 65 can expect to live past 83. The fastest growing segment of our population is people over age 85. Many people now live to age 100 and beyond. The aging population, increased life expectancies, stress on social programs, national debt, and poor stock market results in the last decade have created a perfect storm for many American retirees. They are frightened, confused, and do not know whom they can trust. The capable, trustworthy, and empathetic financial advisor will not lack for prospects needing sound financial planning assistance.

---

**Current Retirement Gap Formula**

1. **Determine current expenses.** (This includes housing, personal expenses, recreation, and so on.)

2. **Calculate existing resources.** (This includes projected Social Security benefits, pensions, savings, investments, and so on.)

3. **Retirement income need = percentage of current expenses. (**The prospect must determine the percentage of current expenses to be calculated for retirement needs. The average is 67 percent of current expenses.)

4. **Retirement income need – existing resources = current retirement gap** (The current retirement gap will provide a figure based on today's dollars, not accounting for the time value of money. The current retirement gap can change in the future as both the economy and the prospect's needs change.)

---

*Working the Calculation.* Consider a couple planning retirement in 10 years to understand how these calculations work. At age 55, their current income is $3,000 a month. Assume a need of 75 percent ($2,250) to retire tomorrow. By the retirement starting date, the mortgage will be fully paid and the children will be independent.

In this case, the figures might look like this:

| | |
|---|---|
| $2,250 | Monthly income goal |
| –375 | Pension benefit |
| –855 | Social Security benefit |
| –500 | Income from savings and investments |
| $520 | Monthly income shortfall existing today |

This couple actually has two needs to address. First, they must find a way to generate the additional $520 of monthly income. Second, they should determine if the additional $520 would still be needed if either spouse should die. Perhaps the $1,720 income would be enough; however, if either spouse will need that $520 as the survivor, the couple should consider cash value life insurance on both spouses. The cash value would help provide additional income while both spouses are alive, and the death benefit would cover the shortfall for the surviving spouse.

***Effect of Longevity.*** More years in retirement require much more money for living expenses, health care, and long-term care. The longevity risk of outliving one's assets has increased with earlier retirements and increased life spans. The U.S. Bureau of Labor Statistics reported that in 2007 the largest expenditure for Americans over age 65 was housing. On average, they spent 32 percent of income on housing and related costs. Other significant expenses were 12 percent for food, 18 percent for transportation, and 12 percent for medical care (Consumer Expenditure Survey, 2007). These costs are for necessities and can rarely be decreased by much.

Inflation is a huge factor in retirement planning. As prices rise with even normal inflation, a retiree's money will gradually lose purchasing power. For example, with a modest rate of inflation of 4 percent, the purchasing power of today's dollar will decline by 50 percent in about 18 years. Many advisors will use the average inflation rate over the last 20 years when building a retirement plan. Since the future is uncertain, a conservative estimate will normally be prudent, especially if we experience very high rates of inflation as in the late 1970s and early 1980s.

### Sources of Retirement Income—Money at Work

Retirement income usually comes from the following general sources:

- government programs, such as the Social Security, military, and federal retirement systems
- private tax-qualified plans such as corporate pensions, 401(k) plans, 403(b) plans or Tax Sheltered Annuities (TSAs), and individual retirement accounts (IRAs)
- personal savings and investments
- life insurance

Advisors need to understand these various sources of retirement income to help prospects and clients pursue their retirement goals. Despite multiple sources of retirement income, many people live on incomes too small to maintain a decent standard of living. Income from one or even two sources is rarely enough. If a client plans properly and early enough, the proper combination of income sources (including life insurance) can provide a comfortable retirement.

***Government Retirement Programs.*** The following government retirement plans offer basic coverage to most workers in the private and public sectors:

- The Social Security Program covers virtually all employed people in the United States and their dependents.
- The Civil Service Retirement Program covers pre-1984 federal employees. Employees hired since 1984 are covered by the Federal Employee's Retirement System (FERS) and by Social Security.
- All military services provide a certain percentage of base pay to retired military personnel, and they offer an optional Survivor Benefit Program (SBP). The SBP will pay a military retiree's surviving spouse a monthly payment (annuity) to help make up for the loss of retirement income when the service member dies.
- Federal employees, state employees, and some municipal employees also have optional survivor benefit plans to replace income if the retiree dies.

Advisors should be very knowledgeable about the most common government program, Social Security. The Social Security Administration sends out an annual benefits statement for every covered employee. Review the last one you received as it contains very useful information. To learn more, the Social Security website (ssa.gov) is a tremendous source of up-to-date information.

**tax qualified**

**pension plan**

**profit-sharing plan**

***Tax-Qualified Retirement Plans.*** Many U.S. employers have established tax-qualified and tax-advantaged retirement plans for their employees. Here the term *tax qualified* means the plans meet federal guidelines that make them eligible for tax advantages. For example, a qualified 401(k) plan provides for pre-tax employee contributions, deductible employer contributions, and tax deferred accumulations. The federal government offers valuable tax incentives to corporations, partnerships, and sole proprietorships to encourage them to establish a qualified *pension plan* and/or a *profit sharing plan*. Public schools, hospitals, and certain nonprofit organizations can set up 403(b) plans that are very similar to 401(k) programs. Any person with earned income is eligible for a tax-favored Individual Retirement Account (IRA).

The message is clear: the government is not going to assume the burden of personal financial security. It is up to individuals to arrange their own retirement savings programs. The government is helping, however, by making these plans available, and encouraging their use through substantial tax incentives.

Tax laws affecting retirement plans change frequently as Congress modifies eligibility rules, contribution limits, and fairness requirements. A recent example is the Deficit Reduction Act of 2005 (DRA 2005), which made many changes to pension plan funding requirements. The trend of legislation in the last decade has been to make corporate, partnership, and sole proprietor retirement plans regulations essentially the same.

---

### Definitions of a Pension Plan and a Profit-sharing Plan

**Pension plan**—There is a defined benefit for each employee and the employer is legally required to make annual payments to the plan. The investment risk is with the employer.

**Profit-sharing plan**—A defined-contribution plan with a separate account for each employee that is held in trust for distribution at death, disability, or retirement. The employer may contribute a portion of company profits for the benefit of employees. The investment risk rests with the employee.

---

For tax-qualified status, plans must conform to a number of requirements. A qualified plan must

- meet minimum participation and coverage requirements
- meet minimum eligibility requirements for employees
- be nondiscriminatory
- meet minimum vesting requirements
- have minimum and maximum funding standards
- provide automatic survivor benefits
- satisfy distribution requirements

This is a highly specialized field. When you find an employer prospect interested in establishing a plan, you can get help from your management team or a home office expert who works with retirement plans.

Most of your individual insurance prospects participate in some retirement plan through their job. Employers must provide an individual summary of benefits to all participants at least once a year. This annual report gives valuable information to help you in building a financial plan for your prospect. For example, the report may give the projected income for retirement at normal retirement age and at earlier ages. It will show if there is a pre-retirement death benefit, and list the amount and the beneficiaries.

Some of the many tax advantages to tax-qualified plans include the following:

- Employers can take a tax deduction for contributions made to the plan on behalf of employees.
- Employees do not pay taxes on amounts contributed, either by the employer or as salary reductions from their own pay, until they withdraw funds (or receive pension payments) from the qualified

plan. This means that all contributions are on a pre-tax basis, and earnings in the plan are tax-deferred.

- Distributions from qualified plans may be rolled over into an IRA (or another employee-sponsored plan) which continues the tax-deferral until the funds are eventually withdrawn.

| Differences Between Defined-Benefit and Defined-Contribution Plans | |
| --- | --- |
| **Defined-Benefit Plans** | **Defined-Contribution Plans** |
| Defines the benefit; the law specifies the maximum allowable benefit payable from the plan—the lesser of 100 percent of salary or a maximum amount published annually by the IRS. | Defines the employer's contribution; the law specifies the maximum allowable annual contribution—the lesser of 100 percent of salary or a maximum indexed for inflation published annually by the IRS. |
| Contributions are not attributed to individual employee accounts. | All contributions are allocated to individual employee accounts. |
| Employer assumes the risks of preretirement inflation, investment performance, and adequacy of retirement income. | Employee assumes the risks of preretirement inflation, investment performance, and adequacy of retirement income. |
| There are unpredictable costs. | There are predictable costs. |

**403(b) plan**

*403(b) Plans.* The *403(b) plan* has traditionally been referred to as a Tax Sheltered Annuity (TSA). It applies to employees of tax-exempt employers, as described in IRS Code Sec 501(c)(3). Organizations eligible for the 403(b) plan include public schools, nonprofit organizations, nonprofit hospitals, charitable foundations, museums, zoos, symphony orchestras, trade associations, and many private schools.

The 403(b) plan shares the following in common with the 401(k) plan. It permits an employee to contribute to the plan by setting aside a portion of his or her salary on a pre-tax basis. As of January 1, 2006, plans are also permitted, but not required, to accept designated Roth contributions. Roth contributions are made on an after-tax basis and qualified withdrawals of associated earnings may be made tax free. The contribution limits are identical to those in the 401(k) plan. Furthermore, employers are able to make matching or nonelective contributions. The assets grow tax-deferred until they are withdrawn (normally after the employee retires), and they may be rolled over into an IRA.

Distributions, or withdrawals, from a 403(b) plan are taxed under the annuity rules of the Internal Revenue Code. If all contributions were with pre-tax dollars, then distributions are taxable as ordinary income in the year received. As with other tax-advantaged plans, a distribution prior to age 59½ triggers a 10 percent penalty tax on the taxable amounts of the distribution.

A 403(b) plan may be funded by annuities (fixed or variable) or custodial accounts invested in mutual funds (such plans are technically known as 403[b][7] plans). IRS final regulations issued in July of 2007 eliminated life insurance products other than annuities as an investment option after September 24, 2007. Certain policies are grandfathered.

To operate in this market you must normally have a securities registration through FINRA (formerly NASD). That registration allows you to sell variable products and/or mutual funds that most 403(b) plans use as investment vehicles. Some reports estimate there are 150,000 organizations in the United States that are prospects for 403(b) plans. However, the IRS final regulations issued in July of 2007 have required substantial changes to the design and administration of plans using multiple providers. It is likely to result in employers limiting the number of providers to keep the administration and coordination of the plan that they are now required to oversee manageable.

**Individual Retirement Account (IRA)**

***Individual Retirement Accounts (IRAs).*** *Individual Retirement Accounts (IRAs)* are tax-advantaged retirement plans available to many people with earned income. Under current law, eligible individuals may contribute 100 percent of earned income up to a maximum annual contribution limit (published on irs.gov). The limit applies to total contributions made to either a Traditional IRA or a Roth IRA, or a combination of the two. For example, in 2009, a person under age 50 could contribute $2,500 to a Traditional IRA and $2,500 to a Roth IRA for a total of $5,000. The annual limit is $6,000 (in 2009) for a taxpayer aged 50 and older.

IRA funds can be held in several investment vehicles such as a custodial bank account, certificate of deposit, mutual fund, brokerage account, and annuity contracts with life insurance companies. IRA owners can invest in gold and certain approved gold and silver coins (of 24-karat quality). Prohibited investments include life insurance and collectibles, such as stamps, rugs, antiques, paintings, and other artworks.

IRAs are a valuable retirement savings opportunity for millions of Americans. While the IRA rules appear complicated, all financial advisors need to understand basic IRA concepts to advise their prospects and clients properly. We will discuss specific rules that apply to Traditional IRAs and then describe the Roth IRA.

**Traditional IRA**

**Traditional IRA.** Any individual under 70½ years with current earned income may contribute to a *Traditional IRA*. The contributions may be fully deductible, partially deductible, or non-deductible. The owner can withdraw assets from a Traditional IRA at any time. However, a 10 percent additional (penalty) tax generally applies if withdrawals occur before the calendar year in which the owner turns 59½. As with all IRAs, investment earnings are tax deferred, and withdrawals are taxed as ordinary income.

A Traditional IRA owner must take the first of his or her Required Minimum Distributions (RMD) from a Traditional IRA no later than April 1 of the year following the calendar year the owner reaches age 70½. Subsequent annual RMDs must be made no later than December 31 each year while the owner remains alive. Distributions are taxed for the calendar year in which they are received. If distributions are not made on time, or if distributions are less than the required minimum distribution, the owner must pay a 50 percent excise tax for that year. This is one of the heaviest IRS tax penalties and the IRS grants few exceptions. Advisors need to learn these rules and advise their clients to avoid penalties. Following are some more important rules for the Traditional IRA:

- Annual contributions are fully deductible if neither the owner nor spouse has a qualified retirement plan available through their employer. If either the IRA owner or spouse is covered by a qualified plan, the deduction phases out based on modified adjusted gross income (MAGI, see box below for definition). For example, in the 2009 tax year, an employee covered by a retirement plan at work and filing jointly could deduct his full contribution to a Traditional IRA if the couple's MAGI is less than $89,000. If the couple's MAGI is more than $89,000 but less than $109,000, then the deductible amount is reduced. For a MAGI above $109,000, none of the contribution is deductible. The situation is different for the spouse who is not covered by a retirement plan at work. The spouse would be able to deduct the full contribution to an IRA if the couple's MAGI is less than $166,000. The deductibility is phased out if joint MAGI exceeds $176,000. The limits are different for a single individual or head of household, and the limits change every year. Current information is on the IRS website (irs.gov).
- Assets from other tax-advantaged retirement plans (for example, 401(k), 403(b), profit sharing, or 457) may be rolled over into an IRA without tax penalty, and the new IRA maintains the tax deferral until the owner takes distributions.
- A person may have multiple IRAs, and he or she may contribute to all of them; however, the combined annual contribution cannot exceed the maximum level set by the IRS.

- An employee may establish a Traditional IRA in addition to other employer-sponsored retirement plans available to him or her. (As discussed above, the tax deductibility of IRA contributions may be decreased or eliminated.)

---

**Modified Adjusted Gross Income (MAGI)**

---

A taxpayer's modified adjusted gross income (MAGI) is usually different from simple compensation. The MAGI includes other income such as interest, dividends, and income from retirement accounts, capital gains, and alimony received. Certain adjustments (subtractions) are made for deductible retirement plan contributions, alimony payments made, and certain interests on student loans.

---

**Roth IRA**

**Roth IRA**. The *Roth IRA* was established in 1997 and has become a very popular vehicle for retirement savings and estate planning. While annual contribution limits for the Roth are the same as for a Traditional IRA, the eligibility requirements for the Roth IRA are quite different. Other important differences include the following:

- Roth IRA contributions are made with after-tax dollars. Thus Roth contributions are never tax deductible.
- Roth IRAs grow tax-free as opposed to tax-deferred under certain conditions. If the Roth IRA has been open for at least five years, and the owner is at least 59½, then both principal and interest withdrawals are tax free.
- There are no required minimum distributions at age 70½, as there are with the Traditional IRA.
- The after-tax contributions to a Roth IRA can be withdrawn at any time, for any reason, and without penalty. This makes the Roth IRA a very flexible vehicle to accumulate retirement funds but also have them available for emergencies, education, and so on.

Other important characteristics of the Roth IRA include the following:

- Annual contributions are subject to income eligibility requirements. For example, in 2009, a married couple filing jointly could contribute the maximum amounts to their Roth IRAs if modified adjusted gross income (MAGI) is less than $166,000. For MAGI between $166,000 and $176,000, the allowable contribution is reduced. If MAGI is above $176,000, then no Roth IRA contributions are allowed. As with other IRA rules, these limits are different for a single individual or head of household, and the limits usually change every year. You can get current information from the IRS website (irs.gov) or tables provided by your company.

- In 2009, a taxpayer (single or married filing jointly) who owns a Traditional IRA may convert it to a Roth IRA without a tax penalty if his or her modified MAGI is less than $100,000 (regardless of income tax filing status). However, ordinary income tax must be paid on all tax-deductible contributions to the Traditional IRA and on subsequent growth inside the account. A big change in this rule is scheduled for 2010. The Tax Increase Prevention and Reconciliation Act of 2005 (TIRPA 2005) will eliminate the MAGI limit and filing status restriction on Roth IRA conversions starting in 2010. Note that limits on taxpayers who can establish and/or contribute to a Roth IRA will remain; however, the income cap on conversion of Traditional IRAs to Roth IRAs will be removed.

- As mentioned earlier, tax-free distributions from a Roth IRA are available under certain conditions. First, the Roth IRA must be in force for at least five years. The five-year test is satisfied beginning on January 1 of the fifth year after the year in which you establish a Roth IRA. Second, the distribution must be a qualified distribution of one of the following types:

  (1) a distribution made after the owner turns 59½
  (2) a distribution made to a beneficiary after the owner's death
  (3) a distribution because the owner becomes disabled according to IRS rules (regardless of his or her age at the time of disability)
  (4) first-time home buyer (up to $10,000 may be applied, and this applies to Traditional IRAs as well)

If a distribution does not meet these criteria, the earnings portion of the distribution is taxable as ordinary income, and a 10 percent penalty tax may apply. Remember, however, that the contributions to a Roth IRA can be withdrawn any time, for any reason, and with no tax or penalty.

**spousal IRA**

**Spousal IRA.** Generally a person must have earned income to contribute to a Traditional or Roth IRA. An important exception is a *spousal IRA* where the spouse with earned income can contribute to an IRA for the non-employed spouse (or for a spouse earning less than the maximum annual IRA contribution limit). This is a good opportunity for a stay-at-home parent (or temporarily unemployed spouse) to build retirement funds. The spousal IRA can be either a Traditional IRA or a Roth. The following requirements apply:

- The employed taxpayer is married to the same spouse at the end of the year, and they file a joint tax return.

- The spouse named in the spousal IRA earns less than the taxpayer.
- The contributions to the IRAs for both spouses do not exceed total joint compensation.
- A spousal IRA can be established even if the employed taxpayer does not contribute to his or her IRA.

### *Personal Savings and Investments*

Your clients can use other methods to accumulate retirement assets in non-qualified, or non-retirement, accounts, including the following:

- equities (for example, common and preferred stock)
- bonds (for example, government, corporate, or municipal)
- mutual funds
- guaranteed fixed investments (CDs, savings accounts)
- annuities
- permanent life insurance

Most advisors recommend that clients take full advantage of retirement plans such as a 401(k) or 403(b), especially when employers match employee contributions. Those plans offer the free money from the employer match, tax-deductible employee contributions, and tax-deferred growth. For your clients in higher tax brackets, the tax deductibility of contributions is extremely valuable. After maximizing use of employer-sponsored retirement plans, most clients will benefit from a deductible Traditional IRA (if eligible) or a Roth IRA, because of the tax advantages described earlier. Annuities, although funded with after-tax dollars, provide tax-deferred growth, and may be annuitized to provide guaranteed, lifetime income.

*Life Insurance.* The cash value of a permanent life insurance policy can supplement retirement income. Permanent insurance cash values grow tax-deferred under current rules. The policyowner may make a tax-free loan using the cash value as collateral, or make a simple withdrawal from some policies such as a universal life (UL) or variable universal life (VUL) contract.

A policyowner may also surrender a permanent insurance contract and select a settlement option that provides regular monthly income for life, or options that guarantee continued payments to survivors.

## Marketing Opportunities

Retirement planning for most clients is very complex. There are many decisions involving employee-sponsored plans, rollover rules, IRAs, Social

Security, income taxation, and many others. Changing tax laws add a huge complicating layer to the process. Most of your prospects will be unable to master all these issues and effectively plan for their own retirement. If you are knowledgeable, competent, and trustworthy, you can provide a great service to your clients and prospects in this important phase of their lives. The rewards for yourself can be in proportion to the valuable service you provide. We will look at a few basic marketing ideas to help you expand your business in the retirement planning field.

### Social Security

Tremendous publicity on Social Security's solvency has made many Americans recognize they need to rely more on their personal funding of retirement than on governmental entitlements. This increased awareness works in the favor of financial advisors. As people grow more concerned about the adequacy and solvency of the Social Security system, they should also be more open to your professional advice on investing for their future. You can help them take the maximum advantage of employer-sponsored plans, IRAs, annuities, and other personal investment methods. An excellent leading question to a prospect is simply: "What role do you feel Social Security benefits will have in your retirement plans?" Many of your younger clients will not want to rely at all on Social Security, because they believe the program will disappear before they retire.

### Employer-Sponsored Programs

Many Americans have employer-sponsored retirement programs, such as a pension plan, profit-sharing plan, or both. You will find that few people really take the time to understand how these plans work. For example, some companies offer plans such as a 401(k) that match an employee's contribution to a maximum percentage of salary. When an employee does not contribute at all, or to the extent of the matched amount, he or she is wasting a valuable opportunity to build retirement assets. Your valuable insight and advice will help the prospect and add to your reputation as a trusted advisor.

*IRAs.* Most prospects will be eligible for either a Traditional IRA, Roth IRA, or both. Some good prospects include the following:

- people who work for companies with no employer-sponsored retirement plan
- people who have a non-working spouse eligible for a Spousal IRA

- people who have contributed up to the employer match in a 401(k) or similar retirement plan, and have additional money to invest toward retirement

***403(b) Plans.*** The 403(b) plan market for implementing new plans is definitely viable. Consider hosting a seminar or meet with employers such as private schools, charitable organizations, or large religious groups to explain how a 403(b) plan works and how it can benefit the employees.

***Annuities.*** There are many market opportunities for annuities in retirement planning for both accumulation and income distribution. Annuities are excellent accumulation vehicles because of the tax-deferred growth feature and solid guarantees. After the severe economic and investment-related problems of recent years, many Americans are looking for the security that annuities provide. Fixed annuities and immediate annuity sales have shown sharp increases as people search for guaranteed products. Some good prospects for annuities are

- the higher-net-worth prospect who has maximized other tax-advantaged options, such as employer-sponsored plans and IRAs
- the prospect who has no employer-sponsored plan and who has maximized all deductible or non-deductible IRA contributions

***Life Insurance.*** Life insurance is important for people approaching retirement or those already retired. A client's retirement decisions for a family must cover two questions: What do we need while both spouses are alive, such as available income, growth of assets, and so on?, and What do we need for the survivor if one spouse dies? We discussed life insurance as an accumulation vehicle for retirement. Now we will look at the unique role life insurance plays in retirement planning (providing for the needs of survivors after the death of a retiree).

Here are some reasons why life insurance is important throughout one's retirement. Life insurance can provide the following:

- liquidity to pay the cost of dying. This includes funeral expenses, debts, administration costs of estate settlement, and estate taxes.
- supplemental income through beneficiary arrangements for a surviving spouse. Proceeds can be paid through settlement options or invested in other income-producing investments to supplement income.
- increases to retirement income. A permanent insurance contract can be surrendered for a settlement option as discussed earlier.

- Social Security income replacement so that a survivor's income level remains sufficient
- bequests to family and charitable organizations

The advisor should carefully review an insured's retirement plan to make sure needed coverage is either available now or obtained before retirement. Many retirees will lose term insurance coverage obtained through their employee, or the coverage may be too expensive to maintain. Those prospects will be good candidates for either a level term policy or permanent policy if they have available funds for the premium. Some prospects may have enough money to purchase cash value policies to provide death benefits and the potential to accumulate sizable tax-deferred savings.

Remember that many life insurers pay current rates of interest substantially higher than those guaranteed in their contracts. If you illustrate a life product with non-guaranteed assumptions, make sure to base income estimates on conservative, guaranteed interest rates. You would not wish a client to experience an income shortage during retirement due to unrealistic projections on your part.

We have just scratched the surface of marketing opportunities related to retirement planning. Later, we will discuss the distribution of income from a client's retirement savings. We will also cover protection of retirement assets through long-term care insurance, and effective legacy and estate planning. Your mastery of these subjects will pay huge dividends for your prospects, clients, and yourself. We will now look more closely at the investment choices your clients have to help build and maintain their retirement assets.

## INVESTMENT CHOICES

Financial planning combines many specialty areas including insurance planning, tax planning, estate planning, and retirement planning. These areas are so interconnected that it is difficult to address any one of them in isolation. For example, taxation affects spendable income, which affects one's retirement plans. Life insurance planning is important for effective retirement planning, especially in providing survivor income. Just as the planning concepts are integrated, so are the financial vehicles to achieve one's goals. Each vehicle has its advantages and disadvantages. Some are appropriate for one client and not for another. No single investment vehicle can do it all.

This section addresses the most common financial products available to your clients to build wealth. We will begin with annuities, a product traditionally associated with life insurance companies. We will then consider products traditionally associated with other entities such as governments, banks, and investment companies. Those products include the following:

- bank savings plans
- treasury bills and treasury notes
- bonds
- stocks
- investment companies and mutual funds
- real estate
- tangible assets
- limited partnerships

We live in a financial environment where the traditional lines are blurred. Today, many banks and brokerage firms sell insurance, and insurance companies sell banking and investment products. Our goal in this section is to help you understand the array of investment choices consumers have for their dollars. This will help you propose an individualized investment portfolio that will best move a client toward his or her retirement goals.

## Annuities

### *What Is an Annuity?*

**annuity**

**annuitant**

**annuity owner**

An *annuity* is a legal contract between an insurer and the annuity owner. Note that the annuity owner is not always the *annuitant*, or person entitled to receive payments from the annuity. The *annuity owner* may purchase the annuity with a single sum of money (single premium annuity), or make flexible purchases (premiums) over time during an accumulation period in which growth inside the annuity is tax-deferred. If the owner wishes, the annuity may start making periodic payments to the annuitant immediately after the purchase (immediate annuity). Another option for annuity contracts allows the invested money to accumulate tax-deferred interest with the insurer until later (perhaps many years), and then begin payments to the annuitant (deferred annuity). A unique feature of a traditional annuity is that it can be annuitized to guarantee an income for the remaining life of the annuitant (life annuity), or for a designated number of years (period certain or fixed-period annuity).

The annuity's tax-deferred growth feature is allowed because the annuity is considered a life insurance product. As such, Congress has granted favorable tax advantages that are similar in some respects to life insurance contracts. The tax-deferred growth in annuities is an extremely attractive and beneficial feature that helps build wealth more efficiently over time by deferring taxes on the growth. Many clients (and unfortunately, many advisors) do not realize that annuities are efficient accumulation vehicles, and they do not require the owner to annuitize the contract. If the owner chooses to annuitize the annuity contract, several distinctive factors apply, as we discuss below.

### How an Annuity Works

An annuity is an insurance product based on the same principles as life insurance. The insurer uses mortality, interest, and expense components to calculate the payout for a given premium amount. With all other factors being equal, an annuity payout for a female will be less than for a male the same age, because the female has a greater life expectancy. In a sense, an annuity is the flip side of life insurance. As you know, life insurance pools the risks of a group of individuals who have a risk of dying prematurely. The insurer, using mortality, interest, and expenses, calculates a premium for each insured to provide a death benefit. If the insured dies much earlier than his or her life expectancy, the insurance company loses on that contract. With the annuity, the insurer uses life expectancies, interest, and expenses to calculate a payout that will distribute principle and interest over the annuitant's projected life span. If the annuitant lives far longer than his or her life expectancy, the insurer loses on that annuity contract. Of course, other annuitants may die sooner than expected, and the insurer would profit on those contracts. It is correct to say, at least for their most basic financial purposes, that life insurance protects against the risk of dying too soon, and an annuity protects against the risk of living too long.

The classic annuity has two phases, an accumulation phase and a payout phase (called an annuity phase in some texts). Let's look briefly at some of the major details about each phase.

**accumulation phase**

*Accumulation Phase.* The *accumulation phase* is the phase when the annuity owner builds up the value of the annuity by making investments called premiums, as with life insurance, and earning interest. The premiums are generally paid with after-tax dollars. An exception is an annuity used inside a deductible IRA or a 403(b) plan. A very important benefit of the annuity is that cash accumulations grow tax deferred, even if the annuity is not used to fund a retirement plan. The longer the accumulations phase of the annuity, the greater the benefit of this tax-deferred feature. In effect, it allows the annuity owner to continue investing the dollars that would have been used to pay taxes on other investments. In a sense, tax-deferred growth acts as if the government is loaning money to the annuity owner by delaying the taxes due. Even though taxes will eventually be paid on all the growth, the annuity owner earns additional interest on the dollars that would have gone to taxes. Additionally, the owner may be in a lower marginal tax bracket later and realize a significant net benefit from tax deferral. Tax-deferred growth is one of the strongest marketing features for annuities.

**payout or annuity phase**

*Payout Phase.* During the *payout or annuity phase*, the annuity contract is annuitized and the insurer makes periodic annuity payments to the annuitant. The amount of the payments depends on the value of the annuity, the age and gender of the annuitant (used to estimate the mortality experience), and the interest rate used by the insurer. Some annuities guarantee payments for a fixed period (for example, 10 years) while others guarantee payments for the life of the annuitant. As we shall see, variable annuities offer a variable payout, based on investment performance inside the annuity. A tremendous benefit of the classic annuity is that the insurer can guarantee that the annuitant will not outlive the income. If a client simply withdraws from a personal savings or investment account, bad markets or periods of low interest rates may cause the annuitant to run out of money before his or her death. The annuity will pay money to the annuitant until death occurs, removing the risk of losing principal and income prior to death. This feature will be more attractive as employers offer fewer traditional defined benefit pension plans for their employees.

### Other Characteristics

*Death Benefit.* The annuity's death benefit should not be confused with a life insurance death benefit. The annuity death benefit applies only during the accumulation phase, or before guaranteed lifetime payouts have begun. The annuity death benefit normally guarantees that a designated beneficiary will receive the greater of the accumulated value, or the premiums deposited minus any previous withdrawals. Any gains in the annuity will be taxable as ordinary income to the beneficiary upon withdrawal. This is unlike a life insurance policy that normally provides a tax-free death benefit to a beneficiary.

*Surrender Charges.* Annuities typically include a declining surrender charge in the first 5 to 10 years. The surrender charges normally decline each year until they reach zero. To give some access to funds, most annuities allow a free withdrawal amount each year of 10 to 15 percent. Surrender charges apply to all withdrawals above the free withdrawal amounts.

*Taxation on Withdrawals.* With annuities, there are two major tax rules about taxation of the gains (or growth) in non-qualified annuities, or those not associated with a retirement plan such as an IRA. First, we will consider withdrawals from an annuity during the accumulation period, which is prior to any annuitization of the contract. If an annuity contract is fully surrendered during the accumulation phase, the owner must pay ordinary income tax on all earnings in the contract. There is no tax on the return of contributions (the owner's investment in the contract).

Partial withdrawals from an annuity in the accumulation phase are taxed on a last in, first out (LIFO) basis. In other words, the first withdrawals from an annuity are earnings, and the owner is taxed on withdrawals until all earnings have been distributed. The owner then receives the contributions tax-free.

There is an exception to the earnings first rule for contributions made to annuity contracts prior to August 14, 1982. Contributions on those older policies are distributed on a first in, first out (FIFO) basis, exactly like life insurance cash values, and the owner is not taxed until contributions are fully recovered. While all current annuity contracts are subject to the new LIFO rules, advisors may encounter some clients who own the older contracts with taxation using FIFO rules.

A 10 percent penalty tax generally applies to taxable distributions from annuities made before the owner reaches age 59½. Exceptions to the penalty tax include distributions:

- as a result of the owner's death or disability
- made in substantially equal periodic payments over the life expectancy of the owner (or joint life expectancy of the owner and a designated beneficiary)
- made under an annuitized contract
- attributable to annuity investments made prior to August 14, 1982

Note that the insurer may also assess surrender charges if they apply.

**exclusion ratio**

If the annuity is annuitized, periodic payments are made to the annuitant according to the annuity option selected by the owner. A portion of each annuity payment represents a return of non-taxable investment in the contract. The balance of each payment is taxable income. The taxable and non-taxable portions of the payments are determined by an *exclusion ratio*, calculated by the insurer. The exclusion ratio for a fixed annuity is the ratio of the investment in the contract to the total expected return under the contract. For example, if the exclusion ratio is .50, then 50 percent of each annuity payment is excluded from tax, or is a non-taxable return of investment, to the annuitant. Once the full amount of the investment in the contract is recovered using the exclusion ratio, additional annuity payments are fully taxable.

***Accumulation and Payout Arrangements.*** Annuities can be categorized as follows according to their accumulation and payout arrangements:

- single premium or installment premium
- immediate or deferred income
- fixed premium or flexible premium

A single premium annuity is purchased with one lump-sum payment. The payout can start immediately, and that contract is a single premium immediate annuity (SPIA). The payout can be postponed until a future date as a single premium deferred annuity (SPDA).

Deferred annuities may be either a fixed premium contract or a flexible premium contract. With the fixed premium annuity, the owner invests a specific amount at preset intervals for a designated period. Under the more popular flexible premium annuity, the owner can make premium payments of any amount at various times subject to minimum premiums set by the insurer.

### Types of Annuities

Annuities are also described according to how the owner's contributions are invested. There are now three major strategies, each with its own set of features and benefits. Fixed annuities, variable annuities, and the newer equity-indexed annuities all have a role in today's financial environment. We will give a short overview of each type; however, you are encouraged to take The American College's course entitled *The Essentials of Annuities* to build your knowledge about this important financial tool.

**fixed annuity**

***Fixed Annuity.*** A *fixed annuity* provides tax-deferred growth as described earlier. When annuitized, a fixed annuity provides a guaranteed income for life of the annuitant at little risk to the owner. Those features make fixed annuities a product much in demand for retirement income planning. Sales of fixed annuities have spiked upward in the last few years in response to a turbulent economy and a long bear market. There are many variations in the contract features of fixed annuities, but we will only cover the most common ones.

During the accumulation period, the insurer pays interest at a current rate that may fluctuate with changes in the insurer's investment experience. However, the interest rate will not fall below a guaranteed rate specified in the contract. During the payout period, the interest used to calculate annuity payments will be set by the insurer, but it will be no less than a minimum annuitization interest rate stated in the contract. When payouts begin from an annuity the interest rate is fixed, and the payout remains level. In recent years, newer contracts have been introduced with a rising income stream during the payout phase. The payouts start lower than traditional fixed annuities but increase by a small percentage each year to help offset inflation.

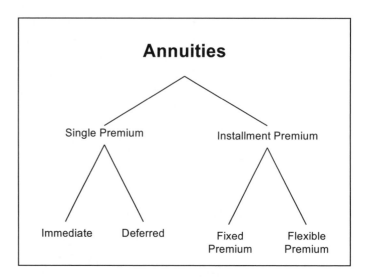

***Variable Annuity.*** A *variable annuity* is a securities product and requires the advisor to have registration through the Financial Industry Regulatory Authority (FINRA), formerly called the National Association of Securities Dealers (NASD). The variable annuity gives the owner a choice of investment options with the tax-deferred feature all annuities possess. The investment options are very similar to mutual funds but are called subaccounts in the variable annuity. These subaccounts invest in stocks, bonds, money markets, or combinations of these. Thus, the accumulated value of a variable annuity contract will rise or fall with the values of the underlying securities within the subaccounts.

***Example:***          Camila purchased a variable annuity with an initial investment of $10,000. She allocated 50% percent of that amount ($5,000) to a bond sub-account, and 50% percent ($5,000) to a stock sub-account. During the following year, the stock fund had a 10 percent% return, and the bond fund had a 5% percent return. At the end of the first year, Camila's account had a value of $10,750 ($5,500 in the stock fund and $5,250 in the bond fund), minus fees and charges.

Variable annuities are attractive because they offer the potential to achieve investment returns that exceed inflation. With the potential for greater returns comes greater investment risk. Advisors must be extremely cautious in determining the suitability of variable annuities, especially for older clients. Many newer contracts offer various guarantees such as a minimum withdrawal benefit, minimum annual step-ups in account values, and guaranteed death benefits. These extra benefits carry an extra charge; however, they have been popular, as investors have sought more security in their portfolios. Many advisors recommend variable annuities for retirement plans such as an IRA, Roth IRA, or rollover from other plans such as a 401(k). Advisors and clients should be aware of the following recommendations taken from the Securities and Exchange Commission (SEC) website:

---

In addition, if you are investing in a variable annuity through a tax-advantaged retirement plan (such as a 401(k) plan or IRA), you will get no additional tax advantage from the variable annuity. Under these circumstances, consider buying a variable annuity only if it makes sense because of the annuity's other features, such as lifetime income payments and death benefit protection. The tax rules that apply to variable annuities can be complicated – before investing, you may want to consult a tax adviser about the tax consequences to you of investing in a variable annuity.

*Source: http://www.sec.gov/investor/pubs/varannty.htm, 3/30/2009*

---

**equity-indexed annuity (EIA)**

***Equity-Indexed Annuity.*** The *equity-indexed annuity (EIA)* is a product introduced in the 1990s that credits interest in an amount that is linked to a stock or other equity index. One of the most commonly used indices is the Standard & Poor's 500 Composite Stock Price Index (the S&P 500®). The return for the EIA will mirror the rate of return for the index to which it is tied. If the index rises by 10 percent over a designated period (for example, monthly, quarterly, or annually) the contract will be credited for a portion of that increase. Most EIAs set a participation rate on the credited interest, which means the annuity may not be credited with the full rate of return of the index. For example, if the XYZ Equity-Indexed Annuity has a participation rate of 90 percent, and the index earned 10 percent, the annuity would credit 90 percent of that return, or 9 percent, as interest in the contract. Many EIAs include a cap, which means the interest credited may not exceed the cap percentage. For example, if the index's rate of return was 15 percent and the cap was 12 percent, the annuity would be credited with 12 percent interest. Another unique feature of the EIA is that when the index value goes down, there is no decrease in the accumulation value of the annuity. This feature, along with the tax-deferred growth, has added to the attractiveness of the equity-indexed annuity, especially for more risk averse investors.

The EIA is currently treated as a variant of a fixed annuity, which means the contracts normally have a guaranteed minimum rate of return, usually about three percent. Since its inception, the equity-indexed annuity has not required a securities registration to sell it. In January 2009, the U.S. Securities and Exchange Commission (SEC) adopted rule 151A, with an effective date in January 2011. The rule will require insurers to register most indexed annuities sold after that date with the SEC as securities. Producers selling the products will need to have the same securities licenses that are required to sell mutual funds and variable products. As we go to press with this publication, a coalition of insurance industry companies has filed a lawsuit to have the SEC decision overturned. The outcome will be watched very closely by companies and producers involved in the EIA business.

## Bank Savings Plans

Banks and savings and loan companies have several types of savings plans available to depositors. These plans offer liquidity, flexibility, and safety for short-term cash equivalent savings. In most cases, the funds are secured by the assets of the institution and are backed by insurance available from the Federal Deposit Insurance Corporation (FDIC) or Federal Savings and Loan Insurance Corporation (FSLIC) on amounts up to $100,000 per depositor per bank. (In late 2008, the guarantee was temporarily increased to $250,000 through December 31, 2009.)

Money deposited in savings accounts can be withdrawn at any time. The money earns interest in the account, but the interest rate is lower than most other plans. No tax advantages are available with these plans.

**NOW accounts**

*NOW Accounts.* Negotiable Order of Withdrawal accounts, or *NOW accounts*, offer the best features of savings accounts (interest and liquidity), and the best feature of checking accounts (check writing). Funds are first deposited in the savings portion of the account, and begin to earn interest. When the customer writes a check, funds are automatically transferred to the checking account to cover the check. More institutional restrictions apply to these accounts than to regular savings accounts. For example, the customer may have to maintain a minimum balance, and the number of checks the customer can write each month is often limited.

**certificates of deposit (CDs)**

*Certificates of Deposit (CDs).* With *certificates of deposit (CDs)*, customers deposit money with the institution for a specific, limited certain period. Typical CD terms are three month, six month, and one to five years. The institution pays interest on the money at fixed or variable rates from the date of deposit to the CD's maturity date. The customer may allow the interest to accumulate or withdraw it periodically. When the CD matures, the customer may either take principal and interest in cash, or roll the money into another CD, usually of the same term. Normally, the larger the deposit and the longer the CD's investment term, the higher the interest rate. Banks normally assess a penalty for withdrawals of the principal before the CD's maturity date. For example, the bank may penalize two to three months of interest, or use another formula to compute the early surrender charges.

### *Treasury Bills, Treasury Notes, and Treasury Bonds*

Treasury bills, notes, and bonds are U.S. Government securities that may be purchased in the over-the-counter securities market. Treasury bills (known as T-bills) are available in amounts from $1,000 to $5,000,000 with maturity dates of 4, 13, 26, and 52 weeks from issue. Treasury notes (T-notes) are available with 2- to 10-year maturities, in amounts between $100 and $1,000,000. Treasury bonds (T-bonds) are available in amounts greater than $1,000 with maturity dates of 10 to 30 years. Both T-notes and T-bonds pay interest every six months. The interest is included in federal income taxes as it is paid. However, the interest is not subject to state or local income taxes. Treasury bills, notes, and bonds pay slightly higher interest rates than most banks and are backed by the full faith and credit of the U.S. Government. Treasury notes and bonds can be purchased directly from the U.S. Treasury under the Treasury Direct program (see savingsbonds.gov).

## Bonds

**bonds**

*Bonds* are debt securities issued by corporate or local (federal, state, municipal) government units. A bond is issued when the investor loans money to the issuer of the bond. The bond is essentially an IOU given by the issuer to the investor with a promise to pay a stated interest (coupon rate), and then repay the invested funds (principal) at a specified (maturity) date. Bonds enable the issuer to borrow money for extended periods and then repay it at fixed rates of interest to the bondholder. The credit quality of the bond issuer is very important to the investor. Various bond-rating agencies give their assessments of many bond offerings, which reflect the credit worthiness of the issuer and the issuer's ability to pay interest and repay principal at the bond's maturity.

**mortgage bonds**

**debenture bonds**

*Mortgage or Debenture Bonds.* There are two broad types of bonds: mortgage bonds and debentures. *Mortgage bonds* are secured by a mortgage on property owned by the issuer; *debenture bonds* are secured only by the credit of the issuing organization. Debentures issued by large, secure organizations carry lower risk (for example, all governmental bonds are debentures). Those issued by smaller organizations generally carry a higher risk element, and the bonds will have to pay higher coupon interest rates to attract investors. Some corporations issue low-quality debentures known as junk or high-yield bonds, which offer considerably higher interest rates than more secure bond offerings. However, the junk bonds involve greater risk, especially in difficult economic times.

Bonds are issued with varying maturities. Short-term bonds may mature in one to five years; medium-term bonds may have 5- to 20-year maturities, and long-term bonds usually mature in 20 years or more. Corporate bonds offer no special tax advantages at any level. Government bonds and municipal bonds do offer attractive tax advantages as described below. Many corporations issue various bonds to raise capital for operating expenses, expansion, and other functions. Subcategories of corporate bonds include the following:

- *bearer bond,* which is payable upon demand to anyone presenting it
- *callable bond,* which may be retired (or called) by the issuer before its scheduled maturity date
- *convertible bond,* which may be exchanged for the issuer's common stock at the holder's option
- *participating bond,* which provides a minimum coupon rate and may pay additional interest if corporate profits warrant
- *zero coupon bonds,* which are purchased at a deep discount from the bond's face value, pay no interest, and are redeemed at the bond's face value. This type is also known as a discount bond.

**U.S. Government bonds**

***U. S. Government Bonds.*** *U.S. Government bonds* are considered safe, reasonably attractive long-term investments. They are viewed as essentially risk-free, but government bonds normally yield slightly less interest than high-quality corporate bonds. The interest is taxable at the federal level and exempt from state and local taxes.

**municipal bonds**

***Municipal Bonds.*** States, cities, and counties, or their agencies (the municipal issuer) issue *municipal bonds*, or muni's, to raise funds. The most attractive feature of municipal bonds is that interest earnings are exempt from federal taxes. If the municipality is located in the same state as the owner, the interest may be exempt from state and local taxes, also. Municipal bond interest rates are normally less than corporate bonds; however, the tax-exempt status of municipal bonds makes their tax-equivalent yield (net yield after taxes) comparable to other bonds. The tax advantages of municipal bonds are more favorable for taxpayers in the highest tax brackets; corporate or government bonds are usually a better choice for lower income taxpayers.

## Stocks

**stocks**

Corporations can raise operating capital by selling ownership in themselves in the form of *stocks*. Investors who buy shares of stock are literally owners of the corporation, and may have voting rights and receive dividend payments. The number of shares available in a company is limited by company policy and by the demand from buyers. Some small or closely held corporations may only issue stock to a limited number of people such as family members or officers of the corporation.

Stocks of large public corporations are sold by brokers or dealers licensed to do business in one of several organized stock markets in the country—the largest of which is the New York Stock Exchange. The NASDAQ (National Association of Securities Dealers Automated Quotations) is the largest electronic screen-based securities trading market in the United States. There are also smaller, regional exchanges, such as the Philadelphia Stock Exchange, and larger foreign cities have exchanges. Many smaller stocks with little trading volume are available in the over-the-counter (OTC) market, through which brokers and dealers match people who want to sell with people who want to buy. The OTC is actually a communications network rather than an organized exchange; broker/dealers do business by telephone and computer. The typical transaction fees are higher for OTC trading than for trading on organized exchanges.

The Securities and Exchange Commission (SEC), an independent agency of the federal government, regulates most stock trading activities. Other organizations such as the Financial Regulatory Authority (FINRA) regulate the companies that buy and sell securities to the public.

Investors who buy stocks hope to make a profit by selling their shares for more than they paid. If the investor sells a stock at a profit, a capital gain is realized in the year the stock is sold. A major advantage of investing in individual stocks is that capital gains can be delayed until the stock is sold. This allows the investor to control much of the taxable income by choosing when to sell.

Many investors buy shares of stock to participate in potential dividends that the stock may distribute to shareholders. The corporation's board of directors must declare all dividends, and the dividends are never guaranteed. Nevertheless, many retirees depend on stock dividends for a substantial portion of their income.

Some stocks are highly speculative and others have historically been very stable; however, all stocks present some risk to the investor. To help you understand some of the complexities of stock investments, we will examine different kinds of stock and define some related terminology.

*Types of Stock.* There are two basic types of stock: common and preferred.

- *Common stock* provides the owner with residual ownership in the company that issued the shares. This means that if the company fails, common shareholders may claim all assets that remain after creditors have been paid.

- *Preferred stock* gives the owner first rights (over common stockholders) to any dividends issued by the corporation. However, preferred shareholders may not have voting privileges in corporate decision-making as do common shareholders, and the corporation usually retains the right to call (or repurchase) preferred stock at any time.

***Diversity of Purpose.*** There are five broad categories of common stocks available to investors. The differences in stocks provide diversity and flexibility as they range from relatively safe, long-term investments to highly speculative ones.

- *Blue chip stocks.* These are considered to be relatively safe, high-yield stocks. Blue chip stocks are stocks of corporations thought to be in excellent financial shape and leaders in their industries. Investors have confidence in the company's continued growth, and the stocks have consistently paid dividends to shareholders.
- *Growth stocks.* These are stocks from companies that are newer, more aggressive companies whose growth is expected to be higher than market averages or for other stocks within their market sector. Companies that issue growth stocks typically invest most of their earnings back into the company, so dividends are sporadic or nonexistent. The attractive feature to investors is the opportunity to enjoy a significant increase in the value of their stock.
- *Defensive stocks.* Quality companies that put stability over growth issue these stocks. Investors expect them to hold their value better in down markets than other stocks, especially growth stocks. Because they are conservative, they are not attractive to the aggressive investor, especially the active trader.
- *Cyclical stocks.* These stocks do well when business conditions are good, and poorly when conditions are bad. Frequently, companies that provide raw materials, such as chemicals or machinery, issue these stocks, which are sensitive to demand from companies that produce finished products. Cyclical stocks attract investors who hope to time their purchases with upswings in the economy and then sell at or near the peak. This is a relatively risky investment strategy.
- *Speculative stocks.* Investors who are looking for quick profits, and who can stand the risk, often look to speculative stocks. These are traded frequently in hopes of realizing short-term profits, with little

thought given to long-term growth potential or the safety of the investment.

*Marketing Stock.* Companies who wish to issue a new stock offering use specialized firms to manage the process. The first stock issued by a corporation is called an initial public offering (IPO). It is a complicated process, and we will look briefly at the major participants who make it possible for large numbers of people to purchase stock.

- *Investment bankers.* These firms or individuals specialize in new stock issues. A corporation wishing to go public with a stock issue will use an investment banker to buy the new stock and sell it as quickly as possible. In some cases, the investment banker acts as a dealer, buying an entire new issue and selling the stock for profit through its own sales organization. In other cases, the investment bank acts as a broker, using its sales apparatus to sell the stock on a commission basis. The investment bank may also underwrite the purchase, which means the investment bank commits to buying any shares it is unable to sell to others within a given period.
- *Brokers.* These firms or individuals act as go-betweens in the sale of stock to an investor. The broker never purchases the stock; instead, the broker administers the transaction and receives a fee or commission in return. Brokers receive commissions from both the sale and the purchase of stock.
- *Dealers.* These firms or individuals purchase securities from the issuing companies and then sell them to buyers at a profit. Dealers charge no commissions. Since they own the stock until they sell it, they hope to make a profit in the net sale price.

*Discount Brokerage.* Stockbrokers and dealers generally offer investment advice to investors as part of their service, and they are paid fees or commissions on the purchase or sale of stock. At one time, commissions for security sales were fixed. In 1975, the SEC ruled that fixed rates for stock transactions were no longer necessary. A relatively new form of securities marketing known as discount brokerage then emerged.

**discount brokers**

*Discount brokers* act as sales representatives only; they merely facilitate the purchase or sale of stock and offer no advice or other extras to the investor. Generally, people who use discount brokers are knowledgeable investors who can plan and execute their own investment strategies. In return for the no-frills treatment, discount brokers usually charge investors commissions much less than full-service brokers.

## Investment Companies and Mutual Funds

A mutual fund is an incorporated investment company whose business is to manage their investors' money. Millions of Americans now own mutual funds in their IRAs, employee-sponsored retirement plans, and other private accounts. Thousands of mutual funds today allow investors to participate in the stock and bond markets without having to invest large sums, or having to analyze, select, purchase, and manage multiple investments. Investors pool their funds as they buy shares, and the fund's managers make investment decisions about what to buy, how much to buy, when to buy, and when to sell securities. Individual investors benefit when the entire portfolio shows a gain, and they share any losses that occur. Because the typical mutual fund owns dozens, or even hundreds of stocks, spread across many sectors and industries, the small investors can easily diversify with just one or two mutual funds.

Investment companies register with the SEC and must provide a prospectus that describes their offering to potential investors. This information helps the investor decide which fund offers the investments that most closely meet his or her objectives. As there are different risks involved with buying stocks, mutual funds carry similar risks that reflect the securities held by the fund.

### *Types of Investment Funds*

***Balanced Funds.*** These funds balance their investments between common stocks, bonds, and cash holdings. They are generally conservative and relatively stable, and offer less potential growth than other types of funds. They are often a good investment choice for the conservative or older client who wants some growth but with reduced risk.

***Diversified Common Stock Funds.*** These funds maintain portfolios which contain only common stock. This makes the fund susceptible to systemic market risk; however, it may be appropriate for a younger or more aggressive investor who understands market risks, invests for the long term, and can accept the inevitable market declines that occur every few years.

***Income Funds.*** These funds invest in securities that generate higher-than-average current investment returns. These funds often invest in dividend-paying stocks, corporate bonds, government-backed mortgages, and preferred stock. They may be appropriate for a conservative investor who wants some growth but may need income for living expenses.

***High-yield Income Funds.*** These funds invest in high-yield (junk) bonds and stocks that pay the highest income available. These funds frequently purchase less familiar and riskier securities in search of high-yield returns. Hence, they are normally less secure than funds that purchase the securities of larger, more secure companies. Clients definitely must understand the risk involved in such funds, especially during a general downturn in the economy, as companies may default on paying interest and/or returning principal to bond holders.

***Preferred Stock or Bond Funds.*** These funds invest only in preferred stock and bonds. They may specialize in one particular type of issue such as utility stocks or very high-grade corporate bonds. The funds are conservative, and are appropriate for more risk-adverse clients who want income that normally exceeds savings account or CD returns. Remember, however, that the funds are not guaranteed and can lose money. Clients must understand their risks with such funds.

***Municipal Bond Funds.*** These funds invest only in municipal bonds offering federal tax exemptions. The tax advantage is passed to the investor. As with individual municipal bonds, these funds offer the most advantage to investors in the highest tax brackets.

***Money Market Funds.*** These funds invest the shareholder's money in Treasury bills and high-quality corporate debt instruments. Money market funds are high-yield, safe investments, generally paying more than similar bank savings accounts. Many money market funds are guaranteed by the FDIC up to published maximums (normally $100,000 per investor account per bank, but temporarily increased to $250,000 until December 2009). In addition, these funds provide a check-writing feature that makes them flexible, liquid, and popular with the public.

### Two Types of Regulated Investment Companies

There are different types of regulated investment companies, as defined by the Investment Company Act of 1940.

***Unit Investment Trusts (UIT) (closed-end investment companies).*** The UIT is a management company that invests in a fixed portfolio of selected securities and holds them for the duration of the trust. It is closed-ended because the portfolio is fixed when the UIT is formed and marketed. No additional trading of the securities inside the trust occurs. Some hold a diverse portfolio, while others invest in only one industry or sector, such as technology or medical equipment. Shares of the UIT are sold just as common stock through the exchanges, and some UITs pay interest on a periodic basis.

***Mutual Funds (open-end investment companies).*** *Mutual funds* are regulated investment companies that issue an unlimited number of shares on demand and redeem them upon request. The number of shares is open-ended, which gives the name to this investment vehicle. Shares in these funds represent ownership in the diversified securities portfolio. Some mutual funds companies sell directly to the public while others work through financial advisors and the firms which support them.

Mutual funds that deal directly with investors, rather than through an advisor, generally do not charge transaction fees to either purchase or sell the fund's shares. They are widely known as no-load funds. With these funds, however, the investor normally does not receive investment advice. When investors buy mutual funds through an advisor, they pay the net asset value of the fund on the day the sale is completed, plus a front-end load or sales charge. The sales charges vary by company, size of the investment, and type of mutual fund share. When shares are sold, the mutual fund generally redeems them with no redemption charges. Some mutual funds offer shares with no front-end loads but do apply a contingent deferred sales charge, or redemption fee. The redemption fee is commonly based on a sliding scale reducing from, say 6 percent to zero over a period of six years. A third class of mutual fund shares charges no front-end load and no contingent deferred sales charge; however, their internal management fees are normally one percent higher than with other shares.

There are many variations on the basic features associated with mutual funds. The advisor must thoroughly learn the important features of funds he or she offers, or those held by a prospect or client.

There are a number of advantages to investing in mutual funds.

- *Diversification.* Most mutual funds invest in a number of securities, spread across different industries and sectors. This diversification reduces overall investment risk and is difficult to achieve by the individual investor with limited assets.
- *Professional management.* Funds offer full-time professional investment research and management, which most investors cannot match. The investor with $1,000 in a mutual fund benefits from the same management expertise as an investor with $1,000,000 in the fund.
- *Liquidity.* All or part of the shareholder's investment may be redeemed on any business day. Some mutual fund companies will transfer the funds directly to the investor's bank account.
- *Convenience.* There is little individual administrative work for the owner of mutual funds. The management company tracks capital gains and dividends, provides statements and fund performance

information, and keeps shareholders informed about the tax status of dividends.

- *Dollar-cost averaging (DCA).* This investment technique takes advantage of fluctuations in the markets. With DCA, an investor - invests the same amount of dollars each period (monthly, quarterly, and so on), regardless of the share price at the time. When prices are relatively high, the invested dollars buy fewer shares. When prices are low, the dollars buy more shares. Over time, DCA results in the average cost per share being less than the average price per share. However, DCA does not insure against market losses. The DCA technique has proved to be very effective, especially for smaller investors who do not have large lump sums to invest.

- *Economies of scale.* Mutual funds are able to buy and sell large numbers of shares, unlike most individual investors who have limited purchasing abilities. This can result in lower transaction fees for the pool of investors in a mutual fund.

- *Attractive to small investors.* Mutual fund investors do not need a large amount of money to begin investments. Some funds can be started with a monthly investment of only $50 or $100. Investors do not have to be market experts to invest in mutual funds; however, they need to understand the risks of investing, and the recommended funds should match the investor's goals and risk tolerance.

## Real Estate

Because there is a limited supply of land, the value of real estate generally increases with time. A review of past real estate values shows that they track closely with the general rate of inflation in the U.S. While there are certainly exceptions and real estate bubbles occur, home values will generally rise at a rate close to the CPI over significant periods. As we have seen in recent years, a geographic area may experience a period of economic decline, which makes real estate difficult to sell, and prices fall with reduced demand. Other factors can cause real estate to lose value, including mismanagement or physical damage to buildings or land. The value of a property can fall due to changing traffic patterns or undesirable property nearby. Many property owners have made huge returns in real estate; however, there is always risk involved with ownership of any asset, including real estate.

There are several ways to invest in real estate. Most often, a buyer will purchase a property outright. Ownership of property is established through a deed, which is a legal document recorded with a local government office, that describes the property's location, dimensions, and owner.

Some advantages of investing in real estate are

- potential appreciation of the property's value
- income earnings from renting or leasing the property
- tax benefits from real estate ownership

Investors can make indirect investment in real estate through government and private investment programs.

- *Fannie Mae*—This stands for the Federal National Mortgage Association, which uses money from private investors to provide funds for buying FHA and VA mortgages. Investors may buy Fannie Mae shares, which pay dividends and may appreciate in value, or Fannie Mae bonds, which pay interest.
- *Ginnie Mae and Freddie Mac*—Ginnie Mae stands for the Government National Mortgage Association, and Freddie Mac for the Federal Home Loan Mortgage Association. Both offer bonds that make monthly payments of interest and principal. The monies from the sale of these bonds are used to fund FHA and VA loans.
- *Real Estate Syndicates*—Investors own shares of real estate syndicates, or organizations that buy property or mortgages on a large scale. Their advantages are similar to those offered by mutual funds.
- *Real Estate Investment Trusts (REITs)*—REITs are similar to closed-end investment companies. REITS deal in real estate and mortgages rather than stocks or other securities. REITs issue shares of ownership, which are traded like stocks on both the over-the-counter and organized exchanges.

## Tangible Assets

Many people own tangible assets that have potential for significant appreciation over time. Some investors buy tangible assets strictly for potential gain, while others value the asset itself and consider the appreciation of secondary importance.

**tangible assets**

*Tangible assets* include almost anything that has a value because the asset is considered valuable in the perception of others, or because the asset is used to produce other goods. As an investment, most tangible assets are highly speculative. Examples include the following:

- *Collectibles*—This includes many items, such as coins, stamps, artwork, antiques, baseball cards, Barbie dolls, and beer cans. Generally, these are sold privately or through dealers.

- *Precious metals and gems*—Gold and silver are traditionally the most popular metals for investors. Gold and silver prices are quoted daily in most newspapers; these metals can be purchased through some brokerage houses and dealers.
- *Commodities*—These include strategic metals such as chromium used in manufacturing. Other commodities are food items such as eggs, pork, sugar, or grains, and industrial inputs, such as wood, petroleum, natural gas, fibers, and steel.
- *Contract Futures*—Futures are contracts to buy or sell quantities of commodities at a fixed price in the future.

## Limited Partnership

**limited partnerships**

*Limited partnerships* are business ventures that attract investors who are willing to take some risk, but do not want to be actively involved in the venture. In other words, the investors want to be limited partners. A general partner is usually the promoter or sponsor of the organization; he or she manages the partnership and is fully liable for its debts. The limited partners (typically investors) have limited liability only to the extent of their investments. The limited partners contribute capital as passive investors, and the general partner provides management talent and assumes liability for the obligations of the partnership. A limited partnership agreement specifies all the rights and obligations of each type of partner. Limited partnerships are created to pursue a specific business objective and continue until the objective is reached.

Although limited partnerships may be high-risk investments, investors can spread the risk by making several smaller investments in more than one limited partnership operation. Some examples include the following:

- *Real estate limited partnerships.* These buy income-producing property, such as rental apartments, shopping centers, warehouses, office buildings, and historical buildings.
- *Oil and gas limited partnerships.* These operations may acquire existing oil and gas property, buy land near existing oil and gas property in hopes of appreciating values, or acquire the rights to exploratory drilling in undeveloped areas.
- *Equipment leasing limited partnerships.* These operations use the limited partners' money to buy assets such as industrial, manufacturing or transportation equipment, drilling rigs, trucks, and office equipment. The assets are then leased to businesses to provide an income stream to the general and limited partners.

## Comparing Investments

As this chapter has shown, there are many investments available to your clients, and advisors should understand how to compare them. Knowledge of the advantages and disadvantages of common investments will prepare you to provide the best possible advice to the public.

### *Rate of Return*

What is the real rate of return of an investment? What is the equivalent taxable yield on a municipal bond, compared to a currently taxable investment? You can compare the rate of return for a taxable CD and a tax-free municipal bond using the following simple calculation:

$$\text{Taxable Return} = \frac{\text{Tax-Free Return}}{(1 - \text{Marginal Tax Rate})}$$

For example, for a taxpayer in the 27 percent tax bracket, a taxable CD would have to earn 8.22 percent to match a tax-free municipal bond returning 6 percent. The calculation is:

$$\text{Taxable Return} = \frac{6.0\,\%}{(1 - 0.27)} = 8.22\%$$

### *Risk*

How much risk is involved? For example, buying individual common stocks may be riskier than buying a mutual fund, because the fund is diversified. Owning a mutual fund or a variable annuity is riskier than a CD or a fixed annuity. Any added risk in an investment should reflect a higher risk-adjusted rate of return: in other words, the greater the risk, the greater the return.

### *Liquidity*

**liquidity**

The term *liquidity* refers to how easily the investor can liquidate an investment to use the money for other purposes? Investments with surrender penalties, or those such as real estate which may be difficult to sell, are considered illiquid to some degree. If an investment is illiquid, the investor should expect a higher return than returns from a more liquid investment with similar risk. For example, a CD that charges a penalty for early surrender is not as liquid as a savings account with unrestricted withdrawals. Compared to a savings account, an investor should expect higher returns from the CD.

One lesson many advisors have learned from the economic downtown in recent years is that liquidity is very important. Some advisors now recommend that clients keep two or even three years of cash equivalents to help them get through difficult times. If clients have good liquidity, they may be more willing to invest in equities for longer-term growth.

In summary, most of your prospects and clients have to make difficult choices about allocating their insurance and investment dollars. If you understand your clients' needs, attitudes, and available options, you can recommend appropriate products and programs to accomplish their objectives.

## CASE HISTORY: AN ETHNIC ENTRÉE

*Advisor.* Sam Fleming has been in the insurance business for several years. Sam has been a leading advisor in his agency.

*The Beginning.* Across from my office there is a small coffee shop where the advisors often go for lunch. The same friendly Asian lady is always there in charge no matter when we go in. It had never occurred to me to approach the owner of this small shop. I thought that Chang Cho, a Korean advisor in our agency, would have already talked to her.

*Prospect's Background.* One Saturday I went in to get a cup of coffee. I started talking to the lady, whom by now I had come to know as Mrs. Pham. It turned out she came to this country as a refugee from Vietnam. In Vietnam she was from a well-to-do family, and when her husband and eight young children came to this country, her husband had a difficult time adjusting to the working class.

Mrs. Pham proudly told me that she babysat, cleaned houses, and worked 14 hours a day, seven days a week for eight years to save enough money to buy this coffee shop. Her children are all on their way to becoming successful professionals. There was a dentist, two computer programmers, a CPA, one was in business school, three were at the state university, and one was in high school. They all worked weekends and evenings in the coffee shop during high school and college. Mrs. Pham still does not take a day off, but she has built up quite a nest egg for her and her husband's retirement years.

Fascinated, I asked her how she saves her money. She said that one-third goes to help other Vietnamese refugees get started, one-third is for her living expenses and her children's education, and the rest goes into expanding her business and for emergencies. I later learned that this money was kept in cash at Mrs. Pham's house.

*Approach.* I asked her if she had any insurance. "Sure, on my shop and my car," she answered. She had no life insurance, no health insurance, and no disability income insurance, yet her entire family depended on the good health and energy of this lady. I asked her if anyone had ever talked to her about insurance. "Yes," she said. "A man from Vietnam, in fact. But he was from a different ethnic group and I didn't trust him."

I asked Mrs. Pham if I could meet with her to discuss different insurance plans. She quickly agreed, but said she wanted me to meet first with her and her daughter, who is a CPA, at the shop. Then Mrs. Pham would talk with her husband.

***The CPA's Questions.*** Mrs. Pham's daughter, Lanh, readily agreed that her parents needed major medical insurance on themselves and for the youngest brother still in high school. She agreed her family had been lucky that they had never had a major health problem before.

As we discussed life insurance, Lanh asked me many questions about my company, its past performance, and how long it had been in business. She also asked me how long I had been an advisor. Indirectly, she politely asked if I would be around if her mother had questions after she bought a policy.

***Advisor's Doubts.*** I wasn't sure how the interview was going. There was a lot of conversation in Vietnamese between Mrs. Pham and Lanh. I had never been asked these types of questions before, and, apparently, I still needed to meet with Mrs. Pham's husband. It was very difficult for me to decide who would make the decisions. All the signals were different from my usual sales calls.

When I left the meeting, I wasn't sure of anything except that I was to call Mrs. Pham after 10 the next night. I would then find out when I could meet with Mr. Pham about the health insurance.

***Meetings.*** Over the next few weeks, I met with various members of the Pham family at unusual times. One Sunday afternoon, Mrs. Pham asked me to go to her oldest son's house. It turned out to be a one-month celebration for Mrs. Pham's new grandson. Afterwards, Mrs. Pham and her husband bought life insurance policies from me. Then they encouraged me to talk with their son, Dr. Pham, the father of the Pham's only grandchild.

I was surprised that Dr. Pham also had no insurance. Yet I found him very receptive to disability income insurance, life insurance, and group health insurance for himself and the small office staff in his dental practice. Mrs. Pham and her husband had set the stage for these sales to their son.

***The Payoff.*** My patience and good service paid off. Mrs. Pham has referred several of her friends to me. Lanh, the CPA, helps many Vietnamese professionals prepare their taxes. She has referred several of her Vietnamese clients to me.

I am regularly invited to Vietnamese celebrations now. I have tried to learn about Vietnamese customs and history so when I'm invited to a Vietnamese New Year celebration, or wedding, I can understand a little bit of what's going on and feel more comfortable.

My Vietnamese clients ask me for service that has never been asked of me before. For instance, last year the father of one of my Vietnamese clients died. The family wanted to have a traditional Vietnamese funeral, but didn't know how to do that in this country. The family asked me to go to the funeral director and help with arrangements for the funeral.

I am considered a trusted friend now when only two years ago, I assumed all Asians in town bought their insurance only from another Asian advisor.

## CHAPTER FIVE REVIEW

*Key terms and concepts are explained in the Glossary. Answers to the review and self-test questions are found in the back of the textbook in the Answers to Questions section.*

### Key Terms and Concepts

| | |
|---|---|
| cost of waiting | exclusion ratio |
| time value of money | fixed annuity |
| current retirement gap | variable annuity |
| tax-qualified | equity-indexed annuity |
| pension plan | NOW accounts |
| profit-sharing plan | certificates of deposit (CD) |
| 403(b) plan | bonds |
| Individual Retirement Account (IRA) | mortgage bonds |
| | debenture bonds |
| Traditional IRA | U.S. government bonds |
| Roth IRA | municipal bonds |
| spousal IRA | stocks |
| annuity | discount brokers |
| annuitant | mutual funds |
| annuity owner | tangible assets |
| accumulation phase | limited partnerships |
| payout or annuity phase | liquidity |

### Review Questions

5-1.   Name the general sources of retirement income available to your clients.

5-2.   Outline the Current Retirement Gap formula.

5-3.   Explain the term *tax qualified* and the associated tax advantages. Then briefly outline types of tax-qualified and tax-advantaged retirement plans.

5-4.   Compare a Traditional IRA and a Roth IRA.

5-5.   What kinds of benefits could life insurance provide during the retirement years?

5-6.   Briefly outline how an annuity works and describe the different types of annuities.

5-7.   Briefly describe the following investments: NOW accounts, stocks, bonds, mutual funds, variable annuities, and REITs.

## Self-test Questions

*Instructions: Read Chapter 5 and then answer the following questions to test your knowledge. There are 10 questions. Choose one answer for each question, and then check your answers with the answer key in the back of the textbook.*

5-1.   A bond that is purchased at a discount, pays no interest, and matures at its face amount is called a

    (A)   bearer bond
    (B)   callable bond
    (C)   convertible bond
    (D)   zero coupon bond

5-2.   A stock mutual fund is an investment vehicle that provides which set of advantages:

    (A)   professional management, diversification, short-term investment vehicle
    (B)   diversification, dollar-cost averaging, short-term investment vehicle
    (C)   professional management, diversification, dollar-cost averaging
    (D)   diversification, short-term investment vehicle, liquidity

5-3.   Changing the retirement triangle into the retirement rectangle results from the addition of which of the following incomes?

    (A)   Social Security
    (B)   employer-provided benefits
    (C)   investment savings and investment plans
    (D)   continued employment during retirement

5-4.  Which retirement vehicle is always funded with after-tax dollars?

(A)   Traditional IRA
(B)   Roth IRA
(C)   Variable Annuity
(D)   Spousal IRA

5-5.  Which of the following statements about the current retirement gap is (are) correct?

I.    The current expenses calculation should not include such items as planned vacations, vehicle purchases, and planned gifts.
II.   Current resources should include estimated Social Security and employer-sponsored retirement benefits.

(A)   I only
(B)   II only
(C)   Both I and II
(D)   Neither I nor II

5-6.  Which of the following statements concerning annuities is (are) correct?

I.    An annuity can provide guaranteed lifetime income to the annuitant.
II.   Annuities may impose surrender charges in the first few years of the contract.

(A)   I only
(B)   II only
(C)   Both I and II
(D)   Neither I nor II

5-7.  Which of the following sources of retirement income are examples of the money at work category?

     I.    government programs, such as the Social Security and federal retirement systems

    II.   personal savings, investments, and life insurance

(A)   I only
(B)   II only
(C)   Both I and II
(D)   Neither I nor II

5-8.  All of the following statements concerning annuities are correct EXCEPT

(A)   A major advantage of annuities is tax-deferred growth of assets.
(B)   Indexed annuities provide direct investments into mutual funds.
(C)   Advisors must have a securities registration with FINRA to sell variable annuities.
(D)   Annuities may be purchased with a single payment, or premium.

5-9.  All of the following statements about investments are correct EXCEPT

(A)   Tangible assets include such items as artwork, precious metals, and gems.
(B)   Investors who buy limited partnerships are generally responsible for all debts of the partnership.
(C)   Municipal bonds are of greatest benefit to taxpayers in the highest tax brackets.
(D)   Mutual funds may decrease overall investment risk by diversifying assets.

5-10.  To qualify for tax-deferred status, tax-qualified retirement plans must do all of the following EXCEPT

(A)   be nondiscriminatory
(B)   meet minimum vesting requirements
(C)   meet minimum participation and coverage requirements
(D)   invest at least 10 percent of assets in company stock

# 6

# *Mature Adults, Medicare, and Long-Term Care*

---

## Learning Objectives

*An understanding of the material in this chapter should enable you to*

---

6-1.  Describe the common characteristics and needs of the mature adult segment.

6-2.  Explain the coverages of Part A, B, C, and D of Medicare.

6-3.  Identify the coverage gaps that Medicare supplement (medigap) policies can insure.

6-4.  Explain what a long-term care policy covers and how it works.

---

This chapter focuses on the mature adult and the needs and insurance products appropriate to this life-cycle segment, including a discussion of Medicare, Medicare supplements, and long-term care insurance.

## LIFE CYCLE: MATURE ADULTS

**mature-adult market segment**

In this section, we will examine some of the common characteristics and needs of the *mature-adult market segment*. For our purposes, we have chosen to describe the mature adult segment as those people ages 59 to 75, the age range during which retirement begins for most Americans. More and more people are reaching this age. The number of retired people in the United States over age 65 is now nearly 40 million people and continues to grow (see the chart below). It is a market with considerable needs and the means to meet those needs.

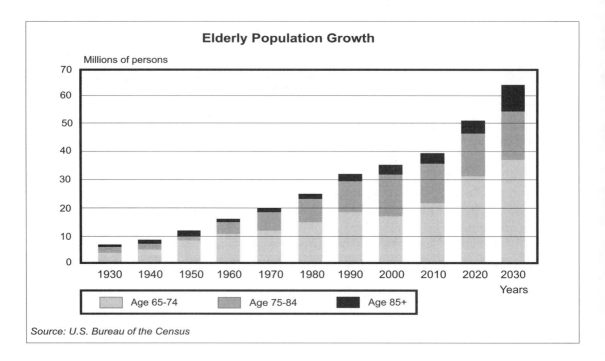

**Elderly Population Growth**

Source: U.S. Bureau of the Census

## Common Characteristics

As we discuss common characteristics, remember that each prospect is an individual, and his or her situation and needs will not be exactly as described. There are great variations in the circumstances we face as we age and in the different ways that we react to and face these circumstances. Describing the average retiree, even if it could be done, would not produce very useful information. They are single, married, and widowed; they have children and do not have children. They are healthy and unhealthy, wealthy and poor, happy and miserable, active and sedentary, sophisticated and naïve. While one mature adult is gearing up to start a new business, another may be taking early retirement. These examples reflect the conflict of market segmentation—the desire to categorize consumers into groups to make marketing manageable and efficient and the realization that no two people are exactly the same because of personal history, genetic inheritance, maturity, and other factors. We want to predict behavior based on a group's similarities, yet we also want to recognize the uniqueness and individuality of our client relationships.

Nevertheless, here are some typical things we expect to see in the mature adult (seniors) segment. These are generalities, but generalities can have value when they express verifiable central themes.

### *Attitudes about Finances*

The principal attitude for the mature market is a desire for safety and security. Primarily they want to preserve the fruits of their labor for their retirement years, which paradoxically requires some amount of market risk to combat the eroding effect that inflation can have on their assets. Correct perception of risk for this segment involves the diminishing time horizon to recover from any financial setbacks, and the necessity to preserve what one has, as it is more difficult to regenerate assets or income at this life stage.

Early in this stage of the life cycle, many will still be concerned with accumulating assets for a future retirement. As they retire, they are apprehensive about spending down their assets. In either situation, they are worried about outliving their resources. What if they misjudge and spend all of their money before they die?

The fear of outliving their financial resources ties in directly with their desire to remain independent. The last thing they want to do is to burden their children financially or otherwise. Older mature adults take great pride in their ability to remain independent and active.

### *Concerns about Healthcare*

For obvious reasons, mature adults are much more sensitive to healthcare issues, especially those related to Medicare and long-term care. They understand the frailties of aging and the need for medical care associated with them, and they are concerned about the affordability of such care if needed.

### *Having More Time*

The primary goal of retirement for most people is to have more time to do things not possible during the child-rearing and working years. Mature adults have time to take trips to exotic places, get involved in community or non-profit organizations, pursue hobbies and interests, and learn new things. They have more time during the day to meet with you, unlike your younger clients or prospects.

### *Being Deliberate*

Mature market clients tend to be more deliberate. This has to do with all of the previously mentioned traits. They have more time, and they are concerned about safety and reduced risk. For these reasons, it may take them longer to make a decision, and their buying cycle may be extended. The key to success in marketing financial products to them is patience and maintaining a low-pressure consultative sales demeanor.

### Anticipating or Entering Retirement

Retirement is something many look forward to with great anticipation. To others, it is something to dread. A major factor in this difference in attitude is the financial preparation made before reaching retirement. Too many people have not given any thought to the amount of money they will need to live on for the rest of their lives.

The lack of planning is compounded by other issues. For example, many people are faced with a number of financial problems that have sidetracked their ability to realize their dreams. These financial problems can arise because people are

- opting for longer mortgages: taking a 30-year or 40-year mortgage over a 15-year or 20-year mortgage
- turning to home equity loans to cover debts
- delaying having children, which pushes the expensive years of child rearing into later life, with college costs coming when people traditionally could save for retirement
- getting divorced more frequently
- living longer, creating the need to fund a longer retirement period
- forgetting to account for inflation

In many cases, these changes have considerable negative impact on retirement income in the later stages of retirement.

Another change is the flexibility in retirement age. In the past, age 65 was considered the universal age of retirement. Now retirement can occur anytime after age 55. However, according to the Bureau of Labor Statistics, the majority of people retire between the ages of 62 and 65. This might be somewhat misleading because many continue to work part-time. A Social Security Administration publication reports that 28 percent of retirees over age 65 receive income from earnings. Many experts feel that this trend toward part-time and even full-time work after the age of 65 will continue, especially as the baby boomers retire. Some will work because they need to work due to longer life expectancies, increased income needs during retirement, or inadequate retirement planning, while others will work because they enjoy remaining active.

### Experiencing Other Life Events

Though not as common among all mature adults, there are some other situations creating new financial and insurance needs. These situations were not as common a generation ago. Here are some examples:

- supporting children returning back to the home due to divorce, unemployment, death, or other needs
- supporting grandchildren in the role of a legal guardian or because of returning children
- raising young children of their own due to late marriages to a younger spouse
- seeking further education due to a career change

### *Redefining Retirement*

Demographic, economic, and societal trends are driving a fundamental shift in the way Americans view retirement. Many retirees will ask themselves, "Is life only about putting the numbers together, or is there more?" The real question being raised by clients is not just, "Will my money be there?" There are also soul-searching questions such as, "How will I spend my time?" "What do I really like to do?" "What will keep me motivated?" "How will my family and I react to my no longer having a job?"

Four factors are shaping this new retirement in the following ways:

- Future retirees will experience a long and active period of retirement.
- Employers expect employees to be more self-reliant in preparing for retirement.
- A growing number of retirees are engaged in postretirement employment.
- Non-financial issues affect quality of life in retirement.

***Longer and More Active Retirement.*** Americans are living longer and today's retirees are generally healthier and more active than those of their parents' generation. Current retirees have greater interest than previous generations in having an active lifestyle that includes postretirement employment. In addition, those looking ahead to retirement, especially baby boomers, are even more likely to view retirement as an opportunity to start a new phase of life with new activities.

In America, a baby boomer will turn 50 every seven to ten seconds. That's more than 12,000 every day and over four million each year for the next decade. Many marketers are not ready to deal with this new class of consumers who have more money to spend than their parents did.

Boomers and older consumers today are affluent. Boomer and older consumers combined are the largest economic group in America. They will continue to set trends for the rest of the population. This is an educated cohort that wants value for their dollar. Those who want to be successful marketing to this group should recognize its need for value.

Another consequence of the aging of America is that marketing, dominated in the past by views, values, and behavior of people under the age of 40, is becoming oriented to those over age 40. Although many boomers hate the idea of aging, as the baby boomers were associated with ushering in youth culture, people generally adjust well to aging. However, be careful what you call them. Terms like elder, mature adult, or senior citizen may turn them off rather than make them feel like you are treating them with respect. Many older people do not like being labeled. They don't generally consider themselves mature, as in old. Don't be surprised to see some of them hop on their motorcycles for a road trip. Many are very active, traveling and trying adventurous activities not previously associated with the older adult.

Developmental changes bring the mature adult toward Maslow's self-actualization concept: a more autonomous, experienced mind, understanding life and reality as shades of gray rather than absolute black and white. Mature people are more relationship minded than their younger counterparts, and respond quite favorably to companies and marketers who see them as whole people, and not merely as prospects for a product or service. This fits well with a client-focused or relationship marketing approach in which customers are not the targets of sales tactics, but humans to be served by a consultative planning process. Marketing is not a game of persuasion but a service-oriented endeavor, and the focus is not on products, but on a positive customer experience.

***Greater Employee Responsibility for Retirement Security.*** Another factor driving new retirement thinking is the fact that employers are increasingly shifting responsibility for a financially secure retirement to their employees. Employees are getting the message that they must take a proactive role in making investment decisions and managing retirement accounts. Yet few have the skills or the knowledge to handle this task. With the shift in employer-type retirement plans from the defined-benefit type to the more employee risk-oriented defined-contribution type, such as 401(k) plans, employees should be advised to contribute to these plans early in their careers and on a consistent basis.

Mature adults should view retirement preparation in the context of the total financial plan—a blueprint for achieving short-, medium-, and long-term goals. These goals should be considered as parts of the whole retirement plan, and be based on a vision for the future that encompasses all areas of life, clarifies a personal vision for the future and, motivates each person to engage in the money management and financial planning activities that will make that vision a reality.

***Postretirement Employment.*** According to a recent AARP survey, 70 percent of workers older than age 45 said they wanted to work during retirement, but in a more flexible framework. This research indicates that boomers want to be more active than the traditional concept of retirement has to offer. They desire a phased-in retirement consisting of more choices regarding employment. Career management therefore should be considered as a process that extends well into the postretirement years. Retirement is increasingly being viewed as a life period with many models that individuals choose and self-define rather than as a single event. [1]

***Retirement Affected by Non-financial Issues.*** A person's retirement experience is affected by factors such as role and relationship changes, time management issues, and a sense of meaning and purpose. These factors can have a profound effect on a retiree's quality of life. Retirement planning today should consider a life management approach that focuses on issues such as health maintenance, enhanced nutrition, developing outside interests, volunteering, stress management, and cultivating positive attitudes.

Individuals who believe they have the power to shape their own lives are more likely to actively seek out new activities and embrace changing roles after retirement. Successful retirees increase their sense of control over the direction their lives are taking and have confidence in their ability to respond to change, to overcome challenges, and to take advantage of opportunities—key elements of successful transitions in every stage of life.

## Common Needs

There are four primary concerns of mature adult prospects and clients:

- financing health care
- increasing retirement income
- reducing taxes
- facilitating estate planning objectives

### Financing Health Care

Seniors are extremely concerned about

- handling the costs of major illnesses
- financing home health care and long-term care facility expenses

This discussion will look at benefits offered by Medicare and the role of private insurance to supplement Medicare. We will also review private long-term care insurance (LTCI). We will discuss the types of LTCI policies available in the marketplace, and why LTCI may be the only way many seniors will be able to stay at home, which is where most wish to receive care as they enter old age.

The increased cost of medical care has created a need for our products. Medicare supplement policies offer seniors a way to fill in the gaps in the system's benefits. LTCI policies offer seniors a method of dealing with the health care costs for chronic conditions that could easily cost $70,000 or $80,000 a year.

The health care needs facing older Americans provide financial advisors with an opportunity to serve their community while growing professionally. Many seniors do not fully understand the risks they face. They know that health care costs are rising and that Medicare has some limitations. They realize that a serious illness can wipe out their life savings. Their problem is that they are unsure of how to manage these risks. Should they simply save more? Should they delay enjoying life in order to set aside extra dollars for potential health care costs? Are there any other ways to handle these problems? Financial advisors who can help seniors find the answers to these questions will prosper as they offer them needed expertise and guidance. The insurance industry has developed products, such as Medicare supplement (medigap) insurance and LTCI that address seniors' health care concerns.

*Medicare Supplement (Medigap) Insurance.* Medicare has coverage gaps. Medicare beneficiaries must pay specified deductibles and copayments. Eyeglasses, hearing aids, and many routine visits to physicians must be paid out-of-pocket. Many seniors can more easily budget these expenses through the purchase of insurance products.

Medicare supplements fill many of the coverage gaps left by Medicare. This type of insurance is highly regulated. There are 12 basic policy variations, referred to as "A" through "L." "A" is the basic only coverage. Added features are available as we move through the alphabet. Marketing medigap insurance is one way to reach the seniors market, and it is likely to remain a viable entry point into that marketplace for the near future.

*Long-Term Care Insurance.* Medigap does not take care of the Medicare nursing home void. As mature adults live longer, the chance of institutionalization increases. The costs of nursing home care are substantial, and often exceed $175 per day. Even affluent seniors find that nursing home stays—typically 2½ years—can deplete their estates.

There often is not enough money to pay for nursing home coverage and still maintain a healthy spouse's standard of living. Single individuals find that retirement income that was sufficient to meet everyday living costs is insufficient to handle the added costs of long-term care (LTC). Assets accumulated during a lifetime of hard work may be quickly spent.

LTCI is one way to avoid these tragedies. This product is designed to pay for LTC facility costs. It is also designed to help your senior clients stay out of nursing homes by offering them home health care benefits. Many seniors who are reluctant to discuss how they will pay for LTC are far more amenable to discussions about ways they can remain at home. As the population ages and government cutbacks become more widespread, more and more seniors will seek your expertise regarding privately funded LTCI.

For prospects and clients in the early years of the mature adult market segment, another sales opportunity for LTCI would be a discussion about LTC coverage for their elderly parents. A more detailed discussion of LTCI occurs later in this chapter.

### *Increasing Retirement Income*

Most individuals are interested in increasing their disposable income, and mature adults are no different. Where seniors differ is in their sources of income. Prospects in the seniors market may or may not be working. What your prospects will typically have in common is a pool of accumulated assets representing a lifetime of savings from working.

There is a variety of privately owned financial products available to assist mature adults augment their retirement income. Among the financial products and concepts that you may be able to offer to clients and advise them about are

- annuities
- mutual funds
- life insurance
- reverse mortgages.

***Annuities.*** The changed workplace creates substantial marketplace needs for senior adults. They can no longer depend solely on employers and Social Security benefits for their retirement income. Annuities offer privately funded alternatives. Younger seniors are finding that many employers no longer offer generous defined-benefit pension plans that continue payments for life. Instead, many younger seniors are retiring with pensions based on accumulations in defined-contribution plans that they may outlive. Many of these individuals are starting to look for guaranteed benefits that earlier generations enjoyed. At the same time, older seniors are finding that taxes are eating up a greater share of their incomes, and that reliable, additional fixed sources of funds are needed to cover recurring expenses.

Annuities are financial products that seniors can use to meet these additional income needs. Because they can provide a source of guaranteed income that cannot be outlived, immediate annuities have a key role in maximizing retirement income. Deferred annuities can also offer guaranteed preservation of principal, or they can be designed to participate in the growth of the equity markets, depending on the individual senior's need.

As more mature adults realize the risks of the financial marketplace and are not misled by the illusion of lower taxes, financial advisors can expect to see increased utilization of annuities in estate planning.

***Mutual Funds.*** Mutual funds also play a role in the retirement income equation. Longer life expectancies have changed seniors' traditional cash equivalent allocation. Today, seniors need to consider anticipated portfolio growth long after they have retired to be sure they do not outlive their assets. Many of you who market mutual fund products will find prospects in the senior marketplace with substantial assets to invest.

***Life Insurance.*** As more mature adults face uncertain retirement incomes, life insurance will increasingly be needed to provide for their survivors. For example, life insurance death benefits can provide an income stream to supplement Social Security retirement benefit payments. Life insurance can also be used to replace income lost at the death of a working spouse or replace pension payments. Like annuities, life insurance can serve as a way to increase personal capital without paying added income taxes. Furthermore, accumulated life insurance cash values can supplement an insured's other accumulated sources of retirement income.

***Securing Loans to Children.*** If elderly parents or other relatives provide funds, either with a loan or an outright gift, to adult children for a down payment to buy a house, it may create a change in the financial planning considerations of your clients. You need to be aware of these changes in circumstances, especially in loan situations. You can customize coverage for the young borrower for life insurance and disability income insurance to protect your senior client or prospect from these risks. Prospects who will not otherwise consider purchasing life insurance beyond basic family protection may well consider additional coverage for collateral or financial security purposes.

***Reverse Mortgages.*** Many seniors are land rich and cash poor. Reverse mortgages offer a way to turn a home into an income source while letting the senior client stay in place. Rather than making monthly mortgage payments, an owner receives income from a lender drawing on the untapped equity in the home. Terms and options vary, depending on the owner's age, marital status, and selected lender. The reverse mortgage income stream or line of credit can then be used as a source of funds for a variety of expenses. Unfortunately, there have been abuses in the use of reverse mortgages. The Financial Industry Regulatory Authority (FINRA) warns: "Be skeptical of reverse mortgages as part of an investment strategy: If someone urges you to obtain a reverse mortgage to make an investment or purchase an insurance product or a security, such as a deferred annuity, be very skeptical, particularly if they are promising high returns." Advisors must know and abide by their company's rules on the use of reverse mortgages and products purchased with the proceeds.

***Retirement Planning.*** In the mature market, people fall into one of three categories: those who are still saving for retirement, those who are about to begin retirement, and those who have retired. In all cases, financial and insurance advice is needed. As you look at retirement for your clients and prospects, several distinct opportunities become obvious.

- There are clients and prospects that fall into the Prime of Life (ages 50 to 60) category. Their income is peaking. They have time to make and implement plans to accumulate further retirement resources. They can arrange their current savings and investment programs to meet their objectives.
- There are clients and prospects on the verge of retiring. This group can be counseled on how to best employ their current resources to maximize retirement income opportunities.
- There are clients and prospects who are retired. Many retirees could benefit from your advice. They may have untapped additional income sources not yet considered.

During this time, income needs are very likely to increase because of increasing health and recreational expenses, inflationary increases, and concerns about leaving an estate. In fact, increasing numbers of potential retirees are opting to plan for no decrease in income from working years to retirement years. They feel they will need the same cash flow.

You may want to assist prospects in assessing their current situations. Here are some important steps to take as you and your clients study the current situation:

- Help them prepare a net worth statement showing their assets and liabilities.
- Help them prepare a current and projected budget.
- Look at their family cash flow.
- Establish what their short-term major expenses are likely to be by retirement, such as purchasing a new car, finish paying for higher education for children or even for the future retiree and spouse, making major repairs to the home, or purchasing a postretirement vacation home.
- Determine how much they are capable of saving and what percentage they are currently saving.

- Review life and health insurance programs, and gather all available details regarding employee benefit programs.

Determine additional facts affecting their retirement planning. Consider if there might be other family members for whom the future retiree will have financial obligations. This may include aging parents, disabled siblings, or children with special needs.

### *Reducing Taxes*

Tax planning is another major financial concern for mature adults. Conventional wisdom holds that individuals pay less in taxes once they are retired. This conventional wisdom will not apply to many of your prospects in today's marketplace.

Retirees' paychecks may have been replaced by generous pension checks. Mortgages may have been replaced by huge amounts of equity in highly appreciated housing. However, once income tax deductions for mortgage interest and exemptions for children are no longer available, many seniors find that they are paying taxes at higher, not lower, rates than in earlier years.

Financial advisors have products that can help seniors to reduce taxes. Lower income taxes can be translated into found premium dollars. Remember, there are individual retirement accounts and other ways seniors can save on income taxes. Keep in mind estate tax reduction techniques as well.

Annuities and life insurance can offer substantial tax benefits. For example, deferred annuities can give seniors a way to shelter interest from current taxation. In some instances, deferred annuities can be used to lower the income taxes seniors pay on Social Security benefits. Life insurance can also offer substantial tax benefits. Current tax law allows for the tax-free accumulation of cash values, along with very generous borrowing terms. Furthermore, the receipt of an income-tax-free sum at the death of a spouse is a welcome resource that can be used to handle unexpected living costs and to replace the deceased spouse's lost pension benefits.

We will also look at the opportunity that long-term care insurance presents to take advantage of a tax deduction. More important, we will consider long-term care insurance as a vehicle to preserve an individual's assets to help create an estate for future generations.

### *Facilitating Estate Planning Objectives*

Throughout this textbook are a variety of tools that prospects can use to meet both lifetime and death-time objectives. Lowering estate taxes and estate settlement costs are traditional planning goals for seniors. It has focused on the disposition of assets at death. Unfortunately, traditional estate planning has often ignored the impact of LTC. Too often, individuals become incapacitated without having formalized plans for health care or asset management. The unfortunate results have been smaller estates with sometimes little or nothing left for heirs.

This situation has created a need for estate planning focused on today's increased longevity, chronic care needs, and the desire to fund the dreams of future generations. Although prospects may have accepted the inevitability of death, you will find that many are still unprepared when it comes to the possibility of becoming physically disabled or mentally incapacitated. As a financial advisor, your access to life insurance, annuity, and LTCI products—combined with appropriate legal tools and your senior clients' financial assets—can make their goals a reality.

---

**Shortcomings of Traditional Estate Planning**

Failure to consider

- increased longevity
- physical disability
- mental incapacity
- increased health care costs
- income replacement for dependents with special needs
- quality of life for elderly
- competition for limited government dollars
- hidden estate settlement costs

---

Legal experts state that a will alone is no longer sufficient for many seniors. Seniors need to consider the use of a will in conjunction with other legal tools, all drafted by an attorney, to facilitate their planning objectives. We will briefly review will clauses, trusts, powers of attorney, and health care proxies to formulate a comprehensive plan aimed at both lifetime and death-time planning.

Financial products dovetail with many of the legal tools and techniques that mature adults are likely to employ. For example, a living trust is just a hollow document unless it has assets to carry out a client's plans regarding lifetime care and death-time asset disposition. Here you may recommend disability income insurance for some clients and long-term care insurance for others. Once again, annuities and life insurance can play a role in bringing plans to completion by making sure dollars are there when needed.

The role of life insurance as a planning vehicle should not be overlooked just because a prospect or client has gray hair. Mature adults often continue to need life insurance in today's economic environment. For many, life insurance represents the best way to provide a sizable inheritance to future generations. In effect, the costs of this inheritance can be budgeted as planning is implemented to bypass the estate and gift tax bite.

Higher-net-worth clients may need to do some sophisticated estate planning. Under current estate tax law, the exemption equivalent amount is $3.5 million in 2009. With the new presidential administration, changes to the existing estate tax rules are expected.

***Income Replacement for Dependents with Special Needs.*** Like elderly parents, children with physical or mental limitations that require special consideration are a major and expensive concern. Providing necessary care for a special-needs dependent can be enormously stressful emotionally and financially. While doing the best that can be done, advisors should warn caregivers not to sacrifice their own health and financial security.

Concerned parents of a dependent with special needs often have a strong desire to see these expenses taken care of on a long-term and guaranteed basis. However, after their deaths, the funds available from government benefits for special-needs individuals may not be sufficient or even available to provide a high level of service and care. With proper planning, you can help ensure these expenses will be adequately discharged regardless of what happens to the provider of support. Various trust, beneficiary, and settlement arrangements are all considerations that should be explored with these clients, as well as the need for adequate life and disability insurance to assure funds for special needs dependents.

## Summary

The mature adult segment has many common needs and characteristics. Because of the universality of retirement income and healthcare needs, this phase of the life cycle is the most homogeneous. Many of their characteristics are a direct result of these two dominant needs. The need for the inevitable retirement income focuses a prospect on finding ways to preserve capital and protect it from inflation. It causes concerns over outliving resources. The increased need for healthcare causes prospects to value independence and activity more. They realize the possibility of becoming a burden to loved ones.

Because of the ramifications of misjudgment, the mature adults facing these decisions will want to make sure they understand the issues more thoroughly. They will be open to education and advice—two things you can provide.

# MEDICARE AND MEDICARE SUPPLEMENTS

**Medicare**

*Medicare* is a federally sponsored health insurance program primarily for people who are age 65 and older. It is administered by the Centers for Medicare and Medicaid Services of the Department of Health and Human Services, and enrollments are handled by the Social Security Administration. For many Americans, it is the only health insurance they have after retirement.

This is a time when many may find their incomes declining while their health needs increase. Without Medicare, the spiraling increase of health care costs would put even the most basic levels of medical care out of reach for many people. Medical care costs can destroy the modest life savings that retirees have worked so hard to accumulate. For these individuals, a viable alternative is Medicare supplemental insurance, which is designed to fill the gaps that exist in the Medicare program. In this section, we will look at Medicare, what it provides, what it does not cover, and the different forms of Medicare supplements that are available.

| **Social Security and Medicare Taxes** An employee and an employer pay a total tax rate of 7.65 percent each: | | |
|---|---|---|
| | OASDI—Old Age Survivors and Disability Insurance (Social Security) | HI—Hospital Insurance (Medicare) |
| Employee | 6.2% | 1.45% |
| Employer | 6.2% | 1.45% |

## Overview of The Current Medicare Program

The Medicare program continually evolves. Hardly a year goes by without some changes. In some years, these changes are minor. In other years, the changes have a major effect on Medicare beneficiaries (recipients) and the providers of medical services. Major changes were made to Medicare in late 2003 by the passage of the Medicare Prescription Drug, Improvement, and Modernization Act. The Act, probably the most significant change to Medicare since its enactment, affects all parts of Medicare.

The current Medicare program consists of four parts:

- Part A—Hospital Insurance
- Part B—Medical Expense Insurance
- Part C—Medicare Advantage
- Part D—Prescription Drug Coverage

**Medicare Part A**

### Part A—Hospital Insurance

*Medicare Part A* is Hospital insurance that helps pay the expense of inpatient care in hospitals, critical access hospitals, and skilled nursing facilities. It also covers hospice care, some home health care, and limited psychiatric hospital care.

**Medicare Part B**

### Part B—Medical Expense Insurance

*Medicare Part B* is medical expense insurance that helps pay for doctors' services, medically necessary outpatient hospital services, X-rays and other diagnostic services, durable medical equipment, and some other services and supplies.

**Medicare Part C**

### Part C—Medicare Advantage

In 1999, *Medicare Part C*, also known as Medicare Advantage, went into effect. It gave more choices to Medicare beneficiaries by allowing them to select one of several alternatives to traditional Medicare Parts A and B. Eligible provider arrangements include the following:

- HMOs
- preferred-provider organizations (PPOs)
- point-of-service (POS) plans. These provide HMO services inside a plan network and out-of-network services if there is a plan referral or in certain emergency situations.
- private fee-for-service plans
- private contracts with physicians

**Medicare Part D**

### Part D—Prescription Drug Coverage

The Medicare Prescription Drug, Improvement, and Modernization Act of 2003 added a voluntary prescription drug program to Medicare referred to as *Medicare Part D*. This legislation provides seniors and people living with disabilities with a prescription drug benefit, more choices, and better benefits under Medicare. It is the most significant improvement to senior health care in nearly 40 years. The act also gives employers a financial incentive to provide or continue to provide drug coverage to retirees as an alternative to enrollment in Part D.

## Who Is Eligible for Medicare Benefits?

Part A of Medicare is financed through Social Security (FICA) taxes paid by workers and employers. In general, it is available without monthly premiums for people age 65 or older who qualify for Social Security retirement benefits. Others who meet certain work requirements in federal, state, or local government employment are also eligible. For those who do not qualify, the Part A coverage can be purchased by paying a monthly premium. Participants in Part A are responsible for paying certain deductible amounts and coinsurance limits.

Part B is optional coverage available to everyone eligible for Part A. It, too, can be purchased by most people over age 65 who do not qualify for Part A. Participants in Part B are required to pay a monthly premium of at least $96.40 in 2009, which covers about 25 percent of the cost of the program as well as certain deductible and coinsurance amounts. Medicare supplement plans, also known as medigap insurance, can be purchased to cover these amounts. The remaining 75 percent of the cost of the program is financed from the general revenues of the federal government. Like Social Security payments, Medicare premiums and payments are indexed to inflation and are changed on an annual basis.

As required in the Medicare Prescription Drug, Improvement, and Modernization Act of 2003, the Part B premium a beneficiary pays each month is based on his or her annual income. Specifically, if a beneficiary's modified adjusted gross income is greater than the legislated threshold amounts ($85,000 in 2009 for a beneficiary filing an individual income tax return or married and filing a separate return, and $170,000 for a beneficiary filing a joint tax return), the beneficiary is responsible for a larger portion of the estimated total cost of Part B benefit coverage. In addition to the standard 25 percent premium, such beneficiaries now have to pay an income-related monthly adjustment amount (see the tables below for specific premiums based on income and tax-filing status).

**FIGURE 6-1**
**2009 Medicare Part B monthly premium rates for those who file an individual tax return or who file a joint tax return.**

| Beneficiaries who file an individual tax return with income | Beneficiaries who file a joint tax return with income | Income-related monthly adjustment | Total monthly premium |
|---|---|---|---|
| less than or equal to $85,000 | less than or equal to $170,000 | $0.00 | $96.40 |
| greater than $85,000 and less than or equal to $107,000 | greater than $170,000 and less than or equal to $214,000 | $38.50 | $134.90 |
| greater than $107,000 and less than or equal to $160,000 | greater than $214,000 and less than or equal to $320,000 | $96.30 | $192.70 |
| greater than $160,000 and less than or equal to $213,000 | greater than $320,000 and less than or equal to $426,000 | $154.10 | $250.50 |
| greater than $213,000 | greater than $426,000 | $211.90 | $308.30 |

---

**FIGURE 6-2**
**2009 Medicare Part B monthly premium rates for those who are married, but file a separate return**

| Beneficiaries who are married filing a separate tax return with income | Income-related monthly adjustment amount | Total monthly premium amount |
|---|---|---|
| less than or equal to $85,000 | $0.00 | $96.40 |
| greater than $85,000 and less than or equal to $128,000 | $154.10 | $250.50 |
| greater than $128,000 | $211.90 | $308.30 |

## Medicare Part A—Hospital Insurance

Medicare hospital insurance helps pay for five kinds of care:

- inpatient hospital care
- inpatient care in a skilled nursing facility following a hospital stay
- home health care
- hospice care
- inpatient mental health care

### Benefit Period

Benefits under Medicare Part A cover inpatient care hospital services for up to 90 days in each benefit period. A benefit period begins with the first day an individual enters a hospital and ends when the patient has been out of a hospital or skilled nursing facility for 60 days in a row (including the day of discharge). A subsequent hospitalization then begins a new benefit period.

---

*Example 1:* Mr. Smith enters the hospital on January 10th. He is discharged January 20th. He has used 10 days of his first benefit period. He is hospitalized again July 5th. Because more than 60 days have elapsed between his two hospital stays, he begins a new benefit period.

*Example 2:* Mrs. Green enters the hospital on August 14th. She is discharged on August 24th. She has also used 10 days of her first benefit period. However, she is then readmitted to the hospital on September 20th. Since fewer than 60 days elapsed between hospital stays, Mrs. Green is still in her first benefit period. Therefore the first day of her second admission is counted as the 11th day of hospital care in that benefit period. Mrs. Green will not begin a new benefit period until she has been out of the hospital (or skilled nursing facility) for 60 consecutive days.

### Inpatient Hospital Care

Medicare hospital insurance helps pay for in-patient hospital care if

- a doctor prescribes inpatient hospital care for treatment of illness or injury
- the kind of care can only be provided in a hospital
- the hospital is participating in Medicare
- a review committee does not disapprove the stay

If these four conditions are met, Medicare Part A will cover up to 90 days of inpatient hospital care in each benefit period. A deductible is charged only for the first admission in each benefit period. If the person is discharged and then readmitted before the benefit period ends, another deductible is not paid.

In each benefit period, covered hospital expenses are paid in full for 60 days, subject to an initial deductible ($1,068 in 2009). This deductible is adjusted annually to reflect increasing hospital costs. Benefits for an additional 30 days of hospitalization are also provided in each benefit period, but the patient must pay a daily copayment ($267 in 2009) equal to 25 percent of the initial deductible amount. Each recipient also has a lifetime reserve of 60 additional days if the regular 90 days of benefits have been exhausted. However, once a reserve day is used, it cannot be restored for use in future benefit periods. When using reserve days, patients must pay a daily copayment ($534 in 2009) equal to 50 percent of the initial deductible amount.

***Major Services Covered with Hospital Inpatient Care.*** Medicare hospital insurance pays for

- a semiprivate room (two to four beds in a room)
- all meals
- regular nursing services

- costs of special care units, such as intensive care or coronary care unit
- drugs furnished by the hospital
- lab tests, X-rays, medical supplies
- use of equipment, such as wheelchairs or oxygen tents
- operating and recovery room costs
- diagnostic and therapeutic items, such as physical therapy
- blood transfusions after the first three pints of blood. Patients must pay for the first three pints unless they or others replace the blood.

Some services not covered when a person is a hospital inpatient include personal convenience items such as a telephone or TV, private duty nurses, or extra charges for a private room unless it is medically necessary. There is no coverage under Part A for the services of physicians or surgeons.

Medicare does not pay for hospital or medical services outside the United States and its territories. Because many retirees travel extensively, a need may exist which can be addressed by most Medicare supplement insurance coverage.

### *Skilled Nursing Facility Care*

Medicare hospital insurance helps pay for inpatient care in a Medicare-participating skilled nursing facility following a hospital stay, if certain criteria are met. An example of such criteria would be if an individual's condition requires nursing or rehabilitation services that can only be provided in a skilled nursing facility and are prescribed by his or her physician. It is important to point out that most nursing homes in the United States are not skilled nursing facilities, and many skilled nursing facilities are not Medicare certified.

Medicare does not cover stand-alone custodial nursing home care services. If an individual needs daily care, Medicare will only cover medically necessary care administered by a medical professional. The patient must require medical attention, such as drugs furnished by the facility, physical therapy, or blood transfusions on a daily basis, to be covered. Custodial care, such as assistance in the activities of daily living (getting from bed to chair, feeding oneself, going to the bathroom, bathing) is not covered. This means that most LTC (custodial) services are not covered by Medicare.

In addition, in order to qualify for Medicare coverage in a participating skilled nursing facility, the individual has to have been in a hospital at least three consecutive days (not including the day of discharge) before being transferred to the skilled nursing facility. It is further required that patients be transferred to the skilled nursing facility within 30 days of leaving the hospital for the same medical condition for which they were admitted.

Medicare pays the first 20 days during each benefit period. For days 21–100, the patient pays a coinsurance amount that is equal to 12.5 percent of the initial hospital deductible ($133.50 in 2009). The patient must pay for all costs after day 100.

### Home Health Care

If the patient needs skilled health care at home for the treatment of an illness or injury, Medicare pays for covered home health services furnished by a participating home health agency. A home health agency is a public or private agency that specializes in giving skilled nursing services and other therapeutic services, such as physical therapy, at home.

Medicare pays for home health visits only if

- the care needed includes intermittent skilled nursing care, physical therapy, or speech therapy
- the individual is confined to home; no prior hospitalization is required
- the individual is under the care of a physician who determines that the patient needs home health care and sets up a health plan for the patient
- the home health agency providing the services is Medicare approved

Once these conditions are met, either hospital insurance or medical insurance will pay for all medically necessary (unlimited) home health services. Services include part-time home health aides, medical and social services, occupational therapy, and medical supplies and equipment provided by the home health agency. It also will pay for 20 percent of the Medicare-approved amount for durable medical equipment such as oxygen tanks and hospital beds.

Medicare pays for

- part-time or intermittent skilled nursing care (this can include eight hours of reasonable and necessary care per day for up to 21 consecutive days)
- physical or speech therapy
- part-time or intermittent services of home health aides
- medical social services
- medical supplies or equipment at 80 percent of the approved amount

Medicare does not cover home services furnished primarily to assist people in activities of daily living, such as housecleaning, meal preparation, shopping, dressing, or bathing.

### *Hospice Benefits*

Hospice care is defined as care provided to terminally ill people, with a life expectancy of six months or less, in their home. It is typically provided by a public agency or private organization and can be received in a facility or, as most often is the case, in the patient's home.

Under the Medicare hospice benefit, Medicare covers medical and support services from a Medicare-approved hospice. Hospice care is designed to provide physical care and counseling, including drugs for symptom control and pain relief, and other services that would not otherwise be covered under Medicare. Medicare pays for services every day and permits a hospice to provide appropriate custodial care including homemaker services and counseling. Benefits are payable if all of the following are met:

- A doctor certifies that a patient is terminally ill.
- A patient chooses to receive care from a hospice.
- Care is provided by a Medicare-participating hospice program.

Medicare will pay for two 90-day benefit periods and an unlimited number of 60-day benefit periods. At the start of each of these benefit periods, the individual's doctor must certify that he or she is terminally ill in order for hospice care to continue. Terminally ill patients may leave the hospice program during any benefit period and return to regular Medicare coverage. They can elect hospice benefits again as long as they meet the benefit requirements. There are no deductibles under the hospice benefit. However, the hospice patient is responsible for modest copayments for outpatient drugs and inpatient respite care.

Medicare hospital insurance pays for the following services for beneficiaries as part of hospice care:

- nursing services
- doctors' services
- drugs, including outpatient drugs for pain relief
- physical and occupational therapy, and speech-language pathology
- home health aide and homemaker services
- medical social services
- medical supplies and appliances
- counseling

- short-term inpatient care, including respite care, is covered by Medicare hospital insurance as part of hospice care

Respite care under the hospice program is a short-term inpatient stay in a facility for the terminally ill Medicare patient. Hospice respite care gives temporary relief to the person who regularly assists with home care. Each in-patient respite care stay is limited to no more than five days in a row. Remember this benefit is only available to the terminally ill; there is no respite care provision for the homebound patient receiving benefits under Medicare home health services.

### Psychiatric Hospital Care

Part A will help pay for up to 190 days of inpatient care in a Medicare-participating psychiatric hospital. The 190-day limit is a maximum lifetime benefit. The benefits are paid following the same rules as other inpatient hospital stays. Psychiatric care in general hospitals is not subject to the 190-day limit and is treated the same as other inpatient hospital care.

## Medicare Part B—Medical Insurance

### Benefits

Medicare medical insurance helps pay for doctors' services, outpatient hospital care, diagnostic tests, medical equipment, and other health services and supplies not covered by Medicare hospital insurance (Part A). These include the following:

- physicians' and surgeons' fees
- diagnostic tests and procedures that are part of treatment
- radiology and pathology services by doctors
- treatment of mental illness
- other services usually furnished in the doctor's office, such as X-rays, services of a doctor's nurse, drugs that can't be self-administered, blood transfusions, medical supplies, and physical or occupational therapy
- medical supplies, such as surgical dressings, splints and casts
- rental of medical equipment, such as oxygen tents, hospital beds, and wheelchairs
- other comprehensive medical services

Medicare medical insurance does not pay for routine physical exams, most routine foot care, exams for prescribing or fitting eyeglasses or hearing aids, most immunizations, custodial care, or cosmetic surgery. For the most part, Medicare only pays for treatment provided by medical doctors. Only very limited coverage is available for services provided by other medical professionals such as chiropractors, podiatrists, dentists, or optometrists.

### *Premiums*

Medicare Part B, Medical Insurance requires a premium payment from its participants. It is usually deducted from the participant's Social Security check each month, and the amount changes from year to year. Beginning in 2007, increases in the Part B premium began to be based on income.

### *Deductibles*

The standard annual deductible is $135 in 2009. This deductible applies to most Part B services. There is one exception, however. In addition to the standard Part B deductible, the recipient must pay for or replace the first three pints of blood used each year, unless the blood replacement was paid under Part A hospital insurance.

### *Coinsurance*

For most services received under Part B, there is a 20 percent coinsurance amount beyond the annual deductible for all Medicare-approved charges. The approved charge for doctor's services covered by Medicare is based on a fee schedule issued by the Centers for Medicare and Medicaid Services, which administers Medicare. A patient is reimbursed for only 80 percent of the approved charges above the deductible regardless of the doctor's actual charge. Most doctors and other suppliers of medical services accept an assignment of Medicare benefits, and are prohibited from charging a patient in excess of the fee schedule. They can, however, bill the patient for any portion of the approved charges that were not paid by Medicare because of the annual deductible and/or coinsurance. They can also bill for any services that are not covered by Medicare. Medicare pays only 50 percent of approved charges for mental health services.

## Medicare Part C—Medicare Advantage

In 1999, Part C of Medicare went into effect. It expands the choices available to most Medicare beneficiaries by allowing them to elect medical expense benefits through one of several alternatives to Parts A and B as long as the providers of these alternatives enter into contracts with the Centers for

Medicare and Medicaid Services. However, beneficiaries must still pay any Part B premium.

The Medicare Advantage plans include the following:

- health maintenance organizations (HMOs). Most of the HMOs previously in the Medicare market became part of the Medicare Advantage program.
- preferred-provider organizations (PPOs)
- provider-sponsored organizations (PSOs). These are similar to HMOs but established by doctors and hospitals that have formed their own health plans.
- private fee-for-service plans
- private contracts with physicians

These plans must provide all benefits available under Parts A and B of Medicare. They may include additional benefits as part of the basic plan or for an additional fee.

The Medicare Prescription Drug, Improvement, and Modernization Act made numerous administrative changes to the program aimed at increasing participation. The method for calculating reimbursement to participating plans was changed, and many plans are receiving larger reimbursements. This has already resulted in some plans increasing benefits and/or lowering premiums. However, under the Obama Administration, the payments to private insurers have been cut. This will result in higher premiums.

Beginning in 2005, PPOs began offering Medicare Advantage plans on a regional basis that is broader than the typical service areas for non-Medicare Advantage participants. These regions were determined by the Secretary of Health and Human Services. This gave PPOs a broader base from which to solicit members and increase competition.

## Medicare Part D—Prescription Drug Coverage

The Medicare Prescription Drug, Improvement, and Modernization Act of 2003 added a prescription drug program to Medicare that became effective in January of 2006.

### *Eligibility*

Part D is a voluntary prescription drug benefit available to all Medicare beneficiaries enrolled in either Part A and/or Part B (original Medicare) or in any of the various Medicare Advantage plans. Each enrollee must pay a monthly premium. No one can be denied coverage because of income level or for health reasons. Hereafter, Part D benefits are referred to as Medicare prescription drug plans.

### *Types of Plans*

Medicare prescription drug plans are private plans offered by insurance companies, managed care plans, and other organizations. These sponsors typically contract with pharmacy benefit managers to design plan formularies. The plans must meet certain standards and be approved by the Secretary of Health and Human Services. Like Medicare Advantage plans, Medicare prescription drug coverage may be marketed directly to Medicare beneficiaries or sold by agents or brokers.

There are two basic types of Medicare prescription drug plans. One type of plan is for persons enrolled in most Medicare Advantage plans. As long as the Medicare Advantage plan has such a prescription drug program, members may obtain their prescription drug coverage only through that program. The other type of plan, referred to as a stand-alone plan, is available to persons enrolled in original Medicare or in Medicare Advantage plans without prescription drug programs. The main differences between these two types of plans are in the process of enrollment and premium payment.

### *Standard Benefit Structure*

The act provides for a standard prescription drug plan but also allows for alternative plans to be approved if certain requirements are met and the plans are at least as generous as the standard plan. Most plans now available provide broader coverage than the standard plan.

The standard prescription drug program has an initial annual deductible of $295 in 2009. This amount and other dollar figures mentioned below will increase in later years if the expenditures for prescription drugs by Medicare beneficiaries increase.

**coverage gap (doughnut hole)**

After the deductible has been satisfied, the plan will pay 75 percent of the next $2,405 (in 2009) of prescription drug costs covered by the plan. Benefits then cease until a beneficiary's total drug costs (including the deductible) reach $6,153.75 (in 2009). The range where no benefits are paid is often referred to as the *coverage gap or "doughnut hole"*. Once the $6,153.75 amount is reached, the beneficiary will have had out-of-pocket costs of $4,350 in addition to the annual premium. For covered drug costs in excess of $6,153.75, the beneficiary will then pay for each prescription the greater of (1) 5 percent of the cost of the prescription or (2) a modest copay (for 2009) of $2.40 for a generic or $6.00 for a brand name drug. For all but inexpensive drugs, this means that the plan will pay 95 percent of the cost to fill a prescription.

All of the above limits apply only to drug costs covered by the plan. If a beneficiary purchases a drug that is not covered by the plan, the beneficiary must pay the full cost for the drug and cannot apply this amount toward the initial deductible or use it to satisfy the previously mentioned limits. In addition, certain other drug costs do not count toward the limits. These include the cost for drugs purchased outside the United States, the cost of drugs specifically excluded by Medicare, and any payments made by most other private or government drug programs. However, drug costs paid by family members and certain state assistance programs do count toward these limits.

The following example shows that beneficiaries with $775 or less in annual prescription drug expenditures will receive no net benefit from the Medicare prescription drug plan, assuming the prescription drug premium is $30 per month. Approximately half of Medicare beneficiaries fall into this category and will need to decide whether they should purchase coverage. The negative side of not signing up when initially eligible, as discussed later, is that there will be a financial penalty for enrollment at a later date when a beneficiary might have significantly higher drug costs.

---

***Example:***        Bryan incurs $775 in covered drug costs during the year.

| | |
|---|---|
| Payment by drug plan | |
| [.75 x ($775 – $295 deductible)] | $360 |
| Minus premium ($30/month) | –360 |
| Net benefit from plan | 0 |
| | |
| Percentage of drug cost paid by Bryan | 100% |

---

The next example shows that Medicare beneficiaries with $6,153.75 or less in annual prescription drug expenditures will also pay a significant percentage of their drug costs.

---

***Example:***        Wendy and her husband Keith have annual prescription drug costs of $2,800 and $6,153.75 respectively. (Wendy's costs are about the average prescription drug costs for Medicare recipients.)

Wendy and Keith will each receive $1,803.75 under their Medicare prescription drug plans. This amount equals 75 percent of the first $2,405 in drug costs exceeding the deductible. In Wendy's case, she will have out-of-pocket costs equal to $1,336.25, or slightly more than 48 percent of her expenditures. This $1,336.25 figure is calculated as follows:

| | |
|---|---:|
| Premium ($30/month) | $ 360.00 |
| Deductible | 275.00 |
| 25% of first $2,405 above deductible | 601.25 |
| 100% of expenses in excess of $2,700 | 100.00 |
| | $1,336.25 |

In Keith's case, his expenses above $2,700 are $3,453.75, and his total out-of-pocket costs and premium are $4,710, or 77 percent of his drug expenditures.

---

The percentage of drug costs that a beneficiary pays drops as costs exceed $6,153.75 because Part D plans pay 95 percent of this excess amount.

Medicare prescription drug plans can incorporate certain cost-saving features found in many other types of prescription drug plans. These include prior approval for certain drugs, quantity limits, and the use of step therapy.

Note that the Obama Administration has proposed the means-testing Part D premiums.

### *Employer Incentives*

One concern of Congress was that employers or unions that provided prescription drug coverage to retirees would drop this coverage and, possibly, other retiree medical expense coverage after the act was passed. To prevent this from occurring, the act provides a subsidy to employers or unions that continue drug coverage as long as it is at least actuarially equivalent to the coverage under a standard prescription drug program.

The Retiree Drug Subsidy (RDS) program provides an annual subsidy to plan sponsors participating in the RDS program. The subsidy in 2009 is equal to 28 percent of the cost of providing a retiree with up to $6,000 in prescription drug benefits, subject to a $295 deductible. After 2009, these dollar amounts will be indexed for inflation.

## Medicare Supplement Insurance

From the explanation of Medicare, it is obvious that most people need a Medicare supplement policy to cover gaps in their coverage, or risk consuming their retirement savings in one lengthy hospital stay. Estimates indicate that about two-thirds of Medicare recipients have some type of coverage to supplement Medicare, with this group being split about equally between those with coverage provided by a former employer and those who purchase coverage in the individual marketplace.

Current policyholders and all those about to turn 65 should begin reviewing their needs and coverage. For example, some retirees have coverage through an ex-employer's group health plan and do not need additional coverage.

### *History and Background*

After the passage of the initial Medicare legislation in 1965, Medicare supplement policies became as diverse as the companies that sold them. As a result, in 1990, the Medicare supplement insurance market became directly subject to federal regulation.

**Medicare supplement insurance (medigap)**

Congress directed the NAIC to develop a standardized array of individual insurance policies, all of which would include at least a common core of basic benefits. The technical name of these plans is *Medicare supplement insurance*, but they are often referred to as *medigap* policies, as they will be here.

In addition to standardizing medigap policies, Congress mandated several other features, including a 6-month open-enrollment period, limited preexisting-conditions exclusions, prohibition of the sale of duplicate coverage, increased individual loss ratios, and guaranteed renewability. When describing the benefits of each of the medigap policies, insurance companies must use the same format, language, and definitions. They are also required to use a uniform chart and outline of coverage to summarize the benefits in each plan. These requirements make it easier for beneficiaries to compare policies and select between them based on service, reliability, and price.

Federal laws have also generated several restrictions on the markets to which medigap policies may be sold. Under these restrictions, known as anti-duplication provisions, it is generally illegal for an insurance company to sell a medigap policy to

- a current medigap policyowner, unless that person states in writing that the first policy will be canceled
- a Medicaid recipient
- an enrollee in a Medicare Advantage plan

A violation of these provisions is subject to criminal and/or civil penalties under federal law.

### *Standardization of Plans*

There are 12 medigap plans (A through L) designed to help fill the gaps in Medicare coverage. Plan A is the basic benefit package. Each of the other 11 plans includes the basic Plan A package and a varying combination of additional benefits, with Plan J providing the most comprehensive coverage of all the plans. Insurers may offer fewer than the 12 standard plans.

State insurance departments determine what policies are available in that jurisdiction. It is important that you understand the coverages that your company offers, but you also need to be familiar with the differences between all 12 forms. (See Table 6-1 for a summary of the differences.) In a competitive situation, you need to be able to explain the differences so your clients will clearly understand what they are purchasing. To do this, you must be sure that you do not mislead the client by comparing apples to oranges.

***The Basic Benefit Plan.*** The basic benefits contained in Plan A, and that must be included in all plans, consist of the following:

- *Hospitalization.* This includes payment of the beneficiary's percentage participation share of Medicare Part A expenses for the 61st through the 90th day of hospitalization and the 60 lifetime reserve days. In addition, full coverage is extended for 365 additional days after Medicare benefits end.
- *Medical Expenses.* This covers payment of the beneficiary's percentage participation share (generally 20 percent) for Medicare-approved Part B charges for physicians' and medical services.
- *Blood.* This covers payment for the first three pints of blood each year.
- *Preventive Care.* This is coinsurance for Medicare-approved preventive care after the deductible.

***Additional Medigap Plan Benefits.*** The other 11 medigap plans include, in addition to the basic benefits, an array of coverage and benefits that are not included in original Medicare. These additions encompass the following:

- paying the hospital inpatient Part A deductible for each benefit period
- paying the Part A percentage participation share for the 21st through the 100th day of skilled-nursing facility care
- paying the annual Part B deductible
- paying charges for physicians' and medical services that exceed the Medicare-approved amount (either 80 or 100 percent of these charges up to the charge limitation set by Medicare or the state)
- paying 100 percent coinsurance (50 percent and 75 percent for Plans K and L respectively) for Part B-covered preventive care services after the Part B deductible has been paid.

- paying 80 percent of the charges after a $250 deductible for emergency care in a foreign hospital (with several limitations) and a $50,000 lifetime maximum
- paying up to $40 each visit for custodial care after an illness, injury, or surgery, up to a maximum benefit of $1,600 a year. This includes at-home recovery while a beneficiary qualifies for Medicare home health care benefits (with certain limitations).

Compared to the 10 original Medicare supplement plans, Plans K and L require cost sharing by the insured for certain covered services, subject to an annual out-of-pocket limit.

***Medicare Supplement Variations.*** Except for conformance with the alternative standards in Massachusetts, Minnesota, and Wisconsin, insurance companies cannot offer medigap policies that differ from these standardized options, and they cannot change the combination of benefits or the letter names of any of the policies. However, there are two allowable variations: high-deductible policies and Medicare SELECT policies.

Companies can offer two standard high-deductible medigap policies. These policies are identical to Plans F and J except that they have a high-deductible amount before the plan pays any benefit. Separate annual deductibles for foreign travel emergencies in Plans F and J also apply. The monthly premium for Plans F and J under the high-deductible option is generally less than the monthly premium for Plans F and J without a high-deductible option. However, the savings may be offset by the out-of-pocket payments for services required before satisfying the deductible.

**Medicare SELECT**

***Medicare SELECT.*** *Medicare SELECT* refers to any one of the 12 standardized medigap insurance policies (although Plans C, D, and F are most popular) in which the beneficiary must use the insurance plan's designated hospitals and doctors for nonemergency services to be eligible for full supplemental insurance benefits. Medicare SELECT policies are issued by insurance companies as PPO products and by some HMOs.

In general, Medicare SELECT policies are required to pay full benefits only if a preferred provider is used for nonemergency services. However, Medicare pays its share of approved charges in any case. Medicare SELECT policy premiums are generally 15 to 25 percent less than the monthly premium for the same plan without the required use of a preferred-provider network.

**TABLE 6-1**
**Twelve Standard NAIC Medicare Supplement (Medigap) Policies - 2009**

| | A | B | C | D | E | F+ | G | H | I | J+ | K | L |
|---|---|---|---|---|---|---|---|---|---|---|---|---|
| **Basic benefits** | | | | | | | | | | | | |
| Hospital coinsurance | x | x | x | x | x | x | x | x | x | x | x | x |
| Part B coinsurance | x | x | x | x | x | x | x | x | x | x | 50%* | 75%* |
| First three pints of blood | x | x | x | x | x | x | x | x | x | x | 50%* | 75%* |
| **Skilled-nursing facility copay (days 21–100)** | | | x | x | x | x | x | x | x | x | 50%* | 75%* |
| **Part A deductible** | | x | x | x | x | x | x | x | x | x | 50%* | 75%* |
| **Part B deductible** | | | x | | | x | | | | x | | |
| **Part B excess charges** | | | | | | 100% | 80% | | 100% | 100% | | |
| **Foreign travel emergency ++** | | x | x | x | x | x | x | x | x | | | |
| **At-home recovery** | | | | x | | | x | | x | x | | |
| **Preventive care** coinsurance for Medicare approved preventive care after deductible | 100% | 100% | 100% | 100% | 100% | 100% | 100% | 100% | 100% | 100% | 100% | 100% |
| **Hospice care\*\*\*** | | | | | | | | | | | 50%* | 75%* |
| **Annual out-of-pocket maximum\*** | | | | | | | | | | | $4,620 | $2,310 |

\*   Pays 100% of Part A and Part B coinsurance for the rest of the year after annual maximum out-of-pocket limit has been spent, and Part B deductible ($135 in 2009) has been satisfied. Charges from doctors that exceed Medicare-approved amounts, called excess charges, aren't covered and don't count toward the annual out-of-pocket limit.

\+   Plans F and J also have a high-deductible option. The insured must pay the first $2,000 (high-deductible in 2009) in Medicare covered costs before the medigap policy pays anything.

\+\+   The insured must also pay a separate deductible for a foreign travel emergency ($250 per year).

\*\*   Plans E and J cover $120 per year for health care screenings ordered by a physician but not covered by Medicare.

\*\*\*   Plan K pay 50 percent and Plan L pays 75 percent of the hospice cost sharing for all Medicare Part A Medicare-covered expenses and respite care.

***Changes to Medicare Supplements in 2006.*** The Medicare Prescription Drug, Improvement, and Modernization Act added a new prescription drug benefit program to Medicare that became effective January 1, 2006. Consequently private insurance companies were no longer allowed to issue new Medicare supplement policies with prescription drug benefits contained in them such as were previously available in medigap Plans H, I, and J. Persons already insured under these medigap policies now have several options. They may continue to renew them with drug benefits included as long as they do not enroll in the Medicare Part D prescription drug program. If they enroll in the Part D program, they may keep in force their existing Medicare supplement policies with the drug benefit eliminated and the premium adjusted accordingly. Alternatively, they can purchase another available Medicare supplement policy that has no drug benefit. Finally, they can enroll in a Medicare Advantage Plan that provides prescription drug coverage. In this case, a medigap policy will be unnecessary because under federal antiduplication rules a medigap policy cannot be sold to someone enrolled in a Medicare Advantage Plan.

***Prospecting.*** Newly retired clients and prospects and those planning for imminent retirement are excellent prospects for medigap coverage. You can help them understand the benefits they will receive under Medicare. As you have seen, this coverage is complicated and is often less comprehensive than people think it will be. Be sure your prospects understand the limitations including the fact that most nursing home care is not covered. This can easily open the door for a discussion and sale of LTC coverage.

Persons aged 65 or older may buy any available Medicare supplement policy, regardless of health status, at any time during the 6-month period after initial enrollment for Medicare Part B benefits.

Help your prospects determine which, if any, of their employer-provided coverages will continue after they retire, and for how long. Some will lose health insurance coverage completely, while others may enroll in a different plan for retirees. These plans may resemble medigap coverage in that they will provide benefits for treatment and services not covered by Medicare. You can help your prospect analyze these new coverages, and if no coverage is provided, the door is open for a discussion and sale of your medigap products.

***Review Existing Policies.*** In working with older retirees, you may encounter medigap policies that were written before the standardization of benefits.

The first priority is to examine the current policy for exclusions and limitations, many of which have been removed from new model policies.

- For example, some older medigap policies exclude coverage for medical care outside the United States. A foreign travel benefit with a separate $250 annual deductible is included in 8 out of 12 new standard policies (a feature regular foreign travelers should look for in their existing policies).
- Remember, any policy not guaranteed renewable can be canceled on the policy anniversary. All new policies will be issued as guaranteed renewable; they will be renewable annually as long as the premiums are paid, regardless of age or health.

In fact, medigap insurance reforms may present an opportunity for some to upgrade their medigap insurance, especially if the present policy has few covered features. In most cases, the client will be able to switch to one of the standard policies without a pre-existing condition clause that would otherwise leave the client uncovered for up to six months for a pre-existing condition.

Companies will, however, be allowed to raise premiums for chronic health conditions, and the attained age could be much older which would consequently raise premiums. Some people will be better off keeping their current policies, especially if they cover current needs, their health has worsened, or they are elderly. It is important to note that a replaced policy should never be terminated until new coverage is in force.

New medigap policies will not cover all health worries. None cover LTC, but the 12 standard provisions make comparing policy features and premiums much easier. Advisors have an opportunity to review present clients' medigap policies and to approach potential senior clients.

# LONG-TERM CARE INSURANCE

In this section, we examine the need for long-term care and the long-term care insurance (LTCI) policies that the insurance industry has created in response to this need. Insurance advisors have long offered cancer and dread disease insurance to the public. These will be discussed at the end of this section.

## Long-Term Care Needs

Although this discussion is placed near the end of the life-cycle material, this does not imply that only older people need this insurance. Younger people have serious accidents and health problems that make them vulnerable to long-term care needs. They may have adequate health insurance through work and not think it important to them. However, a condition that requires continued bed or wheelchair confinement brings new maintenance costs that few health plans would pay.

In general, many people feel the need for long-term care only applies to older people. It is commonly thought of as custodial care, which is help that is needed with activities of daily living.

**long-term care**

The definition of *long-term care* (LTC) has grown increasing complex over the years. It is important to emphasize that LTC is not simply nursing home care; it is much more than that. LTC can best be defined as a broad range of medical, custodial, and other care services provided over an extended period in various care settings due to a chronic illness, physical disability, or cognitive impairment. Knowing the definition of LTC will help you to understand and explain the concept to prospects and clients.

Medical care services imply the supervision of a physician to direct the care provided by skilled, licensed health care professionals, such as nurses and therapists. This care is identified as skilled or intermediate (discussed later).

**activities of daily living (ADLs)**

**instrumental activities of daily living (ADLs)**

Custodial care (or personal care) services include assistance with the *activities of daily living (ADLs)* or *instrumental activities of daily living (IADLs)*. ADLs are those activities geared toward the care of bodily needs that enables an individual to live independently. They include eating, bathing, dressing, toileting, transferring, and continence. On the other hand, IADLs deal more with one's overall ability to function cognitively. IADLs include ancillary activities such as preparing meals, shopping, cleaning, managing money, taking medications, and so on. Custodial care can usually be provided without professional medical skills or training. Family members often provide custodial care at home. Custodial care is normally not covered under individual or group medical insurance policies, Medicare, or most other kinds of insurance.

**care settings**

LTC was once synonymous with nursing home care only. However, the *care settings* for LTC have evolved as technology, services, and market demands have dictated. Now, LTC occurs in a variety of care settings, including the following:

- skilled-nursing facilities, such as an LTC facility or a nursing home
- residential communities, such as an assisted-living facility
- community-based facilities, such as an adult day care
- the home of the person receiving care

**intermediate care**

Some levels of care do require staying in a specified facility, such as a skilled-nursing facility. For example, skilled care that requires medically necessary, 24-hour physician-directed care must be provided in a skilled-nursing facility. Skilled care delivered on an intermittent basis is sometimes referred to as *intermediate care.*

Cognitive impairments, physical disabilities, and chronic illnesses associated with aging (Alzheimer's disease, arthritis, and the general effects aging has on mobility) are the reasons people typically need LTC. However, many people require LTC services because of a disability caused by an accident or a stroke, which is something that could happen to anyone at any age.

### Long-Term Care Trends

The future need for LTC must be discussed with a prospect in light of a few trends that accentuate the need for LTC and the cost of it as well. A brief discussion of these trends follows.

***The Statistics.*** The Health Insurance Association of America (HIAA) estimates that two out of five people age 65 or older will spend some time in a nursing home before they die. The likelihood that LTC services will be needed increases with age. Approximately 25 percent of Americans ages 85 or older are in nursing homes today. The National Center for Health Statistics reports in their National Nursing Home Survey that the average length of stay since admission in 2004 was 835 days (a decline of 35 days from the same figure in 1999), or a little more than two years and three months. One interesting note is that the percentage of residents under aged 65 increased by almost 3 percent from 1999 to 2004.[2]

These statistics do need to be tempered by the fact that they include short-term patients who are in a facility for recovery and rehabilitation.

| Nursing Home Resident Demographics | |
| --- | --- |
| **Age at Interview** | **Percentage of Residents** |
| Under 65 years | 11.7 |
| 65 years and older | 88.3 |
| 65–74 | 11.7 |
| 75–84 | 31.4 |
| 85+ | 45.2 |

*Source: National Center for Health Statistics, Nursing Home Current Residents, 2004.*

***An Aging Population.*** The single greatest predictor of the need for LTC is advancing age. This is due to the gradual decline in physical and mental abilities that usually occurs as one ages. Consider the following often-quoted statistics:

- Approximately 25 percent of Americans between the ages of 65 and 74 "suffer some limitation of activities." The number increases to 62 percent for those older than 85.[3]
- About 55 percent of those age 85 or older who have chronic physical impairments require long-term care.[4]
- Almost 90 percent of all nursing home residents are aged 65 or older and about 45 percent of them are aged 85 or older.[5]

The direct correlation between aging and the need for LTC is the central ingredient for the LTC crisis. This is a fact that medical advances have done very little to change.

***Increased Longevity.*** People are living longer because of advances in medicine, nutrition, and personal and professional health management have developed preventive methods, cures, and treatments for diseases and conditions that were once fatal. Consider that the average life expectancy in 1900 was 47 years; in 2000 it reached 76.9 years. Perhaps more significantly, today people who survive to age 65 can expect to live to age 83. In 1900, they could have expected to live to age 68.

Today, the age-65-or-over segment represents about 11 percent of the population, a figure expected to increase to between 20 percent and 25 percent over the next 50 years. The segment of the population aged 85 and over is growing at an even faster rate. While less than 10 percent of the over-65 group is over 85 today, this percentage is expected to double over the next two generations.

Thus, there are more people entering the time in life in which dependency on others is more prevalent. As life spans increase, the length of time people will need LTC due to such dependency will almost certainly increase as well.

***Changes in the Home.*** Increased longevity is compounded by the significant change in family structure and lifestyles that have occurred over the past few decades in this country. Compared to previous generations, family members are simply less available today to meet the needs of their elderly parents and relatives because of the increased participation of women in the paid workforce, lower birth rates, and the geographic dispersion of families.

Due to economic pressures families face, many have opted for a two-income household. In these households, caring for an aging parent or relative may not be economically feasible or desirable. In other cases, children have moved away, and the care of an elderly parent may fall on the shoulders of only one of the children instead of being equally shared. Thus, many families are turning to organized, formal long-term care, and need money to pay for it.

***Cost of Accelerating Need.*** This accelerating need will continue to drive up the future costs of long-term care because of growing numbers of patients, scarcity of facilities and staff, and continued building of new centers.

**Medicaid**

***Few Sources of Money.*** Many Americans have the misconception that Medicare will cover their long-term care needs. However, Medicare does not provide custodial care for the elderly, and neither does a Medicare supplemental insurance policy. The other government option is *Medicaid*, which provides health care to low-income individuals and families. However, Medicaid requires an individual to exhaust most of his or her assets before qualifying for coverage. This is known as Medicaid spend down. Further, many long-term care facilities no longer accept Medicaid payments, which limits the alternatives for LTC patients.

## Long-Term Care Insurance

Insurance companies have responded with plans that will help individuals ease the burden of these costs. Following is an overview of these products and how they work.

### Differences Among Products

Long-term care insurance (LTCI) is a relatively new and rapidly developing product. It is a complex product, with many variations among companies. As LTC needs have changed, so have LTCI contracts. Policy innovations introduced by one company are rapidly adopted by other companies, with the process continually evolving.

Pricing for these diverse policy features varies greatly. Because LTCI is still relatively new, many insurers have limited claims experience on which to base premium cost projections. This accounts for many of the differences found in pricing this coverage, as each company uses different actuarial assumptions and claims experience in underwriting their products.

Adequate and competitive pricing has been a serious issue for insurers as well as state regulators. A balance between adequate and competitive pricing allows insurers to provide affordable benefits to policyowners, cover expenses, and generate a profit for the company while remaining competitive. Otherwise, company insolvencies and premium increases are inevitable. Conversely, there must be protection for the public against unfair pricing and excessive profits by insurers. Without a solid record of claims experience and with insurer liabilities stretched far into the future, the task of companies and regulators to set prices has been difficult.

Price increases are undesirable because they threaten a policyowner's ability to continue premium payments, and they erode the public's confidence in the products offered by the industry. Underpricing may be even more undesirable as it may make future rate increases inevitable, or it may threaten a company's ability to pay its contractual obligations, or even to remain in operation.

---

**You Get What You Pay For**

In general, comparable policies are competitively priced. If one policy is much lower in price than another being presented to you, there is usually a valid reason. Read the specimen contract carefully. Review the definitions, the exclusions, and the benefit coverage. One policy may be much more limited in its coverage. There may also be policies that are on sale because they are older versions. Most companies do not want to raise premiums on existing blocks of business because of the negative impact it has on consumers. Rather, each time a newer version of the policy becomes active, pricing is always higher than the older policies. However, you should never state that a premium will not be increased in the future. LTCI is a type of health insurance, and no one can predict the future.

---

For many types of insurance, policy provisions are relatively standardized. For LTCI the opposite is true. Significant variations in policy provisions and definitions, and therefore cost, exist from one insurance company to another. A prospect can choose from several different policy provisions. Consequently, properly comparing any two LTCI policies is usually a challenge. Complicating this process even further, many companies offer more than one comprehensive policy, or they offer riders that effectively convert a basic comprehensive policy into an enhanced one. It is difficult for a prospect, as well as an inexperienced advisor, to grasp the many variations in policies and be able to compare them completely and fairly. This, coupled with the wide number of options available to a prospect, makes the evaluation and comparison of LTCI policies more difficult than the evaluation and comparison of most other types of insurance.

When comparing policies, be sure to look carefully at the definitions of policy features. There is a wide variation in definitions and coverage, and these can will affect the price. Some policies may be sold below market value for reasons other than price; however, if a policy is inexpensive, it is usually for a good reason. For example, its benefits may not be as generous or favorable for the insured as those in higher-priced policies. If a policy is priced well below market, be cautious and investigate the reasons for its low price. Never assume those reasons—always read the policy to discover them.

### Types of Care Covered

There are many types of care provided under an LTCI policy. By broad categories, these include facility care, assisted-living, and home and community-based care. A LTCI policy may provide benefits for one, several, or all of these types of care.

nursing home care

***Nursing Home Care.*** *Nursing home care* encompasses skilled-nursing care, intermediate care, and custodial care. All types of care can be viewed as on a care continuum from acute to chronic.

Although some people enter a nursing home for short-term rehabilitation or convalescence after a hospitalization, most people who enter a nursing home for longer stays are experiencing a chronic condition. They may need services for conditions such as dementia, Alzheimer's disease, multiple sclerosis, or severe health conditions resulting from heart disease, stroke, diabetes, or arthritis. They may have lost their ability to perform ADLs, or become too sick or difficult for family members or others to care for them. To ensure that appropriate and high-quality care is provided, insurers require nursing homes, as well as most other care providers, to be properly licensed. Assessment is part of the licensing and license-maintenance procedure for nursing homes, and they must meet high standards on an ongoing basis.

assisted-living facility care

***Assisted-Living Facility Care.*** *Assisted-living facility care* is provided in facilities that care for those who can no longer able care for themselves but do not need the level of care provided in a nursing home. The number and types of these facilities are growing rapidly. Assisted-living facilities are intended to foster independence, dignity, privacy, and the ability to function at the maximum level while maintaining connections with the community.

Assisted-living facilities offer a more home-like atmosphere than a nursing home. They have experienced explosive growth because they offer an effective form of care in the LTC delivery system. Both insurance companies and the government support them because there is a need for affordable alternative settings to the traditional nursing home. We simply cannot afford to put everyone who needs more care than can be provided at home in a nursing home—we need alternatives. Assisted living serves as an intermediate stage of care, between home and community care and a nursing home. It provides cost-effective services for people who need some assistance, but do not need the more intensive care of a nursing home.

home health care

***Home and Community-Based Care.*** *Home health care* provides part-time, skilled-nursing care by registered and licensed practical nurses; occupational, physical, and speech therapy; and part-time services from licensed home health aides under the direction of a physician. Services typically include administering prescription medication, monitoring blood levels, wound care, diabetic care, incontinence management, and injections. Most people desire care at home because it provides emotional well being, control of one's lifestyle, security, familiarity, privacy, and the other comforts associated with home.

Home and community-based care may also include benefits for one or more of the following:

- *Medical equipment, emergency alert systems, and modifications to the home,* such as a ramp for a wheelchair or bathtub grab rails can be purchased, rented, or installed. Insurers find that the cost of equipment or making minor modifications to the home is less than the cost of receiving care in a nursing home. These plans usually provide a benefit for equipment or modifications that is between 20 and 50 times the maximum daily benefit (MDB). For a $150-per-day policy, a benefit of 30 times the MDB would provide $4,500 for medical equipment.

- *Respite care* provides for temporary institutional or home care for a person while the informal caregiver takes a vacation or a break. Respite care can be provided in a person's home or by moving the patient to a nursing facility for a short stay. Insurers limit the number of days for which this benefit is payable, expressed as a maximum number of days or a dollar amount.

- *Adult day-care* facilities offer weekday custodial care to people with light to moderate impairment. They function much like child day care, by providing a supervised, safe environment for people who lack informal caregivers during the day and therefore cannot stay at home and function on their own. Medicine administration, meals, and some skilled nursing services are provided.

- *Caregiver training* provides training for a family member or friend in how to give safe and effective care, so that an insured in need of care can remain at home. Insurers recognize that it is more cost effective to train an informal caregiver than to have the insured go to a nursing home. The amount payable is normally limited to a maximum of three to five times the MDB. For example, if a policy had a $100 per day MDB, the informal caregiver training would pay between $300 and $500. This is normally a one-time maximum benefit.

- *A homemaker companion or home health aide* is normally an employee of a home-health-care agency who assists with homemaker services such as cooking, laundry, shopping, cleaning, bill paying, or other household chores. This benefit also provides personal care services in daily living, such as grooming, personal hygiene, and taking medications.

**hospice care**

***Hospice Care.*** *Hospice care* does not attempt to cure medical conditions but rather treats terminally ill persons by easing the physical and psychological pain associated with death. In addition to providing services for dying people, hospices may also offer counseling to family members to help them with the physical, psychological, social, and spiritual needs of coping with the terminal illness and subsequent death of a loved one. While a hospice may be a separate facility, this type of care can also be provided on an outpatient basis in the dying person's home.

### Policy Features

**reimbursement basis**

Most LTCI products provide daily benefits on a *reimbursement basis*, based on the expenses incurred. The benefits paid are equal to expenses up to the policy's specified limit, the daily benefit amount, or maximum daily benefit. For example, if the covered costs were $120 per day and the daily benefit amounts were $150 per day, the policy would only pay $120—the expenses incurred. If the expenses were $160 per day, the policy would pay the full $150 daily benefit amount and the insured would be responsible for the difference.

**indemnity basis**

In the past, policies that paid on an *indemnity basis* were popular. They paid out a specified amount of money no matter what costs were incurred for care in a nursing home or for home health care. In both of the examples above, the policy would have paid out $150.

---

**"This Is Not For Us"**

I met with a couple in their early 50s who were referred to me. They were in excellent health and had no history of health problems. I went through my usual sales process and could tell their reaction was "This is not for us." Needless to say they did not buy the coverage.

The prospect's father was in excellent health—a kind of physical fitness guru—very fit, very active, and the picture of health. The prospect and his father were traveling to Australia to hike and enjoy outdoor activities. Six or seven months later I got a call from the prospect asking me to see him and his wife again. It seems that a few weeks after returning from Australia, the prospect's father had a major stroke without any warning. In addition to suffering cognitive impairment, he was totally paralyzed on his right side and the family saw no alternative but to place him in a nursing facility.

---

Rather than restricting benefits to a maximum daily amount, some policies base benefits on a weekly or monthly benefit amount, such as $1,000, $2,000, or $3,000 or more. This can dramatically affect the amount of benefits paid. A person may receive both care from a home-care agency and adult day care on a single day. On another day, that same person may receive no services and incur no expenses. Insurers with a weekly maximum allowance may multiply the daily limit times seven to create a weekly amount, or simply have a weekly amount with no reference to a MDB. If a policy is paid on a weekly basis with a MDB, for example, of $100 per day, the insured could incur up to $700 of covered expenses on the same day, and they would all be paid by the LTCI policy, provided the total amount of expenses for the week did not exceed $700. If the monthly benefit is $3,000, based on a $100 per day MDB, the insured could have up to $3,000 of paid services (30 times $100) for the month regardless of the $100 MDB amount. Alternatively, the monthly maximum benefit could be $3,000 without any reference to a MDB. In this case any covered expenses up to the $3,000 monthly maximum would be paid. This manner of accounting for expenses can help explain to some extent the premium differences in policies.

All policies have some outright exclusions, such as self-inflicted injury, acts of war, and chemical or alcohol dependency. A policy will usually contain some form of pre-existing condition exclusion clause. This provides that there is no coverage for any condition for which the insured was previously treated within a certain period.

Although coverage and age-based premiums differ widely, typically very few companies issue new policies beyond the age of 80 or 85. It is on the minimum issue age where you will find the greatest variation. Some companies do not have a minimum issue age. Other companies sell policies to persons as young as age 20. Still other companies have a minimum issue in the 40-to-50 age range.

### The Policy Trigger

The policy begins paying benefits when the policyowner meets certain criteria known as policy or benefit triggers. For example, tax-qualified policy benefits are triggered when the claimant is either cognitively impaired or is unable to perform at least two of five or six activities of daily living (ADLs) such as eating, bathing, dressing, toileting, transferring, and continence. Other criteria may apply for nonqualified policies, such as a physician's certification that long-term care is medically necessary.

Following are some of the features and explanations for the characteristics of a long-term care insurance policy.

### Definitions

Precise, uniform definitions of skilled, intermediate, custodial, and home care coverage do not currently exist. This lack of standardization also applies to the levels of care frequently provided by long-term care policies. Most policies cover skilled-nursing, intermediate, and custodial care, but beyond that policies vary. As you study your company's or a competitor's marketing material for these policies, focus on the definitions that dictate the coverage and the resulting premium. Following are some generally accepted definitions of these levels of care.

*Skilled Nursing Care.* Daily nursing care ordered by a doctor. This care can only be performed by, or under the supervision of, skilled medical personnel.

*Intermediate Nursing Care.* Occasional nursing or rehabilitative care ordered by a doctor. Again, this care can only be performed by skilled medical personnel.

*Custodial Care.* Care primarily for meeting personal needs such as bathing, dressing, toileting, and indoor mobility. This care requires no medical training, but it is administered under a doctor's orders.

*Home Health Care.* Care is received at home, usually on a part-time basis. This can include skilled care, unskilled care, or both.

*Skilled Care.* Care ordered by a doctor can include nursing care, rehabilitative care, and speech and physical therapy. This is given part-time in the home.

*Personal Care.* Help with daily activities such as cooking, cleaning, and washing on a part-time basis.

*Adult Day Care.* Care is provided at a long-term care facility on a day-to-day basis. The policyowner receives assistance with various ADLs with skilled medical care on call.

*Respite Care.* This coverage provides a brief rest period for those who provide care at home. The person receiving care may be cared for at home or placed in a long-term care facility for a short period, usually overnight, so at-home caregivers can rest.

### General Provisions

In addition, it is important to understand the general provisions you will encounter when working with LTCI policies. The discussion below looks at some of the more popular ones.

*Inflation Protection.* This provision adds a certain percentage of additional coverage to the original base amount at a specified time. Most states require that an LTCI policy offer some type of automatic inflation protection as a coverage option. The cost of the automatic inflation option is usually built into the initial annual premium, and no additional premium is levied at the time annual benefit increases occur.

**guaranteed renew-able**

***Renewal Provisions.*** Terms of renewability explain certain limitations regarding cancellation for any reason other than nonpayment of premium. LTCI policies currently being sold are usually *guaranteed renewable*, which means that the premiums cannot be raised for a particular insured. However, premiums can be increased for the entire underwriting class of insureds in the state where the policies were filed.

***Group.*** The employer or association receives a master contract. The insured receives a certificate of coverage. The group can be terminated by the carrier.

***Premium.*** The actual premium is determined by several factors including sex, age, medical history, and benefits. Some plans have regularly scheduled premium increases. These would be in addition to any rate increase for all owners of a particular class of policies.

***Waiver of Premium.*** If a plan includes a provision for waiver of premium, it will state how many days, often 60 or 90, the insured must receive benefits before premiums are waived.

***Benefits.*** Benefits differ between policies and even those offered by a single company. Some of these differences appear in the following areas:

**elimination period**

- *Elimination Period.* The *elimination period* is the duration of time that must pass after LTC commences but before benefit payments begin. Most insurers allow the prospect to select this period from several choices, such as 30, 60, 100, or 180 days. Choices may be as low as 0 days or as high as 365 days. In a comprehensive policy, normally a single elimination period can be met by any combination of days during which the insured is in an LTC facility or receiving home-health-care services. However, some insurers have separate elimination periods for facility care benefits, and home and community care benefits. The two elimination periods may be for the same length of time, and days used for one elimination period may or may not be used to offset each other.
- *Benefit Amounts.* This is the level of benefits payable to the insured. Typically, benefits are expressed in daily benefit amounts of $10 increments ranging from $50 to $500. Some policies base benefits on a weekly or monthly benefit amount.

<table>
<tr><td>

**benefit period**

</td><td>

- *Benefit Period.* The *benefit period* is the maximum duration of time for which benefits are paid. Most insurers make several options available. For example, one insurer offers durations of two, three, and five years as well as lifetime benefits. There are also a few policies, usually of the indemnity (per diem) type, that do not specify a benefit period, but only specify the maximum amount of benefits that will be paid (a stated dollar amount such as $100,000). After the maximum benefits have been paid, the policy terminates.

  Some comprehensive policies have separate benefit periods for stays in a LTC facility and for home health care. For example, if each of these periods is three years, an insured could potentially collect benefit payments for up to six years—three years while receiving benefits at home and an additional three years after entering a LTC facility.

- *Maximum Dollar Benefit of Policy.* Today, the pool of money method is the predominant approach to determining maximum policy benefits. Comprehensive plans base their total benefits on the total sum of money in the pool that can be paid under the policy. Although days are used, it is not in the strict sense of actually counting days of benefits, but as a way of determining the maximum dollar amount payable under the policy. The maximum dollar amount can be calculated by multiplying the number of days (years) of coverage times the MDB amount. For example, if an insured has a two-year benefit period (730 days) and a $150 per day MDB, the pool of money is $109,500 (730 x $150 = $109,500).

  As benefits are paid for the actual charges incurred up to the MDB, the pool of money is reduced by the actual dollar amount of benefits paid. There is actually no need to count the number of days that care is received. For example, if the insured had a two-year, $150 per day MDB, but only used $75 per day, the policy would last four years. If the insured did not receive care every day, the coverage would last even longer.

- *Types of Care Covered.* LTCI policies pay for facility care (nursing home and assisted-living facilities), home and community-based care, or both.

- *Nonforfeiture.* Some states as well as the NAIC model legislation require that such a benefit be offered. With a nonforfeiture benefit, the policyowner will receive some value for the policy if the policy lapses because the required premium is not paid. The most common type of nonforfeiture option is a shortened benefit period. With this option, coverage is continued as a paid-up policy, but the length of the benefit period (or the amount of the benefit if stated as a maximum dollar

</td></tr>
</table>

amount) is reduced. Under a typical provision, the reduced coverage is available only if the lapse is on or after the policy's third anniversary.

- *Shared or Joint Benefit.* Most insurers provide for a shared benefit for a husband and wife. Under this benefit, each spouse can access the benefits of the other spouse. For example, if each spouse has a four-year benefit period, and one spouse has exhausted his or her benefits, benefit payments can continue by drawing on any unused benefits under the other spouse's policy. In effect, one spouse could have a benefit period of up to eight years if the other spouse received no benefit payments. In another variation of benefit sharing, an insurer might allow the transfer of any unused benefits to a surviving spouse's policy, or an insurer might allow the spouses to purchase an extra pool of money equal to the separate pool of money on each spouse. If either or both spouses exhaust their individual pools, this extra pool can be accessed. In addition, at least one insurer offers a shared benefit for family members. Based on the significant difference in money available under these three optional benefits, the total annual premiums of policies within them can vary by as much as 40 percent. These optional benefits demonstrate that it is not enough to know that a policy offers some type of shared benefit. You must carefully study the exact policy language to understand the differences when comparing policies.

- *Bed Reservation Benefit.* Policies that provide nursing home care often provide a bed reservation benefit, which continues policy payments to a LTC facility for a limited time (such as 20 days) if the insured temporarily leaves the facility. It may be that an insured needs to be hospitalized for an acute condition or wishes to temporarily leave the nursing home to attend a family reunion or holiday activity.

- *Spousal (or Partner) Discount.* Most policies today offer some type of spousal (or partner) discount, although they vary considerably in their scope and complexity. Depending on the requirements of the issuing company and the application state, the discounts may depend on whether both spouses are accepted by the same company or only one spouse is accepted. Some states even require that a married person be given the discount whether or not the spouse applies for or is even insurable for LTCI. Some companies offer the discount to unmarried couples or same-sex partners. Living with another person tends to lower the need for LTC, so companies are gradually becoming more favorably disposed to offering these types of discounts.

- *Return-of-Premium (ROP) Rider.* Some policies offer a nonforfeiture benefit in the form of a return-of-premium (ROP) rider under which a portion of the premium is returned if the policy lapses. There are also policies that refund all the premiums paid if the insured dies without claiming benefits on the LTCI policy. As expected, such policies are significantly more expensive that those without the ROP rider.

### *Insurance Reform through HIPAA*

**Health Insurance Portability and Accountability Act (HIPAA)**

In 1996, Congress passed several acts of major importance to those who market or purchase long-term care insurance. The Health Insurance Portability and Accountability Act of 1996 (HIPAA) established standards for LTCI, where there previously were none, and created the tax-qualified product that is eligible for favorable tax treatment. As a result, long-term care contract provisions were required to meet certain specifications.

To be considered a tax-qualified product, a long-term care contract

- must be guaranteed renewable
- can not have any cash-surrender value except for specified refunds of premiums or dividends
- may not duplicate Medicare benefits
- may cover only long-term care services which include necessary and rehabilitative services, and maintenance or personal care services that are required by a chronically ill individual. A chronically ill individual is a person who is unable to perform, without substantial assistance from another person, at least two activities of daily living (ADLs) for a period of at least 90 days, or who requires substantial supervision because of cognitive impairment.
- must meet the consumer protection provisions specified by state law

If these conditions are met, then a business may deduct the premiums it pays for qualified long-term care insurance. If an individual pays the premium, then he or she may deduct the premiums as unreimbursed medical expenses. In order to do this, the employee must itemize his or her medical expenses and meet the 7.5 percent of AGI threshold for the medical expense deduction. Eligible premiums are subject to dollar limitations based on age, as found in Table 6-2. The numbers provided are for the 2009 tax year and are indexed annually. Your company should have information on the changes to these limits.

**TABLE 6-2**
**Tax Deductibility of LTCI Premiums for 2009**

| If attained age before the end of the tax year is | The maximum amount deductible is |
|---|---|
| 40 or less | $320 |
| Over 40 but not more than 50 | $600 |
| Over 50 but not more than 60 | $1,190 |
| Over 60 but not more than 70 | $3,180 |
| Over 70 | $3,980 |

### *Prospecting*

The most natural place for an advisor to start prospecting a new product is among an existing client base. Nearly all clients may need this insurance protection. As you perform annual policy reviews, inform each client of the dangers associated with failing to plan for long-term care. Even a short stay in a long-term care facility without insurance can be financially disastrous to a family. This is avoidable when products such as long-term care insurance can provide the protection.

***Demographics.*** There are four distinct markets for long-term care insurance (some have been penetrated more than others):

- baby boomers
- preretirement-age adults
- retired people
- third-party purchasers (the family)

Due to their longer life expectancy, women have a greater need for long-term care. Consider that women outnumber men in nursing homes three to one. Also, many adult children are willing to pay for LTCI for their parents to ensure they receive long-term care if needed.

***Attitudes.*** As always, people who like to reduce their risk exposure are your best candidates. This is why existing clients are your best prospects. They have demonstrated an understanding of what insurance can do for them in reducing risks and providing financially when it is most needed.

You will also find that people who value independence and self-reliance make good prospects as well, as they do not want to burden their friends and family or depend on the government to provide for them. They want to ensure they can make choices about the care they may receive in the future.

---

### Motives for Buying Long-Term Care Insurance

People buy for many reasons. Here are a few to probe for:

- Does the prospect want to avoid burdening their children or loved with caring for them?
- Is the prospect concerned about outliving his or her resources?
- Does the prospect want to preserve his or her estate for heirs or other reasons?
- Does the prospect want to ensure he or she is able to make choices about here to receive LTC and who will provide it?

---

Long-term care insurance should be introduced as a core part of total-needs planning. Make your prospects aware of the need. When you have a product to sell, illustrate its effectiveness in protecting family assets by shouldering the cost of care. Keep in mind that young clients have parents who need this coverage. Think about prospects age 40 and older. You should be providing long-term care information to them. They should consider LTC coverage while they are insurable and the coverage is reasonably affordable. Many excellent prospects are those adult children or other relatives of persons who have experienced significant LTC episodes.

## Other Related Insurance Products and Benefits

### Accelerated Death Benefits

**accelerated death benefits**

A development in the long-term care market is the introduction of accelerated death benefit riders or provisions attached to life insurance policies. Policies contain a formula that will pay a benefit not only upon death, but also upon a significant health event in a person's life. This might be a catastrophic illness, dread disease, or confinement to a nursing home. This is considered a prepayment of some portion of the death benefit to the insured. Under HIPAA, payments are tax exempt on the federal level and in most states.

### Cancer Expense and Dread Disease Insurance

Cancer expense insurance is similar in some ways to long-term care insurance. Both types of coverage are designed to help cover the cost of care after diagnosis of serious health care problems. In the past, cancer insurance was marketed to younger people who sought financial protection against the medical expenses associated with cancer. Those who have purchased long-term care protection have generally been older. This is beginning to change as companies and advisors come to understand the public's interest in the market for long-term care.

Cancer expense policies are either sold separately or combined with protection offered for other dread diseases. This secondary group of diseases has evolved over time, and may identify for coverage more than 15 illnesses. These range from such health problems as Addison's disease to tuberculosis, polio, and multiple sclerosis.

These policies may be purchased individually or for a family as a unit. The limited medical information required for underwriting helps identify previous diagnosis and treatment for one of the covered health conditions.

The benefits are usually paid on a scheduled basis and may include lifetime benefit limits like many other health plans.

As life expectancy increases and the health care costs associated with aging increase, the need for long-term care will increase even for those who opt to care for aging relatives in their homes. At some point, care in the home may become physically or emotionally impossible, and a long-term care facility will be necessary.

In reviewing the policy, you can see how long-term care insurance can relieve the burden for LTC expenses. This product will appeal to those who want to preserve their estates for their heirs and do not want to burden loved ones with the responsibility of caring for them.

## NOTES

1. Sid Gronerman and Elizabeth Pope, *Staying Ahead of the Curve 2007: The AARP Work and Career Study*, (Washington, DC: AARP Knowledge Management, 2008), 7.
2. National Center for Health Statistics, "Table 12. Number and percent distribution of nursing home residents by length of time since admission (in days) and mean and median length of time according to selected resident characteristics: United States, 2004," Center for Disease Control and Prevention, www.cdc.gov/nchs/data/nnhsd/Estimates/nnhs/Estimates_PaymentSource_Tables.pdf  (accessed May 6, 2009).
3. American Council of Life Insurers. *Long-term Care Insurance: Protection for Your Future,* (Washington, DC: American Council of Life Insurers, 2007), 1.
4. AHIP.org, *Guide to Long-Term Care Insurance*, (Washington, DC: America's Health Insurance Plans, 2004), 3.
5. National Center for Health Statistics, "Table 8. Number of nursing home residents by selected resident characteristics according to all sources of payment at time of admission and at time of interview: United States, 2004," Center for Disease Control and Prevention, www.cdc.gov/nchs/data/nnhsd/Estimates/nnhs/Estimates_PaymentSource_Tables.pdf (accessed May 6, 2009).

## CHAPTER SIX REVIEW

*Key terms and concepts are explained in the Glossary. Answers to the review and self-test questions are found in the back of the textbook in the Answers to Questions section.*

### Key Terms and Concepts

| | |
|---|---|
| mature adult market segment | care settings |
| Medicare | intermediate care |
| Medicare Part A | Medicaid |
| Medicare Part B | nursing home care |
| Medicare Part C | assisted-living facility care |
| Medicare Part D | home health care |
| Medicare prescription drug plans | hospice care |
| coverage gap (doughnut hole) | reimbursement basis |
| Medicare supplement insurance (medigap) | indemnity basis |
| | guaranteed renewable |
| Medicare SELECT | elimination period |
| long-term care | benefit period |
| activities of daily living (ADLs) | Health Insurance Portability and |
| instrumental activities of daily living (IADLs) | Accountability Act (HIPAA) |
| | accelerated death benefits |

### Review Questions

6-1.  What are the common characteristics of the mature adult market segment?

6-2.  What are the common needs of the mature adult market segment?

6-3.  What are the five basic coverages under Medicare Part A?

6-4.  What does Medicare Part B cover?

6-5.  What do Medicare Parts C and D cover?

6-6.  What is a medigap (Medicare supplement) policy and what does it cover?

6-7.  Discuss the reasons for the increasing need for long-term care insurance.

6-8.  Name six activities of daily living (ADLs) that might trigger the benefit of a long-term care policy.

6-9.  What does a long-term care policy generally cover?

6-10.  Describe the basic features of a long-term care insurance policy.

## Self-test Questions

*Instructions: Read Chapter 6 and then answer the following questions to test your knowledge. There are 10 questions. Choose one answer for each question, and then check your answers with the answer key in the back of the textbook.*

6-1. Which of the following services is covered by Medicare Part A?

    (A)   inpatient hospital care
    (B)   doctors' services
    (C)   durable medical equipment
    (D)   outpatient hospital services

6-2. Part A of Medicare is available without premium to

    (A)   people who retire
    (B)   people who meet the means test
    (C)   Social Security recipients age 65 or older
    (D)   Social Security recipients at age 62 or older

6-3. The policy trigger that determines if a person is eligible for benefits from a long-term care policy is

    (A)   the date of hospitalization
    (B)   the end of the benefit period
    (C)   the date at which the policy goes into effect
    (D)   the date at which the inability to perform certain activities of daily life (ADLs) occurs

6-4. The principal attitude for the mature market regarding finances is

    (A)   spending down assets as quickly as possible
    (B)   accepting of market risk to accumulate wealth
    (C)   indestructibility and invincibility
    (D)   safety and security

6-5.   What is the total percentage of compensation an employee pays towards OASDI and HI?

   (A)   1.45%
   (B)   6.20%
   (C)   7.65%
   (D)   15.30%

6-6.   Long-term care policies that pay a specified amount per day regardless of actual costs incurred for care pay benefits on a

   (A)   reimbursement basis
   (B)   indemnity basis
   (C)   facility-only basis
   (D)   maximum-daily-benefit basis

6-7.   Which of the following statements is (are) correct regarding Medicare coverage?

   I.    Part A covers hospital insurance.
   II.   Part B covers medical and surgical outpatient service and diagnostic tests.

   (A)   I only
   (B)   II only
   (C)   Both I and II
   (D)   Neither I nor II

6-8.   Which of the following statements is (are) true about Medicare?

   I.    It covers long-term care custodial costs.
   II.   It covers persons over the age of 65 eligible for Social Security.

   (A)   I only
   (B)   II only
   (C)   Both I and II
   (D)   Neither I nor II

6-9. All of the following are activities of daily living used to trigger long-term care insurance benefits EXCEPT

(A)   bathing
(B)   dressing
(C)   transferring
(D)   cooking

6-10. All of the following are common characteristics of mature adults EXCEPT

(A)   They have a greater concern about healthcare.
(B)   They have more time.
(C)   They are more deliberate.
(D)   They have no tolerance for risk.

# *Delivery, Service the Plan, and a Basic Marketing Plan*

---

## Learning Objectives

*An understanding of the material in this chapter should enable you to*

7-1. Explain the steps that will help achieve the objectives of a good policy or contract delivery.

7-2. Identify the cost of a lapsed or cancelled product to the client, the company, and to you.

7-3. Explain the monitoring process and its role in client building.

7-4. Describe and explain the importance of the multiple service level strategy of providing service to differentiate your clients.

7-5. Describe how to create a basic marketing plan.

7-6. Summarize the role of compliance, regulation, ethics, and professionalism in the financial advisor's marketing activities.

---

This chapter begins by looking at the last task of plan implementation (Step 7 of the selling/planning process) for some financial products: delivering the product. When applicable, the delivery of a product is an excellent opportunity to lay the foundation for the eighth and last step of the selling/planning process: service the plan. The chapter then examines how to service the plan with the objective of creating and retaining clients, increasing referrals, and enhancing the advisor's business. The chapter closes with a look at applying the concepts described in this textbook to create a basic marketing plan that utilizes the target marketing strategy.

## POLICY OR CONTRACT DELIVERY

**purpose of delivery**
Helping new prospects properly address their financial needs is always satisfying, but providing service to existing clients to keep their plans current is often the most professionally and financially rewarding part of the job. The *purpose of delivery* of a policy, contract, or plan is an important step in

laying the foundation for future service contacts with a new client because it can achieve three objectives:

(1) *It can reinforce the sale by reemphasizing the objectives of the purchase.* New clients who clearly understand how the product meets their needs will be less likely to let it lapse or move their accounts to a competitor.

(2) *It can help the advisor gain the new client's trust, and it sets expectations for future service and repeat sales.* Set the expectations and schedule for future services such as periodic reviews of their insurance, investment, or financial plan. In addition, you can discuss other immediate or future needs identified during the selling/planning process. This may lead to follow-up sales or lay the groundwork for them down the road.

(3) *It can offer another opportunity to obtain referred leads.* A satisfied new client can be your best source of referrals. What better time is there to ask for the names of people, for whom your services and products might also be of value, than at policy delivery?

**steps of an effective delivery**

Accomplishing these objectives involves more than simply handing over or mailing the financial product, or completing required paperwork. The *steps of an effective delivery* involve managing the issuance process, preparing for the delivery, executing the policy or contract review, establishing expectations for an ongoing relationship, and asking for referrals.

## Managing the Issuance Process

For insurance products, there is an issuance process, namely underwriting, which results in a delay between the closing of the sale and the receipt of the product. Note that during this interim, the prospect is often referred to as an applicant and not a new client, as the application may be denied by the company or not accepted by the applicant.

Sometimes a similar delay may occur for investment and other financial products as well. However, for investment and other financial products, prospects move directly to a new client classification.

Regardless of which type of product is involved, it is critical that the advisor monitors the issuance process and takes appropriate action as needed.

### *Insurance Products*

Managing the issuance process for insurance products begins with communicating reasonable expectations during the closing interview. Let applicants know what to expect in terms of any contacts, exams, and so on related to the underwriting process. Also, provide a timeline if possible.

Monitor the underwriting process and keep the applicant informed throughout, especially if there are delays in issuing the policy. Contact the applicant at various appointed times in the process to communicate the status of the application and whether additional information may be needed. For example, if an attending physician's statement (APS) or a physical exam is needed, communicate this requirement to your applicant so he or she will feel a part of the process and will not be surprised. Remaining actively involved during the underwriting process demonstrates you are not so eager to sell your next case that you cannot be bothered with your applicant's present situation.

When you receive the policy, review it to make sure it that the policy type and amount of insurance are correct. If any changes have been made, such as a rated premium or an exclusion rider, be sure you can explain the situation to the applicant. Check the accuracy of the applicant's information, premium amounts, mode of payment, beneficiary designations, and optional benefits. The policy will need to be amended (corrected) if a mistake has been made.

### *Investment Products*

Occasionally, investment products may take several weeks or even months to be processed and placed. For example, a rollover of funds from a 401(K) into an IRA may be delayed by the custodian of the 401(k). That custodian may require specialized forms, signed by the customer, to authorize the rollover. Tax-free exchanges (for example, 1035 exchange) may also be delayed. You should ensure you have an adequate follow-up system to track the process and personally intervene when unexplained delays occur. As with insurance products, inform the new client when delays are encountered.

### *All Products*

If you have not already done so, update the new client's contact record with pertinent information about the policy or investment product in your records. Do not let this important work backlog—do it as it comes across your desk. Note any important information regarding contacts, activities, and services rendered to the client. Describe any agreements you made with the client such as future meetings or the respective responsibilities of the client or yourself. In addition, for marketing purposes, indicate the target market to which the new client belongs as well as the financial and emotional reasons for buying the product.

## Preparing for Delivery

As you prepare for delivery, here are a few important tasks to complete. Note that from this point on, we will refer to the applicant/new client as a client.

### *Tie Up Loose Ends*

If you promised your client you would contact another advisor, or speak with a lawyer or accountant, be sure to follow through. Prepare a brief report on your follow-up during the delivery interview. The same holds true if your prospect gave you a referral during the sales interview, suggesting that you contact the person soon. Do not put it off until it is convenient. Follow up on the referral before delivery. If the matter was important enough to your client to bring it to your attention, show that you thought it was important too.

### *Call for an Appointment*

Determine how much time you will need to explain the product, to establish expectations for future service, and to get referred leads. Call the client for an appointment to deliver the product. The amount of time needed for the appointment will probably be less if you are delivering one product or if you are dealing with an existing client. When delivering more than one product (or a financial plan) to a new client, you will want to take more time to review the reasons for the purchase (or the details of the plan). Plan the meeting accordingly so that you are not rushed.

### *Add a Few Professional Touches*

A few professional touches go a long way. A product portfolio or policy wallet is an inexpensive way to add flair to your delivery. It gives the client a place to keep the product and related information, and provides a place for your business card for future reference. A large portfolio will do the above and provide room for other financial and insurance products that the client owns or may buy from you in the future. Insert the policy, your business card, and any other information you wish to include before the appointment. Do not do it in the car at the last minute.

### *Include Any Required Information*

Check with your company to see what is required for an insurance policy or investment product delivery. For example, you are required to include the illustration of an issued life insurance policy. A new illustration is required if the policy issued differs from the one for which the client applied. It must comply with state and company delivery requirements.

Investment products are closely regulated, and client-approved pieces are normally included in the investment contract or portfolio statement. You must know and follow your company's compliance procedures. Be sure that all handouts or information piece are compliance-approved.

### *Add Backup Information*

Product review checklists or summaries can be printed on letterhead, or may be provided by your company. These can be inserted in the portfolio or policy wallet. Checklists, summaries, and illustrations will be very useful in reviewing the product that was purchased. All of this backup information serves to reinforce the purpose and need for the product. Use your strongest materials that communicate your expertise, your caring attitude, and the other services and products you provide.

Other useful support items include your company-approved consumer information brochures, a list of service suggestions, and information on claims procedures (for insurance products) that will be valuable to the client and family members. Some advisors also recommend including a copy of the company's annual report, explaining in the interview, "Now that you are one of our clients, I thought you'd like to know a little more about the company and its operations. Here's a copy of our latest annual report."

Check with your company to see what types of compliant support materials are available. Goodwill items, like company calendars and pens can add a personal touch to your message saying, "I care about you and appreciate your business."

### *Practice Your Presentation*

Once you have put your delivery package together, outline what you want to say and rehearse the presentation. Make it smooth and professional. Plan ahead to set the stage for future sales to cover needs discovered but not yet addressed. Consider how you will ask for referrals.

When you have prepared your presentation, make a short list of items (an agenda) you plan to cover; take it to the interview and use it to keep yourself on track. By preparing well and rehearsing in advance, your presentation will be smoother and you will be less likely to forget to cover an important point.

## Executing the Policy or Contract Review

The last step for an effective delivery is to execute the policy or contract review. Reviews involving insurance policies tend to be more involved than those involving investment contracts. This section will look at conducting an involved policy review for life insurance products, as well as a contract review for an investment product. This section closes with a look at reselling the need, if necessary.

### Review the Policy: Life Insurance Products

***Explaining the Policy as Valuable Property.*** A life insurance policy is property with a value that goes well beyond the face amount of protection. Since the life insurance policy is valuable property, point out that dropping a policy and replacing it with another is generally not a good practice, and it can be a costly one. The policyowner would have to pay the start-up costs again, including a new sales commission, and would be starting a new contract at an older age.

Ask your clients to contact you if another advisor attempts to sell them additional protection or tries to induce them to drop the protection they own. Remind them that you have done your best to review fully their life and health insurance needs. Let them know that you would be happy to discuss the opinions of another advisor who might suggest that a different approach or product would be more suitable to their needs.

Inform your clients if your state requires a policyowner to sign a special replacement form when a policy is sold to replace an existing policy (check your state and company requirements). Advisors who attempt to replace life insurance policies without submitting the form are violating state regulations.

***Meeting the Delivery Requirements.*** States have adopted policies promoted by the National Association of Insurance Commissioners (NAIC) in its Model Life Insurance Solicitation Regulation. This regulation provides a system of comparison and disclosure to which life insurance companies and advisors must comply. Compliance involves furnishing a "Policy Summary" and "Buyer's Guide" at policy delivery (or before taking the application). Your company can provide these brochures and directions on their use.

*The Buyer's Guide.* This brochure, prepared by the NAIC, presents basic facts about life insurance in a simple manner. It covers topics such as the selection of the proper amount of coverage, the differences between the main types of insurance (permanent and term), what the interest-adjusted cost indexes are and how they should be used, and a summary explaining that illustrative cost indexes are not the only consideration. Quality of service rendered by the advisor and the company are also important factors.

*Policy Summary.* This contains information about the policy. It shows premiums, cash values, illustrative dividends (if applicable), guaranteed death benefits, interest-adjusted indices, and the policy loan interest rate. Separate pages for each term rider are included.

*Signed Illustration.* The NAIC Model Illustration Regulation has become law in most states and policy in many companies. This regulation establishes guidelines for companies and advisors regarding the content and presentations of sales illustrations. The regulation covers all life insurance products except face amounts under $10,000 and variable life. It requires that an illustration matching the issued policy be presented to the customer. The advisor and policyowner must sign this illustration; one copy is given to the policyowner, one is returned to the company, and one is retained in the advisor's client file.

*Delivery Receipt.* Most companies and some states require that the advisor and customer sign receipts upon policy delivery. This form typically contains information regarding guaranteed and non-guaranteed elements in the policy and information regarding proper policy delivery. The client and advisor sign and retain one copy each; another copy is returned to the insurer.

*Client File.* A client file must be kept as long as a policy is in force. After a policy is no longer in force because it has lapsed, was surrendered, or a claim was paid, a file must be kept for five to eight years, depending on your jurisdiction. When litigation or other disputes occur, files should be kept even longer. Individual companies and states may have their own rules for documents to be maintained in files, but these are the typical requirements:

- complete illustrations, including signed NAIC illustrations
- all sales materials used in solicitation of the sale
- fact finder and related materials
- replacement forms and related materials
- copy of policy delivery receipts
- contact sheet used to keep records of the dates and content of all client contacts
- substantive correspondence concerning contractual changes or concerns of client
- no original documents should be in the file, especially signed, blank documents

Check with your company for its specific requirements.

### Review the Contract: Investment Products

Thoroughly review the account statements related to the investment product. Make sure the customer knows how to read the statements and when to expect future statements. If they have any problems, ask them to call your office— not the home office of the investment company.

### Resell the Need—Rekindle the Motivation

**buyer's remorse**

A delay between closing and delivery provides time for *buyer's remorse* to occur, in which a new client wonders if he or she made the right decision. Be prepared to address potential doubts by reestablishing the need for the purchase, and rekindling the motivation for addressing the need.

After some opening pleasantries, begin reviewing your client's objectives and financial situation as discussed in the fact-finding interview. Check for agreement.

Reestablish the shortfall between existing benefits and immediate or future needs. Illustrate again your proposal for filling this gap in cash or income requirements. If appropriate, revisit your discussion of the long-term nature of insurance and investment products, and carefully review surrender charges, annual fees, and free withdrawal amounts.

Review the product and show why it will perform as you said it would. Your purpose is to help the client recapture the sense of urgency that led to the purchase decision. The amount of detail you use will depend on several factors:

- the length of time since the closing interview
- the client's personality
- the product and whether it is meant to satisfy a single need or is part of a comprehensive financial plan
- whether you are dealing with a new client or an existing one

In some situations, the financial product you are delivering may be just the first of several to meet the various needs and objectives detailed in the financial plan. Show your client exactly where this product fits into the big picture and how subsequent additions will help complete the overall plan.

## Establishing the Expectations for an Ongoing Relationship

If your new clients feel good about their purchase and about you, they will feel committed to both their plan and to you. In turn, you must make a commitment to be there to monitor and service the plan. Product delivery is the time to set the stage for a solid, long-term relationship by selling your customer on the idea of becoming your client. You can do that by explaining the difference between a customer and a client, describing the services that you offer, and agreeing to expectations about your ongoing relationship.

### Explain the Difference Between Customers and Clients

The term *client* is often used to refer someone who has purchased an insurance or other financial product. In fact, we might also refer to them as a customer. Are the terms *customer* and *client* interchangeable? For the purposes of writing about how to market financial products, we use them interchangeably to keep things simple. However, there is a difference you can use when establishing the terms of your ongoing professional relationship with a new client.

**customer**

**client**

According to the Merriam-Webster dictionary, a *customer* is "one that purchases a commodity or service."[1] A *client*, on the other hand, is defined as "one that is under the protection of another; a person who engages the professional advice or services of another."[2] It follows then that all clients are customers, but not all customers are clients. Clients are customers who follow your advice consistently, buy from you again, and refer you to others.

---

### Customer or Client

What do people who have purchased your products and services say about their relationship with you? Do they consider themselves customers or clients? What do people working in your agency say? Are they busy getting new customers or committed to developing clients?

A customer buys a policy from you, but a client is different. A client seeks your advice on coverage. A client respects your time. A client responds promptly to your request for information. A client may occasionally take quotes, but when he gets a lower price, he asks you why. A client does not expect you to personally attend to all the details of his or her account. A client values your opinion. A client pays bills on time. A client sends you referrals.

There is a big difference between a customer and a client. Every advisor must be able to recognize the difference and then find ways to turn customers into clients. The rewards are a stable book of business and quality referrals.

---

The key to converting customers to clients is the ongoing service and relationship building you provide. It means establishing the service you will provide and the standards to which you will commit yourself. Then you must fulfill or exceed those promises of service. Frequent contacts and updates are necessary, and these entail more than simply responding to customer service requests. As clients grow, the advisor grows, and more doors are opened through referrals and the development of clients' other financial needs and wants.

Take the time with new customers to explain the difference between a customer and a client. Point out the ways they would benefit from working with you, such as the professional advice and the convenience (if you sell multiple products). Indicate your intentions to keep the commitments you make in delivering quality and professional service. That will give you the opportunity to describe the services you offer.

### Describe the Services You Offer

For new customers, begin by explaining the services you provide in terms of changes he or she may want to make to the policy or contract. Tell customers that you are only a phone call away and will respond to them as soon as possible. Let them know you will ensure that any action completed by agency personnel or the home office is followed up in a timely manner.

Then describe the annual or periodic review that you recommend and offer every 12 to 18 months. Explain the process and its importance. In addition, clearly state the benefits to the customer.

Finally, take time to review other products and services you provide. This includes educational seminars and other complimentary services that you offer your clients. An example is helping clients understand their Social Security benefits.

### Agree Upon Expectations for Your Ongoing Relationship

Common expectations of a strong client relationship dictate that neither the customer nor the advisor should expect surprises. Take the time to ask the customer about his or her expectations for an ongoing relationship. What does he or she want in an advisor? It may be that the customer does not want a client-advisor relationship. Knowing this will help you determine the level of service the client expects, and you can adjust accordingly.

Before leaving, set a date for the annual review. Mark it on your calendar and ask your customer to do the same, making it a mutual commitment to meet even if the date is changed. As you leave, thank your client for the confidence he or she is placing in you.

## Asking for Referrals

Product delivery is one of the best opportunities you will have to ask a new customer for referrals, especially personal introductions. Your new customer is satisfied with the purchase and may even feel grateful toward you for assisting in the process. However, your business will wither on the vine unless you are able to add new names to your prospect pool.

Many advisors get about 60 percent of their business from their present clients and from referrals by these people. That statistic supports the value of client relationships and setting the stage for future sales at delivery. It also underscores the importance of referred leads to your ongoing career success.

## Relationships are Everything
### By Brian Tracy

**Your Foundation For Success**

Relationship selling is the core of all modern selling strategies. Your ability to develop and maintain long-term customer relationships is the foundation for your success as a salesperson and your success in business. Relationship selling requires a clear understanding of the dynamics of the selling process as they are experienced by your customer.

**Propose A Business Marriage**

For your customer, a buying decision usually means a decision to enter into a long-term relationship with you and your company. It is very much like a "business marriage." Before the customer decides to buy, he can take you or leave you. He doesn't need you or your company. He has a variety of options and choices open to him, including not buying anything at all. But when your customer makes a decision to buy from you and gives you money for the product or service you are selling, he becomes dependent on you. And since he has probably had bad buying experiences in the past, he is very uneasy and uncertain about getting into this kind of dependency relationship.

**Fulfill Your Promises**

What if you let the customer down? What if your product does not work as you promised? What if you don't service it and support it as you promised? What if it breaks down and he can't get it replaced? What if the product or service is completely inappropriate for his needs? These are real dilemmas that go through the mind of every customer when it comes time to make the critical buying decision.

**Focus On The Relationship**

The reason why choosing the right career, why doing what you love to do is so important, is because unless you really care about your work, you will never be motivated to persist at it until you become excellent. And until you become excellent at what you're doing, you can't move ahead.

**Build A Solid Trust Bond**

In many cases, the quality of your relationship with the customer is the competitive advantage that enables you to edge out others who may have similar products and services. The quality of the trust bond that exists between you and your customers can be so strong that no other competitor can get between you.

**Keep Your Customers For Life**

The single biggest mistake that causes salespeople to lose customers is taking those customers for granted. This is a form of "customer entropy." It is when the salesperson relaxes his efforts and begins to ignore the customer. Almost 70 percent of customers who walked away from their existing suppliers later replied that they made the change primarily because of a lack of attention from the company.

Once you have invested the time and made the efforts necessary to build a high-quality, trust-based relationship with your customer, you must maintain that relationship for the life of your business. You must never take it for granted.

**Action Exercises**

First, focus on building a high quality relationship with each customer by treating your customer so well that he comes back, buys again and refers you to his friends. Second, pay attention to your existing customers. Tell them you appreciate them. Look for ways to thank them and encourage them to come back and do business with you again.

There are reasons why delivery is a good time to get referrals. First, the atmosphere is relaxed. The decision to buy has been made and the tension is less than it has been for all concerned. Second, you have delivered the product, completed the buying process, and have reinforced the customer's trust in your recommendations and the decision to follow them. You have established yourself as a professional who is committed both to future service and to earning the right to call the customer a client. Now, perhaps more than at any other time, the customer wants to feel good about you, and that means it is a good time to ask.

## SERVICE THE PLAN

In the beginning of this textbook, we set our overall goal to be turning prospects into clients. The intermediate result is the creation of a customer—where the prospect has purchased a product but not bought you; that is, you have not yet been able to establish a client-advisor relationship. Each step in the selling cycle contributes to the creation of a client. You cannot have a client without creating a customer and you cannot have a customer unless you execute an effective insurance planning session. In the servicing step, your goal is to turn your good customers into clients who consistently follow your recommendations and enthusiastically recommend you to others. They believe in you and the products and services you provide.

This section will begin with the objectives and benefits of providing excellent service. Then we will examine how to monitor the plan through annual reviews. The discussion of service looks at differentiating service activities for clients, potential clients, and customers. This discussion will provide the background to examine servicing opportunities, and how to stay in touch with your clients.

### Objectives of Service

**objectives of service**

Client building does not happen without providing quality service. As one top producer explains it, "I believe the essential factor for most of us in transforming a customer into a client rests basically with the type of service we provide." By service, we mean two things. First, we mean the monitoring of the insurance or financial plan through annual reviews. Second, we mean responding to customers' requests and providing some personal-touch optional services. Together, they work to achieve the following *objectives of service* as it relates to client building:

- to facilitate customer retention
- to obtain repeat sales and referrals
- to lower expenses

### *To Facilitate Customer Retention*

A strong client relationship can help prevent competitors from replacing your business. In this competitive climate, service is clearly a necessary defensive strategy. Maintaining a high profile with clients through your various service activities and other contacts will help clients feel loyal and committed to the business you have done together. A customer who feels no such loyalty or commitment is not likely to think twice about accepting the next attractive proposal that comes along. Your retention will suffer unless you take steps to keep your clients in the fold.

### *To Obtain Repeat Sales and Referrals*

Client building is also part of a smart offensive marketing and sales strategy as we see in the selling process. Experienced advisors report that as much as 75 percent of their new business comes from existing clients or referrals provided by these clients. If you are relatively new to the business, preoccupied with generating production and first-year premiums, or struggling to find a market, consider the difference it would make if most of your sales were to people who had already bought from you or those they referred. Remember that people have a tendency to refer those like themselves. If the client values your products and services, there is a good chance those they refer will also.

### *To Lower Expenses*

Another consideration is the cost of developing clients. What are your marketing and sales costs for finding one qualified prospect and going through a multiple-interview sales process? Factor them all in: the cost of the lead, sales promotion, telephone, secretarial and mail expenses, other overhead expenses, automobile costs, meals, computer time, and presentation materials. Multiply what you get by the number of prospects it takes to make a sale. By being able to sell primarily to clients and people they refer, you can drastically lower your sales and marketing costs.

## Monitoring the Plan—Annual Reviews

**monitoring**

*Monitoring* is the servicing aspect that separates a financial product from a financial plan. Financial products are often thrown into a drawer and never reviewed. If the advisor does not follow-up, the advisor-client relationship and client-building process is defeated. Conversely, a financial plan is monitored and revised to ensure that it is doing what the client intends for it to do. Because of this important distinction, we have identified monitoring as a separate topic from the other servicing activities. It is the backbone of client-building service activity. Effective monitoring is the key that professional advisors use to maintain their clients and continually improve their business. It distinguishes the professional from the stereotypical product pusher.

Monitoring should be a part of your basic service package offered to everyone who owns a product. What follows is an overview of what an advisor should monitor. It ends with a discussion of how to set up and conduct an annual review.

### Monitor Changing Needs and Circumstances

A person's personal and financial situation changes over time. Age, marriage, births, divorce, deaths, and other life events cause a person's insurance and other financial needs to change. (Incidentally, the life cycle is one way to frame the need for monitoring.) We will review some of the more common changes here.

***Insurance Coverages.*** First, there's a need to check that any insurance coverage is adequate to protect the needs the client desires to protect. In particular, it means evaluating whether or not the insured has the right coverages and the right amount of those coverages. Changes in insurance coverage could occur for various reasons including the following:

- additional needs discovered but not insured. For example, the original needs analysis may reveal that the new client needs more life insurance or disability income protection than could be afforded at the time of the original purchase.
- additional needs due to life events. For example, the client may marry or remarry, give birth or adopt a baby, divorce, earn a promotion, or buy a new home. All of these events could trigger new insurance needs.
- amount of current need increases. For example, inflation may spike for several years, salary and expenses may increase, or the original need may have been underestimated. An increase in assets may indicate that a personal umbrella liability policy is needed.
- changing needs due to life events. For example, when the client's adult children leave home the need for income protection may diminish, but other needs, such as long-term care coverage, may be more important. Becoming eligible for Medicare creates the need for Medicare supplement insurance products.

By updating a needs analysis periodically, you can help the client discover new needs, which could result in additional coverage.

***Life Insurance Policy Values.*** For permanent insurance, there is a need to track cash values and policy dividends (if applicable) to ensure they are going to achieve any anticipated cash goals for retirement or other future goal. Here are two examples:

- interest sensitive products such as universal or variable universal life. Because of the fluctuating values, it's important to look for times when the original cash goals may be affected by depressed interest rates or market values.
- traditional life insurance products with dividends. Dividends will need to be reviewed if paid-up additions are expected to help life insurance coverage keep pace with inflation. They would need to be reviewed if it is anticipated that they will be used to pay future premiums using the premium offset concept.

***Life Insurance Type of Need.*** For life insurance, sometimes the type of need changes. Here are two examples:

- term conversions. A client may have purchased a term policy to cover educational expenses and at some point realizes he or she will probably have needs beyond retirement. Perhaps the client's estate has grown or he or she would like to provide money for a charity.
- universal life death benefit option change. A client may find that his or her insurance needs have diminished and wants to focus on supplementing retirement income. If the client currently has a death benefit Option 2 (increasing death benefit), this is a time to consider changing to an Option 1 (level death benefit).

***Automatic Transactions or Changes.*** The greatest client-building tool is honest communication. When automatic changes occur, communication with the client can help them adjust or perhaps take advantage of them. Here are some examples of automatic transactions:

- children's term rider. Some companies will allow children insured through a children's term rider to convert to a permanent policy without evidence of insurability. If this is the case, you have the opportunity to help a young adult get started with an insurance plan.
- term premium increase. If the client or customer has purchased a guaranteed renewable term policy the rates will increase at the renewal. This is an opportunity to explain the increase and examine conversion possibilities.
- guaranteed insurability options. If the client has purchased the guaranteed insurability rider you can help him or her take advantage

of it. Some life insurance policies allow for an early exercise of the option if someone gets married or has a baby. A client may not be aware of that or may not remember.

*Investment Needs.* Life events often affect a person's need for various investment products or ability to fund them. Consider the following:

- A client's graduation from college is a perfect opportunity to discuss the need to create or increase an emergency fund, or a savings plan to accrue funds for a wedding or a down payment on a house.
- The arrival of a baby in the household may indicate a need for education planning products such as a Coverdell education savings account or a 529 plan.
- A change of employers could create a need for a rollover into an IRA or Roth IRA.
- A pay raise may indicate an opportunity to increase regular investment amounts.

*Investment Asset Allocation.* An investment portfolio rarely remains constant over the years. It is important to review the client's asset allocation for investment products to ensure it remains within the client's risk tolerance. In addition, a client's risk tolerance may change over time. For instance, as a client ages, it is appropriate to consider a more conservative asset allocation.

*Law Changes.* Sometimes the concepts used to sell the product may be affected by changes in laws. This would require monitoring to be sure that the plan performance will take place as anticipated; otherwise, changes may need to be made. Tax law changes often provide new sales opportunities. The most common areas impacted are income tax planning, retirement planning, and estate planning.

Tax law changes occur almost constantly, and you should keep abreast of them for opportunities and threats to yourself and your clients. Congressional acts commonly create changes in estate taxation and exemption amounts, income tax on capital gains, and income tax rates. Some changes occur automatically, such as annual contributions limits and deductible amounts for IRAs, which statutorily increase to keep pace with inflation. These changes are opportunities to talk with your clients about how they are affected.

### The Annual Review

annual review

Without the *annual review*, the customer meets the Merriam-Webster definition of a customer: a purchaser of a commodity. However, a person who responds favorably to an annual review is well on the way to becoming a client. Several key points regarding the annual review are outlined below.

***Set the Expectation.*** Lay the groundwork early in the process; it can be as early as the first interview when you explain to a prospect how you conduct your practice and the services you offer. State that you help people uncover their insurance and financial goals, create and implement a plan to achieve them, and monitor their plan to make adjustments as needed. This helps the prospect understand how you intend to service their plan after it is implemented.

***Keep Good Records.*** Record keeping is extremely important. An updated master folder and/or computer record will help you prepare for the annual review. Keeping good records will shorten your preparation time and provide a professional image. Make sure you record things like children's names and ages, grandchildren, and so on. Some advisors also record personal interests to help them reestablish rapport. Also, keep any notices that contain pertinent information on things such as cash value, investment performance, and so on.

***Confirm the Appointment.*** Call to confirm the appointment. You can let them know in advance to bring any documentation they may need. For example, if you were following up with a disability income plan, a W-2 and Social Security benefits statements may be needed. Some advisors send a preapproach letter reminding the client of the annual review service they offer. The advisor also follows with a phone call to set the appointment.

***Prepare for the Appointment.*** If you have kept good records, preparing will be much easier. Refresh your memory by reviewing the needs analysis and any financial information, such as a budget, that the client provided you. Look at your interview notes to remember attitudes and values. Rerun projections of the client's plan. This may involve running policy projection reports (illustrations on in-force life insurance policies), updating projected account values for investments, and updating pro forma financial statements (cash flow statement and personal balance sheet). Compare the projected values with current values and evaluate if changes are needed. Put together a list of areas where additional needs may exist.

***Conduct the Review.*** Review with the client the personal and financial situations, and status of insurance and other financial plans. Discuss progress in implementing recommendations, noting any trouble spots, and taking appropriate action. If necessary, recalculate needs and note any shortfalls. Using a client-focused selling approach, inquire about any changes in their current or future financial situation. Listen carefully and note any opportunities. Implement any plan changes and set necessary follow-up appointments.

***Ask for Referrals.*** An annual review is a perfect time to ask clients if they know anyone who might share their same values and goals. There is a very high probability that they value and trust you because they agreed to have you review their financial plan.

## Providing Service Packages

service package

Monitoring the plan and responding to customer or client requests for changes and information are often combined with other services the advisor offers in a *service package*. It is advisable to offer standard services to everyone, and offer extra services to those who meet your criteria to be a client (consider the ABC method for differentiating your clients).

### Standard Service Package

standard service package

Excellent customer service is now the price of admission in financial services. It is the expected level of service and not the exception. This means you need to create a high quality *standard service package* for dealing with routine requests for changes and information for everyone, regardless of their value to your business. You need a system that ensures all customers and clients receive the service they need and allows you to capitalize on new marketing opportunities.

***Define It.*** Define your standard service package. What services will you provide everyone and at what level? Your standard services may include the following:

- annual or periodic reviews (monitoring of the plan should be offered to everyone)
- prompt handling of changes and inquiries
- claim kit and assistance for beneficiaries (for life insurance)

You should also define the level of service they can expect, such as

- accessibility—When can they reach you? What after-hours services do you have?
- response time—How quickly will they receive a response to their phone call, e-mail, or letter?

***Communicate It.*** Once you have defined your standard service package, communicate it to your customers. Tell them what they can expect. The best times to do this are either during the closing interview or during the policy or contract delivery. Many advisors provide a flyer that describes pertinent servicing information.

***Deliver It.*** The next step is to hold yourself and your staff to what you have committed. Here are some basic tips as a matter of review:

- When you receive a request, let clients know how long it may take or when you will get back to them.
- Contact your clients after service requests to make sure that the information received or action taken was what they needed. Make sure that the service was prompt and efficient. Take the opportunity to discuss any unresolved issues related to the service request.
- Provide a claims kit that gives information for how to file an insurance claim. Offer to work closely with the insured or family members to ensure claims are promptly paid and other matters, such as settlement options, are explained and arranged.
- If your client moves to another city or state, try to arrange to keep in contact and to retain the business. If you are unable, offer to review their plan with their new advisor. Remember to discuss any protection or plans that need to be completed.

***Take Care Plus.*** Excellent service is necessary because it puts you in a position to inquire about other relevant needs. You can take care of clients and market other products and services you provide. The keys to recognizing opportunities are listening carefully and asking a few relevant questions. Here are some examples related to life insurance to get you started:

- Beneficiary changes may reveal a need to revisit the plan. For example, the insured may be changing the beneficiary due to a new spouse or baby.
- Disbursement requests (policy loan, dividend withdrawals, universal life partial surrenders, and so on) indicate that a service call is needed. They may reveal financial trouble or that the client is opening a new business or paying for a wedding. Ask what prompted the loan request. Make sure the paperwork is handled promptly and that the client understands the need to repay interest, if not principal, in order to keep the protection from eroding. Policy loans often come before a lapse, so stay in close contact with your clients and customers after they request loans.

As always, anytime someone is pleased with what you have done for them, ask for referrals.

### Extra Frills Package

**extra frills package**

For some of your clients, you will want to provide an *extra frills package*, which is simply a higher level of service that includes other ancillary services. This means you will need to identify what services you will provide as frills.

***Purpose of the Extra Frills Package.*** The purpose of the extra frills is to make every contact an opportunity to market. By this we mean that you accomplish one of three things:

- Create visibility. You do not want clients to think of anyone else when they think of insurance and financial products unless it is a product you do not sell.
- Create awareness of the products and services you provide. You want clients to associate your name with any product you sell and any service you provide. For example, you want them to know you sell mutual funds and have the expertise to help them plan for their retirement.
- Create a sense of personal touch. You want clients to associate you with insurance and other products and services you provide, and you want them to think of you as a person who cares about them. You want them to see you as someone who provides what they need, when they need it, and how they want it.

***Define the Frills Package.*** Effectiveness will vary from advisor to advisor—what works for some may not work for you. What works will also depend on the customer or client. What one client finds interesting another may find annoying. Perception is everything. In the following examples, we refer to the audience as clients. Some of these may be directed at customers as well, especially those you might want to convert to clients.

- Send birthday and holiday cards to your clients and their families. Appropriate cards are available for this purpose from various commercial vendors of greeting cards. They can be imprinted with your name and address, and the selection of messages is wide enough so that you will be able to find one or more cards that fit your style. Ask your manager if greeting card catalogues are available. The cost is deductible as a business expense, so keep track of the postage and number of cards sent.
- Contact clients at other important dates such as marriages, christenings, bar/bat mitzvahs, births, weddings, home purchases, new jobs, or promotions. Do not limit your concern to happy occasions. You should show your sympathy and support when there are

deaths in your clients' families, or if your client or client's spouse loses a job. Your sympathy or regrets in these situations will be appreciated. Your support and, more importantly, your advice and assistance may be even more significant both to your client and to your business.

- Handwritten notes add a real personal touch. Sending copies of news clippings that are of special interest to your clients demonstrates you know who they are. A good practice is to scan the local newspaper every day for articles about or of interest to your clients. When you see an announcement about a client's family or business, send a copy of it with a brief personal note. (Be sure to include publication name and date of appearance.) This source of news about your clients can also uncover new sales or service opportunities for which you will want to follow up. For example, you may find out they are a member of a community club or professional organization that may be a great target market for you.

- Commercial (as always with company approval) or company-sponsored newsletters offer a wide selection of tax and financial information that you can send to your clients either monthly or quarterly. In many cases, the letters can be personalized with your name, address, logo, and photograph. You may also be able to enclose a return mail card that the client can use to request more information about the topics covered in that issue. Ask your manager about the availability of these newsletter services and their costs.

- Contact clients by phone to let them know the general results of any contacts you have had with people they referred to you. Thank them for their support.

- Follow up by phone when the first premium is due to make sure that the amount and timing of the premium notice are correct, and that the billing department has the insured's correct name, address, and policy number. Also, ask if everything is all right and if there is anything else you can do for them.

- To keep their names in front of clients and customers, many advisors give imprinted calendars, refrigerator magnets, pens, and other items. Look for package offers and quantity discounts on larger purchases.

- Look for articles of interest in the business or general press and send copies of these items to appropriate clients. Consumer-oriented brochures can be used in the same way.

- Offer special client events, such as a client appreciation event or an educational seminar. Send a special invitation. One prospecting strategy is to send tickets for the client, a spouse, and a friend (a potential prospect).

Take the time to define what frills you will offer. Make sure that you can deliver and that they are cost effective from both a monetary and time standpoint.

***Commit Yourself to It.*** Commit yourself to your frills package by including it in your business plan and preparing a list of your services that you may give to your clients at product delivery, on annual reviews, or in a special mailing. Let them know these are the services you provide to the people you value as clients.

### Classifying Clients—The ABC Method

**ABC method**

The purpose of monitoring and servicing is to build client relationships. Realistically, not everyone who purchases a product will want to become your client. Conversely, there will be people who buy from you that you would prefer not become your client. This means you will need to identify whom you want to be a client. A great way to do this is the *ABC method* in which you segment your book of business into three categories or grades:

- "A" clients—These are people who believe in you and the products you sell. They are a source for repeat sales and referrals. Your long-term goal is to only deal with these clients. They merit your very best service.
- "B" clients—These are customers whom you wish to turn into clients, or customers who have purchased financial products from you in the past year, but who have not yet committed to a full client relationship. These are your "B" clients. To the "B" group you will offer a broader range of services than the "C" group. Your goal is to eventually drop them to the basic service group or to raise them to client status.
- "C" clients— These are people who have either demonstrated that they do not wish to enter into an ongoing client relationship with you, or you do not want to do more than your existing business with them. These are your "C" clients to whom you offer only basic services (for example, annual reviews, and follow up on information and service requests).

***Why Classify?*** In the same way you would not place most of your money into low-yielding investments, you cannot afford to place most of your time, energy, and money in the low-profit segment of your book of business. Have you ever noticed in other businesses that the perks go to the people that generate the most revenue? Why should it be any different for an advisor's practice?

***How Do I Know?*** Exercise some caution here. Do not focus solely on income or how well you get along with the client. Look at their impact on your business. You can measure this in three ways:

- Are they a source or potential source for repeat business? For example, Matt may be a young man who does not have a lot of business with you now. However, he has demonstrated an appreciation for financial planning and he has the motivation and ability to improve his income over the years.
- Are they a source or a potential source for referrals? In the previous example, Matt may be a plumber who is part of a trade union. The union meets regularly for programs on interesting topics. Could this be a seminar opportunity?
- Are they a good client? In other words, are they easy to get along and not high maintenance? Stay away from high-maintenance, low-value clients. You will spend a lot of time and energy and have a negative net return.

***How It Works.*** Identifying "A" clients, "B" clients and "C" clients allows you to treat each accordingly in terms of the discretionary services you provide.

In selecting which services to offer, distinguish between basic and discretionary services. Clearly, you have an obligation to process policy changes and handle other requests for information or service; and you may want to send every one of your customers a calendar each year. You can be selective, however, in how you spend your service budget for items such as product portfolios, greeting cards, lunches, receptions, and other gifts. You are not obligated to include all of your customers in your newsletter mailing list or to send special clippings from the local newspaper to everyone with a personal note. These can be expensive and time-consuming gestures, and would be wasted on some clients. For example, you may take your "A" clients out to lunch or host receptions for them as a way of showing your appreciation for their business. One advisor who lives near the water and owns a sailboat makes a point of inviting some of his best clients on board for evening or weekend sails. This has been an excellent way to strengthen the association between this advisor and his clients. Golf outings, tennis matches, or running dates are other ways to share non-business interests you have in common with your clients.

### Measuring the Impact

Measure the impact of service by looking at whether or not it produces a measurable level of sales revenue. To create that revenue, monitoring and servicing will have predictable costs such as overhead, staffing, supplies, marketing, and sales costs attributable to its operation. The amount of profit is determined by a simple formula:

$$\text{Profit} = \text{Income} - \text{Costs}$$

Determine how profitable your client-building and service efforts are by identifying the income and expense items associated with these activities for any given period.

---

**How Profitable Is Your Service Work?**

Period: From _____ to _____

| Income Items | | Expense Items | |
|---|---|---|---|
| Renewal commissions: | $ _____ | Travel: | $ _____ |
| Persistency bonuses: | $ _____ | Office: | $ _____ |
| New sales to customers | | | |
|   (first year commissions): | $ _____ | Word processor costs: | $ _____ |
| | | Supplies: | $ _____ |
| | | Postage : | $ _____ |
| | | Lunch with Clients | $ _____ |
| Number of prospect leads | | Product portfolios: | $ _____ |
|   from service calls: | $ _____ | | |
| Number of sales from | | Calendars: | $ _____ |
|   prospect leads: | $ _____ | Newsletters: | $ _____ |
| | | Others (list): | $ _____ |
| | | | $ _____ |
| | | | $ _____ |
| | | | |
| Total income from service work: | | | $ _____ |
| Total expenses attributable to service work: | | | $ _____ |
| Profit from service work: | | | $ _____ |

---

The income items listed on the chart above will be the actual commissions or bonuses paid to you in each category for the period. Some of the expense items entered, such as product portfolios, business cards, and client lunches, will represent costs that are fully attributable to service activity. Other general office and staff expenses, including word processing, telephone, and secretarial costs will have to be estimated and apportioned.

effectiveness in performing the key sequential prospecting and sales activities as they relate to each other as well as attaining desired production goals. Usually your ratios are based on your activity from the previous year.

Each ratio is calculated by taking the first number and dividing it by the second number. Thus to calculate the phone calls to contacts ratio, you would take the number of calls you made and divide it by the number of times you talked to a prospect. The ratios needed for a basic marketing funnel include the following:

- phone calls to phone (or face) contacts
- phone (or face) contacts to appointments set
- appointments set to initial meetings
- initial meeting to fact finders completed
- fact finders completed to closing interviews conducted
- closing interviews conducted to sales
- first year compensation to sales

Other ratios of interest that are not a part of the marketing funnel but are valuable for analyzing target markets include the following:

- leads to appointments
- referrals to sales

Construct funnels for each target market and general market (every lead that is not from a target market).

### Determine Income Objectives

To determine your FYC income objective, begin by estimating next year's personal expenses, business expenses, and savings goals. Budget amounts for each category of cash outflow you expect, and for the money you want to save for the upcoming year (see Appendix C for a sample form).

Pay special attention to your marketing budget. If you plan to grow your business, you most likely will need to expand your marketing efforts, and consequently your marketing expenses. One approach is to take the marketing budget from the previous year and divide it by FYC for the previous year. Then take this ratio and multiply it by the amount you anticipate your FYC increasing. Adjust this estimated figure up or down based on factors such as anticipated efficiency gains, increased cost of current marketing approaches (such as advertising, membership dues, and telephone directory listings), and so on.

Next, determine the new income objective to meet your cash outflow and savings goals. Start with the gross income you desire; then subtract anticipated renewal commissions and other business income to arrive at your net FYC objective.

### Calculate Activity Objectives

Now you can determine the prospecting and sales activity objectives you need to achieve your FYC income goal by using the marketing funnel.

First, estimate the percentage of FYC you anticipate will be derived from each target market and your general market. Use the previous year's numbers as a benchmark. Simply determine the percentage of income derived from each target market by dividing the estimated FYC from each target market by total FYC. Adjust this percentage based on anticipated changes you plan on making. Multiply the percentage by the total FYC goal.

---

***Example:***     Madison earned $100,000 in FYC last year. $25,000 of her FYC was derived from business she wrote with female businessowners. She anticipates increasing her efforts this year such that 30 percent of her FYC goal of $110,000 for next year will come from members of the local Businesswomen's Association. Thus the FYC goal she will run through her marketing funnel calculation would be 30 percent x $110,000 = $33,000.

---

For each target market and your general market, begin by dividing the FYC income goal by the average FYC per sale to determine the number of sales you need to meet your goal.

Using last year's prospecting and sales effectiveness ratios and working backwards, start by multiplying the number of sales you need by the number of closing interviews it takes to produce one sale. Continue the same process to calculate the necessary level of each prospecting and sales activity to reach the number of sales required to meet your FYC goal. Complete this for each target market and your general market.

---

***Example:***     Madison runs her FYC goal for the Businesswomen's Association target market through her marketing funnel. The following activity goals result:

- $33,000 ÷ $1,000 per sale = 33 sales
- 33 x 1.5 per sale = 50 closing interviews
- 50 x 1.33 per closing interview = 67 fact finders

- 67 x 1.5 per fact finder  = 101 initial meetings
- 101  x  1.33  per  initial  meeting  =  135 appointments
- 135 x 2 per appointment = 270 contacts
- 270 x 2 per contact  = 540 phone calls

See the completed marketing funnel in Figure 7-2.

To break this down by month and by week you would divide the annual figures by 12 and 52, respectively.

**FIGURE 7-2**
**Sample Marketing Funnel**

| | Activity Summary | Suspects (Leads) | Activity Objectives |
|---|---|---|---|
| Phone Calls | 400 | <u>2.00</u> phone calls to produce 1 contact | 540 |
| Contacts | 200 | <u>2.00</u> contacts to produce 1 appointment set | 270 |
| Appts Set | 100 | <u>1.33</u> appointments set to produce 1 initial meeting | 135 |
| | | **Prospects** | |
| Initial Mtgs | 75 | <u>1.50</u> initial meetings to produce 1 fact finder | 101 |
| Fact Finds | 50 | <u>1.33</u> fact finders to produce 1 closing interview | 67 |
| | | **Qualified Prospects** | |
| Closing Interviews | 38 | 1.50 closing Interviews to produce 1 sale | 50 |
| Sales | 25 | <u>$1,000</u> FYC per each sale | 33 |
| FYC | $25,000 | Referrals | $33,000 |
| | | FYC ← Clients | |

## Defining To Whom You Are Marketing

The ideal situation is marketing in a monolithic target market with an endless supply of prospects. Most likely, that will not be the case. Instead, you will probably have a few main target markets that you supplement with your general (undifferentiated) market. If you do not have a few target markets identified, you can do so by completing steps one and two of the target marketing process: segmenting your market and targeting a market. In other words, at this point, you will need to have

- segmented your natural market using relevant segmentation variables
- identified market segments and created profiles
- created selection criteria
- conducted market research
- assessed other factors
- selected and even tested a few target markets

Your basic marketing plan should include a brief profile of your target markets, defining the common characteristics and common insurance and financial needs, regardless of whether or not you can meet them. It may also be helpful in looking for marketing ideas to specify some common nonfinancial needs as well, if there are any readily identifiable. In addition, you may want to include the following information:

- size of the market (how many potential prospects)
- average income and assets
- communication networks (informal and formal)
- preferences for how they buy your products and services
- attitudes toward financial products and services you sell

When you are identifying common needs, and if you are working with a quasi-target market—a group of people who have common characteristics and a communication system but lack common financial needs—it would be helpful to segment the group by life cycle and identify common financial needs within each life-cycle market segment identified.

## Defining What You Are Marketing

From the common financial needs you identified, select those needs that you are able to meet based on the products you sell and your level of training and experience. Take a few minutes to define what you are marketing by examining the financial and emotional needs of each target market that are satisfied by your products.

***Example:***        Harry sells life insurance. His target market is parents at the Menses School, a private grade school for middle- and upper-middle-class families.

| Financial Needs | Emotional Needs |
|---|---|
| • income replacement<br>• education funding for private school and college<br>• debt liquidation | • feel like they are taking care of their families<br>• love for their families<br>• peace of mind |

## Strategizing How You Will Market

Your next step is to determine how you will market to your target markets. This includes the following:

- creating and implementing a position for your personal brand
- implementing prospecting methods for identifying prospect names and contact information
- implementing methods for creating awareness and interest of your products
- creating and using scripts to set appointments
- anticipating objections
- outlining additional services you will offer to increase retention

### *Positioning Your Personal Brand*

Based on the information you have gathered about your target markets and your competition, write your positioning statement and your value proposition. They should be relevant to the target market. You may have separate ones for each target market. Remember, a value proposition is how you will answer the question, "Why should I do business with you?" This may include ancillary products and services you will provide or relevant expertise in working with the needs of people in your target market.

Then outline how you will create awareness of your personal brand within the target market. Identify specific ways that you will build prestige so that your reputation within the target market will precede you. Prestige methods include the following:

- community involvement
- writing

- speaking to groups
- radio or television opportunities
- personal brochure
- internet presence
- newsletters
- advertising

Estimate the anticipated costs involved. It would be extremely helpful to track and categorize expenses associated with each target market going forward. This will enable you to estimate the net-profit margin (first year compensation minus associated marketing and selling expenses) for each target market. This information will enable you to evaluate target markets relative to one another and to your general market.

### Selecting Prospecting Methods

In your marketing plan, identify the prospecting methods you will use and map out how you will implement them. For instance, if you are planning to use a center of influence, identify whom that is and how you will approach him or her to ask for prospects. If you are already working in the target market, create a script for asking for referrals and an ideal client profile to guide the referrer (or simply include the one you are using already).

Create a prospect list, tracking also the source of the prospect. This will help you identify the best sources and methods so you can devote more time developing them.

### Implementing Methods for Creating Interest in Your Products

The marketing plan should also identify preapproaches you plan to use to create interest in your products. The most common preapproaches are

- seminars
- letters and postcards
- third-party influence

### Creating Approach Scripts

Create or select appropriate approach scripts to set appointments. Most likely, this will involve telephone approaches. However, for multiline agents, a pivot from a service transaction would also be an excellent time to ask for an appointment. Specifically, include in your plan the "Creating Interest" component of the script.

### *Anticipating Objections*

As the Boy Scout motto says, "Be prepared". Include in your plan how you will handle the most common objections. The purpose of this is not to write a script, but to think through the questions you would want to ask and the points you would want to make beforehand.

### *Outlining Additional Services for Retention*

Client retention is very important to most practices. Improved retention will translate into more repeat sales as well as referrals. If it is appropriate, outline any additional services you will provide that are relevant to your target markets.

## Evaluating Your Results

The last part of a basic marketing plan is a plan for evaluating your results. Furthermore, this process will lay the groundwork for planning your next income period.

### *Review of Daily Activity*

Some advisors prefer to monitor their daily activity. For newer advisors, a review of the day's activity at the end of the business day can help them stay on track, and ensure they execute their plans and manage their time effectively.

---

**Twenty Points for a Successful Day**

Your goal is to achieve twenty points every working day. Your day isn't over until you do. There are no carry forwards from one day to the next. There are no carry backs. Each day stands alone. Your workweek requires a minimum of ninety points. Give yourself the afternoon off if you earned 10 points in the morning and 20 points every previous day to reach your 90 points for the week. A suggested point system is

- one point for each referral
- two points for each appointment requested
- three points for each appointment made
- four points for each closing interview
- five points for each sale

---

Many successful advisors use a daily or weekly point system for monitoring their progress (see the box entitled "Twenty Points for a

Successful Day"). Such a system provides motivation and keeps advisors on track to achieve their sales activity objectives.

On a monthly basis, examine your prospecting and sales ratios, comparing them to the ones used to construct your marketing funnel. Notice that the funnel used in this text divides the prospecting and sales process into three distinct conversion points: from suspects (or leads) to prospects, prospects to qualified prospects, and qualified prospects to clients. (For the purposes of the marketing funnel, the term *client* refers merely to someone who has purchased an advisor's product or service.) For each conversion point, there are associated activities that can affect an advisor's conversion rate. Thus, the conversion points enable the advisor to analyze and evaluate specific aspects and tasks of the marketing plan to determine possible causes for success or failure. Let's look at them now.

***Conversion of Suspects (Leads) to Prospects.*** Look at the ratios of contacts to appointments and appointments to initial meetings. These ratios are affected by the following:

- the quality of your leads. Do they need your products and services? Can they afford them?
- prospecting methods. How are you accessing these leads? Is there a better, more natural method? Are you asking for referrals? All things being equal, centers of influence and referrers are typically the best methods for tapping into a target market.
- your prestige-building activities. How are you creating awareness of your personal brand? Do the members of a target market know who you are before you call? Prestige building is critical for penetrating new target markets in which you are not well known.
- preapproach activities, approach scripts, and telephone skills

Note that the information discussed in this textbook is most relevant to the items above.

***Conversion of Prospects to Qualified Prospects.*** Examine the ratios of initial meetings to fact finders and fact finders to closing interviews (conducted). Activities that will affect your success include the following:

- building rapport. How did you attempt to build rapport? Was it established in a manner that reflected the prospect's social style?
- establishing the need. What approach did you use to establish the general need for your products and services? Did you ask enough open-ended questions? Did you establish prospect goals? How did

you present your products and services as the best solution for addressing their needs?

- handling objections. Why did the prospect not grant a fact finder or closing interview? What objections arose? How did you attempt to address them? Would another approach have been more successful?

***Conversion of Qualified Prospects to Clients.*** Review the closing interviews to sales ratio (closing ratio). Consider the following:

- analyzing the information and developing the plan. Did the plan adequately address the prospect's needs within the prospect's budget?
- presentation skills. How well did you present the plan? Did you adequately present relevant features and benefits?
- closing skills. How did you ask for the sale? Was there too much pressure? Did you adequately demonstrate the consequences of not acting now?
- handling objections. What objections arose? How did you attempt to address them? Would another approach have been more successful?

Conduct an analysis for each target market and your general market. Make adjustments accordingly. Without periodic review and adjustment of your prospecting and selling activities, it will be difficult to improve your marketing efforts.

## COMPLIANCE, ETHICS, AND PROFESSIONALISM

Your career as a financial advisor places a tremendous responsibility upon you. You will approach friends and strangers and offer to help them plan for their future financial security. You will then ask them to accept your advice, trust your recommendations, and purchase financial products. In this business, you must maintain the highest ethical standards of professional behavior.

As you assist your clients, many areas of financial planning are difficult for the average person to understand. Your training, specialized knowledge and especially your ethical behavior can elevate your selling/planning activities to the level of a career professional. That should be your goal as a financial advisor.

In today's financial services marketplace, there is a tremendous emphasis on ethical business practices and legal compliance issues. How do professional advisors live up to their responsibilities? Certainly, an advisor must comply with

- state regulations for the sale of all insurance products
- federal regulations for the sale of securities and registered products
- company rules and procedures for all marketing activities
- codes of ethical conduct
- principles of professionalism

## State Regulation

Today, insurance companies and insurance products are regulated primarily at the state level. Each state has its own department of insurance to regulate the insurance activities within the state. State legislative bodies pass laws that regulate the insurance industry, and state insurance departments enforce the laws and set procedures for companies and producers. The states regulate the insurance business in several key areas:

- insurance company licensing
- producer licensing
- product regulation
- market conduct
- financial regulation
- consumer services

States look closely at insurers' financial solvency and their ability to cover their policyowners' claims. The states also regulate market conduct, which covers the sales and marketing practices of insurance companies and producers. The top priority of each state insurance department is to protect their state's consumers from unfair business practices within the insurance industry.

### *Licensing*

*Insurance Companies.* An insurer must normally be licensed by a state's insurance department to sell insurance products within that state. After it is licensed, the insurer must have approval from the insurance department for individual products sold in the state.

*Producers.* A producer must obtain a license to sell insurance products in a particular state. Producers can have licenses in more than one state. Often a producer will maintain a resident license in his or her home state and hold nonresident licenses in other states.

The producer must also obtain an appointment to sell an insurance company's products. During the appointment process, the insurance company will verify the producer's license and will usually conduct financial and criminal background checks. If a producer sells for several insurance companies, he or she will need an appointment with each company.

Securities products such as variable life insurance, variable annuities, and mutual funds require registration with The Financial Regulatory Authority (FINRA, the successor to the NASD). FINRA is the largest non-governmental regulator for all securities firms doing business in the United States. A special license to sell variable products may also be required by individual states.

Although state laws that regulate insurance company and advisor licensing vary, state insurance commissioners work together through the National Association of Insurance Commissioners (NAIC) to identify and publicize the most important consumer issues. NAIC also helps standardize insurance regulation by developing model legislation for the states. Although NAIC has no enforcement authority, it has helped increase the commonality of insurance laws and procedures among the states.

---

**Unauthorized Entities**

Regulation of insurance products and services varies from state to state. In Florida, for example, regulations prohibit doing business with an unauthorized insurance entity. An unauthorized entity is an insurance company that has not gained approval to place insurance in the jurisdiction where it or a producer wants to sell insurance. These carriers are unlicensed and prohibited from doing business in that state. In most cases, where these carriers have operated they have characterized themselves as one of several types that are exempt from state regulation. It is the financial advisor's responsibility to exercise due diligence to make sure the carriers for whom they are selling are approved by the department of insurance in that state.

---

### *Advice*

States are concerned with what advisors call themselves and the advice they give to the public. In many states, advisors who call themselves financial planners or financial consultants may be breaking state laws unless they have special licenses.

In contacts between an advisor and a prospect or client, the discussion may touch on legal or tax matters. Although discussing legal or tax matters with clients in very general terms is allowed, the advisor cannot give specific advice in those areas without the proper credentials. Giving specific legal or tax advice can be construed as practicing law without a license, which is illegal. If people ask for specific advice, you should recommend they consult an attorney or tax advisor.

## Federal Regulation

Although the states are the primary regulators of the insurance industry, the main responsibility for regulation of securities products rests with the federal government. Securities products include the variable life insurance and variable annuity products many insurance companies now offer. Without a securities registration, an advisor cannot legally discuss equity-based investment products with the public.

### *Selling Securities Products*

As we mentioned previously, an advisor must register with the Financial Regulatory Authority (FINRA) to sell securities products. FINRA establishes procedures and monitors compliance to ensure fair practices for the industry and protect the public interest. FINRA's regulatory responsibilities include registration and testing of securities professionals, approval of members' advertising and sales literature, and arbitration of investor disputes. Representatives registered through FINRA must provide personal information, including prior employment and existence of any securities-related disciplinary action.

An advisor must be affiliated with a broker/dealer to obtain a FINRA registration. Most large life insurance companies have broker/dealer subsidiaries, and they will sponsor their advisors for FINRA registration. For independent advisors, there are many broker/dealers available to establish an affiliate relationship.

### *Marketing Securities Products*

The regulations for marketing securities products are extensive. The Securities and Exchange Commission and the advisor's broker/dealer must approve all advertising materials, correspondence, and sales literature. An advisor's stationary and business cards must even be approved. Failure to follow securities rules can lead to the suspension or loss of licensing, significant fines and penalties, and a suspension of a company's right to do business. The laws also require a prospectus, which describes the security in detail, be delivered to all purchasers of the security.

### *Registered Investment Advisor*

The Investment Advisers Act of 1940 defines an investment advisor as a person who, for compensation, advises others on the value of securities or the advisability of buying or selling them. Most people who fall within the act's definition of an investment advisor, and who make use of the mail or any tool of interstate commerce, must register with the SEC as a registered investment advisor (RIA).

Merely dealing with a security does not necessarily make one an investment advisor. In the 1980s, the SEC issued three tests to determine if individuals must register as an investment advisor. If all three tests are answered affirmatively, registration is required (unless it is waived). If any of the tests is answered negatively, there is no need to register as a RIA. To require RIA registration, the individual or entity must

- give advice or analysis concerning securities (security advice test)
- be engaged in the business of advising others regarding securities (security business test)
- be in receipt of compensation (compensation test)

The SEC's purpose for these three tests is to protect clients from fraud and other abusive situations. The SEC does not guarantee the competence or investment abilities of any individuals who register under the act. The SEC merely seeks to discourage unethical behavior by requiring full disclosure to clients.

Registered Investment Advisors must follow very strict rules for registration, record keeping, and compliance. Many states also have a qualifying exam for those wanting to operate as an RIA.

### *Financial Planners*

There is no special federal licensing or registration requirement for financial planners. Most financial planners analyze their clients' financial situations, help set achievable financial goals, and develop, implement, and monitor financial plans. Advisors may recommend the purchase or sale of securities, and they may charge a fee for planning services. Generally, if the financial planner meets the three tests cited earlier, he or she must register as a Registered Investment Advisor with the SEC.

Many states require special licenses for those who use the name financial planner, or for those who charge a fee for financial advice. Other states are considering similar legislation. Contact your State Securities Commission for the latest information on state licensing requirements.

Additionally, in some states, it is illegal for an advisor to charge a fee for planning and collect commissions from products sold to the same client. If you have questions concerning these requirements, contact your broker/dealer to clarify your position immediately.

## Company Rules and Procedures

The rules and procedures of a financial services company are enforced to make certain the company and its advisors meet all state and federal regulations. The company must have complete and accurate information to supervise the sales of suitable financial products to its customers.

As a financial advisor, you are an agent of the companies you represent. In simple terms, an agent represents a company, and has a limited right to speak and act for the company. The actions and words of an agent may be binding on the company even if they are incorrect. Understandably, financial services companies carefully protect themselves from possible misbehavior of agents who represent them. Rules, procedures, guidelines, and reporting all reflect the actions of the company to protect themselves and their clients.

Company rules also help advisors to meet all applicable legal requirements. In today's litigious society, that is a valuable benefit. Advisors should appreciate a company that maintains high standards, and be wary of companies whose compliance functions are loose. Remember that most financial products are legal contracts between the owner and the financial services company. If a contract is not properly executed, the result may be serious legal complications for the owner, the company, and the advisor.

### *Advertising*

Many compliance problems occur with advertising. Financial advisors must only use advertisements that are accurate and understandable. Advertising that contains untrue, unclear, incomplete, or deceptive statements is both illegal and unethical. State and federal laws specifically prohibit such advertising. The laws apply to materials from the home office, agency, and those created by the financial advisor. If you prepare customized materials for your clients, always get home office approval before using the materials.

## Ethical Considerations

### *Suitability*

Your professional obligation to prospects is to help them determine and carry out the most suitable solutions to meet their financial planning needs. In identifying the need for financial products that address prospects' concerns, helping prospects understand how certain products meet those concerns, and implementing solutions to prospects' financial planning needs, you have fulfilled your professional obligation.

***Client Needs.*** Clients should expect their financial advisor to make accurate analyses and recommend only suitable products to satisfy their needs. The advisor must conduct thorough fact finding to identify a client's needs, personal and financial goals, time horizon, and risk tolerance. A primary rule of financial planning is to know your client. It is dangerous, unprofessional, and bordering on unethical to recommend any financial product without having enough information to determine the product's suitability for the client.

### Compliance and Ethics

compliance

*Compliance* means following the laws and regulations, including company rules, which apply to the sale of all financial products. These are the minimum standards. Ethical behavior is doing the right thing, which always requires you to put the prospect's best interests ahead of your own. It is treating the client in a way you wish to be treated. The ethical advisor will maintain the highest possible standards of behavior in all business dealings. Ethical advisors keep their word, and their clients can depend on them. Ethical advisors continually improve their knowledge and skills to provide the best possible service. They feel the public's scrutiny and the heavy responsibility to represent the financial services industry, their companies, and other advisors in the best light.

Conflicts often arise between the prospect's need for a product and a company's underwriting requirements or ratings rules. These conflicts can create both compliance and ethical concerns. A common example involves reporting a client's use of tobacco on an application for life insurance. The advisor may be tempted to shade the truth to get a better rating for the client. The ethical advisor will not go down that road. He or she knows that telling the truth is not only the ethical way; it is the smart way to do business.

Professionalism and ethical conduct demand more than mere compliance with laws and regulations. Following rules and procedures is the first, and very important, step in professional conduct.

### Professional Code of Conduct and Ethics

professional ethics

*Professional ethics* is behavior according to principles of right and wrong—a code of ethics—accepted by one's profession. By adopting, embracing, and practicing a professional code of ethics, the financial advisor will likely achieve the high standard of professionalism demanded by a career in financial services. The advisor's ethics affect the reputation of the profession and the confidence of the public in the industry and its practitioners. An advisor's breach of professional ethics must make the advisor subject to disciplinary action to protect the public and the profession itself.

All professional organizations within the financial services industry publish pledges and ethical codes for their members. These codes rest on common sense, ethical virtues, and other common themes. Some common characteristics of these codes are as follows:

- Every code calls on professionals to look out for the best interests of the client.
- Most codes require professionals to conduct themselves with fairness, objectivity, honesty, and integrity.
- Each code requires professionals to protect the confidential information of their clients.
- Most codes require that professionals present enough information to allow the client to make an informed decision.
- Each code requires professionals to continue the learning process throughout their careers.
- Each code asks professionals to conduct themselves in a way that brings honor to themselves and to their professions.
- Most codes specify that financial services professionals should comply with the law.

A clear understanding and appreciation of the codes will help to better deal with today's complex marketplace. It is impossible to write a rule for every situation in any business. The ethical advisor will be guided by firm principles to decide the ethical behavior when conflicts arise. The American College code of ethics is a time-tested standard of professional behavior that all advisors would do well to follow (see Figure 7-3).

## Being a Professional

### *Professionalism*

professionalism

The successful financial advisor must be a professional advisor. *Professionalism* means mastering the technical knowledge to provide meaningful support and accurate advice to your prospects and clients. As a competent financial services professional, you must know the legal and tax ramifications of your recommendations. In addition, you must present both positive and negative implications of the options available so prospects and clients can make informed purchasing decisions. Thus, you must thoroughly understand your products, problems confronting your prospects and clients, and solutions your products can provide.

***Client Focus.*** The professional advisor is client-centered, which means putting clients' interests ahead of any others. While selling products is a big part of the business, your job goes far beyond simply making a sale. Focus on the client's problems, needs, and attitudes. Be informed enough to make suitable recommendations, and then relax because sales will follow as a natural by-product of a job well done.

***Client Confidentiality.*** Prospects and clients are entitled to a high level of confidentiality with personal information they give the advisor. Advisors must keep this information private, protect it, and certainly not share it with any unauthorized person or organization. In an age of frequent identity theft, be extremely careful with data files, faxes, and e-mails that contain clients' personal information such as SSN, birthdates, and phone numbers. Also, make sure you do not discuss a client's financial situation with family members, other clients, or prospects. It is not only wrong, but it may get back to the client and cause very unpleasant consequences.

---

**FIGURE 7-3**
**The American College Code of Ethics**

To underscore the importance of ethical standards for Huebner School designations, the Board of Trustees of The American College adopted a Code of Ethics in 1984. Embodied in the code are the Professional Pledge and eight canons.

The pledge to which all Huebner School designees subscribe is as follows:

*In all my professional relationships, I pledge myself to the following rule of ethical conduct: I shall, in light of all conditions surrounding those I serve, which I shall make every conscientious effort to ascertain and understand, render that service which, in the same circumstances, I would apply to myself.*

The eight canons are

I. Conduct yourself at all times with honor and dignity.

II. Avoid practices that would bring dishonor upon your profession or The American College.

III. Publicize your achievement in ways that enhance the integrity of your profession.

IV. Continue your studies throughout your working life so as to maintain a high level of professional competence.

V. Do your utmost to attain a distinguished record of professional service.

VI. Support the established institutions and organizations concerned with the integrity of your profession.

VII. Participate in building your profession by encouraging and providing appropriate assistance to qualified persons pursuing professional studies.

VIII. Comply with all laws and regulations, particularly as they relate to professional and business activities.

### Professional Responsibility

Financial advisors must consider themselves professionals and conduct themselves accordingly. The public expects advisors to act professionally, as do the courts. Financial advisors advertise themselves as having special skills to provide financial guidance to their clients. Such advertising creates a higher legal standard of performance for the advisor's work. Truth in advertising demands it; ethics and professional responsibility demand it.

Part of your professional responsibility is to educate and encourage prospects and clients to take actions to improve their own financial security and their family's. A good financial advisor is a good teacher, and a good teacher must first be a good learner. An educated prospect is likely to make a good long-term client if your products and services meet his or her planning needs.

### Professional Development through Education

To educate your prospects and clients, you must first educate yourself. You must understand basic concepts of financial planning and continue studying advanced concepts and changes that constantly occur. New product innovations, legislative trends, and tax rulings affect your ability to provide the highest possible level of service. You can gain additional knowledge and skills by pursuing the recognized professional designations of the financial services industry. Such designations as LUTCF, FSS, CLU®, ChFC®, and CFP® after your name are marks of your ongoing commitment to self-improvement.

Membership and participation in industry professional organizations, such as the National Association of Insurance and Financial Advisors (NAIFA) and the Society of Financial Service Professionals, offer opportunities for networking and continuing education. You should also explore the various training and educational programs provided by insurance companies, universities, proprietary training organizations, and other professional organizations. *Advisor Today* (the magazine of NAIFA) and *Life Insurance Selling* magazines are excellent sources of insurance news and sales ideas.

Formal programs can supplement your personal self-improvement regimen of daily and weekly readings in financial literature. For more information on additional training resources aimed at enhancing the skills and knowledge of the dedicated financial services professional, log on to The American College's website at www.theamericancollege.edu.

## NOTES

1. customer. Merriam-Webster.com. *Merriam-Webster Online Dictionary*. 2009. http://www.merriam-webster.com/dictionary/customer (accessed March 25, 2009).
2. client. Merriam-Webster.com. *Merriam-Webster Online Dictionary*. 2009. http://www.merriam-webster.com/dictionary/client (accessed March 25, 2009).

## CHAPTER SEVEN REVIEW

*Key terms and concepts are explained in the Glossary. Answers to the review and self-test questions are found in the back of the textbook in the Answers to Questions section.*

### Key Terms and Concepts

purpose of delivery
steps of an effective delivery
buyer's remorse
customer
client
objectives of service
monitoring
annual review
service package

standard service package
extra frills package
ABC method
marketing funnel
prospecting and sales effectiveness
  ratios
compliance
professional ethics
professionalism

### Review Questions

7-1.   Explain the three objectives a good product delivery can achieve, and steps of an effective delivery.

7-2.   What is the difference between a customer and a client, and why is the distinction important?

7-3.   Why is it important to provide excellent service to your clients?

7-4.   What are some of the more common client circumstances an advisor should monitor?

7-5.   What are the key points to preparing for the annual review?

7-6.   What are the two levels of service, or service packages, that you can offer your customers and clients?

7-7.   Discuss the ABC method of classifying clients and what service distinctions are made between these groupings.

7-8.  List the five questions that are answered in a basic marketing plan. Briefly explain each.

7-9.  Explain the difference between compliance and professional ethics.

## Self-test Questions

*Instructions: Read Chapter 7 and then answer the following questions to test your knowledge. There are 10 questions. Choose one answer for each question, and then check your answers with the answer key in the back of the textbook.*

7-1.  A financial services client is

    (A)  any customer who has purchased a financial product from you
    (B)  any person who has a strong interpersonal relationship with you
    (C)  any customer who has given you a referral
    (D)  a customer who follows your advice consistently, buys from you again, and refers you to others

7-2.  The booklet prepared by the National Association of Insurance Commissioners (NAIC) that provides objective advice and comprehensive cost comparisons for those purchasing life insurance is called

    (A)  The Buyer's Guide
    (B)  The Consumer's Resource Book
    (C)  The Insurance Guide
    (D)  Choosing the Policy that Fits

7-3.  Which of the following aspects of marketing and selling affects the conversion of suspects to prospects?

    (A)  handling objections
    (B)  prospecting methods
    (C)  establishing needs
    (D)  building rapport

7-4. Which of the following statements about classifying your clients is correct?

(A) "A" clients are only those who have done the most business with you.
(B) "B" clients are those you wish you did not have.
(C) "C" clients receive basic services only, such as annual reviews.
(D) "B" and "C" clients should receive the same exact services.

7-5. Which of the following statements regarding strategies for how you will market is (are) correct?

    I.    Prestige building methods include writing books and advertising.
    II.    Creating approach scripts is a task associated with strategizing how to market.

(A) I only
(B) II only
(C) Both I and II
(D) Neither I nor II

7-6. Which of the following statements concerning the marketing funnel is (are) correct?

    I.    A marketing funnel is used to calculate the activity goals needed to achieve one's income goal based on first year compensation.
    II.    The funnel analogy is used because a funnel's shape illustrates how it takes many suspects to produce a smaller number of clients.

(A) I only
(B) II only
(C) Both I and II
(D) Neither I nor II

7-7.  Which of the following statements concerning compliance and ethics is (are) correct?

      I.    Ethics is a code of behavior concerning right and wrong, embraced in a code of ethics.

      II.    If an advisor follows all company rules and regulations, ethical behavior will be assured.

    (A)   I only
    (B)   II only
    (C)   Both I and II
    (D)   Neither I nor II

7-8.  An effective insurance policy or investment contract review should accomplish all of the following EXCEPT

    (A)   reestablish the need for the financial product and reasons for its purchase
    (B)   emphasize that a life insurance policy is a valuable property
    (C)   replace other insurance policies the customer may own
    (D)   ensure the customer knows how to read investment account statements

7-9.  A properly conducted policy or contract delivery can accomplish all of the following EXCEPT

    (A)   offer another opportunity to obtain referred leads
    (B)   set expectations for future service
    (C)   reinforce the sale by reemphasizing the objectives of the purchase
    (D)   provide an opportunity to close the sale

7-10.  All of the following are objectives of monitoring and servicing customers EXCEPT

    (A)   facilitating customer retention
    (B)   making repeat sales to customers
    (C)   improving your web-based lead generation program
    (D)   obtaining referrals to new prospects

# Old-Age Adults, Estate Planning, and Distribution Planning

---

## Learning Objectives

*An understanding of the material in this chapter should enable you to*

---

8-1.  Describe the distinguishing characteristics and needs of the old-age adult segment.

8-2.  Explain how seminars can be used as an approach to senior prospects.

8-3.  Explain the concepts of property, wills, estate and gift tax, and applicable credit amount as they relate to estate planning.

8-4.  Explain the key elements of distribution planning for retirees.

---

This chapter focuses on the needs, characteristics, and insurance products appropriate to the old-age adult market segment. It also introduces some estate planning topics and discusses distribution planning considerations.

## LIFE CYCLE: OLD-AGE ADULTS

**old-age adult market segment**

This section covers the common characteristics of the *old-age adult market segment*—those aged 76 and older. As with the other segments in the life cycle, we focus on common characteristics and needs for this group.

### Old-Age Market Segment

Old age is really a social category defined differently by various cultures. In the United States, we define old age in a number of ways:

- Age 40 is the age at and beyond which a person may not be discriminated against in employment (Age Discrimination in Employment Act or ADEA).
- Age 55 is the age at which low-income individuals may qualify for subsidized employment and subsidies to learn new work skills (Title V of the Older Americans Act).

- Age 60 is the age of eligibility for Older Americans Act services. Due to limited funding, however, services are targeted to those older people who are most needy (Older Americans Act of 1965).
- Age 62 is the earliest age at which persons can begin receiving Social Security retirement benefits on their own earnings record (The Social Security Act).
- Age 65 has been the traditional retirement age, coinciding with full retirement age for Social Security benefit purposes. However, because of longer life expectancies, full retirement age has increased for people born after 1938. It ranges from 65 to 67 depending upon the year of the recipient's birth (The Social Security Act).
- Age 70 has been the mandatory retirement age for members of some professions.

**young-old**

**old-old**

Rather than categorizing everyone past a certain age as being old, some social gerontologists make a distinction between the *young-old* (ages fifty-five to seventy-four) and the *old-old* (ages seventy-five and older). Still other gerontologists add a middle-old category between the other two categories.

However the aged are categorized, aging is a highly individual experience. Chronological age may differ considerably from a person's functional age, and age-related changes occur at different rates for different persons. Age-related changes do not begin at the same time nor do they all occur simultaneously. The typical beginnings of change in the five senses are as follows:

- hearing in the mid 40s
- vision in the mid 50s
- touch in the mid 50s
- taste in the late 50s
- smell in the mid 70s

### Common Characteristics

People are living longer. The number of people reaching the old-age adult segment in life is growing significantly. In 1990, there were 3.6 million people aged 85 and older. As of July 2007, this number had grown to 5.5 million. Sixty-five percent of the over-85 populations are women.

Because of the burgeoning size and heterogeneous nature of our nation's aging population, today's advisors need to understand the financial issues of aging. This segment is growing so significantly that a new discipline called financial gerontology has developed, dedicated to understanding the financial needs and related issues of the older population. Topics such as life settlements, Medicare benefits, Medicaid, reverse mortgages, retirement planning, post-retirement planning, annuity regulation, sales conduct issues regarding senior citizens, long-term care, and estate planning are just a few of the senior planning issues in this field.

Where once it was unusual for families to have three living generations, today it is common for families to have four living generations. Many persons experience full lives for two to four decades past age 60. In fact, many are quite capable of fully enjoying life until the end of their lives. While advisors must be careful about stereotyping the older population, here are some of the common characteristics within this age group.

***Cognitive Changes.*** For most, an ability to learn does not decrease with age until very late in life. In fact, some areas of intelligence increase with age. The old adage, "use it or lose it" seems to apply when it comes to the brain. There is a declining ability to acquire new intelligence, but a sustained ability to apply existing knowledge (for example, wisdom is maintained, wit declines). Aging has little effect on the size of working memory, but it does impair the transfer of information from the short-term to long-term storage. For some older persons, advisors may need to present information more slowly or repeat it to reinforce understanding.

On the other hand, many people over age 60 are adept at handling their finances on the computer, surfing the Internet, taking courses, and performing mental activities that challenge even the brightest 21 year old. You see more and more seniors skydiving, rock climbing, and doing other physical activities far from the rocking chair on the porch. Many in this age group are as active as they ever were.

***Physical Changes.*** Hearing loss is very common and often one must speak louder or repeat oneself with an older person. The loss of existing knowledge (for example, knowing how to dress oneself) is a pathological change, not a normal consequence of aging. There is a slowing down of motor response, reaction time, and the ability to complete complex tasks. In some tasks, this slower response time may cause older people to spend more time checking results and making sure they are accurate. If given the time and opportunity, they can compensate for slower reactions by shifting emphasis from speed to accuracy. Overall, these age changes have little effect on the capacity of older adults to perform well at home and on the job.

***Psychological Changes.*** The elderly have to come to terms with their changing role in life, and individuals respond in different ways. Society causes many older people to assume a dependent role through retirement and pensions. Some elderly people are quite content to accept these changes, while others deny that they are occurring or may even become depressive as a result. Many use the extra time to take up additional activities and interests and have a fulfilling old age.

There are strong emotions and new realities that must be dealt with in the old-age segment of the life cycle. It is a time when relatives, friends, and spouses die. Consequently, there is an increased awareness of death as the final reality. There is a strong sense of nostalgia for the past, often accompanied by a sadness and loneliness when the future is considered.

Some older adults have difficulty concentrating because of outside situations and events. Caregiving responsibilities, the illness or loss of a spouse, changing roles in different social groups (particularly the family), bouts of depression, and the side effects of medication can affect their ability and interest in tasks.

***Nursing Homes and Assisted Living.*** Many in this age group require long-term care in their homes, assisted living facilities, or nursing homes because of fragile health. Long-term care insurance and Medicare supplement insurance are important issues as an older person deals with the effects of aging.

***Desire to Leave a Legacy.*** The next generation takes on a new importance when people reach old age. A reconciliation of spiritual values and a final conclusion as to the meaning of life often prompt a desire in older persons to leave a legacy to the next generation. They attempt to pass on their wisdom and knowledge about life. The liquidation and distribution of any remaining estate is important. For many, finding the proper way to pass assets on to children and grandchildren is the most important objective. Many older adults will want to contribute to a favorite charity. There are significant sales opportunities for charitable, financial, and estate planning.

### Common Needs

***Updated Will.*** As with all ages, a properly executed will ensures that an older person's estate is dealt with in the manner he or she desires. By this phase in the life cycle, if a will has not been updated, beneficiaries may have predeceased your client, or relationships with the beneficiaries may have changed, making the will out of date. An advisor can provide good service by reminding clients to create, or by this phase in life, update an existing will. Advisors must remember the prohibitions against the unauthorized practice of law, and clients should be referred to an attorney skilled in elder law.

***Lifetime Income.*** One of the biggest concerns for many people in the old-age market segment is the possibility of outliving their assets. The majority of old-age prospects and clients realize that Social Security is not adequate to sustain their desired standard of living. This need is even more acute for those who do not receive pension benefits from an employer.

If prospects have not purchased an immediate annuity already, they ought to consider it, especially if they are healthy and longevity runs in their family. An immediate annuity provides lifetime income. For fixed products, the income is level and guaranteed. Together with Social Security, the immediate annuity can help provide a basic standard of living that the annuitant cannot outlive.

***Gifts to Children or Grandchildren.*** Some members of the old-age market segment will want to leave a legacy to children and/or grandchildren. This objective may be achieved through bequests at death or gifts made during one's life.

Bequests at death may involve the distribution of assets, such as a house or investments and savings. Life insurance proceeds are another method for creating a legacy. The prospect or client should be encouraged to update the beneficiaries on any existing policies. Life insurance enables the prospect to increase the value of the bequest, as a dollar of premium purchases more than a dollar of death benefit. The interested prospect who can afford and qualify for a new policy should consider this option.

For most prospects in this stage of the life cycle, purchasing life insurance is too expensive. From this standpoint, many people in the old-age market are not good prospects for insurance for themselves. However, for those who would like to pass on a gift to their children or grandchildren, life insurance remains a method.

A good way for a grandparent to show his or her love for a child is to purchase permanent life insurance on a grandchild, thereby starting that child's life insurance program at an early age. By the time the child becomes a young adult, the cash value of that permanent plan can prove useful. It could provide the down payment on a home or an emergency fund. When that child eventually reaches retirement, it could be a source of supplemental income. With the addition of a guaranteed insurability rider, this policy could also guarantee the ability to purchase additional insurance in the future.

### Working with Older Persons

We must be careful not to let stereotypes—that old age adults are unable to learn, are slow to understand new concepts, are confused, unable to concentrate, and so on—get in the way when working with our older clients. Ageism is defined as stereotyping and discrimination against a person on the basis of age. Stereotypes are a composite of attitudes and beliefs about people as a group. When people act based on these beliefs, they can be guilty of age discrimination.

In working with older persons, present your information in the context of their lives, not as isolated items. Do not overuse facts or statistics. Present only the most significant information. Give mature adults an overview, and let them know what to expect in terms of what will be covered and how long it will take (this is recommended for people of all ages). Seniors are excellent at understanding the big picture because of their life experience and knowledge. Break a presentation down into smaller segments. Encourage interruptions and reviews as you progress. Older people like to ask questions. Slow down your presentation. Provide handouts so they can review them at their leisure. Do not ask them to complete worksheets or other complex tasks, especially with time constraints. They need to be able to work at their own pace. Be aware that some older persons may have a decreased ability to hear and see well.

## Approaching Senior Prospects through Seminar Marketing

Seminars are a proven strategy for prospecting in the senior market. Unlike other prospecting methods, seminars appeal more to the senior market than to other personal markets. Typically, seminars appeal to prospects who need information and have the time to seek it —a description that fits older prospects.

In general, seniors feel a heightened need for information when making decisions, especially financial ones. Whether they are pre-retirees or retirees, they are looking for safety, security, and ways to avoid unnecessary risks. They understand that time is critically important when it comes to making financial decisions. Younger prospects can afford to make a mistake because they have time to recover from it. Seniors realize they do not have that luxury. Thus, they want to have as much information as they can process before they make financial decisions. Unlike books, videos, web sites, and magazine articles, a seminar enables seniors to interact directly with a financial expert who can answer their questions immediately.

Seniors have more time to devote to finding the information they need. Many seniors have retired or work part time and have the time to attend daytime seminars, which gives the financial advisor the advantage of being able to work with seniors during normal business hours. Even seniors who work full time generally have more time than younger prospects because they no longer have dependent children and the obligations associated with them.

### *Seminar Topics*

Four key topics typically generate a great deal of interest among seniors: financing health care, increasing retirement income, reducing taxes, and facilitating estate planning objectives. Relating your products and services to any of these four topics will enable you to use seminars effectively. In some cases, you will need to bring in experts, such as a CPA or eldercare attorney. However, relying on outside experts does not minimize your need to keep your knowledge regarding these topics current. Continuing education is critical.

### Education and Motivation—Not Manipulation

Unfortunately, some unethical advisors in the financial services industry have used seminars to exploit seniors. Therefore, it is important to maintain the purpose of the seminar, which is to impart information. This is the implicit promise you make when you send a seminar invitation, so be sure to keep it. The seminar's purpose is not to make an on-the-spot sale.

Your goal, rather, is to enlighten seminar attendees by making them aware of the exposures they face. For example, a seminar on health care can give attendees information on Medicare nursing home benefits. Many seniors are still under the false impression that Medicare will take care of their long-term care needs. Once they realize the limitations of the Medicare system, they are more likely to seek alternatives, such as LTC insurance, for funding their long-term care needs.

Educating seniors in a seminar setting facilitates the eventual sales process. Prospects can get the facts from which to draw their own conclusions. This reduces the time you must spend educating seniors on their needs during face-to-face appointments. When you make the individual appointment, you can then devote more time to work on ways to meet specific objectives. The seminar education process, in effect, maximizes a financial advisor's time.

## Summary

This ends our review of the life cycle. You can see that throughout the life cycle there are ever-changing insurance and financial needs. Because of the dynamic nature of these needs, you have opportunities with prospects and clients to help them to understand, plan, and protect their financial futures and dreams.

## ESTATE PLANNING

Throughout this textbook, we have examined many planning concepts. They are interdependent and are parts of the larger discipline of financial planning. This section provides an overview of some basic estate planning concepts that affect the overall planning process for all prospects and clients, especially those with a high net worth. We begin with a review of how property passes at death. We then discuss federal estate and gift taxes, and how life insurance can be used to achieve estate planning goals.

### What Is Estate Planning?

estate planning

There is a common misconception that an estate is only the property that one leaves at death. In reality, the estate is much more than that. In its broadest sense, the term *estate planning* encompasses the accumulation, conservation, and distribution of an estate. The overall purpose of the estate planning process is to develop a plan that will enhance and maintain the financial security of the client and family, and carry out his or her final intentions at death. Estate planning has evolved to include lifetime financial planning that may lead to an increase in the client's estate as well as the conservation of existing assets. Estate planning should provide financial security during retirement years, and facilitate the intended and orderly disposition of property either during one's lifetime or at death.

Although many people consider that the primary goal of estate planning is to reduce and/or minimize estate transfer taxes, frequently the central issue is accomplishing the goals of the client for the distribution of assets after death. Financial advisors should seek to optimize the client's goals in light of tax considerations, rather than to simply maximize tax deductions. Advantages of effective estate planning are in Figure 8-1.

---

**FIGURE 8-1**
**Advantages of a Well-Planned Estate**

- Property distribution according to the decedent's wishes
- Tax-saving options
- Appropriate ownership of assets
- Disability and last illness preparedness
- Liquidity needs assessment
- Personal peace of mind

---

Advisors often find that clients are reluctant to engage in estate planning because they consider anticipating their own death to be morbid. Procrastination, as with many aspects of financial planning, is a frequent obstacle. Additionally, family issues such as blended families resulting from second or third marriages will make it difficult for some clients to decide how to treat their own children and stepchildren equitably. Frequent obstacles to effective estate planning are shown in Figure 8-2.

---

**FIGURE 8-2**
**Obstacles to Effective Estate Planning**

- failure to plan for death
    - not executing or updating a will
    - not taking the time to think about who gets what and when
    - believing the state succession statutes will cause property to pass the way the estate owner would want it to
- outdated plan
    - birth and death of family members
    - tax law changes
- overlooked provisions
    - guardianship
    - simultaneous death of spouses
    - tax apportionment
- improper tax planning
- improper ownership of assets
- failure to plan for disability, illness, or changes in or loss of employment
- failure to consider inflation
- lack of liquidity
- psychological factors
    - dealing with mortality
    - procrastination

---

### How Property Transfers at Death

**operation of law**

**right of contract**

Generally when a person dies, property he or she owned will pass to heirs in one or more of the following ways:

- by *operation of law*. A typical example of this method is a home owned jointly (with right of survivorship) by a husband and a wife. At the death of the first spouse, the surviving spouse gains full ownership of the jointly held property. Property not passing by contract, a will, or operation of law passes under the laws of intestate succession.
- by *right of contract*. The prime example of this is life insurance that is paid directly to a named beneficiary. Other examples include annuities, Individual Retirement Accounts (IRA), and qualified retirement plans such as a 401(K).
- by will. If there is a will, the remaining property passes under the terms of the will once it has been admitted to probate. If there is no

will, remaining property passes according to the state's laws of intestacy.

- by trust. A trust is an arrangement in which a trustee administers your assets for the benefit of others in a manner that you specify.

### Wills

**will**

Everyone who owns property should have a will whether single or married, old or young, healthy or infirm. A *will* is a legal declaration of an individual's wishes for the disposition of his or her property at death. It describes matters to be taken care of after death. The will becomes legally enforceable at death and is not operative until that time. Prior to one's death, a will may be amended, revoked, or destroyed by the maker at any time.

Younger couples should name a guardian in their wills to care for their minor children in the event they become orphaned. Another crucial function of the will is to designate someone as the estate's executor. This is the person who will be responsible for taking inventory of all property, paying estate taxes and creditors, and ultimately distributing the probate estate among the heirs.

**intestate**

***Dying Intestate.*** When a person dies without a will (*intestate*), the courts take control of the estate and, in effect, write a will in accordance with the state's intestate laws. It is unlikely that the state's distribution would match most people's personal wishes. For example, in most states a spouse does not automatically inherit all property when there are children. One state's intestacy law awards a spouse $4,000 plus one-third of the balance of the estate. The rest is evenly divided among the children, regardless of their ages or any special needs. In most cases, that distribution is not what the deceased person desired, and dying intestate may create severe hardships for the surviving spouse.

In the absence of a will, the probate court must also appoint an administrator of the estate and a guardian for minor children. Normally, the court prefers a relative as administrator, but if one is not available or willing to serve, the estate could end up in the hands of a professional administrator. This official generally charges 3 to 5 percent of the estate in fees each year. This arrangement offers little incentive to settle an estate quickly or to minimize the estate for tax purposes. The court would also select a relative as guardian if the children were orphaned, but without any guarantee of the choice the parent might have made. Because the court's appointment does not carry the moral weight of the parent's wishes in a will, children could become the object of a prolonged and acrimonious custody battle.

***Helping Clients Obtain a Will.*** Considering the anguish it prevents, a will is a bargain. If the estate is simple, a person can expect to pay $300 to

$500 to have an attorney draw up a will (including a general power of attorney, health care proxy, and living will). You should advise your clients and prospects to have a will prepared as soon as possible.

**testator**

No one should undertake to make a will without legal assistance. Regardless of how simple and straightforward the individual's wishes may be, one small error can void the whole effort. Consulting an attorney within one's resident state assures that all details comply with the laws of that state. The attorney should be familiar with the applicable state laws and should draft the will according to the state law and the wishes of the *testator* (person making the will).

As a financial advisor, you are uniquely positioned to assist your clients by helping them focus on the dangers and uncertainties of not having a will. Point out that the client's family can be best served by careful planning and proper execution of a valid will. At times, it is difficult to face up to this disagreeable task, but it must be done and will save the family much grief at the death of a loved one.

***The Requirements of a Will.*** The will must meet technical and legal requirements, such as the following:

- The testator must be of legal age as defined by the state (age 18 in most states).
- The testator must be mentally competent and not under duress at the time the will is executed.
- It must be in writing and properly executed according to the state's laws.
- The will must be signed to indicate intent.
- It must be attested to (verified) by the appropriate number of witnesses (varies by state).

The will does not take effect until the death of the testator. Therefore it can be changed at any time during the life of the testator. A new will can be written to revoke prior wills.

Because only the original will is valid, it is important to keep it in a safe place that others know. A bank safe-deposit box is not suggested because access to it is often restricted. Only limited copies of the will should be made and distributed. The original should be left with the estate executor or attorney for safe keeping.

### *Probate*

**probate**

Whether a person writes a will or not, at death an individual's worldly effects are generally subject to the legal process known as probate. *Probate* is the act or process of proving a will. To probate the will means to prove to the court that the document presented is the last will of the deceased person. The jurisdiction of the probate court extends only to the probate assets of the decedent. Probate assets are the property that passes under and is subject to the terms of the will or, if no will exists, the property is subject to administration by the court due to intestacy.

At this time the executor, or the court-appointed administrator, values the assets, pays off creditors, files estate tax returns, and pays taxes (if any are due), and finally distributes what is left to the heirs. Probate occurs under the supervision of a local court known in different states as probate, surrogate, or orphan's court.

In addition to approving the will—or applying the state's laws of intestacy for the person who died without a will—the probate court rules on the legitimacy of creditors' claims against the estate and supervises the actions of the executor until all business of the estate is completely settled. If minor children inherit any property directly, the court also oversees the guardian's use of that property until the children reach legal adulthood. All guardians, including the child(ren)'s surviving parent, must keep records of their routine use of the child(ren)'s inheritances and must petition the court for any unusual expenditures on the child(ren)'s behalf. It is not a good practice to leave property to minors. A contingent trust for life insurance proceeds is often a sensible alternative.

A major problem with probate is that even with an efficient court and executor, the process takes a minimum of four to eight months. If disgruntled relatives contest the will, or if property was owned in another state, heirs might have to wait longer, sometimes even years. Administrative and legal expenses during probate may run between 5 and 10 percent of the estate. Naturally, the longer an estate lingers in probate, the greater the costs.

### Trust

**trust**

A *trust* is a legal vehicle with four key components: corpus, grantor, trustee, and beneficiary. The property transferred into the trust is called the trust corpus. The person who transfers the property into the trust is called the grantor. The person for whom the trust assets are to be used is called the beneficiary. The trustee holds and manages the corpus for the benefit of the beneficiary, according to a trust agreement. The trust agreement is a contract between the grantor and trustee, who will have actual legal ownership of the trust corpus, which is the cash, or property in the trust. The trust agreement contains the directions to the trustee from the grantor regarding what can and cannot be done with the trust.

**revocable living trust**

***Revocable Living Trust.*** In a narrow sense, a *revocable living trust* (or living trust) is generally established to avoid the cost and the public nature of probate. By transferring ownership of all you own to the living trust, you avoid the costs, the time lag, and the public record aspects of probate.

In a broader sense, the living trust is more like a will, except that it bypasses probate. A will is still needed to direct possessions not included in the trust, whether intentionally or inadvertently. The living trust focuses on the management and distribution of assets during both life and death. It does not have tax savings as an objective. An attorney prepares it. The owner retains full control, and it is revocable and amendable at any time. Since the living trust is revocable, the trust assets are fully included in the estate at the owner's death.

The living trust can include decisions about what the owner wishes to take place in the case of disability or death. The owner names someone to be responsible for the distribution of property and can include advance directives that indicate his or her wishes in advance of a medical crisis.

Everything that is to pass through the living trust must have its title changed to ownership by the trust. This includes any property the owner wishes to include, such as real estate, vehicles, stocks, and other investments. Most personal property lacks formal title documents, so the trust instrument simply uses wording that sweeps all of the non-titled personal property into the trust.

The potential advantages of a revocable living trust include the following:

- *Asset control*—the owner has a way of controlling assets in good or poor health. There is no judicial interference or supervision, even in the case of incompetence (such as in Alzheimer's disease). This control can be extended through the use of a durable power of attorney.
- *Indefinite life*—the trust vehicle is designed to survive the death or disability of the grantor, or even the trustee or successor trustee, through the trust terms.
- *Protection against mismanagement*—As opposed to court-appointed supervision, the grantor of the living trust can select a trustee based on business acumen, expertise, and trustworthiness. A relative or friend and a professional trust company can serve as cotrustees to form an internal checks and balances system within the trust.
- *Effective planning vehicle*—Where minor children or grandchildren are involved, the living trust provides both management and distribution of assets during the child(ren)'s minority. This contrasts with the delays that can occur through the judicial process when a guardian is appointed to manage the assets of minor(s). The living trust can also be designed to deal with specific needs of each minor.

It can also deal with physical incapacity or mental incompetence among the heirs.

- *Achieving privacy*—the probate process leaves financial and personal matters exposed to public scrutiny. A living trust enables a person to avoid this public process completely.
- *Reduce or eliminate probate expense*—Probate costs result from court supervision according to state statute. Executor commissions and attorney fees are generated.
- *Avoid delays in estate administration*—Property distribution may be time consuming, depending on the complexity of the estate, will disputes, and the jurisdiction.

**pour-over will**

**power of attorney**

The components of a living trust include the following:

- *Pour-over will.* The pour-over will is a short will containing provisions specifying which assets are transferred to a living trust. It can also state that any property inadvertently left out of the living trust be brought in at death. The property is then distributed as part of the living trust plan.
- *Power of attorney.* A power of attorney (POA) is a document legally signed by one person authorizing another person to act on behalf of the signer. For example, a POA can be used at a house closing when one spouse cannot be present, or to allow a parent to give an adult child access to a bank account. Rather than have an elderly parent travel to the closing of the family home, a daughter with a POA can help a senior manage his or her day-to-day affairs.

There are two types of powers of attorney: a general power and a durable power. A general power is effective as long as the person granting the power remains in good health. Failing health is often a reason for using powers of attorney, but a general power becomes legally ineffective in cases of mental incompetence or medical incapacity. Durable powers of attorney solve this problem by allowing designated family members or advisors to step in and manage financial affairs at the point of the grantor's incapacity.

Advisors should know that while a revocable living trust has several advantages (privacy, avoidance of probate, and so on), it does not protect a person's assets from Medicaid spend down if the owner of the trust needs long-term care. Because the living trust is revocable, Medicaid will require that assets in the trust be used to spend down (or self pay) for nursing home care before the owner of the trust can qualify for Medicaid assistance. Unfortunately, some seniors have established revocable living trusts with the belief that their assets in the trust would be protected from Medicaid spend-down requirements. This is another complex area, and advisors must be familiar with state and local Medicaid regulations.

**advance directives**

*Advance Directives.* Individuals by law have a right to make their own medical choices based on personal values, beliefs, and wishes. But what happens if a person has an accident or suffers a stroke and can no longer make decisions? Would the person want to have his or her life prolonged by any means necessary, or would he or she want to have some treatments withheld to allow a natural death? Usually *advance directives* will go into effect only when the person cannot make and communicate his or her own health care decisions. Preparing an advance directive lets the physician and other health care providers know the kind of medical care the individual wants, or doesn't want, if he or she becomes incapacitated. It also relieves family and friends of the responsibility to make decisions regarding life-prolonging actions.

**living will**

There are two kinds of advance directives:

**health care proxy**

- *Living will.* A living will is a legal document that describes the types of medical treatment an individual wishes to receive and chooses not to receive. The purpose of a living will is to let others know of your medical wishes when you are terminally ill and in a vegetative state or unable to communicate.
- *Health care proxy*, or *health care power of attorney*. This is also a component of a well-drafted living trust. A living will makes the medical treatment wishes of a person known. A living will does not guarantee that these wishes will be followed. Someone still has to make the necessary decisions about whether to continue treatment. This is a difficult, emotional decision. Sometimes close relatives are reluctant to let their loved one die. A health care proxy is a signed and witnessed legal document in which an individual names another person to make medical decisions about his or her care. As with a living will, the health care proxy goes into effect only when the person is no longer able to make health care decisions. Sometimes this is incorporated in a durable power of attorney. Depending on state law, which varies widely in directives they officially recognize, it may have to be drafted as a separate document.

### Advice to the Advisor

You should prepare a list of three to six attorney's names that you have researched, along with their fee range, to give to clients or prospects who may need an attorney. It is good to avoid endorsing a single attorney. Give prospects or clients several good alternatives and allow them to make the choice. This will also protect you from claims of ethics violations, collusion, or poor judgment.

You should establish a network of professionals including attorneys and bank estate planning officers. They will normally welcome an opportunity to work with you, your clients, and prospects, and may even refer their clients to you.

You should develop a working knowledge of the laws of intestacy and probate for your own state. This will provide a source of motivating or disturbing questions for complacent prospects, and you will know about possible solutions and pitfalls. A final caution: these subjects are complex and require the advice of a qualified attorney. Avoid giving advice beyond what you are licensed to do.

## Federal Estate and Gift Taxes

The federal transfer tax system consists of three components—gift taxes, estate taxes, and generation-skipping taxes. We will discuss gift and estate taxes in the following sections.

**federal estate tax**

The *federal estate tax* is imposed on the transferor's estate and is based on the privilege to transfer property. Inheritance taxes, found at the state level, are taxes to the recipient of property based on the privilege to receive property by inheritance. To avoid estate tax-avoidance schemes to dispose of property during lifetime, the federal tax system is coordinated with the federal gift tax, which is a tax imposed on transfers of property by gift during the donor's lifetime.

### The Federal Estate Tax

The federal estate tax is calculated on the value of the property transferred at death. It is a tax on the right to transfer the property; it is a graduated tax beginning at 18 percent. The tax then builds up to a maximum percentage that is changing each year from 2002 to 2009 for amounts of $3.5 million and more. Apart from congressional action in 2009 (which is probable), the federal estate tax is to be repealed for 2010 and return in 2011 using 2001 tax rates and limits. The tax rate in 2011 would return to 55 percent on taxable estates greater than $1.0 million or more.

Individual states may impose an additional inheritance tax on the assets of the deceased that are received by the estate's heirs. It can be arranged to have the estate pay inheritance taxes to protect the interests of the heirs.

**taxable estate**

***Taxable Estate.*** The *taxable estate* is the value of all property or partial interest in property, owned or controlled by the deceased, reduced by allowable deductions. These allowable deductions include reasonable funeral expenses, administrative expenses (court costs, attorney/executor fees), claims against the estate, unpaid mortgages, debts, as well as bequests to charities and the surviving spouse.

Three additional deductions are allowed: the marital deduction, the charitable deduction, and the state death tax deduction. These will be covered shortly.

As you may know, the details regarding the calculation of estate taxes can get quite complex. For example, determining what property is includible in the estate is not that straightforward. There are intricate rules that often bring property that the deceased did not own outright at the time of death back into the taxable estate.

marital deduction

***Marital Deduction.*** An important part of estate taxes is the *marital deduction* provision that permits a deduction of 100 percent of property passing to a spouse either by gift or at death. To qualify for the deduction, the property generally must pass to the surviving spouse in such a manner that he or she has sole power of control during life or at death. In effect, the estate of one spouse can be passed to the other completely free of taxation, as long as it qualifies for the marital deduction.

Although there are exceptions to this general rule, further discussion is beyond the scope of this textbook. In effect, using the marital deduction is merely a postponement of taxation at the death of the first spouse. The property that passes to a surviving spouse will be taxable at his or her subsequent death. Much estate planning is directed toward minimizing this result.

charitable deduction

***The Charitable Deduction.*** An estate tax *charitable deduction* is allowed for the full value of property transferred to a qualified charity, but only if the property is included in the donor's gross estate. The charitable deduction allows an unlimited deduction for assets passing to a qualified charity. Examples of qualified charitable organizations include corporations operating exclusively for religious, charitable, scientific, literary, or educational purposes.

state death and inheritance taxes

***State Death and Inheritance Taxes.*** Many states also impose *state death and inheritance taxes* on the transferred property of the deceased. In some states, this is an estate tax. In other states it is an inheritance tax that taxes the share received by the beneficiary.

Frequently, the consideration of state death and inheritance taxes is overshadowed by the attention given to the federal estate tax. Ironically, the federal estate tax affects a very small percentage of all estates, whereas most estates are within reach of state death and inheritance taxes. Learn how your state's death and inheritance taxes work. Your clients will appreciate the information and may be open to discussing your ideas about how to plan for this, such as buying life insurance to meet the corresponding expenses.

Until 2005, the federal estate tax gave a state death tax credit. However, this provision was repealed by the Economic Growth and Tax Relief Reconciliation Act of 2001 (EGTRRA). Beginning in 2005, the state death tax credit is repealed and replaced with a deduction for any amount of state death taxes paid. This change has caused many states, especially those states with only a federal estate death tax credit, to legislate new state death tax laws.

| **2001 Federal Estate Tax Law Change** As changed by the Economic Growth and Tax Relief Reconciliation Act of 2001 (EGTRRA) | | | |
|---|---|---|---|
| **For Decedents Dying During** | **Top Estate Tax Rate** | **Applicable Unified Credit Amount** | **Exemption Equivalent** |
| 2002 | 50% | $345,800 | $1,000,000 |
| 2003 | 49% | $345,800 | $1,000,000 |
| 2004 | 48% | $555,800 | $1,500,000 |
| 2005 | 47% | $555,800 | $1,500,000 |
| 2006 | 46% | $780,800 | $2,000,000 |
| 2007 | 45% | $780,800 | $2,000,000 |
| 2008 | 45% | $780,800 | $2,000,000 |
| 2009 | 45% | $1,455,800 | $3,500,000 |
| 2010 | Repealed | N/A | N/A |
| 2011 | 55% | $345,800 | $1,000,000 |

**applicable credit amount**

*Applicable Credit Amount.* Once the taxable estate is calculated, the estate tax is figured. From this amount, the estate can subtract the *applicable credit amount*. The credit is an amount that can be applied directly against any gift or estate tax due. This amount is $1,455,800 in 2009. This means that a person with assets less than $3.5 million dying in 2009 generally will have no federal estate tax payable. The $3.5 million is called the exemption equivalent. Note that without further Congressional action, the tax is set to repeal in 2010 and return in 2011. However, it is anticipated that the Congress will take action on the estate tax law in 2009.

The applicable credit amount coordinates the estate and gift taxes. In other words, whatever portion of the applicable credit amount someone uses during his or her lifetime to gift substantial sums of money will reduce the amount of the applicable credit available for estate tax purposes. The applicable credit for gift tax purposes is $345,800 based on an exemption equivalent of gifted property of $1,000,000.

### *Federal Estate Taxation of Life Insurance*

The death proceeds of life insurance owned by the decedent or the decedent's estate is fully includible for estate tax purposes. This is true even if the proceeds are to be paid directly to a named beneficiary. If the decedent had owned a life insurance policy on someone else's life, meaning the decedent was not the insured, the cash value of that policy would also be included in the decedent's estate.

Frequently, life insurance is the single largest asset or group of assets in the gross estate. Including life insurance can often mean the difference between having a federal estate tax liability and having none. For this reason, it is important to know when life insurance is included in the decedent-insured's gross estate for federal estate tax purposes. Factors include the following:

- Life insurance proceeds payable to the executor (that is, to or for the benefit of the insured's estate) are includible in the estate, regardless of who owned the contract or who paid the premium.
- Life insurance proceeds are included in the estate of an insured if the deceased possessed an incident of ownership in the policy at the time of his or her death.
- Life insurance proceeds are included in the gross estate of a deceased insured who transferred incidents of ownership in the policy within three years preceding his or her death.

***Life Insurance Payable to the Executor.*** In general, life insurance should not be made payable to a decedent's estate. There are many reasons besides avoiding federal estate taxation why estate planners seldom recommend such a beneficiary designation. Reasons include the following:

- Insurance payable to a decedent's estate subjects the proceeds to the claims of the estate's creditors.
- Insurance payable to a decedent's estate subjects the proceeds to costs of probate administration, such as executor's fees, but provides no corresponding advantages.

**incidents of owner-
ship**

***Possession of Incidents of Ownership.*** *Incidents of ownership* refers to a number of rights to, and degree of control of, the policyowner or the policyowner's estate in the economic benefits of the policy. Examples of contractual rights that reflect incidents of ownership include the following:

- the right to surrender or cancel the policy
- the right to make policy loans
- the right to assign the contract
- the right to name and change the beneficiary

***Ownership and the Three-year Rule.*** One strategy for decreasing the value of an estate is to transfer ownership of life insurance from the estate owner to some other person or a trust. However, the value of any life insurance is included in the estate if the transfer is for less than full consideration (for example, a gift) and occurs within three years prior to the death of the owner. Therefore, one must relinquish all incidents of ownership and remain alive for at least three years after the date of transfer for the life insurance to avoid inclusion in the estate. Note that a sale to a third party for the full fair market value of the policy will not cause the death benefits to be included, even if the sale occurs within three years of the insured's death.

***Example:***     Brenda, a widow, transferred ownership of three whole life insurance policies to her daughter, Sara, six years ago. However, it was clear at the time of the transfer that Brenda still had the right to borrow against the policies' cash values and the right to change the beneficiary by written notification to the insurance company. Although Brenda effectively transferred title in the policies to her daughter, the policies' proceeds will still be included in her gross estate for federal estate tax purposes because she retained the right to borrow against these policies and to change the beneficiary. To have successfully removed the proceeds from the gross estate, Brenda should not have reserved these rights.

For new life insurance policies, the best approach to keep the policy out of the insured's estate is for another person or an irrevocable trust to own it outright from inception. No three-year rule applies if the insured never possessed incidents of ownership in the policy.

### *Uses of Life Insurance in Estate Planning*

***Insurance Used to Increase Estate Value.*** The ways life insurance can be used in estate planning depend upon the client. For most people, life insurance is bought to provide for surviving family members. These are the clients that most of us serve. It could be the young family buying insurance as income replacement, to fund college educations for their children, to provide for mortgage redemption, or to build a nest egg for retirement. Life insurance provides the immediate estate to replace income if the breadwinner of the family should die prematurely.

***Insurance Used to Provide Estate Liquidity.*** For older clients and those who have built wealth, life insurance is often used to provide estate liquidity. Their children's support and educational expenses are usually no longer their obligations. In addition, these older clients are nearing the end of their income-producing years, and should have less future income to replace. They can purchase life insurance to provide death proceeds equal to the size of the anticipated shrinkage of their estate due to settlement and taxes. The estate liquidity/wealth replacement needs include the following:

- *Probate expenses.* Estate settlement costs usually increase with the size of the estate. The cost for professionals, such as executors, attorneys, accountants, and appraisers, to settle an estate is often based on a percentage of the total size of the probate estate. Generally the larger the estate, the greater the complexity and need for expensive professional help. One excellent advantage of life insurance is that it avoids probate if paid to a named beneficiary.
- *Death taxes.* As discussed above, federal estate taxes and other taxes also increase with the size of the estate. Federal estate taxes (and state death taxes in many states) are based on a progressive rate schedule. Thus, wealthy individuals often desire life insurance to replace the wealth lost to death taxes.
- *Liquidity needs.* Wealthy clients often face an additional problem. Frequently, their accumulated wealth contains assets that are not liquid. For example, wealthy individuals often own closely-held businesses or real estate that may be illiquid or unmarketable to outsiders. Death taxes and other estate settlement costs are based on the full value of such assets owned by the estate and must be paid in cash. The liquidity problems faced by an estate often result in the forced sale of estate assets on undesirable terms.

An estate must normally be settled in nine months after the owner's death. The liquidity of life insurance provides a ready fund for this. Other assets which cannot be easily liquidated are protected and preserved for the heirs. This is a common use of life insurance for estate planning.

Life insurance is the most effective way to supply needed dollars to meet federal estate tax obligations. First, the dollars, in the form of death proceeds, are free of federal income taxation. Second, if the life insurance is owned by someone other than the insured (or some entity such as a trust), the policy's face amount will not be included in the decedent's gross estate. Finally, as with all life insurance policies, a sizable death benefit may be purchased for pennies on the dollar.

### Estate Planning Techniques

Among the practical uses of life insurance in estate planning are the following:

- *Transferring policies to family members.* When the three-year rule of transfer is not met, no greater penalty will occur than the inclusion of the policies back into the value of the estate. The insured/owner will be no worse from an estate tax standpoint because the policy would have been included if the transfer had not occurred.
- *Creating irrevocable life insurance trusts* (ILIT). These are often used in estate planning for wealthy individuals to provide estate liquidity. The irrevocable trust should be set up before an application for life insurance is submitted. If the application is written prior to the trust's existence, the government treats it as a transfer of ownership and the three-year rule applies. By having the trust serve as applicant, owner, and beneficiary of the life insurance policy, the insured possesses no incidents of ownership, and the proceeds will not be included in the insured's estate.
- *Creating revocable trusts.* These are sometimes used to receive the proceeds of life insurance to ensure proper management of the distribution of assets. An example would be a family situation where a spouse and young children were to be protected. The revocable trust is designed to become irrevocable at the death of the grantor, and a trustee manages the proceeds for the benefit of the remaining family members. The proceeds are includible in the estate of the deceased grantor.
- *Equalizing inheritance among heirs.* An example is a family business where one or several children will inherit the enterprise, and other family members will be excluded. Life insurance is frequently purchased to provide an equal inheritance for children who would be excluded from the business inheritance.

***Example:***   Marcus is president and sole shareholder of Zipper-Do, Inc., a highly successful manufacturer of snag-proof zippers. He has three adult children—two sons and one daughter. The daughter and one of the sons work for Marcus and would like to take over the business when Marcus retires. The other son, a musician, has no interest in the business. Marcus arranges for the two employee-children to receive the business at his retirement or death. He also acquires life insurance on his life in an amount equal to the anticipated fair market value of Zipper-Do, Inc. that each employee-child will receive. Marcus pays the premiums, and the musician son is the designated beneficiary of the policy. Equity of inheritance has been achieved.

• *Creating survivorship life insurance plans.* With the federal estate tax unlimited marital deduction, taxes are postponed but not eliminated. The estate values from the first marriage partner's death are added to the second partner's assets at death, usually leading to a higher overall tax when the second partner dies. Greater planning is needed for the second spouse. The survivorship life insurance plan, also commonly called the second-to-die plan, is designed to protect the overall estate by creating liquidity at death. It jointly insures the husband and the wife, and proceeds are not paid until the death of the second spouse. The proceeds provide needed estate liquidity. When children or a trust owns the policy, the proceeds will be paid outside the estate and escape estate taxes.

### Gift Taxes

**gift tax**

The *gift tax* is a federal tax on an individual's right during life to transfer money and property by gift to others. It is levied on the donor. The annual exclusion for 2009 is $13,000 (inflation-adjusted in $1,000 increments) to each donee, provided the gifts are outright and of a present interest. A present interest means the gift is complete, transferred for less than full and adequate consideration, and the donee (recipient of the gift) has full possession and the immediate right to use, possess, and enjoy the gift.

**annual gift tax exclusion**

A person is entitled to give annually to any number of recipients with no gift tax payable, up to the *annual gift tax exclusion* amount. For a married couple, each spouse can give up to the annual exclusion per recipient and together exclude two times the annual exclusion per recipient. This is referred to as a split gift and a gift tax return must be filed to accomplish this. Therefore it is possible to transfer significant amounts of property out of an estate during one's lifetime, without a gift tax. As a practical matter, most people limit their lifetime gifts to small amounts and only to their children and grandchildren.

| 2001 Federal Gift Tax Law Change As changed by the Economic Growth and Tax Relief Reconciliation Act of 2001 (EGTRRA) | | |
|---|---|---|
| **Calendar Year** | **Exemption Equivalent*** | **Top Gift Tax Rate** |
| 2002 | $1,000,000 | 50% |
| 2003 | $1,000,000 | 49% |
| 2004 | $1,000,000 | 48% |
| 2005 | $1,000,000 | 47% |
| 2006 | $1,000,000 | 46% |
| 2007 | $1,000,000 | 45% |
| 2008 | $1,000,000 | 45% |
| 2009 | $1,000,000 | 45% |
| 2010 | $1,000,000 | 35% |
| 2011 | $1,000,000 | 55% |
| * This is a lifetime transfer exemption applying to gift taxes. | | |

Gift taxes are levied only after someone exhausts the lifetime gift exemption equivalent of $1 million. Any use of this lifetime gift exemption equivalent will reduce the applicable credit amount available for gift and estate tax purposes by the amount of the corresponding gift tax.

Note that only the gift tax amount associated with gifts that exceed the annual gift tax exclusion will reduce the applicable credit amount. For example, if during the course of a year, a single mother gives $40,000 to her son, no taxes will be due on the $27,000 that exceeds the annual exclusion (for 2009) as long as she has not exceeded the $1 million lifetime exemption equivalent for gifts. The net effect is that her applicable credit amount for gift and estate tax purposes would be reduced by the gift tax amount associated with this $27,000 gift. The exception would be donations to charities, which do not reduce the applicable credit amount. `

***Charitable Gifts through Life Insurance.*** People make gifts to their favorite charities because they believe in the work of the charity and because they want to do something good. Unfortunately, for most of us, the amount we can give is limited and we are influenced by the tax benefits of our gifts. The use of life insurance to fund a charitable gift has many advantages.

Charitable gifts can produce three federal tax benefits:

- income tax. When the donor itemizes deductions, charitable donations during the donor's lifetime are usually deductible.
- gift tax. With a few exceptions, qualified charitable gifts or bequests are exempt from gift taxes.
- estate tax. Charitable gifts that become effective after the donor's death may qualify for an estate tax deduction.

More people are beginning to realize the advantages of using life insurance in a charitable giving situation as an alternative to giving cash or other assets to a charity. Many charities have established life insurance programs that they publicize to their most loyal supporters. Some of the advantages your clients will realize by using life insurance as the vehicle of gifting are

- leveraging the contribution, so it will become a larger gift than otherwise possible with a straight cash contribution. It becomes a gift made on the installment plan through annual premium payments for the life insurance.
- receiving a current income tax deduction for donations made to pay premiums on a policy owned by the charity
- receiving a future estate tax deduction for life insurance proceeds paid to a charitable organization upon the death of the donor
- creating a new asset and not depending upon other owned assets to make the gift
- avoiding the probate process for the life insurance that would create costs, delays, and publicity which connects the charitable gift to the settlement of the estate
- avoiding possible challenges by the potential heirs
- avoiding creditor claims that could be attached to the other assets that pass by will
- creating, through life insurance, a self-completing gift that is fairly simple to arrange

Estate planning is complex process that requires a significant amount of study, training, and experience. However, in writing even the simplest life insurance policies, these basics must be understood, as these principles of effective estate planning will potentially affect your client's taxable estate. This section should help you to see opportunities in this area, and to better understand your role in advising your client and using life insurance most effectively in your client's financial plan. With this information, you can also determine whether you want to pursue the skills and knowledge necessary to target clientele with estate planning needs.

## DISTRIBUTION PLANNING

Most of your older clients will have several different sources of post-retirement income, including the following:

- Social Security benefits
- tax-advantaged employer plans such as 401(k), 403(b), SEP-IRA
- Individual Retirement Accounts (IRAs)
- investment income from mutual funds, stock dividends, bond interest, rental from investment real estate, and so on
- pensions such as corporate, military, federal, or state employment
- income from trusts set up by the client or for the client's behalf
- income from part-time work such as consulting

Your client may also inherit assets or be the beneficiary of life insurance policies on others such as a spouse or other relative. These sources of income may be intermittent or last for only a few years. Some income sources are subject to cost of living increases (for example, Social Security benefits and federal pensions), while some will remain level. The task of planning for a client's income distribution can be very complex, with many moving parts and assumptions about such things as future inflation rates, investment returns, and spending requirements. The entire field of income distribution is evolving into a financial specialty in itself with its own practitioners, associations, and publications. While it is beyond the scope of this textbook to deal thoroughly with the subject, it is safe to say that as a practicing financial advisor, you will have opportunities to assist clients with this important issue. Thus, you will need to know the basics of distribution planning.

Many recent consumer surveys have highlighted the concern that retirees have for their retirement income security. Along with concerns about their personal health, risks of needing long-term care, and loss of their independence, retirees consistently reveal their strong fear of outliving their assets before they die. They know of others who retired with a comfortable middle-class lifestyle in their 60s who were struggling and debt-ridden in their 70s and 80s. Advisors must acknowledge these fears in the older client, and help them take the steps to ensure their future financial success.

## Maintaining Purchasing Power

One of the major challenges for older retirees is maintaining the purchasing power of their money, thus maintaining their standard of living. Two major threats to all retirees are inflation and taxes. Inflation is often compared to high blood pressure as a silent killer, as even normal inflation constantly reduces purchasing power of the dollar by increasing costs over time. For example, at a relatively low annual inflation rate average of 3.5 percent, the purchasing power of $100,000 would erode to approximately $70,000 after just 10 years. The costs of many goods and services heavily used by seniors, particularly health care and prescription drug costs, are increasing at rates three or four times the general rates of inflation measured by the Consumer Price Index (CPI). Thus if income sources and investment returns do not increase with time to keep pace with inflation, purchasing power inevitably declines along with the retirees' standard of living.

Tax rates vary considerably by areas of the nation. However, it is a safe assumption that taxes will increase for nearly everyone over the next decades. The huge need to fund social services for the large baby boomer population, the pressing need for infrastructure improvements, and the economic difficulties of recent years make tax increases inevitable.

Finally the increased life expectancies of Americans make retirement periods lasting 30 or more years a real possibility. Inflation risk will thus be a much greater threat to today's retirees than it was for their parents or grandparents who normally lived only a few years after they retired. Modern retirement planning must carefully consider longevity issues and seek ways for clients' income and investments to accommodate inflation over much longer retirement periods.

## Cash Flow and Spending Plan

For most of your clients, with the exception of those with considerable wealth, it will be critical to make a careful projection of income and expenses, that is, a cash-flow analysis. This step is often given lip service by some advisors, and many clients are reluctant to develop it because it highlights areas of excessive spending or careless recording of checks and other financial records. There is a valuable discipline required to compile an adequate cash-flow analysis, and it will almost always reap benefits for your clients.

When considering the client's income, pay special attention to whether the income source is adjusted for inflation. Many older corporate pension plans are fixed, while most state, federal, and military pensions are inflation adjusted. That can make a significant difference in meeting future income needs.

Many advisors find a three-tiered analysis of income goals helpful, which places retirement spending into three categories: needs, desires, and aspirations.

- **Needs**: These include the necessities of life such as food, rent or mortgage, utilities, insurance, and debt repayment. They are expenses which would be the last to go if the client experienced financial difficulties.
- **Desires**: These include convenient, but unnecessary, items such as vacations, cruises, hobbies, gym membership, and gifting to children or charities. These are expenses, which could, and would, be eliminated if the client experienced financial difficulties.
- **Aspirations**: These are dreams a client may have such as returning to college, studying abroad for a year, or leaving a large inheritance to children or grandchildren. While emotionally important to the client, these aspirations may have to be eliminated if financial difficulties occur.

After the different spending categories are determined, the advisor and client will be better equipped to understand the true nature of the client's financial situation. For example, if secure income sources such as government pension and social security benefits are adequate to meet the basic needs of the client, then additional dollars can comfortably be spent for the desires and aspirations, or they may be invested with greater confidence on the part of the client. On the other hand, if the secure income sources are not enough to meet basic needs, other strategies must be used. For example, some of the client's assets such as stocks, bonds, or mutual funds may need to be liquidated to provide the additional income.

Advisors must understand that some clients may be at risk by withdrawing too much from their investment portfolios, because they have unrealistic expectations of future market returns. While the specifics are beyond the scope of this textbook, much of the recent research studies project sustainable withdrawal rates of only 4 to 4.5 percent per year from a diversified investment portfolio (for example, a mix of stocks, bonds, and cash). Thus, a client with a diversified portfolio of $100,000 should withdraw only about $4,000 to $4,500 per year (pre-tax) to increase the probability that the portfolio will last over his or her expected life span. This concern for outliving one's assets has generated interest in immediate annuities.

## Individual Annuities

More and more advisors are taking a new look at the advantages of annuities to provide secure income to their clients, especially to meet the basic needs when a shortfall exists. We assume you have a basic familiarity with annuities from your previous studies. In this section, we will review some general definitions and examine alternative payout or settlement options—different ways to structure annuity payouts. Remember, these same annuity payout alternatives can be used with life insurance cash values or death benefits, often referred to as optional modes of settlement.

**annuity**

In its most basic form, an *annuity* is a legally enforceable contract between an individual and an insurance company which can convert assets into an income stream. The income is in the form of regular, periodic payments such as annually, quarterly, or monthly. The income may be guaranteed in some cases for the life of the annuitant (usually the owner), or the guarantee may be for shorter periods.

Annuities can be categorized in several ways. There are immediate annuities and deferred annuities. There are single-premium and flexible-premium annuities. Also there are fixed and variable annuities. These distinctions are briefly described below.

### Immediate Annuity

**immediate annuity**

An *immediate annuity* provides periodic payments in return for a lump sum investment of money, with the payments beginning one annuity period (for example, annual or monthly) after the contract issue date.

| | |
|---|---|
| ***Example:*** | Barbara, a 65-year old widow with no close, living relatives, purchases an immediate annuity for $100,000 from the High Life Insurance Company on January 1st. Her monthly payments of $575 begin one month later on February 1st. With the payout option that Barbara selected, her monthly payments are guaranteed for her life and will cease at her death. |

### Deferred Annuity

**deferred annuity**

With a *deferred annuity*, the income payments are deferred for a period longer than one annuity period after the contract's issue date. The period from the initial purchase until income payments begin is called the accumulation period. The payout period, also known as the annuitization period, begins with the first payment to the annuitant.

| | |
|---|---|
| ***Example:*** | Robert, at age 50, purchased a deferred annuity using a $50,000 inheritance to provide retirement income beginning at age 60. For the 10-year accumulation |

period, the annuity earned interest which was tax-deferred under current income tax rules. At age 60, the value of the annuity was almost $78,000. Robert then chose to annuitize the contract, and he began receiving annual payments of $4,600 exactly one year after the annuitization date. Those annual payments are guaranteed to Robert for the remainder of his life.

### Single-Premium Annuity

A single premium annuity is funded by only one lump-sum premium payment by the contract owner to the insurer. All immediate annuities are also single-premium annuities.

### Flexible-Premium Annuity

In contrast to a single-premium annuity, the flexible-premium annuity allows the contract owner to vary the frequency and amounts of premium payments into the annuity during the accumulation period. Thus a contract owner may periodically make both monthly premium payments and occasional lump-sum payments, perhaps from a tax return or inheritance. All flexible-premium annuities are deferred annuities.

### Fixed Annuity

**fixed annuity**

A *fixed annuity* specifies a minimum guaranteed interest rate which is the lowest rate the insurer will credit to the contract owner. The current interest rate, also known as the credited rate, is the rate the insurer pays for a given period. The current interest rate is equal to or higher than the guaranteed interest rate.

*Example:*     James purchases a single-premium fixed annuity from the Very Old Life Insurance Company. The insurer guarantees a first year interest rate of 5.25 percent, and a rate of 4.25 percent for years two through six. After the sixth year, the contract guarantees a minimum interest rate of 3 percent.

### Variable Annuity

**variable annuity**

The *variable annuity* has accumulation values that fluctuate with the performance of one of more specified investment funds. The funds may be managed by the insurer, or they may be provided by outside investment companies. Variable annuities do not guarantee either principal or interest of investment accounts, although many variable annuities have a fixed account option which may pay a low guaranteed rate for a specified period of time.

## Life Insurance Settlement Options

Life insurance death benefits can be critical for the financial futures of surviving loved ones. In such situations, the proper disposition of the policy proceeds through policy settlement options is important. A number of different options are available. The selection of the specific settlement option may be established prior to death by the policyowner or left to the beneficiary's choice.

### *Lump-sum or Cash Proceeds*

Most payments to beneficiaries are taken as a lump sum. All of the contract proceeds under this arrangement are paid to the named beneficiary in a cash payment by check or, for most companies, into an interest-bearing checking account for immediate use or future disposition. These accounts work much like a check-writing money market fund. The beneficiary can withdraw the total proceeds in one transaction or make partial withdrawals of funds by writing checks. The balance in the account continues to earn interest until withdrawn. Even with these conveniences, over 90 percent of beneficiaries still choose a single lump-sum withdrawal and take possession of all the proceeds.

In deciding whether the proceeds should be paid in a lump sum, remember that this option offers no protection against the creditors of the beneficiary. The choice of other options, discussed later, can provide protection against creditor rights to the proceeds. Lump-sum distributions allow the beneficiary to manage the money, either reinvesting it at a higher rate, using it to pay estate settlement costs or debts, or for any purpose they choose. For many beneficiaries, however, especially those who are relatively inexperienced in money management, receiving guaranteed payments in installments may be safer and more desirable.

### *Supplementary Contract*

settlement options

supplementary
contract

When proceeds are to be paid under one of the *settlement options*, other than the cash settlement, a new contract called a *supplementary contract* is issued. Insurance companies guarantee the safety of the funds and keep them invested at a contractual rate of return.

The insurance company can prepare illustrations and figures for any of the settlement options you may wish to discuss with a client or beneficiary. A list of the most common arrangements follows. You will recognize these as the same as those offered in annuity contracts. Most companies permit arrangements not specifically granted in the contract, but are more liberal in working out different settlement plans adopted by the policyowner before death than for unusual requests by a policyowner beneficiary after death.

### Payout Choices

*Interest Income.* Under this settlement option, the insurer holds the proceeds and makes regular interest income payments to the beneficiary based on a rate of return guaranteed in the policy, or a higher rate based on current interest rates. This selection preserves the capital for the future and protects the capital from creditors of the beneficiary. The option can also be set up to enable the beneficiary to make cash withdrawals from the proceeds at any time. This option is designed to distribute the full proceeds at a later date, when the beneficiary is ready to receive them, or at the beneficiary's death. The most flexible of all available settlement options, the interest option is also the only one in which income is fully taxable (from the interest, not the death benefit) to the recipient. (Note that with the other options, income is made up of principal and interest and only the interest portion is taxed. We will revisit this later.)

*Fixed Period Income.* Here, the company pays out both policy proceeds and interest earned in installments over a specified period. The income received depends on the amount of proceeds, the interest credited, and the time period selected. The fixed period payout for insurance proceeds offers no flexibility to the beneficiary and is not appropriate unless a clearly-defined purpose and time frame for need can be established.

*Example:* Janice, a 61-year-old widow, recently received a death benefit of $50,000 after the death of her mother. Janice needs income for the next five years to supplement her salary until she retires at age 66 and begins drawing Social Security benefits. As the beneficiary, she chose a settlement option which will pay her $900 per month for 60 months, after which payments will cease. Each monthly payment consists of a taxable portion due to the interest paid by the insurer, and a tax-free portion from the death benefit.

*Specified Amount.* Under this option, policy proceeds, plus interest, are used to pay out a specified amount of income at regular intervals for as long as the proceeds last. The larger the payment, the shorter the period of income. This option is similar to the fixed period settlement choice except that excess interest above the return guaranteed by the company extends the length of time for the payout. This option is selected when the beneficiary determines that a specific amount of income is needed.

| | |
|---|---|
| ***Example:*** | Nancy was the beneficiary of a $50,000 life insurance policy on her father who recently passed away. Nancy has determined she would like a monthly payout of $600 per month for as long as the proceeds (and interest accumulations) will last. The insurer provides Nancy a supplemental contract which will guarantee her the $600 monthly payment for 93 months, with a small residual payment of the remaining account value. |

***Life Income.*** The life income option is a settlement choice unique to the insurance industry. The promise is to pay a stated income as long as the beneficiary lives. At death, the contract ends. This describes a pure no-refund annuity. Whether the beneficiary lives to 110 or dies next year, the annuity reverts to the company at death. Even though it may offer the highest amount of income to the beneficiary during life, this option is used sparingly. A more popular and commonly used life income settlement builds in a refund or period-certain guarantee.

| | |
|---|---|
| ***Example:*** | Malcolm, a 70-year-old retired factory worker with no living relatives, received a $100,000 death benefit when his wife passed away. Malcolm desired the maximum monthly payout and was not concerned with leaving a legacy. The insurer provided a supplemental contract with a life income option that guaranteed Malcolm an income of $625 per month, which he accepted. After only five years of payments, Malcolm died from a stroke. The value of the annuity reverted back to the insurer. |

***Life Income with Refund.*** The life income with refund option guarantees payments for the life of the annuitant. If the annuitant should die before all the proceeds have been distributed, the balance of payments would be paid, either in a lump sum or installments, to the annuitant's beneficiary or even a third beneficiary, until all proceeds are depleted. The annuitant is assured through this option that all proceeds will be paid out.

---

***Example:***        Carlos, a 65-year-old retiree, was the beneficiary of a $100,000 insurance policy on his father. Carlos accepted a life-income-with-refund payout from the insurer. Under the contract terms, Carlos is guaranteed a monthly payout of $550 for the remainder of his life. If he should die before the full $100,000 has been paid, the remainder will be paid in a lump sum to Carlos's daughter Maria.

---

***Life Income with Period Certain.*** Under a life income with period-certain payout option, the annuitant receives payments for his or her entire life. In addition, the annuitant is guaranteed that if he or she should die within a certain period, such as, 10, 15, or 20 years, the payment will be paid to a beneficiary for the balance of the period.

---

***Example:***        Scott selects a life income option with a 10-year period certain. If he died three years later, his designated beneficiary would receive payments for seven years, which is the balance of the period certain. If Scott should live longer than the 10-year period, he will have income for the rest of his life under the life income portion of the payout. At his death, no further payments are due.

---

***Joint and Survivor Life Income.*** Under this settlement option, income is provided for two people. It is most commonly used by married couples for payment of retirement benefits. It can be set up to expire at the second death or to have the refund or period-certain guarantees built into the settlement. The joint income may be set up so that the survivor's income continues at 100 percent of the amount paid when both annuitants were alive. This is called a joint and 100-percent survivor income. This can be varied so that survivor income is reduced to a percentage of the full amount. The common arrangements are joint and two-thirds or joint and one-half.

---

***Example:***        David is the sole beneficiary of a $100,000 life insurance on his sister who recently passed away. David selects a joint-and-survivor life income option which will pay $600 per month to him and his wife Diane while they both remain alive. If either spouse dies, the surviving spouse will continue to receive 75 percent of the $600, or $450, for the remainder of his or her life. After the second spouse dies, no further payments are made by the insurer.

### Other Options

You may find that one option is not enough when the issue is the distribution of large sums of money. For example, estate settlement costs must be paid before proceeds are dedicated to income-producing vehicles such as annuities or an investment. Annuities may be too narrow of a method for managing all funds from a single situation, and other forms of investment may be indicated for diversification. However your clients choose for distribution of cash proceeds from their insurance policies, they should consider three objectives:

- income needs
- growth of principal
- safety of principal

If you are making recommendations on the allocation of the proceeds, you should know these objectives and attempt, through questioning, to understand your client's views on them.

## Death Claims

There is an old observation about death claims. When someone dies, many will come offering sympathy. Many others will come with hands out, because death creates expenses that must be paid. Only the life insurance advisor can come offering financial support at the time it is needed most.

You will not fully understand what it means to be a life insurance advisor until you have delivered the first claim check on a policy that you wrote. This role for advisors is an extremely difficult yet important experience. It validates the message you have shared with your clients and prospects in a highly personal, emotional way. In some cases, it is best to delay major decisions until the beneficiary has had some time to adjust to the loss, especially if the deceased was a close loved one.

Respond quickly to deaths of your customers or clients. Although this is a hard time for the family, your help in initiating the claims process will provide a much-needed and appreciated service. Always start a separate client file for death claims. Record the summaries of conversations you have with claims personnel in the insurer's home office. Do not accept unnecessary delays in processing the claim. Find out early if there are questions that may delay the claim, such as investigation of an insured's death within the policy's contestability period. Best practice is to not discuss with family members or beneficiaries exactly how much the death benefit will be. Remember, the death benefit may be adjusted for outstanding policy loans, interest payments, misstatement of age or of gender, and other reasons. When you deliver the first check—and you should do so in person—you will then know the amount, and you will be able to ease the trauma of the situation.

In addition, when you contact family members, you may find that they need your help in filing claims for other benefits to which the deceased was entitled, such as Social Security, other insurance policies, or veteran's benefits. You can assist your clients and customers in this often time-consuming and confusing chore by providing them written instructions in advance for filing these claims. These instructions become part of a claims kit that you prepare and present to your customers during the delivery interview or at the first product review. In a death claim situation, you may provide additional assistance by helping clients with the paperwork for these claims.

### Claims Kit

A claims kit can include any number of items that will be helpful to your customers and their surviving family members. The cover letter explaining the deceased's life insurance plan, which you discussed during the product delivery and in subsequent annual reviews, should be in the kit. So should any brochures or booklets that offer solid, supportive advice for your insured or the surviving family members, particularly a spouse. Many of these are available from your company or commercial publishers. The subjects covered are typically about the importance of wills, community property arrangements (where applicable), and other more personal advice such as budgeting.

Generally a claims kit will also include some form of record-keeping booklet in which the insured can list important information that the surviving spouse will need. The names and phone numbers of financial and legal advisors, policy numbers, amounts, company information, location of life insurance policies, information on employee benefits, and veterans and Social Security eligibility and benefit information could be listed. Two copies of this booklet should be prepared, one for the surviving spouse and one for the client's attorney.

As in all aspects of your business, service during the death claims process is crucial. Your words, actions, and especially the financial assistance you can offer are important to the deceased's survivors and to you and your business. You will see first-hand what life insurance and other great financial products can do for the families you serve.

---

**How to File a Life Insurance Claim**

### Life Insurance Benefits

1.  Contact your agent as soon as possible. He or she is qualified to advise you regarding any benefits to which you may be entitled, and will also help you secure necessary claim forms.
2.  If you are unable to contact your agent, notify the nearest office of the insurance company. Be sure to provide the date of death and the policy number(s). If there is no local office, contact the home office of each company, using the address that appears on each policy.
3.  Your policies may provide various methods by which the company will distribute the death benefit to beneficiaries. Ask for an explanation of the available settlement options so you can select a payment plan to fit your income needs. You may wish to obtain counsel from your agent, attorney, or other financial advisor.

### Social Security Benefits

Apply immediately for any benefits at the nearest Social Security field office. A delay in filing your claim may result in a loss of benefits. You will need the following papers:

1.  insured's Social Security card
2.  insured's military discharge, if any
3.  marriage certificate (if applicable)
4.  birth certificate of each child who is under 16, or under 19 if a full-time secondary student, or who is severely handicapped before age 22
5.  federal tax W-2 forms for year of death

### Veterans Benefits

Apply for the following benefits at the Veterans Administration Field Office nearest you:

1.  National Service or U.S. Government Life Insurance. You will need:
    a.  a certified copy of the death certificate
    b.  a certified copy of your birth certificate (if you request a life income option)
    c.  Form VB 26-4125, obtainable from the Veterans Administration
2.  Burial Benefit. You will need:
    a.  a certified copy of the death certificate
    b.  a certified copy of the military discharge
    c.  statement from the coroner showing the amount of itemized funeral expenses and by whom paid
    d.  Veterans Administration Form 21-530
3.  Spouse's and Children's Pension and Compensation. The spouse or children of deceased veterans may be entitled to certain income benefits. Your life insurance agent or the Veterans Administration can help you determine if you have a valid claim. If you or your children are eligible, you will need:
    a.  a certified copy of the death certificate (include certified death certificate of prior spouse(s), if any)
    b.  a certified copy of marriage certificate (include certified divorce decree of any prior spouse)
    c.  a certified copy of your birth certificate
    d.  a certified copy of each child's birth certificate
    e.  a certified copy of military discharge
    f.  Veterans Administration Form VB 21-534
4.  Compensation for Dependent Parents. You will need:
    a.  a certified copy of the death certificate
    b.  a certified copy of the birth certificate of the deceased veteran showing the names of both parents
    c.  Veterans Administration Form 21-535

If you are filing claims for more than one veteran's benefit, it is not necessary that you provide more than one copy of any form.

### Dealing with the Beneficiary

When a life insurance beneficiary is considering the most appropriate payout option, there are some considerations that do not appear in other situations. Keep in mind that you are dealing with a beneficiary rather than an insured. Once the life insurance proceeds have been paid to a beneficiary, that money is the sole property of the beneficiary. Both the insurance company and the policyowner lose control over the policy proceeds after they have been distributed.

***Avoid Emotional Decisions.*** The loss of a loved one makes decisions emotionally charged, and immediate concerns may seem unrealistically more important than long-term needs. You must be careful to advise your clients properly, and may suggest leaving the proceeds with the insurance company at interest—for six months or longer. Later, when life has calmed down for the survivors, and they have adjusted to the loss, you may suggest steps that will assure they reach their long-term objectives using the proceeds of the life insurance.

Other options, even for the short-term situation, may be useful. You might consider certificates of deposit, money market certificates, NOW accounts, or even regular passbook savings, if they yield more than what the insurer pays.

Often, survivors recall instructions or suggestions from the deceased, perhaps in a letter that states how the deceased thought the money might be used. If the advice or wishes are outdated and there are other, better ways to apply the policy proceeds, your client may have a difficult time deciding to deviate from those wishes. As you counsel your clients, consider these and any other pertinent aspects of each situation. Do not be hesitant to suggest waiting or bringing other experts into counsel.

***Considerations.*** With any investment opportunity, beneficiaries need to weigh their objectives against such factors as safety of principal, rate of return, liquidity, and ease of management. Our purpose in looking at the several payout options is to learn how they might help beneficiaries meet their different financial objectives.

When you help the beneficiaries select their most appropriate payout options, you build a reputation as an adept financial-services professional who stays with your clients throughout the entire process of identifying and satisfying their financial needs.

## CASE HISTORY: GREATEST ASSET

*Advisor.* Tony Spadetti has been in the life insurance business for more than 12 years, the last two years as a general advisor. An LUTC graduate and CLU, Tony is married and has four children. The agency's marketplace is a large industrial area.

*Prospect.* Before I called the prospect, 37-year-old Mary, I knew very little about her. The lead came from the agency's file of orphan policyholders. Many years ago, her father had purchased a $25,000 policy for her, but the father, recently deceased, was still carried as the owner.

Some checking in the city directory revealed that Mary was now the owner of a small industrial equipment manufacturing business started by her father. In the course of my first interview, I found that she was divorced and has five children, the youngest one year old and the eldest 14. None of the children was insured through our agency.

*Approach.* I phoned and introduced myself:

"I am calling in connection with the policy you hold with our company. I plan to be near your office on business tomorrow morning, and I would like to stop by to meet you. I would be glad to bring you up to date on some recent changes in the tax laws and in Social Security to see how they might affect your life insurance. Will you be free at 10:30, or would 11:00 suit you better?"

She replied that she had no desire at all to talk to me about life insurance but would permit me five minutes of her time the next morning, just to make her acquaintance. I could hear the noise of heavy machinery in the background.

*Initial Meeting.* As soon as I entered her office, she removed her watch and placed it on her desk, stating that she would give me five minutes and no more. Then she opened a desk drawer and produced a large number of life insurance proposals. Tossing them across the desk to me, she said, "These are souvenirs from the last dozen insurance salespeople. If you've got any intention of showing me proposals or drawing any fancy charts, don't waste my time. I've seen them all."

She concluded her greeting by telling me she had not the slightest interest in any "fancy business insurance plans," and frankly didn't believe life insurance was of any value to her, although she very generously conceded that for "the average working person," it is probably necessary. She was obviously proud of her station in life, probably due to her running the plant and a home with children at the same time. She was accomplished at an early age.

She was on the defensive. It was easy to see that any routine presentation would be useless. Many had tried before and failed. While she talked, I decided on an approach I hoped would be completely new to her. Life insurance would not be mentioned. First, there was the difficult task of gaining her confidence.

My one way to capture her attention was my knowledge of her policy. She was the insured, but not the owner. Wouldn't she prefer to transfer ownership of this property to herself? Yes, she would. In fact, she was very interested because her father had died without a will and the policy was now in his estate. I told her I would come back at a later time with the necessary forms if she would obtain a letter of administration to make the change of ownership. She promised to do this.

On her office wall was the picture of a man I assumed to be the father and founder of the company. Having confirmed my guess, I seized the opportunity to ask how long her father had been in the manufacturing business and how the company had developed so rapidly.

Mary was eager to talk about her father's success. For the next 15 minutes, she spoke fondly of the progress the firm had made under her father's leadership, expressing a great deal of respect for her father and revealing a deep emotional disturbance over his recent death. It was an interesting discussion, and the time we spent talking about her father helped in establishing confidence and friendship. I listened attentively.

I had to remind her of the original time limit. She laughed and thanked me for being courteous enough to listen to her. In return, she said she would listen to any idea I might have, but she hastily added that she would buy no more life insurance.

***Establishing the Need.*** I spoke about human life values. I explained that she is an asset to herself, her family, and her business. I made reference to a formula that she could use to assess her value as an asset in actual dollar figures. This aroused her interest and she challenged me to prove it, indicating doubt that her worth could be measured.

As I worked out the formula, I explained that because she was then 37, she had 28 years of earning power before she would reach 65. Her current earnings were $75,000 a year and it would be reasonable to expect no reduction in this. Multiplying that by 28 showed $2.1 million of anticipated future earnings. Then I included her own costs for maintenance and taxes, cutting the figure by 50 percent to yield the total value to her family and business to be at least $1 million. Even at conservative rates, an investment of her value would yield over $80,000 per year.

Comparing this "asset" to other assets, such as her home, the manufacturing plant, and the heavy machinery, I pointed out that she should not leave these other valuable physical assets unprotected. Yet the most precious asset she owned—her income-producing ability—was grossly neglected and sadly uninsured.

I stressed that when she was gone there was no guarantee that someone could continue her business. It might have to be liquidated. Because the value of the company was now largely due to her skill and knowledge as its leader, there would be a tremendous loss.

During the discussion she had become absorbed with the analysis of her position. Now she asked how much $100,000 of new life insurance would cost. Here again was a key point in the interview. The great temptation was to quote a rate and try for the easy sale.

I controlled my first impulse. I replied that I would not think of insulting her by suggesting she buy $100,000. This would be like proposing that she insure only the windows in her factory. A person in her position—an investment worth over $1 million—should never be insured for anything less than $250,000, and even that might be low considering her personal situation with the children and the business.

This startled her, but I could see the idea beginning to take hold. Telling her that permanent coverage was probably the best recommendation in her case, I suggested we review the figures on $250,000. As I explained the estate, or creative values, and the accumulation of contingency funds as living benefits, I emphasized that this was not just a sheet of paper with unintelligible legal clauses. Life insurance was property in every sense of the word. I completed my presentation by showing her the income power of the annuity feature, and painting a rosy picture of retirement for her.

*Close.* It was time again for restraint. Up to this point she had listened attentively, but had been unresponsive to any leading questions. I decided to keep quiet. We sat in silence for a long time. To me it was like two hours. It was a nerve-wracking struggle not to speak, but I was successful.

"How much does this cost?"

Again I resisted the impulse to name a figure. I replied that I couldn't answer yet because it depended on her qualifications, but she could be assured it would be a fair premium based on her health and other considerations. The first step to securing an answer involved a thorough medical examination. Unless she could meet the company's rigid standards, she could not have the insurance, no matter how much she might be prepared to spend. Was there any reason for thinking she might not qualify?

As a matter of fact, there was. Since birth she had had a heart murmur. Several doctors had advised her that it was not a serious defect and was nothing she should worry about. Because she had already been insured at standard rates, I did not believe she would fail. But I emphasized the potential problem to impress her with the need to be examined.

After much hedging, during which she repeatedly asked the cost, she agreed to be examined for $150,000. She even agreed that if the premium was fair (standard), she might consider the additional $100,000. Feeling that I had obtained the advantage, I began to fill in the application that I had put on her desk under the policy data card at the beginning of the interview.

After arranging the examination, I made several attempts to get a binder, but she refused. She said she would pay only after the goods were delivered to her satisfaction. I settled for her promise that she would pay for at least the $150,000 if the company issued it.

When I submitted her application, I ordered two policies, one for $100,000, the other for $150,000. The investigation was lengthy; a second medical was requested. At last the contracts were issued, but rated. Although the rating was moderate, I knew the toughest part of the sale was still ahead.

**Delivery**—I arranged an appointment to review the policy. Mary was very upset about the rating. Although she had no idea about the difference in premium between standard and a special class, she was irate that she had not been offered the lowest price. After a long discussion about the company being impartial, and that it must charge as it does for all the compelling reasons, she told me she felt the company had not been fair. She did not intend to accept the policy.

I reminded her of our agreement that she would buy the basic $150,000, which she obviously needed. At the same time, I attempted to show that she was fortunate because if the company had not felt she was a good risk, she would not have been granted the option to secure the additional $100,000. Many times a company will make an offer in the interest of harmony and service, but if the client once refuses, there may not be a second chance at such favorable rates. She could even be turned down, completely.

I asked if the children would feel that the company had been unfair if she were killed in an accident that night. She did not answer right away, but maintained a thoughtful silence.

*Final Crisis.* After a moment, she spoke. She said she had a suggestion. In her business, she explained, it is common for the company to lower its price or the salesperson to cut commissions when negotiations bog down. She liked me, she went on, and would be glad to have me as her insurance adviser. Her offer was that if I "made her a deal" we could "do business."

I was purposely silent for a moment. When I spoke I chose my words very carefully. This prospect could not be expected to know the ethics and rules of my business. The suggestion had to be turned down flatly, but there was no call for offending her because she had naturally assumed that what is all right in one sales situation is all right in another.

I said that I had never and would not now "make a deal," for three reasons. First, life insurance is not a commodity that can be bartered. It is a contractual property and professional service. As such, it is governed (just as medicine and law are) by a code of ethics, and that code forbids any life insurance advisor to make deals for service. Second, proper conduct of the life insurance business is governed by state statutes that, among other things, make price cutting an offense for which both parties are punishable by law. Third, the compensation I earn for my services is fair. I would feel I was cheating myself if I gave them for less than their just worth.

I won't tell you about the debate that followed for almost half an hour. Suffice it to say that she grudgingly (as she put it) admired my stand in the face of possibly losing the sale. She bought the entire $250,000, arranging to pay the premiums through the business, because she needed the protection.

*Comment.* There were many lessons in this sale. I made the sale because I conducted myself as a professional life underwriter through knowledge and sales skill, thorough preparation, careful analysis of the prospect, and flexibility in the selling interview. It means I was an advisor and a salesperson, not an order-taker, and it means I stood by principles of integrity in a difficult situation.

My client respected me for being a professional. Since then she has purchased $75,000 more from me, and we are in the process of reviewing her program for a third time because she is presently reorganizing her business. She has also referred me to a number of her competitors and suppliers who are now among my best policyowners.

## CHAPTER EIGHT REVIEW

*Key terms and concepts are explained in the Glossary. Answers to the review and self-test questions are found in the back of the textbook in the Answers to Questions section.*

### Key Terms and Concepts

| | |
|---|---|
| old-age adult market segment | federal estate tax |
| young-old | taxable estate |
| old-old | marital deduction |
| estate planning | charitable deduction |
| operation of law | state death and inheritance taxes |
| right of contract | applicable credit amount |
| will | incidents of ownership |
| intestate | gift tax |
| testator | annual gift tax exclusion |

probate                          annuity
trust                            immediate annuity
revocable living trust           deferred annuity
pour-over will                   fixed annuity
power of attorney                variable annuity
advance directives               supplementary contract
living will                      settlement options
health care proxy

## Review Questions

8-1.  What are the common characteristics of the old-age market segment?

8-2.  What are the common needs of the old-age market segment?

8-3.  Explain how seminars can be used to approach senior prospects.

8-4.  List and explain four ways property may pass at death.

8-5.  Explain what happens if a person dies without a will.

8-6.  What are some of the requirements of a will?

8-7.  Define the following items:

- applicable credit amount
- marital deduction
- three-year rule

8-8.  Explain the uses of life insurance in estate planning.

8-9.  Name three federal tax benefits that can occur as a result of making charitable gifts.

8-10. Explain some of the advantages your clients will realize by using life insurance as the vehicle of gifting.

8-11. Explain the concepts and methods of distribution planning.

## Self-test Questions

*Instructions: Read Chapter 8 and then answer the following questions to test your knowledge. There are 10 questions. Choose one answer for each question, and then check your answers with the answer key in the back of the textbook.*

8-1.  Which of the following statements concerning the federal gift tax is correct?

(A)  Federal gift taxes are paid by the recipient of the gift.
(B)  Any person can give an amount up to the annual gift tax exclusion to any other person with no federal gift tax imposed.
(C)  Federal gift tax rules are unrelated to the federal estate tax rules.
(D)  Any person may make unlimited gifts to any other individual without federal gift taxes being imposed.

8-2.  John, age 62, was the beneficiary of a $100,000 life insurance policy on his father who recently died. John chose a settlement option which guarantees him $550 per month for the rest of his life. Upon his death, all payments will cease. This settlement is a

(A)  life income
(B)  life income with refund
(C)  fixed period income
(D)  specified amount

8-3.  Which of the following statements about how property transfers at death is correct?

(A)  If a person has no will, the property will always go to a spouse, or nearest kin.
(B)  Property will pass by contract, only if there is no will in effect.
(C)  Advisors should recommend that clients have a valid will or other arrangement to ensure an orderly disposition of assets upon death.
(D)  The provisions of a will take precedence over beneficiary designations.

8-4. Which of the following statements concerning seminars for seniors is (are) correct?

    I.    Financing healthcare, increasing retirement income, and reducing taxes are good seminar topics for seniors.

    II.   It is important to maintain the purpose of the seminar, which is to impart information.

    (A)   I only
    (B)   II only
    (C)   Both I and II
    (D)   Neither I nor II

8-5. Which of the following statements about advance directives is (are) correct?

    I.    A living will lets others know your medical wishes when you are terminally ill and/or unable to communicate.

    II    A healthcare proxy is effective even in cases where the patient is able to communicate his or her healthcare decisions.

    (A)   I only
    (B)   II only
    (C)   Both I and II
    (D)   Neither I nor II

8-6. Which of the following statements concerning estate planning is (are) correct?

    I.    Estate planning encompasses the accumulation, conservation, and distribution of an estate.

    II.   The major objective of estate planning should be to minimize estate taxes.

    (A)   I only
    (B)   II only
    (C)   Both I and II
    (D)   Neither I nor II

8-7.   Which of the following statements regarding a will is (are) correct?

    I.   If an individual dies without a will, all states allow the property to be divided equally among his or her remaining relatives.

    I.   The laws of intestacy, which vary by state, determine how a deceased person's property will pass if he or she died without a valid will.

    (A)   I only
    (B)   II only
    (C)   Both I and II
    (D)   Neither I nor II

8-8.   Which of the following statements concerning a revocable living trust is (are) correct

    I   One advantage of a revocable living trust is that assets in the trust avoid probate upon the trust owner's death.

    II.   Assets within a revocable living trust are protected against Medicaid spend-down requirements if the owner requires care in a nursing home.

    (A)   I only
    (B)   II only
    (C)   Both I and II
    (D)   Neither I nor II

8-9.   All of the following statements about aging in America are correct EXCEPT

    (A)   Aging is a highly individual experience, affecting different people in different ways.
    (B)   Social gerontologists distinguish between the "young-old" and "old-old" segments of our aging population.
    (C)   You can safely assume that most clients over 60 cannot learn new material.
    (D)   For some older people, advisors may need to repeat information or speak louder to them.

8-10. When a person dies, his or her property will normally pass to heirs in all of the following ways EXCEPT

 (A) by a lottery system among eligible heirs
 (B) by operation of law, such as jointly-held property
 (C) by right of contract, such as with life insurance beneficiaries
 (D) by a will or trust arrangement

# *Appendix A*
# *Ideal Client Profile*

An ideal client profile describes the type of prospects with whom the advisor prefers to work. It is slightly different from a target market profile in that it concentrates on personality traits and attitudes. The ideal client profile typically tells you the type of person you think you would enjoy working with, focusing less on, but not totally ignoring, the need for your product. It follows that ideal clients are a subset of each of your target markets. They are the type of people in each target market with whom you would prefer to work.

To create an ideal client profile, make a chart with two columns. The first column heading should be "What I Want." The second should be "What I Don't Want." Then think about your 20 best and worst clients, and note the demographics and attributes that correspond with each, placing them in the appropriate column. For example, if some of your worst experiences were with very analytical prospects, that characteristic should appear in the "What I Don't Want" column. The following is an example of characteristics and attributes of one advisor's best and worst clients.

| *Example:* | *What I Want* | *What I Don't Want* |
|---|---|---|
| | • has household income of $70,000 or more<br>• has investable assets of $100,000 or more<br>• desires face-to-face interaction<br>• values family<br>• is thinking about retirement and/or education planning | • very analytical<br>• unreliable<br>• price shopper<br>• do-it-yourselfer |

You can now create a profile from the lists of traits you want your ideal client to have and those you do not want him or her to have. As you create the profile, convert the negative traits into positive ones. For instance, if you do not want a do-it-yourselfer, you want a delegator or someone who seeks advice. Using the two columns in the example above, you can describe the ideal client as shown below.

---

***Example:***          My ideal client is someone who

- has a household income of $70,000 or more
- has investable assets of $100,000 or more
- wants a face-to-face relationship
- desires advice from a competent professional about retirement and education planning
- is family-oriented
- appreciates the value of good advice and is willing to pay for it
- is reliable

---

The most obvious application for your ideal client profile is to focus your prospecting activity. Compare your new or current prospects with the profile to determine whether you should continue to pursue these prospects, eliminating those who do not match the profile. In addition, you should periodically repeat the profiling process to see if your ideal client has changed. You may discover, for instance, that you are now working predominantly with prospects who have investable assets of $150,000 or more instead of the $100,000 or more you originally listed on the profile.

Another application is to determine who your "A" clients are—the clients to whom you provide your top level of service. This will enable you to create a service strategy that caters to your top clients (see Chapter 7).

Additional worthwhile applications (some of which are mentioned in this textbook) are as follows:

- Use the profile to guide you in your marketing strategies and materials.
- Post your ideal client profile on your website and in your office.
- Give the profile to friends, family, current clients, and centers of influence. (These are influential people who know you, have a favorable impression of you, and agree to introduce or recommend you to others.) That way, these people will know the type of client with whom you want to work.

# *Appendix B*
# *Activity Tracking Forms*

**Note to Advisors:** *The following forms provide examples for how to track your prospecting and selling activities while accounting for target markets and prospecting methods. Forms like the ones that follow enable you to analyze the success you are having in your general market and your target markets. This will help you to compare your effectiveness in each market and make well-informed decisions. In addition, such analysis will help you identify strengths and weaknesses in the prospecting and selling process, and take the appropriate action to capitalize on things gone right and change things gone wrong.*

*What follows is an overview of each form. Then you will find a copy of each approach and samples illustrating how to use them. If you adopt them for use in your practice, consider creating them in a spreadsheet to automate the calculation process and make the analysis easier. For example, a spreadsheet version of the* Prospect Activity Tracker *would enable you to use the sort and filter functions of the spreadsheet to sort by target market and prospecting method.*

**Daily Activity Tracker:** *This tracking form will provide data for analysis as well as self-accountability to engage in activities that will create sales. With it, you can set a daily point goal and have feedback at the end of each day for how you spent your time and energy. Many successful advisors use this type of scorekeeping to keep their production on track. Here are a few tips to help you to understand and use this form.*

*The first column lists each of the activities to be tracked. Most are self-explanatory. What follows is an explanation of the more ambiguous ones:*

- Contacts*: Record a contact only when you actually talk to a prospect and ask for an appointment (either on the phone or face-to-face). If you get an answering machine or talk to the prospect's teen-aged daughter, a contact is not recorded.*
- Appointments*: Indicate an appointment for any type of interview or meeting.*

- Initial Meetings: *Tally any meeting with a prospect in which you are able to explain what you do and ask the prospect to agree to complete a fact finder.*

*The next five columns are where you place your tally marks (or letters). Use the* General/Other *column if the prospect is from your general market or a target market not listed in the other four columns. Label the other four columns with the names of your target markets. Place a tally mark for an activity in the appropriate column.*

*The* Act *column should be used to total up all of the occurrences for each activity. Multiply this sum by the number of points awarded per occurrence indicated for each activity in the first column. Record this product in the* Pts *column. Total the numbers in the* Pts *column and record it on the* Daily Total *line.*

*Instead of using tally marks, you can use letters to indicate the prospecting method used to obtain the client. For example, you would use an* R *for a referral, an* L *for a purchased list, a* C *for a lead obtained from a center of influence, an* N *for someone you met through networking, and so on. You are then able to compare your results for various prospecting methods.*

***Prospect Activity Tracker:*** *The* Prospect Activity Tracker *tracks activity based on the prospect rather than the day. You simply list your prospects and tally.*

## Daily Activity Tracker

**Day/Date:** _____

| | General/ Other | Target Markets (up to 4) | | | | Total | |
|---|---|---|---|---|---|---|---|
| | | | | | | Act | Pts |
| Phone Calls (1 pt. each) | | | | | | | |
| Contacts (no points) | | | | | | | |
| Appointments (2 pts. each) | | | | | | | |
| Initial Meetings (3 pts. each) | | | | | | | |
| Fact Finders (5 pts. each) | | | | | | | |
| Sales Presentations (5 pts. each) | | | | | | | |
| Closing Interviews (5 pts. each) | | | | | | | |
| Sales (10 pts. each) | | | | | | | |
| 1st Yr Comp (no points) | | | | | | | |

**Daily Total:** _____

## Daily Activity Tracker
## (SAMPLE)
## Day/Date: Monday, 6/21

| | General/ Other | Target Markets (up to 4) | | | | Total | |
|---|---|---|---|---|---|---|---|
| | | *Little League Parents* | *Female Business* | *Kiwanis* | | Act | Pts |
| Phone Calls (1 pt. each) | *RRRRR* | *NNNNNRR* | *NNRRRLLCCC* | *NN* | | *24* | *24* |
| Contacts (no points) | *RR* | *NNN* | *NRRRLCC* | *N* | | *13* | *N/A* |
| Appointments (2 pts. each) | *R* | *N* | *NRC* | | | *5* | *10* |
| Initial Meetings (3 pts. each) | | *N* | *N* | | | *2* | *6* |
| Fact Finders (5 pts. each) | | | | *R* | | *1* | *5* |
| Sales Presentations (5 pts. each) | | *N* | *R* | | | *2* | *10* |
| Closing Interviews (5 pts. each) | | *N* | *R* | | | *2* | *10* |
| Sales (10 pts. each) | | *N(2)* | *R* | | | *3* | *30* |
| 1st Yr Comp (no points) | | *$1,500* | *$300* | | | *$1,800* | |

*Daily Total:*    95

## Prospect Activity Tracker

| Prospect | Target/Meth | A | C | APT | IM | FF | CI | Sales/Comments | R |
|---|---|---|---|---|---|---|---|---|---|
| | | | | | | | | | |
| | | | | | | | | | |
| | | | | | | | | | |
| | | | | | | | | | |
| | | | | | | | | | |
| | | | | | | | | | |
| | | | | | | | | | |
| | | | | | | | | | |
| | | | | | | | | | |
| | | | | | | | | | |
| | | | | | | | | | |
| | | | | | | | | | |
| | | | | | | | | | |
| | | | | | | | | | |
| **TOTALS:** | | | | | | | | | |

**Target/Meth**= the target market or the default of general market/prospecting method, **A** = attempt to contact, **C** = contact made, **APT** = appointment set, **II** = initial interview conducted, **FF** = fact finder completed, **CI** = closing interview, **Sales/Comments** = product line[s] and amount of first year compensation or comment on why the sales process stalled, **R** = referrals

**Prospecting Activity Tracker**
**(SAMPLE)**

| Prospect | Target/Meth | A | C | APT | IM | FF | CI | Sales/Comments | R |
|---|---|---|---|---|---|---|---|---|---|
| George Washington | General/Ref | *11* | *1* | *11* | | | | | |
| Thomas Jefferson | Kiwanis/Net | *1* | *1* | | | | | *Has agent* | |
| John Adams | Kiwanis/Net | *11 11* | | | | | | | |
| James Monroe | Little League/Net | *1* | *1* | *111* | *1* | *1* | *1* | *2 Life - $500* | *1* |
| Ben Franklin | General/List | *11 1* | | | | | | | |
| Dolly & Neil Madison | Female Business/Net | *1* | *1* | *11* | *1* | | | | |
| Harriet Tubman | Female Business/Net | *11 1* | *1* | *111* | *1* | *1* | *1* | *DI - $300* | *2* |
| Betsy & Jon Ross | Female Business/Dir | *1* | *1* | *11* | *1* | *1* | | | *3* |
| Stony Banks | Little League/Net | *1* | | | | | | | |
| Wally Cleaver | General/Ref | *11* | | | | | | | |
| Barbara Seville | General/Net | | | | | | | | |
| Hugh Gofers | General/List | | | | | | | | |
| | | | | | | | | | |
| | | | | | | | | | |
| | | | | | | | | | |
| TOTALS: | | *19* | *6* | *12* | *4* | *3* | *2* | *L 2 - $1,500, DI 1 - $300* | *6* |

**Target/Meth**= the target market or the default of general market/prospecting method, **A** = attempt to contact, **C** = contact made, **APT** = appointment set, **II** = initial interview conducted, **FF** = fact finder completed, **CI** = closing interview, **Sales/Comments** = product line[s] and amount of first year compensation or comment on why the sales process stalled, **R** = referrals

# *Appendix C*
# *Expense Estimates and Income Objectives*

|  |  | Monthly Total | x 12 | Annual Total |
|---|---|---|---|---|
| **Fixed Expenses** | Rent or mortgage payments | $ |  |  |
| **(Nonbusiness)** | Utilities |  |  |  |
|  | Property, auto, and life insurance |  |  |  |
|  | Property taxes |  |  |  |
|  | All health insurances |  |  |  |
|  | Income taxes |  |  |  |
|  | Social Security taxes |  |  |  |
|  | Other |  |  |  |
|  | **Total Fixed Nonbusiness Expenses** | $ | X 12 | $ |
| **Variable Living** | Food |  |  |  |
| **Expenses** | Clothing |  |  |  |
|  | Laundry and dry cleaning |  |  |  |
|  | Outside meals (nonbusiness) |  |  |  |
|  | Transportation (nonbusiness) |  |  |  |
|  | Medical—doctor, dentist, drugs |  |  |  |
|  | Other |  |  |  |
|  | **Total Living Expenses** | $ | x 12 | $ |
| **Business Expenses** | Rent |  |  |  |
|  | Sales promotion, advertising, and mail |  |  |  |
|  | Telephone |  |  |  |
|  | Transportation |  |  |  |
|  | Entertainment and meals |  |  |  |
|  | Administrative assistance |  |  |  |
|  | Self-development |  |  |  |
|  | Association dues |  |  |  |
|  | Other |  |  |  |
|  | **Total Business Expenses** | $ | x 12 | $ |
| **Miscellaneous** | Charity, gifts, church |  |  |  |
| **Expenses** | Recreation, vacation |  |  |  |
|  | Hobbies, clubs |  |  |  |
|  | Other |  |  |  |
|  | **Total Miscellaneous Expenses** | $ | x 12 | $ |
| **Savings** | Savings |  |  |  |
| **Accumulations** | Investments |  |  |  |
|  | Other |  |  |  |
|  | **Total Savings Accumulations** | $ | x 12 | $ |

**Total Annual Income Objective**     $ _____

     Less: Estimated Renewal Commissions    $ _____

         Other Income    $ _____

**Annual First-Year Commission Objective**     $ _____

# Answers to Review Questions and Self-test Questions

## Chapter 1

### *Answers to Review Questions*

1-1.  The five questions that must be answered when constructing a basic marketing plan are

- *What are my objectives?* You market and sell for a reason, to earn income. Your marketing plan must begin with income objectives that will translate into activity objectives (the level of various marketing activities needed to attain income objectives).

- *What am I marketing?* The key to answering this question is to view financial products and services as tools that enable people to achieve and/or protect their dreams. To market financial products successfully requires helping people connect the idea of achieving their goals and protecting the necessary assets and income for achieving their goals with the products and services designed for these very purposes. Therefore it is important for the advisor to describe and discuss his or her products and services in terms of the results they will achieve for the prospect.

- *To whom am I marketing?* Ideally, the advisor will set appointments with qualified prospects—people who need and want the advisor's products and services, can afford them, can qualify for them, and can be approached by the advisor on a favorable basis. Imagine the increased efficiency and effectiveness of the advisor's marketing efforts if he or she could market to a large group of such prospects that share identifiable common characteristics and needs, and have a communication (networking) system. Such a group of people is known as a target market.

- *How will I market to them?* For each target market selected, the advisor must choose and apply prospecting methods to access qualified prospects. These prospecting methods should reflect the prospecting source, the most probable financial needs and goals, and the target market's preferences. In addition, the advisor must identify and implement appropriate ways to position his or her personal brand and products and create awareness of them. Finally it includes using effective methods for approaching prospects effectively to set appointments.

- *How effective am I?* A basic marketing plan identifies metrics to measure and evaluate marketing effectiveness. The most common measures are effectiveness ratios.

1-2.  The eight steps of the selling/planning process are

- *Identify the Prospect.* Effective selling begins with getting in front of qualified prospects. This step involves target marketing, which operates on the premise that people tend to congregate with people of like values and characteristics. By definition, a target market has a networking system. If the advisor behaves professionally and provides valuable products and services, referrals are very likely.

- *Approach the Prospect.* In this step, the advisor contacts the prospect with one objective in mind: to set an appointment. The approach should be based on a relevant, potential need the prospect may have.

- *Meet with the Prospect.* In the initial meeting with a prospect, the advisor's objectives are to establish rapport, describe his or her services and the process involved, ask some thought-provoking questions, and listen attentively. Based on the prospect's responses, the advisor establishes a mutually beneficial reason to do business, describing it in the form of a value proposition.

- *Gather Information and Establish Goals.* Using a company-approved fact finder, the advisor asks a lot of questions to gather personal information, qualitative data, and quantitative data.

- *Analyze the Information.* The advisor analyzes the information gathered by creating and/or examining appropriate financial statements; identifying obstacles to desired goals; looking at the prospect's current insurance coverages, savings and investments; analyzing possible alternatives; and so on.

- *Develop and Present the Plan.* The advisor develops a plan. In addition to summarizing the client's situation and the findings of your analysis, the plan should include recommended actions.

- *Implement the Plan.* If recommendations are based on the information gathered using a properly completed fact finder, implementing the plan should simply be the logical next step in working together. That does not mean the prospect will not have some concerns or objections. This is the step in which they will arise typically. An advisor should be prepared to address them as well as to motivate prospects to take action in general. Finally the advisor should assist the prospect with acquiring any necessary products and services.

- *Service the Plan.* This is the step in which you turn customers into lifetime clients. Service cements the relationship with a customer, giving you the opportunity to make additional sales and obtain referrals. Some service is reactive: the customer initiates it by requesting a needed change. What differentiates one advisor from another, however, is the proactive element of his or her service strategy. Proactive servicing strategies, such as monitoring the plan through periodic financial reviews and relationship-building activities enable an advisor to stay in touch with customers. It is this high-contact service that builds clientele.

1-3.  In a client-focused approach to selling and planning, the objective is to cultivate a mutually beneficial, long-term relationship with a client, someone who follows your advice consistently, buys from you again, and refers you to others. (Note that for our purposes, a person who pays an annual retainer, asset management fee, and so on is a repeat buyer.) In other words, the end result is an ongoing relationship that benefits both parties. The initial sale is an intermediate, rather than final, step.

1-4. Target marketing is a process in which the advisor aims products and services at a well-defined target market. A target market is a group of prospects that meets the following criteria:
- The group is large enough to provide a continual flow of prospects.
- Members in the group have common characteristics that distinguish them from nonmembers. At least one common characteristic provides a basis for customized marketing messages and approaches.
- Members in the group have a common need or common needs, usually attributed to a common characteristic.
- The group shares information through a formal or an informal communication or networking system, making it more likely for an advisor to be referred and for the advisor's reputation to precede him or her. A communication system is the most important criterion in defining a target market.

The advantages of a target market include the following:
- Successful target marketing will result in enhanced referability due to the communication network.
- Concentrating on a few target markets enables the advisor to tailor postsale service strategies to facilitate deeper relationships, which generally translate into increased loyalty.
- Gaining a reputation within a target market for being the expert will discourage other advisors from trying to penetrate the market.
- Target marketing results in higher profits through lower acquisition costs.
- Working with people with whom the advisor has a lot in common typically will increase the advisor's job satisfaction.

1-5. The first step of the target marketing process is to divide your natural market into market segments, groups of people with common characteristics and common needs. The segmenting step involves one of two approaches:
- A very basic and effective approach to segmenting your natural markets is to analyze your personal background and history. Brainstorm to identify the types of people with whom you think you would like to work. In some cases, you will readily identify groups (markets), in other cases you will identify types of personalities for which you will need to take an additional step of identifying where you might find such people.
- A second approach is based on the process used by marketers in other industries. Although it is applied here toward past personal production, it can easily be applied to segment a newly appointed agent's friends, family, and acquaintances list. Furthermore, one could apply it to the undifferentiated, or general, market. This approach involves completing the following:
    a. Identify your top 20 clients. These are people you enjoy working with and not necessarily those who generate the highest amount in commissions or fees.
    b. Select relevant segmentation variables. There are generally four types of segmentation variables that marketing experts use to divide a market: geographic,

demographic, psychographic, and behavioristic. Choose variables that will help you find groups of qualified prospects.

c.   Apply the segmentation variables. Make a chart with columns for the client's name and for information corresponding to each of the demographic variables you chose. Enter the information for each client.

d.   Identify market segments and create profiles. Analyze the information you have gathered for commonalities. Look for groups with a communication network. Examine the segmentation variables that would indicate that a client belongs to a group with a system for networking. Groups may be found  through variables such as occupation, employer, hobbies or other interests, social or religious organizations, and neighborhood or homeowners associations. Look at commonalities of product, need, and motivation. Finally assess variables related to profit generation, including compensation, and quantity and quality of referrals.

1-6.   In the targeting a market step, you narrow your target market options and select one or a few to test and pursue. The following activities are recommended for completing this step:

- *Create selection criteria.* Take the top five or so market segments you identified and compare and prioritize them using criteria of your choosing. Such criteria will depend largely on your product mix (including services). You can group criteria into three main categories: fit of resources to segment's needs, level of potential compensation, and level of competitiveness.

- *Conduct market research.* If you do not know enough about the market segments you have identified to evaluate them accurately, you will need to conduct market research. You can begin your initial research on the Internet or at the local library. The information does not have to be precise; a very rough estimate will do fine. Select your best potential target markets from the market segments you have chosen, and prepare and conduct a market survey.

- *Assess other factors.* Advisors who sell only one product will typically utilize a product specialization strategy in which they market one product to multiple target markets. One best practice is selecting target markets that are related to one another. A second strategy, the single-segment concentration, involves marketing one product to a single market segment. This approach is applicable for advisors who are targeting high net worth clients (dentists, doctors, professional athletes, and so on). Advisors who sell multiple products will choose from a selective specialization coverage strategy, which involves marketing a few products to multiple target markets, or a market specialization strategy that specializes in one market's needs. Advisor's who sell property and casualty insurance along with other insurance and financial products can use an undifferentiated full-market coverage strategy for the auto and homeowners insurance but use one of the other coverage strategies for their other products. You may identify some market segments that do not have a communication network. Most likely, this will happen if you segment by need and motivation. Look a little deeper to see if there is the potential for targeting this market segment within larger undifferentiated groups that do have a communication network or some reasonable proxy. If you find a strong correlation between certain characteristics and buying behaviors, ask the question: "Where can I find people like this?" Often a group of people may lack common financial needs. If there is a communication network and a perpetual supply of new members, consider segmenting the market segment by life cycle (age) and/or life stage (marital and family status) and targeting them according to the unique needs of each of the resulting market segments.

1-7.   Positioning your personal brand and products involves the following:

- Your personal brand is an amalgamation of the qualities, characteristics, personal experiences, and skills that make you who you are. It is critical to identify the relevant, unique aspects of your personal brand and position them appropriately in your target market. The process includes the following steps: identify a relevant, unique position; put it in writing; test it; establish your position; and monitor and protect it.

- Advisors need to help prospects see the need for their products and services. Just as advisors must provide a compelling reason to be chosen as advisors, they must also provide a compelling reason for a prospect to purchase products. An advisor must appeal to the prospect's logic by identifying relevant facts that pertain to the needs of the target market and individual prospects. In addition, an advisor must appeal to the prospect's emotions by identifying the emotional reasons to buy that flow from the financial need that the prospect has for the products.

1-8.   Common prospecting methods used to identify people who know you favorably include the following:

- Service transactions are typically initiated by the client (a change to a policy, contribution amount, mutual fund account, and so on). When clients contact an advisor for service, they are thinking about financial matters. This is a perfect time to see if prospects need other products or services.

- The purpose of a periodic financial review is to monitor the client's progress in meeting financial goals and identify any new financial needs they may have. They are a staple in every advisor's prospecting arsenal, and applicable to nearly every financial product or service.

- Seminars for clients are better thought of as client education events that are designed to achieve one or both of the following objectives: to create awareness of financial needs and methods for addressing them, and to help clients with ancillary aspects of their goals that cannot be addressed with your products and services.

- Introduction of your practice involves meeting with friends and family and giving a concise 10-minute overview of what you do for a living. A more indirect approach is to use your friends and family as a sounding board for the various target markets they represent. The advisor can ask their friends and family members to answer a market research questionnaire, to respond to particular marketing ideas, to provide feedback on telephone approaches, or to role-play the interview process.

1-9.   Common prospecting methods used to identify people recommended by those who know you favorably include the following:

- Personal recommendations are the referrals an advisor receives from clients, friends, and family. Personal recommendations are the dominant prospecting method among most advisors.
- A second way to generate referrals is by identifying a center of influence (COI) within a desired target market. A COI is an influential person you know, who knows you favorably, and who agrees to introduce you or refer you to others. Using a COI is indicated when you can identify a person or persons whom the target market looks to for guidance and leadership. For example, all of the businesses may use a particular CPA or attorney. The president of an association is a potential COI.
- Networking is the process of continually sharing ideas, resources, and prospect names by non-competing businesses that target the same market. It is indicated when there are other professionals and businesses that specialize in working with your target market. Two forms include tips clubs and NetWeaving.

1-10. Common prospecting methods used to identify prospects among people who do not know you at all include the following:

- Personal interaction requires mastering the art of listening and the art of small talk, and showing a genuine interest in others. It also requires an ability to ask meaningful but innocuous questions that help you qualify a prospect. A good interaction is subtle and natural and avoids the appearance of shameless personal marketing.
- Another prospecting method is to sponsor or establish a formal presence at a public event that appeals to your target market. You could sponsor a child safety fair at a local school, coordinating your efforts with the local police department.
- Once you have established a good reputation, you will have the opportunity in some target markets to conduct group presentations, in which you educate a group of your target market constituents about a particular topic on which you are an expert. It is different than a seminar in that, in most cases, it is not appropriate to give a sales pitch.
- Another prospecting method is direct response, which involves sending letters with reply cards that prospects can return if they are interested in an appointment or more information. Sometimes, the letter will offer a small gift, such as a road atlas or a free booklet, to prospects who respond to the direct mail letter and agree to a free consultation with the advisor. An alternative is to use e-mail, if e-mail addresses are available. If prospects are not on a do-not-call list, advisors may follow up with a phone call to set an appointment.

### Answers to Self-test Questions

| | | |
|---|---|---|
| 1-1. | B | page 1.2 |
| 1-2. | B | page 1.5 |
| 1-3. | D | page 1.18 |
| 1-4. | C | page 1.26 |
| 1-5. | D | pages 1.23–1.24 |
| 1-6. | C | pages 1.32–1.33 |

1-7.   B     pages 1.33–1.39
1-8.   D     pages 1.13–1.14
1-9.   A     pages 1.36–1.39
1-10.  A     page 1.8

## Chapter 2

### *Answers to Review Questions*

2-1.   Life-cycle marketing operates on two generalizations:

- From birth to death, people experience common life events that affect their financial and insurance needs. Many life events inherently create or increase a prospect's need and/or ability to pay for insurance and/or other financial products. Life events serve as a trigger that raises a prospect's awareness of financial needs or increases his or her interest in meeting them. More often than not, life events are partial triggers that require some advisor-initiated contact to raise awareness of the resulting financial need and/or opportunity.

- In the past, life events occurred in a fairly predictable pattern over a person's life. The evolution of societal norms has changed the order and timing of some of these events. For example, people are marrying later in life. Despite these changes, the life-cycle paradigm is viable because life events still tend to occur within certain age ranges, or life-cycle market segments. The five segments are as follows:

    a.  *Youth—Ages 0 to 19.* These are the growing and learning years marked by dependency on adults. Youth is characterized by physical, emotional, and intellectual development. This is the stage of life when people are most impressionable. Toward the end of this phase, the teenage years involve a search for identity.

    b.  *Young Adulthood—Ages 20 to 37.* The early part of this phase involves transitioning from depending on parents to becoming independent and establishing one's own identity. It is often a time for making commitments to work, marriage, and family. Toward the middle of the phase, one tends to reexamine commitments made to career, marriage, assumed roles and lifestyles.

    c.  *Middle-Years Adulthood—Ages 38 to 58.* In the earlier years of this phase, many people begin searching for real meaning to life and/or attempt to hold onto lost youth. Some may experience a mid-life crisis as dreams and reality are reconciled. Toward the middle of the phase, the realities of life have been generally accepted. For most, the importance of one's career increases with the decreasing responsibilities as a parent. Toward the end of this phase, some may be in the position of retiring. Those who are not are making preparations for retirement.

    d.  *Mature Adulthood—Ages 59 to 75.* These are the fulfillment and yearning years. Many people achieve some self-actualization during these years. It is common for a renewed focus on the spiritual dimension to emerge. The early part of this phase is usually when people are preparing for retirement or retiring. Wealth accumulation is important early on; toward the end of this phase more attention is placed on seeking new achievements and education, working in the service of others, and enjoying leisure time and accumulated wealth.

e. *Old Age—Ages 76 and up.* Old age is when a person becomes a seasoned citizen. It is the wise and fragile phase of life, a time to remember and recall the past. This phase encompasses the consumption and distribution of wealth. Long-term care is a key issue and often a major concern. Demographically, there will be three times as many women as men.

2-2. Prestige building is your public relations campaign to position your personal brand favorably in your target markets. The limit to prestige-building activities is your imagination. Methods for prestige building include the following:

- Social mobility refers to a person's movement within and impact on a community. The result of social mobility is a reputation within the community. Some of the more common ways to increase social mobility include the following:

    a. Community Involvement. If the target market coincides with a social, civic, business, charitable, or religious organization, this is usually the preferred method for creating awareness of who you are and what you do. Remember to involve yourself only with organizations and causes that you support personally. In addition, determine a realistic view of your capacity for involvement to help you make decisions regarding your level of commitment. Aim for visibility and not shameless self-promotion. There are four levels of involvement to consider: sponsorship and giving, volunteering, joining, and leading.

    b. Writing. If you can write short articles and your target group has a newsletter or reads certain publications, then write an article and have it approved by your compliance department.

    c. Speaking to Groups. Some organizations will offer their members free educational seminars about pertinent topics. If this opportunity is available and you are comfortable speaking to groups, let the appropriate persons in the organization know your availability and the topics about which you would be willing to address. The goal of these speaking engagements is first and foremost to establish your reputation as an expert. Keep promotional information to a minimum—a business card and/or a personal brochure.

    d. Other Media Opportunities. There are other media opportunities, including local radio and television. There are many financial advisors who host their own 1-hour radio or television show on local public access channels. Others find their way on to local radio talk shows and local television news, and into newspaper articles as financial experts. Let local media know you are available, and inform them of the topics on which you can provide expert opinion. If they call you, the exposure is free and will help establish you as an expert in your field.

- The personal brochure is typically a one-page (usually front and back) document that introduces the advisor. Treat it as the prospect's first impression of you. It should impress, inform, and create interest. Your brochure should communicate your value proposition and should appeal to your target market.

- An Internet presence should be considered especially if your target market consists of members who are younger (although increasingly, older people are utilizing the Internet to conduct research).
- Although traditionally geared to relationship building and marketing to current clients, newsletters can be used with prospects as well.
- Advertising is the use of persuasive messages communicated through the mass media. The ultimate goal of advertising is to create new clients. For the purposes of financial products, advertising seems best suited to create awareness of an advisor's personal brand rather than to induce prospects to purchase specific products. The premise for using advertising is that prospects typically want to work with advisors with whom they have some level of comfort and trust. All things being equal, they will want to work with an advisor they have at least heard of rather than a total stranger. Advertising promotes in a prospect a level of familiarity with the advisor. It may predispose the prospect to a favorable response when the advisor does finally approach him or her. In using advertising, it is helpful to determine how members of your target market find advisors like you; identify places a high concentration of your target market frequents; select advertisements that are appropriate to your target market; and implement methods to track the effectiveness of your efforts.

2-3. A preapproach is any method used to stimulate the prospect's interest and precondition him or her to agree to meet with you about potential financial needs.

2-4. A seminar is a prospecting method in which you, alone or as a part of a team of professional advisors, conduct an educational and motivational meeting for a group of people. Seminars are distinct from speaking to groups in that a seminar's objective typically is to produce appointments.

- Advantages of seminars include the following:
  a. Prospects who agree to a follow-up appointment are really coming to a fact-finding interview because they already have an understanding of their potential need and how the product can help them. In other words, a seminar is like conducting an initial interview for several prospects at one time, which is a tremendous time saver.
  b. Assuming that you and any other presenters give educational and motivational presentations, seminars build your credibility as an expert.
  c. Seminars allow you to maximize your public speaking skills.
  d. The natural next step of a seminar is either asking for an appointment or setting the expectation that you will be calling for one.
- Important steps for conducting seminars include the following:
  a. Define your objective. Determine what you want the seminar to accomplish.
  b. Set a budget and work to stay within this constraint.
  c. Determine how many people to invite. Start by setting a goal for the number of attendees you wish to have. You will need to invite more than the desired number

of attendees. One rule of thumb is to invite 10 people for each desired attendee. Once you have determined how many people to invite, create a list of names from your prospecting sources.

d. Choose content that is relevant to your target market's needs. Make sure it is approved by compliance.

e. Select the presenters. This may mean using another speaker, such as a company expert, to present the bulk of the material.

f. Choose a date and time that avoids holidays and dates that coincide with important local or national events that interest your target market. Also consider how the time of day may affect your target market's willingness or ability to attend.

g. Select a site convenient for the members of your targeted group. Parking may be a prime consideration in urban and suburban areas. The location should also be neutral. It is generally recommended that you do not use your office.

h. Announce the seminar. The invitation should clearly inform the prospect that the seminar will be educational in nature. It should provide the topic, date, time, and length of each seminar session as well as any fees to be paid. The seminar title should be clear and relate to the perceived needs of the targeted audience. In addition to the invitation itself, your letter should contain a response mechanism (a telephone number, e-mail address, or a stamped, self-addressed postcard) for more information. It is important to monitor both the mailing of the invitations and the response rate. Careful monitoring will allow time for you to make adjustments, if necessary.

i. Check the facility by visiting it while another meeting is in progress. This will give you the opportunity to evaluate the lighting, the sound system, and the visibility of any screens you will use with a projector. You can assess how well everyone in the room can see the speaker and judge whether the ambiance of the room reflects the feeling you wish to convey to your audience. Consider what audiovisual equipment or visual aids, such as an easel or whiteboard, you will need before you begin calling facilities.

j. Prepare a feedback mechanism that asks for attendees to provide their names, addresses, and phone numbers.

k. Address miscellaneous details such as nametags, pens, paper, and handouts.

l. Conduct an effective follow-up campaign. Many advisors end their presentation by telling their audience that the advisor will contact each attendee to answer any questions that might result from the seminar. Others bring their appointment book to the seminar and schedule appointments right then and there.

2-5. Guidelines for choosing effective preapproach letters include the following:

- Select letters that reflect your target market's needs.
- Generally the shorter the better.
- Postcards are often more effective than letters because there is no envelope to open.

2-6. If you feel your company's standard letters are not adequate, obtain company approval to draft your own.

- The objectives for writing a preapproach letter are to trigger your prospect's interest by highlighting briefly a problem or need; to communicate the relevant parts of your value proposition related to meeting that problem or need; to prepare the prospect for your call, or to request for written permission to call if the prospect is on a do-not-call list.
- Guidelines for writing include the following:
  a. Aim to write something that grabs the prospect's attention.
  b. If possible, establish a basis for your contact by referring to how you heard of the prospect.
  c. Describe the most probable and acute financial need that the prospect faces and you can address.
  d. Link that financial need to an appropriate emotional need.
  e. Do not overstate the need; that is manipulative.
  f. In communicating your value proposition, keep it to one or two sentences. Avoid platitudes and clichés.
  g. Confirm the credibility of any statistics you use, and use them responsibly and appropriately (do not overuse them).
  h. Pay strict attention to wording, grammar, spelling, and punctuation.
  i. Ensure that the letter conveys an image of professionalism by using quality stationery and typeface.
  j. Ask a current client from your target market to review the letter's message and appearance.

2-7. The logistics for using preapproach letters include the following:
- No letter is good enough to do a selling job by itself. An efficient and effective follow-up system is crucial to the success of any direct mail program. Do not send letters to more prospects than you can follow up with in a week.
- Consider addressing letters by hand. Some advisors have found that handwritten addresses increase the probability that prospects will open the letters.
- Affix postage with an individual stamp rather than a postage meter. Some advisors highly recommend the use of commemorative stamps.
- Consider including an attention-getter in the envelope. One advisor includes a dollar bill to pay the prospect for reading the letter. Another advisor includes a Band-Aid with a health insurance preapproach letter.
- E-mail is another way to send a preapproach letter. If you are dealing with a technically savvy target market, e-mail may be more effective than regular mail.

2-8. The steps for creating an effective telephone approach script include the following:
- *Greeting.* In the greeting, you will introduce yourself and confirm that the prospect is willing to talk to you. This is your opportunity to make a good first impression. Open your conversation with "Good morning" or "Good afternoon." Identify who you are and what company you represent. As a matter of courtesy, ask the prospect if he or she has time to talk. Pushing your agenda on the prospect may turn a "not right now" into "not ever."

- *Creating Interest.* In this step, you will explain why you are calling and implement a method designed to pique the prospect's interest so he or she will agree to meet with you. There are at least two different methods used to create interest. On the one hand, some advisors take a direct approach and simply address the prospect's most probable financial needs as indicated by the prospect's life-cycle segment. A second method for achieving this objective is to ask an open-ended question that allows you to uncover potential needs the prospect has. The advisor can provide a list of the most probable needs, applying the life-cycle marketing strategy, and asking the prospect which of these needs he or she considers most pressing. Depending on the prospect's answer to the question, you can follow-up with questions designed to uncover a logical basis for the appointment. In other words, you are looking for a good logical foundation upon which to position your request for an appointment.
- *Asking for the Appointment.* This is the reason you are calling. In asking for the appointment, you are going to first offer a value proposition, a clear and compelling reason why the prospect should meet with you based on the prospect's most probable need.
- *Prequalifying.* For those advisors who believe in prequalifying, this would be an appropriate time to do so. Prequalifying involves asking the prospect a few questions to ensure the meeting will not waste the prospect's and the advisor's time. The questions are related to underwriting issues (for insurance) and/or suitability issues. Some advisors ask a question to identify any third party who may influence the prospect's decision, such as a CPA or an adult child.
- *Ending the Call.* In this step, you confirm the appointment and affirm your desire to meet the prospect. Depending on where you meet, you may either have to give or obtain directions.
- *Handling Objections.* Unfortunately, prospects often have objections to meeting with you. You will find that they will usually fall into one of four categories: no hurry, no money, no need, and no trust. Rather than be caught off guard and have no idea how to handle objections, write a script for each of the more common ones you face. A common strategy for handling objections is to use the "Feel, Felt, Found" technique. This technique works well for objections that the advisor feels need no further clarification and are simple to handle. The "Acknowledge, Clarify, Resolve" technique works for all objections. The steps are as follows: acknowledge the objection; clarify the objection; resolve the objection; and use an escape close.

2-9. The do-not-call regulations place limitations on telemarketers.
  - Some of the important limitations include the following:
    a. Sales calls to persons who have placed their residential or mobile phone numbers on federal or state DNC lists are prohibited.
    b. Calls cannot be made before 8 a.m. or after 9 p.m.
    c. Sellers must maintain an in-house DNC list of existing customers who do not want to receive sales calls.
    d. Sales callers must, at the beginning of every sales call, identify themselves, the company they represent, and the purpose of the call.

e. Telemarketers may not intentionally block consumers' use of caller identification.

- The exceptions to these limitations are the following:
    a. Established business relationship. A business relationship exists in which a product or service is in place, and for 18 months after that product or service is no longer in effect or active. Several states have stricter requirements. If a consumer contacts an advisor, whether by phone, mail, e-mail, or in person, to inquire about a product or service, an existing business relationship exists for three months after that inquiry.
    b. Business-to-business. The DNC regulations do not apply to business-to-business calls.
    c. Prior written permission. Advisors may make calls to persons on the DNC lists if they have a signed, written agreement from the consumer in which he or she agrees to be contacted by telephone at a specified telephone number. An e-mail from the prospect that clearly grants permission and identifies a number to call should suffice. Advisors may not call persons on the DNC list to ask for written permission to be called.
    d. Personal relationship. Calls may be made to people with whom an advisor has a personal relationship, including family members, friends and acquaintances.

- Advisors cannot contact prospects who are referred leads unless they receive written permission from the prospects to do so. They can work within the rules by doing any of the following:
    a. Ask for personal introductions. An arranged meeting over lunch, a cup of coffee, a round of golf, and so on would be ideal. This would give you a little more time to build rapport and probe for needs.
    b. Ask for an e-mail recommendation. The best method for using e-mail is to have the referrer write an e-mail recommending you to the prospect and letting the prospect know that you will be in contact with him or her. The referrer should carbon copy (Cc) you so that you have the prospect's e-mail. Then you may send an introductory e-mail along with a requesting for permission, a phone number, and a best time to call. Have your e-mail approved by your compliance department, if necessary.
    c. Send a direct mailer with response cards. If the prospect does not have an e-mail address or the referrer is reluctant to give it out, consider sending a prospecting letter with a compliance-approved response card. The card should request a signature and a phone number to call.
    d. Invite the prospect to a seminar. Ask the referrer to jot a recommendation on a 3 x 5 index card. For example, "Lance really helped me make some important financial decisions." Mail the recommendation along with an invitation to a seminar you are holding. If the prospect comes to the seminar, you will have an opportunity to gain permission to call face to face.

2-10. Two aspects for projecting a professional phone image are the following:
- Attitude:

a.  Be cheerful and smile. Your smile can be heard over the telephone.
b.  Wear proper business attire to help you feel more professional; it will show in your voice.
c.  Stay low-key, relaxed, and do not press too hard.
d.  Stay healthy. Illness and fatigue will affect how you sound. Many people stand up to aid both their energy level and breathing.
e.  A good way to start a telephoning session is to stand up and stretch, especially your stomach muscles to relax your diaphragm.
f.  Breathe from your stomach, not your lungs, to relax your voice and give it more presence.
g.  Be courteous. Listen to the prospect and do not interrupt.
h.  Pay attention to what is said, think about it, and then respond. Pausing to think about what your prospect has said does not show weakness; it shows consideration.
i.  Approach every call like it's the only one you will make that day. Act as if that person is the most important person in the world.
j.  Speak conversationally. You are prepared and you have practiced the script, but it should be so well prepared and practiced that it sounds spontaneous.
k.  Practice your telephone approach until you know it by memory, but keep it in front of you when you make your calls. Its presence will give you extra self-confidence.
l.  Keep your conversation brief.
m.  Use the prospect's name once or twice; avoid overusing it like telemarketers do. Remember, though, that no one is flattered if you mispronounce it.
n.  If you are calling with a referral or a reference of any kind, use it. It will help establish you as a person to be taken seriously.
o.  Always watch your use of words. Speak carefully using proper grammar. Don't stammer. Try to eliminate non-words (like "um" or "er") completely.

- Voice:
  a.  Speak in your natural voice. You should sound relaxed and sincere. Try to make every call sound as if you are calling a good friend.
  b.  Speak clearly. It takes the listener a few seconds to get used to a new voice, so your first few sentences are critical.
  c.  Keep a good posture. Sit up straight or stand up to get the most out of your voice.
  d.  Listen to what others give back as feedback. If you are asked to repeat yourself often, you may need to improve your enunciation.
  e.  Speak distinctly. If this means slowing down, then slow down. Your message is worth it.

2-11.  Prospecting and selling activities:
- Activities you will want to track include the following:
  a.  number of contacts attempted
  b.  number of contacts made (spoke to the prospect)
  c.  number of appointments made

    d.  number of initial meetings or interviews
    e.  number of fact finders conducted
    f.  number of closing interviews
    g.  number of sales made
    h.  number of hours spent setting appointments
    i.  amount of commission and/or fees

- Keeping accurate records of your daily prospecting and selling activities enables you to generate effectiveness ratios for setting appointments and making sales. These ratios will provide valuable data you can use to make decisions about target markets, approach scripts, interviewing techniques, and so on.

### Answers to Self-test Questions

| | | |
|---|---|---|
| 2-1. | B | pages 2.5–2.6 |
| 2-2. | B | page 2.17 |
| 2-3. | C | pages 2.35–2.36 |
| 2-4. | A | pages 2.24–2.25 |
| 2-5. | C | pages 2.28–2.29 |
| 2-6. | B | pages 2.36–2.37 |
| 2-7. | D | pages 2.38–2.39 |
| 2-8. | D | pages 2.2 and 2.4 |
| 2-9. | B | page 2.8 |
| 2-10. | C | page 2.20 |

## Chapter 3

### Answers to Review Questions

3-1. When you work with clients using an integrated planning approach, you aim to propose recommendations regarding their products within the context of the prospect's overall financial situation and needs. This will involve being aware of the client's needs in the following planning areas: general financial situation, insurance planning and risk management, employee benefits planning, investment planning, income tax planning, retirement planning, and estate planning. For those areas that you lack expertise, consider referring prospects to non-competing advisors who can assist them. You may even form a team of specialists and serve as its manager, coordinating the team's efforts as well as contributing your expertise in your field of specialization.

3-2. Budgeting and cash flow management are the most basic tools of financial planning. Communicating the importance of these processes and helping the client through them can be among the advisor's most valuable services. Budgeting is the process of creating and following a specific plan for spending and investing the resources available to the client. A working budget model should be established, followed by a comparison of actual and expected results. By monitoring the budget, the client and advisor can recognize problems as they occur and even anticipate problems, providing a means for financial self-evaluation and a guideline to measure actual performance.

3-3.   The financial planning pyramid uses four levels: wealth foundation, wealth accumulation, wealth preservation, and wealth distribution. The pyramid in its entirety represents an integrated and comprehensive financial plan. The individual blocks illustrate how most people feel comfortable building their financial plans—one or a few blocks at a time. The term *building-block approach* is used to describe this incremental approach. The various levels provide some guidance as to a general order in which to address financial needs. The first level represents the foundation, the basic needs that should receive primary attention. Failure to address these needs leaves any savings and investments vulnerable should an uncovered loss occur. Thus basic insurance products, a simple will, and an emergency fund form a wealth foundation.

Once the foundation is in place, a person can begin buying products in the wealth accumulation level such as CDs, stocks, bonds, mutual funds, real estate, and so on. Once assets are acquired, wealth preservation tools are needed. When the accrual of assets reaches a threshold, a person will need to consider products such as umbrella liability and long-term care insurance to preserve assets from lawsuits or the potential need for long-term care. Most likely, with increased wealth will come additional property that will need to be insured, such as a summer home, a boat, a jet-ski, and so on. At the wealth distribution level, products are needed to manage retirement income to ensure it will last. In addition, estate planning tools are used to conserve the estate for heirs and provide for charitable causes.

3-4.   The young-adult market segment can be grouped into the following subsegments:

- single—individual with no partner and no kids
- dual income with kids—individual with a partner and kids
- dual income with no kids—individual with a partner and no kids (referred to as DINKs)
- single income with kids—individual with a partner and kids where the partner is not employed outside of the home. Also included in this grouping are single parents.

Common characteristics in the young-adult market segment include the many firsts that a person experience: the purchase of a first car and first house, a first marriage, first child, and first divorce.

Common needs in this segment include the following:

- Final expenses—Final expenses are needed to cover burial, probate and administrative costs, any state inheritance or federal estates taxes due, and any medical expenses associated with death.
- Emergency Fund—This is the recommended three to six months of living expenses needed to keep a person afloat in the event of losing a job or being disabled. For a single person, three months would be adequate while six months would be more appropriate for those individuals with children.
- Debt Liquidation—Credit card debt begins to mount during this phase. You could provide some wise counsel regarding the advantages of paying off these balances and providing for their liquidation at death. Car or personal loans would also fall under this category.

- Disability—Protection against loss of income due to disability should be addressed as soon as a person begins earning an income. For young adults, it now becomes a pressing need.
- Retirement—It's never too early to begin saving for retirement. Systematic saving over a working lifetime is a key to supplementing other retirement programs. The old rule of thumb is to tuck away 10 percent of annual income. Young families with modest incomes should start with something, even if they cannot make a total commitment to this 10 percent guideline at first.
- Will—This is the point in life when most people should have a first will.

3-5. While the need for life insurance receives a great amount of attention, the need for disability income insurance is often obscured or never discussed. But studies show that

- a 30-year-old has a 24 percent chance of being disabled for at least 90 days before reaching age 65
- at age 45, the chance of suffering a disability is only reduced to 21 percent
- a person disabled for 90 days will probably go on to be disabled for at least four years.
- Despite these statistics, very few people have adequate protection against long-term disability. The public may purchase life insurance for their family's protection, but they have largely neglected their own income protection, even though the odds are far greater for a person to be disabled than to die. Statistics comparing the incidence of disability as compared to death at various ages show that up to age 42 the chance of suffering a disability of at least 90 days is at least three times greater than the chance of dying.

3-6. Terms associated with disability income insurance:

- *Total disability*. The definition of disability differs from one company to another, and from one contract to another. These differences become extremely important to the eventual payment of a claim. The definition can be very narrow, providing very limited coverage. An example of this kind of definition is the inability to do any kind of work. Conversely, the definition can be more specific, defining disability more liberally and providing coverage that is more comprehensive. Defining disability as the inability to perform your own occupation is a more specific definition and more beneficial to the insured. Policies may also have a mixed definition of disability, using, for example, the own-occupation or own-occ definition for an initial period of disability (typically two years), then changing to a less liberal definition. Such a provision would pay benefits for the first two years if the insured is unable to perform the material and substantial duties of his or her occupation, but would only continue paying benefits beyond the two-year period if the insured was unable to work in any occupation for which he or she was reasonably suited by education, training, or experience.
- *Elimination period*. This is the period the insured must be disabled before benefits are payable. It may range from 30 days to one year (although 30- 60- and 90-day elimination periods are most common). The longer the waiting period for benefits, the lower the premium will be.

- *Residual disability.* Residual benefits in disability policies represent a further refinement in the partial disability definitions. Under residual disability coverage, benefits are proportionate and based on a percentage of lost income. If needed, they are usually payable for the contract's entire benefit period instead of the limited time available under a partial disability definition. Thus the residual benefit encourages the disabled to return to work. The definitions are numerous, some even incorporating various qualification periods as trigger dates to enact benefits. Study these details to fully understand the policies you sell, or are selling against.

- *Cost-of-living adjustment rider (COLA).* The benefit provided by this rider attempts to adjust the base amount of coverage to reflect cost-of-living changes due to inflation. The insured usually must be disabled for at least 12 months. Some companies offer a flat percentage of the base amount while others tie the payment to the Consumer Price Index. The cost-of-living rider is used only at claim time. When the insured recovers, benefits return to the original level unless a special rider is provided to maintain the increased level of benefit.

- *Future increase option (FIO).* As in a similar rider to a life insurance policy, the future increase option allows the insured to increase coverage at stated future dates as income eligibility increases without any medical underwriting. Income verification is required.

## *Answers to Self-test Questions*

| | | |
|---|---|---|
| 3-1. | A | pages 3.33–3.34 |
| 3-2. | B | page 3.14 |
| 3-3. | A | page 3.6 |
| 3-4. | B | page 3.33 |
| 3-5. | D | pages 3.31–3.32 |
| 3-6. | C | pages 3.12–3.13 |
| 3-7. | B | page 3.33 |
| 3-8. | B | page 3.35 |
| 3-9. | D | page 3.22 |
| 3-10. | C | page 3.24 |

## Chapter 4

### *Answers to Review Questions*

4-1.  The more carefree days of young adulthood for most people eventually give way to a more serious outlook on life. Somewhere during the young adulthood phase, some people have begun new careers. Others have found a partner and some have had children. Toward the end of the young adult phase, people have begun to establish themselves, as they transition into the middle years of adulthood. By this time, people tend to be established in their careers. They may change jobs or employers, but typically not what they do for a living. Tenure in their field means they are moving toward the peak of their earning potential, and as they approach the middle of the phase they begin to grow more aware of their need to prepare for retirement. Some parents experience an empty nest as their children move out and become independent. The empty nest brings an emotional adjustment as parents face the reality that they no longer have financial responsibilities for their children. For many, this is exhilarating and reintroduces parents to situations they have not experienced since the onset of parenthood. It also means having more disposable income and more time. For others, it may be a sad time that calls for reflection and a reordering of life as their children depart the home to venture out on their own. In this segment, you will find people who must begin dealing with aging parents and decisions that older people have to make. Some in the sandwich generation will begin caring for a parent or another elderly relative. For some, this phase of the life cycle means receiving inheritances in the form of gifts from living parents or estates from deceased parents.

Needs of this segment include emergency funds, mortgage cancellation, final expenses, income replacement, education planning, debt liquidation, disability, retirement planning, wills, estate planning, and long-term care planning.

4-2.  Term insurance policies provide a death benefit if death occurs during the period of time that the policy is in force. The policy period is expressed as a number of years, such as 1, 5, or 30, or until a certain age of the insured, such as 65 or 70. If the insured dies during the policy period, the face amount of the policy will be paid to the beneficiary. If the insured survives to the end of the policy period the insurance company pays no benefit and the coverage ends. Term insurance is tied directly to the cost of mortality, which increases as the individual grows older. The premium is initially relatively low and increases periodically in most types of term insurance to reflect the increased mortality of the insured. The older a person is and the longer the period of coverage, the higher the premium and mortality costs will be.

The main types of term include:

- Level face amount. Most term life insurance sold today provides a level death benefit over a specific period. The premiums on these policies normally increase with age at renewal or may remain level at younger ages.

- Increasing premium contracts. Many term policies have increasing premiums with level death benefits and are renewable. The ART may be referred to as yearly renewable term (YRT) by your company. The premiums increase each year for the length of the renewal duration, which may be one, 5, 10, 20, 30 years, or to age 70. Some plans extend to age 100 and have a large number of rate bands for sums ranging from $100,000 to $1 million. Many offer different premium categories based on underwriting qualifications such as standard/preferred, tobacco user/nonuser, and various combinations of these.

- Decreasing term life policies. Some term insurance products have face amounts that decrease over time. The premium remains fixed for the length of the contract, while the face amount gradually decreases. Decreasing term premium may be significantly higher than for the same initial amount of level term. Advisors should be aware of this difference and recommend level term if appropriate for the clients.

- Term riders. Most companies allow policyowners to add term riders to either a term or permanent policy. The convenience of term insurance as a rider, and the advantages of combining different types of protection under one contract, have earned term riders a lasting place in your portfolio. Because a policy fee is charged for the contract as a whole, the term rider will save the cost of an additional policy fee for most company plans. A level term rider can provide temporary additional term protection for a specific number of years. They may also be used to insure other family members, such as a spouse and/or children.

4-3. The different variations of whole life insurance include:

- Ordinary life provides level death benefit protection for a level premium. Premiums are paid to age 100, and the policy builds guaranteed cash values, which equal the face amount at age 100. At that time, if the insured is still alive and has paid all the premiums, the policy will mature. The cash value will equal the face value of the original policy and will be paid to the policyowner. Ordinary life offers the most permanent protection for the least premium.

- Limited-pay life policies are designed for people who need permanent protection, but who want accelerated cash accumulation or who prefer not to pay premiums to age 100. With limited pay plans, insurance protection extends to age 100 when the policy endows as it would with ordinary life, but the premium payments stop before age 100 resulting in higher premiums and cash values. Generally the shorter the premium payment period, the higher the premium and the faster the cash value accumulation.

- Modified whole life insurance is a whole-life product that offers a lower premium for a period of time (such as three to five years) and a level face amount. After a premium increase, the premium stays level for the rest of the life of the contract. This product is used for clients who may not have the money to purchase level premium whole life now, but expect to be able to afford the premiums in a few years.

4-4. Universal life combines the features of renewable term insurance with a tax-deferred cash value account that earns competitive market interest. Policyowners are able to pay premiums on a flexible, nonscheduled basis. The policyowner can increase or decrease the amount of death benefit protection of the policy at any time within company and IRS rules. Universal life policies have either a front-end or a back-end load. With a front-end load, the company's fixed expenses are deducted before the premiums are added to the cash value account. With a back-end load, fixed expenses are recovered from surrender charges by reducing the account value if surrendered. With a Level Death Benefit Option, the amount of the term protection, or net amount at risk, decreases as the cash value account increases. With the Increasing Death Benefit Option, the net amount at risk remains level with the increasing cash value account used to increase the death benefit. Most universal life policies offer the full range of additional benefit riders available with other personal permanent policies. A monthly deduction from the cash value is made to pay for this additional protection.

4-5. Non-variable, interest-sensitive life insurance products also include:

- *Current Assumption Whole Life.* This is a variation of whole life that uses current mortality charges and interest earnings that are based on current yields rather than overall general account yields. It does not offer the premium flexibility of universal life.

Sometimes it is described as universal life with fixed premiums. Despite this oversimplification, as the premiums may be restructured at specified anniversary years, it describes how CAWL differs from a traditional policy. If premiums are paid on schedule, CAWL guarantees a death benefit and a minimum guaranteed interest rate to be credited on cash values.

- *Interest-Sensitive Whole Life.* Some companies guarantee the mortality charge and the expense charges in current assumption plans. When the mortality and expense charges are guaranteed, the policy is often referred to as an interest-sensitive whole life policy because interest credited to the cash value becomes the only element not guaranteed in the contract.

4-6. The key differences of variable life and variable universal life from their fixed versions are as follows:

- *Variable Life Insurance.* This was the first life insurance policy designed to shift the investment risk to policyowners. It offers a combination of permanent life insurance protection and the growth potential of variable fund investments. The policy's cash value is invested in an account made up of one or more funds of equities, money market accounts or bonds. The policyowner decides where to invest the money and within contract limits may transfer funds from one fund account to another. The policy guarantees a minimum death benefit, but the actual death benefit paid may be higher if the investments perform well. The cash value also fluctuates with the investment performance. The cash values are not guaranteed. If the investments to which the cash values are linked perform poorly, the variable life cash values may grow at a lower rate than in traditional products or not at all. The premium is level for the duration of the policy. Each premium is reduced by an amount needed to maintain the minimum guaranteed death benefit. It offers traditional product provisions such as loan privileges and the usual variety of optional additional benefit riders. Variable life is considered to be both a life insurance and an equity product. Advisors who sell variable products must be licensed and registered with FINRA. Variable life is regulated by both state law, where applicable, and by the SEC. The company selling variable life must have a prospectus available that the advisor must mail or give to prospects prior to or during the sales interview. This fixed-premium policy offers a unique feature by guaranteeing a minimum death benefit regardless of investment performance. If all of the required premiums are paid, the insurance company guarantees that the death benefit will be paid even if the investment funds are otherwise inadequate to support the policy.

- *Variable universal life.* This is also known as flexible premium variable life and combines features of variable and universal life insurance. It offers policyowners the flexibility of universal life with the investment growth of variable while discarding the fixed-premium aspects of variable life. With variable universal life, the policyowner selects an initial insurance amount and premium level. Premium dollars can be directed to one or more investment funds and switched from one fund to another as in variable life. The same registration with NASD and licensing are required to sell variable universal life insurance as is required to sell variable life insurance. Because it is a registered product, it also requires delivery of a prospectus to the prospect. Policyowners decide how much premium to pay into the policy and when to pay it, just as in universal life. Likewise, the cash account must always be large enough to pay the monthly cost of the term insurance element and administrative expenses. Within certain legal limits, policyowners can adjust the combination of cash value and term insurance in the policy by making larger or smaller premium payments. It offers the same two death benefit options, the ability to change options, and other such features.

4-7. Premiums paid for individual life insurance policies are usually considered a personal expense and are not deductible for income tax purposes. There are some exceptions to this, but in these situations, life insurance premiums can be deductible because they also fit the definition of some other type of deductible expense, not because they are life insurance premiums. For example, premiums paid for life insurance in an alimony agreement may be deductible as alimony payments. Premiums paid for life insurance that is owned by and paid to a charity as beneficiary may be deductible as a charitable contribution. The premium is deductible because it is treated as a charitable contribution, not because it is a life insurance premium. Similarly, in business situations, employers are allowed to deduct premiums for life insurance protection if paid in the form of a bonus to an employee. The employer may then deduct the amount of the bonus paid to the employee as compensation and thus as a business expense. If life insurance is part of a pension plan, the premiums are deductible as part of a contribution by the employer to a tax-qualified plan. Again the deduction for the premium is based on the fact that it is a contribution to a tax-qualified retirement plan rather than a life insurance premium.

4-8. Living benefits refer to the use of cash values and dividends of a permanent insurance policy while the insured is alive. To the extent living benefits are taxable, they will be treated as ordinary income and not capital gains. In addition, the taxable amount is the amount the taxable benefit exceeds the tax basis. The tax basis is initially calculated by adding the total premiums paid into the policy and subtracting any dividends paid by the insurer. If nontaxable withdrawals have previously been made from the policy, those amounts reduce the policyowner's basis. Living benefits include:

- Loans. The policyowner is given the right to borrow a percentage of the cash value in the policy. The policyowner is charged interest on the borrowed amount, and the interest is not tax deductible. If the policyowner does not pay the loan interest, it is added to the loaned amount. Unless a policy is a modified endowment contract (MEC), policy loans are non-taxable providing the policy remains in force.

- UL and VUL partial surrenders (withdrawals). UL and VUL policies offer the ability to withdraw cash value from the policy, known as a withdrawal, a partial withdrawal, or a partial surrender. The death benefit and cash value are reduced dollar for dollar by the amount of the partial surrender. Partial surrenders are taxable when the total amount of all withdrawals exceeds the cost basis of the policy. The exception is when the policy is a MEC; in that situation, harsher tax rules apply. In some cases, surrender charges may apply as well.

- Dividends. Mutual insurance companies pass along favorable experience in mortality, interest, and expenses through a return of premium called dividends. Policies eligible for dividends are called participating policies. In most cases, mutual insurance companies that provide participating insurance plans build a margin into their premium for contingencies. Dividends are not taxable unless the total amount of all dividends paid exceeds the total premium paid. Because policy dividends are a nontaxable return of premium, they reduce the policyowner's basis. If total dividends paid exceed total premiums, additional dividends are taxable. Divideds may be paid as cash, applied to reduce premiums, left with the company to accumulate at interest, used to purchase paid-up additions, or used to pay for one-year term insurance equal to the current cash value.

- Cash surrenders. Income tax is payable on the surrender of all policies for cash (or the maturity of an endowment) if the amount received over the life of the contract exceeds the net premiums paid (excluding premiums for supplementary benefits). Net premiums paid determine the cost basis and equals the gross premium less any dividends received. If the amount the policyowner receives upon surrender exceeds the net premiums paid (cost basis), then the excess is fully reportable as a taxable gain in the year received. An exception to this rule would be for certain government policies or GI insurance. Any gains realized with these types of policies are tax exempt.

- Section 1035 policy exchanges. A special situation arises when a policyowner exchanges an existing policy for a new one in accordance with the Internal Revenue Code Section 1035. In a properly executed Section 1035 Exchange, no taxable gain is realized on the exchange. The adjusted cost basis of the old policy is carried over to the new one.

4-9.   The modified endowment contract (MEC) came into being because some people were using life insurance primarily as a tax-deferred investment vehicle. This went against the premise that life insurance was to be used primarily to provide a death benefit. A 7-pay test was devised to determine if a policy should be classified as a MEC. This establishes limits to the amount of premiums that can be paid into a life insurance policy within a period of seven years. If the policy is overfunded, it becomes a MEC and distributions from the policy are subject to different taxation rules not applied to non-MEC policies.

   If a material change occurs to a policy once it is in force, the 7-pay test period is reset. Examples of changes include an increase or decrease in coverage, or an added rider or benefit. If a policy is or becomes a MEC, it is treated the same as any other life insurance policy with one exception—some distributions from a MEC are taxed on a LIFO (last-in-first-out) basis to the extent there is gain in the policy. In addition, the taxable gain is subject to a 10 percent penalty unless the distribution is made after age 59½, or death, disability, or annuitization occurs.

4-10.  The face of America continues to change. There are dramatic ethnic population shifts in many states and most large cities in this country. By 2050, Hispanics are projected to make up 24 percent of the U.S. population and minorities in general will make up 47 percent of the population. In assessing any market, you should consider what penetration your services and products have in that market as well as how receptive the market will be. One particular opportunity you will find with emerging markets is the first-to-market strategy in which you penetrate a market where a particular product or service has little or no representation. The goal is to create loyalty and to grow with the market. Loyalty is high in these situations and that is the key to the success of this strategy.

Diverse markets qualify as target markets. They share common characteristics in their language, culture, and many times their lifestyle. They share common needs, sometimes because of their culture or simply because they are now away from the natural support system of their relatives and friends. Most importantly, they have a communication system. The latter is critical in defining a target market because it is the factor that creates a perpetual flow of prospects. Two of the biggest misconceptions are that you have to be of the same ethnicity and/or you must speak the language to sell in these markets. Undoubtedly possessing one or both of these characteristics will help you tremendously, but lacking them does not eliminate you.

Look for opportunities within your natural market. Do you currently have someone in your book of business that is a part of that market? Do you know a businessperson who is a member of that market or does business in that market? Are there businesses run by members of that particular ethnic community? In this situation, if you do not speak the language, a center of influence will be necessary. The best way to approach a new community is to find a few professional friends in the target community and ask them to help you. If you don't know anyone, try finding a professional, such as a doctor, a non-competing insurance advisor, or a lawyer who works with members of that community. After you have done your market research, look to work with other professionals in that community. Referrals from non-competing advisors, attorneys, and other financial services professionals will build your prestige in that community.

4-11.  Each divorce or separation case will present a unique set of challenges. You must deal with them in a sensitive but direct manner. Your response will be dictated largely by four factors: (1) the personal terms under which the spouses are parting, (2) the legal conditions of the separation or divorce set down by the court, (3) the number and ages of the children involved, and (4) the wishes of the couple.

You will want to express your regret and let your clients know that you are ready to help them any way you can. Tell them that there are several considerations that they should be aware of, both with their present life insurance and any new coverage that is made part of the settlement. Suggest that the three of you need to go over these points and decide the best way to proceed. Meeting with the two spouses is usually less complicated than trying to act as a go-between unless the situation is such that it is not practical for the former spouses to meet with you at one time. Determine if the divorce is amicable or otherwise. You need to be sure that no necessary coverage is inadvertently lost. Review with your clients their plans to keep their present life insurance protection in force after divorce. Discuss any change of beneficiary designations that may be necessary. Life insurance is valuable property and in recent years has begun to figure prominently in the court's judgment. In these situations, your role should be that of a professional advisor who both facilitates the various policy arrangements and, when possible, recommends the most favorable approach to both parties.

4-12.   There are many financial aspects of divorce because marriage typically involves the joining of many financial arrangements that must now be untangled. A major part of a divorce or separation is the transfer of property from one spouse to the other. Depending on how the married couple kept their financial affairs, there may be property that is commingled and other that is separate. That property may have been brought to the marriage or acquired during marriage by one party, and it is intended to stay that way. The treatment of this and other property upon divorce will vary from state to state.

When a divorce is taking place, legal instruments such as wills and trusts must be reviewed, and if necessary, modified based on the changes the divorce brings about. The federal estate tax marital deduction will no longer be available to the taxpayer. The divorced persons may need to reconsider choices for estate representatives (administrator or executor) and legal guardians for minor children. Estate planning alternatives for children may need to be reconsidered and the establishment of trusts and other legal instruments executed. Property, such as a home, retirement plans, and other assets may need to be re-titled and beneficiary designations changed. Jointly held property may need to be distributed and/or re-titled. It is also important to consider the consequences of remarriage on the family. This is particularly important where there are children from a prior marriage or prior marriages. The parent may want to consider children both from this and other marriages after his or her death.

Divorce may leave one or both parties with little or no accumulation of pension benefits or other private sources of retirement income. If the marriage lasted 10 years or longer, divorced persons are eligible for Social Security based on their former spouse's earnings record. In addition, a spouse may be entitled to a portion of the former spouse's retirement benefits if the divorce decree includes a qualified domestic relations order. Qualified domestic relations orders are judgments, decrees, or orders issued by state courts that allow a participant's plan assets to be used for marital property rights, child support, or alimony payments to a former spouse. Divorce may change the family relationship, but it does not alter the basic fact that both spouses will continue to have insurance needs. The plans established to provide protection for their children may be even more important now than before. Life, health, property, and other forms of insurance will need to be continued, and possibly changed.

4-13.   There are two general tax rules to keep in mind when dealing with divorce: Alimony payments are tax deductible for the payor, and child support payments are not tax deductible for the payor. Different tax rules also apply to life insurance in divorce situations. Whether premiums are deductible depends upon the premium payor, the owner, the beneficiary, and the purpose of the insurance in the divorce. Similar factors will determine whether premiums are income to an ex-spouse.

## *Answers to Self-test Questions*

4-1.   C     page 4.29
4-2.   B     page 4.14
4-3.   B     page 4.3
4-4.   C     page 4.8

4-5.   A     pages 4.18–4.20
4-6.   C     pages 4.22–4.23
4-7.   C     page 4.46
4-8.   B     page 4.25
4-9.   C     pages 4.2–4.3
4-10.  D     pages 4.33–4.34

## Chapter 5

### Answers to Review Questions

5-1.   There are only three sources of income available to any of us at retirement: people at work, money at work, and charity. With planning before retirement, your clients will not need to work unless it is something they do to stay active and involved. Work will not be something they have to do to pay the bills. The financial need to continue working may be the result of bad luck, but it may be the result of a failure to plan and implement that plan. Money at work is the money you have working for you. This includes government-sponsored personal retirement and savings programs, and permanent cash value life insurance. Without savings or planning, only charity is available to make up the shortcomings. Charity is not an option that any of us would look forward to having to live on, either from our children or government subsidy programs.

5-2.   The current retirement gap formula is determined by the following calculation:

1.   *Assume your prospects will retire tomorrow.* Determine their current expenses, including housing, personal expenses, and recreation.
2.   *Calculate existing resources.* Determine what current resources they have to meet expenses, including estimated Social Security and employer-sponsored retirement benefits, cash values from existing permanent life insurance, and other long-term investments intended for this use.
3.   *Retirement income need = percentage of current income.* Determine a percentage of the current income that will meet the retirement income needs. Your prospect may not wish to discount the current income. It could be viewed as an inflation hedge. For many people 70 percent of current expenses seems realistic. Whatever figure your prospect chooses will work. It must be their goal.
4.   *Retirement income need – existing resources = current retirement gap.* The difference between tomorrow's needs and today's resources is the current retirement gap. It produces a dollar figure for today, not accounting for the time value of money. Today's calculations will change in the future as both the economy and the prospect's needs change.

5-3.   The term *tax-qualified* means that the plans are eligible for certain tax advantages such as deductible employer contributions or tax-deferred accumulations. To qualify for tax-qualified status, plans must conform to a number of requirements: a plan must meet minimum participation (including minimum age and service) and coverage requirements, be nondiscriminatory, meet minimum vesting requirements, have minimum and maximum funding standards, provide automatic survivor benefits, and satisfy distribution requirements. Tax advantages to tax-qualified plans include the following: (1) the employer can take a tax deduction for contributions made to the plan, and (2) employees do not have to pay taxes on amounts contributed, either by the employer or as salary reductions from their own pay, until they are withdrawn. This means that contributions are made on a pretax basis, earnings in the plan are made on a tax-deferred basis, and distributions from these plans can be rolled into an IRA with continued tax-deferral until the funds are withdrawn.

The various types of plans include:

- Defined-benefit (DB) plan—In a DB plan, the benefit is defined and guaranteed, based on a formula in relation to earnings, years of service, and other considerations. The employer makes the contributions on a tax-deductible basis, and assumes the investment risk.

- Defined-contribution (DC) plan—In a DC plan, the employer defines the contribution, but does not guarantee or define the retirement benefit. The employee assumes the risk of inflation, investment performance, and adequacy of the retirement income.

- 403(b) plan—The 403(b) plan has traditionally been referred to as a Tax Sheltered Annuity (TSA). It allows employees of tax-exempt employers, as described in IRS Code Sec 501(c)(3), to set aside a portion of their earned salary income for deferring compensation for retirement. Eligible organizations include public schools, nonprofit organizations, nonprofit hospitals, charitable foundations, museums, zoos, symphony orchestras, trade associations, and many private schools and colleges. Contributions are typically made by the employee, but are administered by the employer, who may also contribute to an employee plan. Each year's taxable income is reduced by the amount of that year's contribution to the plan, and investment growth is not currently subject to income tax. 403(b) plans are designed to be self-directed by the employee. These plans are meant to accumulate money during working years to be distributed through settlement options during retirement. Like IRAs, they have named beneficiaries and are owned by the participant.

- Individual Retirement Accounts (IRAs)—IRAs are tax-advantaged retirement plans available to many people with earned income. Under current law, eligible individuals may contribute 100 percent of earned income up to a maximum annual contribution limit. The limit applies to total contributions made to either a Traditional IRA or a Roth IRA, or a combination of the two. In 2009, a person under age 50 could contribute $2,500 to a Traditional IRA and $2,500 to a Roth IRA for a total of $5,000. The annual limit is $6,000 (in 2009) for a taxpayer aged 50 and older.

5-4. The Traditional IRA and Roth IRA have the following differences:

- Contributions can be made into a Roth IRA provided the accountholder has earned income. For a Traditional IRA, the accountholder must also be under age 70 ½.

- Traditional IRA contributions may be fully deductible, partially deductible, or nondeductible. A Roth IRA's contributions are always nondeductible.

- Withdrawal of earnings at any time results are taxable for a Traditional IRA. Earnings received through a qualified withdrawal from a Roth IRA are received tax free.
- Income limits restrict the deductibility of contributions into a Traditional IRA if the taxpayer/accountholder is a participant in an employer-sponsored retirement plan, whereas income limits restrict a taxpayer's ability to fund a Roth IRA and participation in an employer-sponsored retirement plan is not a factor at all.
- The required minimum distributions at age 70 ½ that apply to a Traditional IRA are not applicable for a Roth IRA.

5-5.  Life insurance can provide the following benefits in retirement:
- Liquidity to pay the cost of dying. This includes funeral expenses, debts, administration costs of estate settlement, and estate taxes.
- Supplemental income through beneficiary arrangements for a surviving spouse. Proceeds can be paid through settlement options or invested in other income-producing investments to supplement income.
- Increases to retirement income. Permanent insurance can be surrendered for one of various settlement options.
- Social Security Income replacement to ensure that the beneficiary's income level remains at a desired level.
- Bequests to family and charitable organizations.

5-6.  An annuity is a legal contract between between an insurer and the annuity owner. The annuity owner may or may not be the person entitled to receive the payments from the annuity (the annuitant).
- The annuity has two phases. The first phase is the accumulation phase in which the annuity owner builds up the value of the annuity by making investments called premiums, as with life insurance, and earning interest. The premium may consist of one payment (as with a single premium immediate annuity or single premium deferred annuity) or multiple payments (as with a flexible premium deferred annuity). The earnings grow tax-deferred. The second phase is the payout or annuity phase which occurs when the annuity contract is annuitized and the insurer makes periodic annuity payments to the annuitant. The amount of the payments depends on the value of the annuity, the age and gender of the annuitant (used to estimate the mortality experience), and the interest rate used by the insurer. Some annuities guarantee payments for a fixed period (e.g.,for example, 10 years) while others guarantee payments for the life of the annuitant.
- The annuity has a death benefit, which applies only during the accumulation phase, or before the guaranteed lifetime payouts have begun. The annuity death benefit normally guarantees that a designated beneficiary will receive the greater of the accumulated value, or the premiums deposited minus any previous withdrawals. Any gains in the annuity will be taxable as ordinary income to the beneficiary upon withdrawal.
- Annuities typically include a declining surrender charge in the first 5 to 10 years. The surrender charges normally decline each year until they reach zero. To give some

access to funds, most annuities allow a "free withdrawal" amount each year of 10 to 15 percent.

- Partial withdrawals are taxed on an a last in, first out (LIFO) basis. The first withdrawals from an annuity are earnings, and the owner is taxed on withdrawals until all the earnings have been distributed. The contributions are then received tax free. A 10-percent penalty tax applies to the taxable distributions made before the owner reaches 59 ½. Exceptions include those distributions made as a result of the owner's death or disability, in substantially equal periodic payments over the life expectancy of the owner, under an annuitized contract, or attributable to investments made prior to August 14, 1982.

The various types of annuities can be categorized as follows:

- *Fixed annuities* provide a guaranteed, lifetime income at little risk to the policyowner, making them an ideal long-term investment for purposes such as retirement income planning. During the accumulation period, the interest rate fluctuates with changes in the underlying investments. However, the annuity never earns less than the guaranteed rate specified in the contract. During the payout period, the interest used to calculate payments will also be at least the minimum interest rate stated in the contract.

- *Variable annuities* pay a rate of return during both the accumulation and payout periods that may rise and fall depending on investment results. The owner of the annuity assumes the investment risk and allocates premium to a range of mutual fund type investment options called subaccounts.

- In *equity-indexed annuities (EIAs)*, accumulated value is tied to a stock index of companies such as the S&P 500. Returns mirror the rate of return for the index to which it is tied. Usually there is a participation rate on the rate of return, meaning that the annuity will earn a percentage of the rate of the return of the index. For example, if XYZ Equity-Indexed Annuity were tied to the A&B Index and the A&B Index returned 10 percent, the annuity may only pass on 90 percent of that return, or 9 percent, to the annuitant. The rate of return may be capped, meaning the interest credited will not exceed the cap amount. For example, if the rate of return is 15 percent and the cap is 12 percent, the annuity would be credited with 12 percent.

5-7.  Investments other than annuities include:

- *Negotiable Order of Withdrawal (NOW)*. These accounts offer features of savings accounts: interest, liquidity, and withdrawal by check. Funds earn interest and are automatically transferred to the checking portion to cover checks. Restrictions on minimum balances or a limit on the number of checks may apply.

- *U.S. Government securities*. Treasury bills, notes, and bonds are U.S. Government securities that may be purchased in the over the counter securities market. Treasury bills (known as T bills) are available in amounts from $1,000 to $5,000,000 with maturity dates of 4, 13, 26, and 52 weeks from issue. Treasury notes (T notes) are available with 2 to 10-year maturities, in amounts between $100 and $1,000,000. Treasury bonds (T-bonds) are available in amounts greater than $1,000 with maturity dates of 10 to 30 years. Both T-notes and T-bonds pay interest every six months. The interest is included in federal income taxes as it is paid. However, the interest is not subject to state or local income taxes.

- *Bonds*. These are securities issued by public or private corporations or federal, state, or local government units. They are an IOU given by the issuer to the purchaser with a promise to repay the principal, plus interest, at a specified future date. Mortgage bonds are secured by a mortgage on specific property owned by the issuer; debentures are secured only by the credit of the issuing organization. Debentures issued by large, secure organizations offer lower risk.

- *U.S. government bonds*. These are very secure and may yield just slightly less than high-quality corporate bonds. They are exempt from federal taxes, but not from state and local taxation, and are generally considered safe, reasonably attractive long-term investments.

- *Municipal bonds*. These are offered by local (municipal) governments to raise money. Interest earnings are exempt from federal taxes, and are generally exempt from state and local taxes.

- *Stocks*. Stocks represent ownership in a public or private corporation as a way to raise operating capital. The number of shares available is limited by company policy as well as by the demand from buyers. The tax advantage is the deferral of tax payments on growth until the stock is sold by the owner. Common stock provides the owner with ownership in the company that issued the shares. If the company fails, common shareholders may claim all assets that remain after all other creditors have been paid off. Preferred stock gives the owner first rights to any dividends issued by the corporation. Preferred shareholders may not have voting privileges in corporate decision-making as common shareholders do, and the preferred stock may be callable. Stock types are recognized according to investment object: blue chip, growth, defensive, cyclical, and speculative.

- *Unit investment trusts* (closed-end investment companies). These are management companies that invest in fixed portfolios of specific securities. Some hold a variety of diverse securities while others invest solely in one geographic area or industry. They neither redeem outstanding trust shares nor sell new shares on an ongoing basis. The investments are close-ended because they are fixed at the time of purchase.

- *Open-end investment companies* (mutual funds). These companies issue an unlimited number of shares on an ongoing basis and redeem these shares on demand. Shares represent ownership in the diversified securities portfolio. Types include balanced, diversified common stock, income, aggressive income, preferred stock, municipal bond, and money market funds. For the small investor there are a number of advantages to investing in mutual funds, such as diversification, professional management, liquidity, convenience, dollar-cost averaging, and economies of scale.

- *Real estate*. Ownership in real property, either directly or indirectly, is considered real estate. Advantages include appreciation, income from renting or leasing, and tax benefits. Investors can also participate in federal mortgage programs, such as Fannie Mae, Ginnie Mae and Freddie Mac, or in real estate syndicates or real estate investment trusts.

- *Tangible assets*. This refers to property that has intrinsic value and potential for appreciation. Such property includes collectibles, precious metals and gems, commodities, and contract futures
- *Limited partnerships*. These are used to attract investors who do not want to be actively involved in a venture. A limited partnership is an association of two or more persons with at least one general partner and one limited partner. The limited partner has limited liability up to the limits of his or her investment as a passive participant (investor), and is not involved in management. The general partner provides everyday management duties.

## *Answers to Self-test Questions*

| | | |
|---|---|---|
| 5-1. | D | page 5.29 |
| 5-2. | C | pages 5.36, 5.37 |
| 5-3. | D | page 5.4 |
| 5-4. | B | page 5.15 |
| 5-5. | B | page 5.7 |
| 5-6. | C | page 5.21 |
| 5-7. | B | page 5.5 |
| 5-8. | B | pages 5.21–5.27 |
| 5-9. | B | pages 5.30–5.39 |
| 5-10. | D | page 5.11 |

## Chapter 6

### *Answers to Review Questions*

6-1. Common characteristics in the mature adult market segment include the following:

- *Attitudes about finances*. The principal attitude for the mature market is safety and security. They want to preserve the fruits of their labor for their retirement years, which paradoxically requires some amount of market risk in order to combat the eroding effect that inflation can have on their assets. Early in this stage of the life cycle, many will still be concerned with accumulating assets for a future retirement. As they retire, they are apprehensive about spending down their assets. In either situation, they are worried about outliving their resources. What if they misjudge and spend all of their money before they die? Outliving resources ties in directly with their desire to remain independent. The last thing they want is to burden their children financially or otherwise. Older mature adults take great pride in their ability to remain independent and active.
- *Concerns about health care*. Mature adults are sensitive to health care issues, especially those related to Medicare and long-term care. They understand the frailties of aging and the medical care associated with them, and they are concerned about the affordability of such care if it is needed.
- *Having more time*. The primary goal of retirement is to have more time to do things not possible during the child-rearing and working years. Mature adults have time to

take trips to exotic places, get involved in community or non-profit organizations, pursue hobbies and interests, and learn new things. They have more time during the day to meet with you, unlike your younger clients or prospects.

- *Being deliberate.* Mature market clients tend to be more deliberate, because they have more time and are concerned about safety and reduced risk. For these reasons it may take them longer to make a decision and the buying cycle may be extended. The key is patience and to maintain a low-pressure sales approach.

- *Anticipating or entering retirement.* Retirement is something many look forward to with great anticipation. To others, it is something to dread. A major factor in this difference in attitude is the preparation made before reaching retirement. Too many people have not given any thought to the amount of money they will need.

6-2. Common needs in the mature adult segment include the following:

- *Financing health care.* Seniors are concerned about handling the costs of major illnesses, financing home healthcare, and nursing home fees. The increased cost of medical care has created a need for insurance. Medicare supplement policies offer seniors a way to fill in the gaps in the system's benefits. Long-term care insurance policies offer seniors a method of dealing with the health care costs for chronic ailments that could easily cost $50,000 or $60,000 per year.

- *Increasing retirement income.* Most individuals are interested in increasing their spendable income; seniors are no different. Where seniors differ is in their sources of income. Prospects in the seniors market may or may not be working, but they will typically have a pool of accumulated assets representing a lifetime of work. There are a variety of privately-owned products that financial advisors can market to assist seniors in augmenting their retirement income, including annuities, mutual funds, and life insurance.

- *Reducing taxes.* Tax planning is another major financial concern of seniors. Some individuals pay less in taxes once retired, while others may actually pay more. Retirees' paychecks are commonly replaced by generous pension checks. Mortgages may be replaced by huge amounts of equity in appreciated housing. However, with income tax deductions for mortgage interest and exemptions for children no longer available, many seniors find that they are paying taxes at higher, not lower, rates than in earlier years. Annuities and life insurance can offer substantial tax benefits. Deferred annuities can give seniors a way to shelter interest from current taxation, and can be used to lower the income taxes on Social Security benefits. Life insurance can also offer substantial tax benefits, allowing tax-free cash value accumulation, along with generous borrowing terms. The receipt of an income-tax-free sum at the death of a spouse can be used to handle unexpected living costs and replace the deceased spouse's lost pension benefits.

- *Facilitating estate planning objectives.* Lowering estate taxes and estate settlement costs have typically been planning goals for seniors. Traditional estate planning has accomplished this by focusing on the disposition of assets at death. Unfortunately, traditional estate planning has often ignored the impact of long-term care. Too often individuals become incapacitated without having formalized plans for health care or asset management. The unfortunate results have been smaller estates with sometimes little or nothing left for heirs. This situation has created a need for estate planning focused on today's increased longevity, chronic care needs, and the desire to fund the dreams of future generations. Although prospects may have accepted the inevitability of death, you will find that many are still unprepared when it comes to the possibility of becoming physically disabled or mentally incapacitated. As a financial advisor, your access to life insurance, annuity, and long-term care insurance products—combined with appropriate legal tools and your senior clients' financial assets—can make their goals a reality.

6-3.   Medicare Part A Hospital Insurance helps pay for five kinds of care: inpatient hospital care, inpatient care in a skilled nursing facility following a hospital stay, home health care, hospice care, and inpatient mental health care. Benefits under Medicare Part A that cover inpatient care in a hospital or skilled nursing facility are based on a benefit period. A benefit period begins with the first day one enters a hospital and ends when the patient has been out of a hospital or skilled nursing facility for 60 days in a row (including the day of discharge). A subsequent hospitalization then begins a new benefit period.

6-4.   Medicare Part B Medical Insurance helps pay for doctors' services, outpatient hospital care, diagnostic tests, medical equipment, and other health services and supplies not covered by Medicare hospital insurance (Part A). Premiums are usually deducted from the participant's Social Security check each month, and the amount changes from year to year. The standard annual deductible is $135 in 2009. For most services received under Part B, there is a 20 percent coinsurance amount beyond the annual deductible for all Medicare-approved charges. Medicare helps pay for covered services received from a doctor in his or her office, in a hospital, in a skilled nursing facility, at home, or any other location in the United States. Medicare medical insurance helps pay for medical and surgical services, diagnostic tests and procedures that are part of the treatment, radiology and pathology services by doctors, treatment of mental illness, and other services usually furnished in the doctor's office, such as X-rays, services of a doctor's nurse, drugs that cannot be self-administered, blood transfusions, medical supplies, and physical or occupational therapy.

6-5.   Medicare Part C (Medicare Advantage) expands the choices available to most Medicare beneficiaries by allowing them to elect medical expense benefits through one of several alternatives to Parts A and B as long as the providers of these alternatives enter into contracts with the Centers for Medicare & Medicaid Services. However, beneficiaries must still pay any Part B premium. The Medicare Advantage plans include HMOs (most of the HMOs previously in the Medicare market became part of the Medicare Advantage program), preferred-provider organizations (PPOs), provider-sponsored organizations (PSOs), private fee-for-service plans, and private contracts with physicians. These plans must provide all benefits available under Parts A and B of Medicare.

Part D Medicare The Medicare Prescription Drug, Improvement, and Modernization Act of 2003 added a prescription drug program to Medicare. Since spring 2004, most Medicare beneficiaries have been able to purchase a drug discount card. These cards can be sponsored by insurance companies, retail pharmacies, Medicare Advantage plans, and pharmacy benefit managers. Sponsors are required to pass any discounts they negotiate on the purchase of drugs to cardholders, and to publish a price list of the drugs they cover. Certain low-income seniors will also be eligible for annual subsidies to help them pay the cost of prescription drugs. In 2006, Medicare Part D replaced Medicare-approved drug discount cards. Part D is a voluntary prescription drug plan that is available to all Medicare beneficiaries entitled to Part A and enrolled in Part B.

6-6.   Most people need a medigap (Medicare supplement) policy to cover gaps in their coverage, or they risk consuming their retirement savings in one lengthy hospital stay. Medigap policies are designed specifically to cover deductibles and any coinsurance payments under Medicare. Most policies pay 100 percent of inpatient hospital care expenses for an additional 365 days after Medicare benefits are exhausted. These additional days are limited to 365 over the individual's lifetime. There is a limit on the number of different medigap policy formats that can be sold. These regulations provide for standardized benefits and establish rules for selling medigap coverage. Although most companies do not offer all forms, there are 12 different approved forms for medigap policies (Plans A through L). State insurance departments determine what policies are available in that jurisdiction.

6-7.   Reasons for the increasing need for long-term care and long-term care insurance include the following:

- *An aging population.* The single greatest predictor of the need for LTC is advancing age. This is due to the gradual and inevitable decline in physical and mental abilities that usually occurs as one ages.

- *Increased longevity.* People are living longer because advances in medicine have developed preventions, cures, and treatments for diseases and conditions that were once fatal. There are more people entering the time in life in which dependency on others is more prevalent. As life spans increase, the length of time people will need LTC due to such dependency will almost certainly increase as well.

- *Changes in the home.* Increased longevity is compounded by the significant change in family structure and lifestyles that have occurred over the past few decades in this country. Compared to previous generations, family members are simply less available today to meet the needs of their elderly parents and relatives because of the increased participation of women in the paid workforce, lower birth rates, and the geographic dispersion of families.

- *Cost of accelerating need.* This accelerating need will continue to drive up the future costs of long-term care because of growing numbers of patients, scarcity of facilities and staff, and continued building of new centers.

- *Few sources of money.* Some have the misconception that Medicare will cover their long-term care needs. However, Medicare does not provide custodial care for the elderly, and neither does a Medicare supplemental insurance policy. Medicaid requires an individual to have used up his or her assets before qualifying for coverage. Further, Medicaid payments are accepted by only some of the available long-term care facilities, limiting the alternatives from which an individual will be able to choose.

6-8.   Six activities of daily living (ADLs) that might trigger the benefit of a long-term care policy include bathing, dressing, transferring, toileting, continence, and feeding. Other criteria may apply for nonqualified policies, such as a physician's certification that long-term care is medically necessary.

6-9. Benefits provided under a long-term care (LTC) insurance policy include the following:

- Facility care (nursing home care) encompasses skilled-nursing care, intermediate care, and custodial care. Care is on a continuum from acute to chronic. An emerging, more sophisticated integration of care techniques and facilities can accommodate people along the continuum and offer a wide variety of services for different levels of care. Although some people enter a nursing home for short-term rehabilitation or convalescence after a hospitalization, most people who enter a nursing home for longer stays are experiencing a chronic condition. They may need services for conditions such as dementia, Alzheimer's disease, multiple sclerosis, or severe health conditions resulting from heart disease, stroke, diabetes, or arthritis. They may have lost their ability to perform ADLs, or become too sick or difficult for family members or others to care for them.

- Assisted-living facility care is provided in intermediate facilities for those who are no longer able to care for themselves but do not need the level of care provided in a nursing home. The number and types of these facilities are growing rapidly. Assisted-living facilities offer a more home-like atmosphere than a nursing home. Their relatively recent appearance as an LTC provider has witnessed explosive growth because they offer an effective form of care in the LTC delivery system.

- Home and community-based care provides for part-time, skilled-nursing care by registered and licensed practical nurses; for occupational, physical, and speech therapy; and for part-time services from licensed home health aides under the direction of a physician. Services typically include administering prescription medication, monitoring blood levels, wound care, diabetic care, incontinence management, and injections. Most people desire care at home because it provides an important foundation of emotional well being, control of one's lifestyle, security, familiarity, privacy, and other comforts.

6-10. Most long-term care (LTC) insurance products today provide daily benefits on a reimbursement basis, based on the actual expenses incurred. The benefits paid are equal to the actual expenses up to the policy's specified limit, the daily benefit amount, or maximum daily benefit. The other method of providing benefits is an indemnity policy. These pay out a specified amount of money no matter what costs are incurred for care in a nursing home or for home health care. Rather than restricting benefits to a maximum daily amount, some policies base benefits on a weekly or monthly benefit amount, such as $1,000, $2,000, or $3,000 or more. This can dramatically affect the amount of benefits paid.

As with life insurance benefits, inflation is a concern. Fortunately, most policies do offer inflation protection to help the daily benefit amount keep pace with future increases to long-term care costs. All policies have some outright exclusions such as self-inflicted injury, acts of war, and chemical or alcohol dependency. A policy will usually contain some form of pre-existing condition exclusion clause, excluding coverage for any condition for which the insured was previously treated within a certain time frame.

Although coverage and age-based premiums differ widely, typically very few companies issue new policies beyond the age of 80 or 85. Some companies do not have a minimum issue age. Other companies sell policies to persons as young as age 20. Still other companies have a minimum issue in the 40-to-50 age range.

### *Answers to Self-test Questions*

| | | |
|---|---|---|
| 6-1. | A | page 6.18 |
| 6-2. | C | page 6.16 |
| 6-3. | D | page 6.43 |
| 6-4. | D | page 6.3 |
| 6-5. | C | page 6.15 |
| 6-6. | B | page 6.42 |
| 6-7. | C | page 6.16 |
| 6-8. | B | pages 6.16–6.20 |
| 6-9. | D | page 6.43 |
| 6-10. | D | pages 6.2–6.4 |

## Chapter 7

### *Answers to Review Questions*

7-1.  A well-executed product delivery can achieve three objectives:

   (1) *It can reinforce the sale by reemphasizing the objectives of the purchase.* New clients who clearly understand how the product meets their needs will be less likely to let it lapse or move their accounts to a competitor.

   (2) *It can help the advisor gain the new client's trust, and it sets expectations for future service and repeat sales.* Set the expectations and schedule for future services such as periodic reviews of their insurance, investment, or financial plan. In addition, you can discuss other immediate or future needs identified during the selling/planning process. This may lead to follow-up sales or lay the groundwork for them down the road.

   (3) *It can offer another opportunity to obtain referred leads.* A satisfied new client can be your best source of referrals. What better time is there to ask for the names of people, for whom your services and products might also be of value, than at policy delivery?

The following techniques are recommended for a successful policy delivery:

   • For insurance products, there is an issuance process, namely underwriting, which results in a delay between the closing of the sale and the receipt of the product. It is critical that the advisor monitors the issuance process and takes appropriate action as needed. Communicate reasonable expectations during the closing interview, alerting applicants to any contacts, exams, and so on related to the underwriting process. The advisor should communicate with the applicant throughout the issuance process, especially if there are any delays. When the advisor receives the policy, he or she should review it to make sure that it is correct.

- Prepare for the delivery. Tie up any loose ends, making contact with any other advisors or referred leads as promised and being able to provide a report. Call to set up an appointment to deliver the product. Add a few professional touches, such as a product portfolio or policy wallet. Include any required information, such as an illustration or prospectus. Add any backup information. This includes product review checklists, summaries, company-approved information brochures, a list of suggestions, and information on claims procedures (if insurance product). Practice your presentation.

- Execute the policy or contract review. Briefly explain the policy or contract. Meet any delivery requirements, collecting any signatures or handing out required information. Review how to read annual statements. If necessary, resell the need to combat any perceived buyer's remorse.

- Establish the expectations for an ongoing relationship.

7-2.  According to the Merriam-Webster dictionary, a customer is "one that purchases a commodity or service." A client, on the other hand, is defined as "one that is under the protection of another; a person who engages the professional advice or services of another." It follows then that all clients are customers, but not all customers are clients. Clients are customers who follow your advice consistently, buy from you again, and refer you to others. The difference is important because a client values the relationship he or she has with the agent and will not defect simply to get a lower price. A client pays bills on time and has greater potential for repeat business and referrals. Thus a client is better for the advisor's bottom line.

7-3.  It is important to provide excellent service to clients for three main reasons:

- To facilitate customer retention. A strong client relationship can help prevent competitors from replacing your business. In this competitive climate, service is clearly a necessary defensive strategy.

- To result in repeat sales and referrals. Client building is also part of a smart offensive marketing and sales strategy as we see in the selling process. Experienced advisors report that as much as 75 percent of their new business comes from existing clients or referrals provided by these clients. Remember clients tend to refer people like themselves.

- To lower expenses. By being able to sell primarily to clients and people they refer, you can drastically lower your sales and marketing costs.

7-4.  An advisor should monitor a client's circumstances for the following:

- *Insurance coverages.* First, there's a need to check that any insurance coverage is adequate to protect the needs the client desires to protect. In particular, it means evaluating whether or not the insured has the right coverages and the right amount of those coverages. Changes in insurance coverage could occur for various reasons including the following:

  a. additional needs discovered but not insured—For example, the original needs analysis uncovers that they need more life insurance or disability income protection, but they could not afford to cover these needs in full at the time of the original purchase.

      b.  additional needs due to life events—For example, if the client gets married or remarried, gives birth or adopts a baby, gets divorced, gets a promotion, or buys a new home, these events could trigger new life insurance or disability needs.

      c.  amount of current need increases—For example, if inflation spikes for several years, salary and expenses increase, or the original need was underestimated, there may be a greater need for coverage.

      d.  changing needs due to life events—For example, if the client's children have left home, the life need may diminish, but a long-term care need may be felt more.

- *Life insurance values.* For permanent insurance, track cash values and policy dividends (if applicable) to ensure they are going to achieve anticipated cash goals for retirement or any other future goal. This is especially true with interest-sensitive and variable products, and participating policies where dividend values are of concern. Sometimes the amount of the need does not change but the type does. Here are two examples:

      a.  term conversions—A client may have purchased a term policy to cover educational expenses and at some point realizes he or she will probably have needs beyond retirement. Perhaps his or her estate has grown or he or she would like to provide money for a charity.

      b.  universal life death benefit option change—A client may find that his or her needs have diminished and now would like to focus on supplementing retirement income.

- *Automatic changes.* When automatic changes occur, communication with the client can help them adjust or perhaps take advantage of them. Some companies will provide for children insured through a children's term rider to convert to a permanent policy without evidence of insurability. If the client or policyowner has purchased a guaranteed renewable-term policy the rates will increase at the renewal, and this presents an opportunity to communicate the increase and examine conversion possibilities. If the client has purchased the guaranteed insurability rider you can help him or her take advantage of it.

- *Investment needs.* Life events often a person's needs for various investment products or his or her ability to fund them.

- *Investment asset allocation.* An investment portfolio rarely remains constant over the years. It is important to review the client's asset allocation for investment products to ensure it remains within the client's risk tolerance. In addition, a client's risk tolerance may change over time.

- *Law changes.* Sometimes the concepts used to sell the policy may change due to law changes. This would require monitoring to be sure that the plan performance will take place as anticipated, otherwise changes may need to be made. Tax law changes often provide new sales opportunities. The most common areas impacted are income tax planning, retirement planning, and estate planning.

7-5.  There are several key points to consider regarding the annual review:

- Lay the groundwork for the annual review at the first interview when you explain how you work and the services you offer. Tell the prospect that you help people uncover their insurance and financial goals, create and implement a plan to achieve them, and then continue to monitor their plan to make adjustments as needed. This enables the prospect to understand how you expect to service their plan after it is implemented. At the policy delivery, your goal should be to leave with a date for your next review.

- Record keeping is extremely important. An updated master folder or computer record will help you prepare for the annual review. Keeping good records along the way will not only shorten your preparation time, it will also provide a more professional image. Make sure you record things like children's names and ages, grandchildren, and so on. Record personal interests to help reestablish rapport. Also keep any policy notices that contain pertinent information on things such as cash value.

- Call to confirm the appointment. You also can let the client know in advance to bring any documentation he or she may need. Some advisors send a preapproach letter reminding the policyowner or client of the annual review service that they offer. They then follow up with a phone call to set the appointment.

- Refresh your memory by reviewing the needs analysis and any financial information that the client provided. Look at your interview notes to remember attitudes and values. Rerun policy illustrations if applicable, and compare the projected values with current values. Put together a game plan of areas where needs may exist. Review the client's insurance plan and current progress in the plan. If appropriate, recalculate needs and note any shortfalls.

- Inquire about any changes in their current or future financial situation. Listen carefully and note any opportunities. Implement any plan changes or set any necessary follow-up appointments. An annual review is a perfect time to ask a client for referrals. There is a very high probability that they value and trust you because they agreed to have you review their insurance plan.

7-6.  Two levels of service, or service packages that can be used in servicing clients based on your relationship with them, and them with you are:

- *The standard service package.* Excellent customer service is now the price of admission in financial services. It is the expected level of service and not the exception. This means you need to create a high quality standard service package for dealing with routine requests for changes and information for everyone, regardless of their value to your business. You need a system that ensures all customers and clients receive the service they need and allows you to capitalize on new marketing opportunities. Define what that package is. Communicate it to your customers. Deliver as promised. Excellent service puts you in a position to inquire about other needs. You can take care of clients and market other products and services you provide.

- *The extra frills package.* For some of your customers and clients, you will want to give a better service package that includes other services and frills. This means you will need to identify what services you will provide as frills. The purpose of the extra frills is to make every contact an opportunity to market by doing one (or all) of three things: create visibility, create awareness of the products and services you provide, and create a sense of personal touch. Define your frills packages and deliver them. Make sure they are relevant, you can deliver them, and they are cost effective from both a monetary and time standpoint.

7-7. The purpose of monitoring and servicing is to build client relationships. Not everyone who purchases a product will want to become your client, and there will be people who buy from you that you would prefer not become your client. You will need to identify whom you want to be a client. With the ABC method, you segment your book of business into three categories or grades:

- "A" clients—These are people who believe in you and the products you sell. They are a source for repeat sales and referrals. Your long-term goal is to only deal with these clients. They merit your very best service.
- "B" clients—These are customers whom you wish to turn into clients, or customers who have purchased financial products from you in the past year, but who have not yet committed to a full client relationship. These are your "B" clients. To the "B" group you will offer a broader range of services than the "C" group. Your goal is to eventually drop them to the basic service group or to raise them to client status.
- "C" clients— These are people who have either demonstrated that they do not wish to enter into an ongoing client relationship with you, or you do not want to do more than your existing business with them. These are your "C" clients to whom you offer only basic services (for example, annual reviews, and follow up on information and service requests).

Once you have identified the three classes of clients, you can treat each accordingly in terms of the discretionary services you provide. In selecting which services to offer, distinguish between basic and discretionary services.

7-8. The marketing plan will apply target marketing concepts and will be built by answering the following questions:

(1) What are my objectives? The first step of building a basic marketing plan is to identify your objectives, specifically, your income and activity objectives. There are three basic steps: (1) construct marketing funnels for your target markets and general market, (2) Determine income objectives, and (3) calculate activity objectives using applicable marketing funnels.

(2) To whom am I marketing? Your basic marketing plan should include a brief profile of your target markets, defining the common characteristics and common insurance and financial needs, regardless of whether or not you can meet them.

(3) What am I marketing? From the common financial needs you identified, select those needs that you are able to meet based on the products you sell and your level of training and experience.

(4) How will I market to them? Your next step is to determine how you will market to your target markets. This includes the following: creating and implementing a position for your personal brand, implementing prospecting methods for identifying prospect names and contact information, implementing methods for creating awareness and interest of your products, creating and using scripts to set

appointments, anticipating objections, and outlining additional services you will offer to increase retention.

(5) How effective am I? The last part of a basic marketing plan is a plan for evaluating your results. This process will lay the groundwork for planning your next income period.

7-9. *Compliance* means following the laws and regulations, including company rules, which apply to the sale of all financial products. These are the minimum standards. *Professional ethics* is behavior according to principles of right and wrong—a code of ethics—accepted by one's profession. By adopting, embracing, and practicing a professional code of ethics, the financial advisor will likely achieve the high standard of professionalism demanded by a career in financial services.

## *Answers to Self-test Questions*

| | | |
|---|---|---|
| 7-1. | D | page 7.9 |
| 7-2. | A | page 7.6 |
| 7-3. | B | page 7.34 |
| 7-4. | C | pages 7.22–7.23 |
| 7-5. | C | pages 7.31–32 |
| 7-6. | C | pages 7.25–7.26 |
| 7-7. | A | pages 7.41–7.42 |
| 7-8. | C | pages 7.6–7.8 |
| 7-9. | D | page 7.2 |
| 7-10. | C | page 7.13 |

## Chapter 8

### *Answers to Review Questions*

8-1. Common characteristics of the old-age market segment include the following:

- *Psychological changes.* There is a declining ability to acquire new intelligence, but a sustained ability to apply existing knowledge. Aging has little effect on the size of working memory, but it does impair the transfer of information from the short-term to long-term store. Hearing loss is very common. The loss of existing knowledge (for example, how to dress oneself) is a pathological change, not an aging one. The elderly have to come to terms with their changing role in life. Society causes the elderly to assume a dependent role through retirement and pensions.

- *Dealing with death.* Strong emotions and an increased awareness of death emerge as relatives, friends, and spouses die. There is a strong sense of nostalgia for the past, often accompanied by sadness and loneliness when the future is considered.

- *Nursing homes and assisted living.* Many in this age group face nursing home and assisted-living choices because of fragile health. Long-term care insurance and

Medicare supplement (medigap) insurance are often issues of importance as a person begins to deal with the effects of aging.

- *Leaving a legacy.* The next generation takes on a new importance when people reach old age. A reconciliation of spiritual values and a final conclusion as to the meaning of life often provide members of this stage of life a legacy to leave to the next generation. They attempt to pass on their wisdom and knowledge about life. The liquidation and distribution of any remaining estate is considered. To many, the proper way to pass assets on to children and grandchildren is the most important objective. Many mature adults may have charitable intentions.

8-2. Common needs of the old-age segment include the following:

- *Updated will.* As with all ages, a will ensures that a person's estate is dealt with in the manner he or she desires. By this phase in the life cycle, a will may not have been updated in a while, and relatives and friends may have predeceased your client or relationships with children have changed, thus making the will out of date. An advisor can provide good service by reminding clients to create a will, or update an existing will.

- *Lifetime income.* One of the biggest concerns for many people in the old-age market segment is the possibility of outliving their assets. The majority of old-age prospects and clients realize that Social Security is not adequate to sustain their desired standard of living. This need is even more acute for those who do not receive pension benefits from an employer. Immediate annuities are good products for this market segment.

- *Gifts to children and grandchildren.* Some members of the old-age market segment will want to leave a legacy to children and/or grandchildren. This objective may be achieved through bequests at death or gifts made during one's life. Bequests at death may involve the distribution of assets, such as a house or investments and savings. Life insurance proceeds are another method for creating a legacy.

8-3. A seminar is an effective way to approach seniors. It is an educational and motivational meeting for people interested in your topic. The seminar's purposes are to create awareness, motivate prospects to take action, and to set an appointment with you. They are not an attempt to make an immediate sale. The only selling that takes place in the seminar is the selling of yourself and your ideas; this will open up opportunities for one-on-one follow-up meetings in which selling of products can take place. Typically, seminars appeal to prospects who need information and have the time to seek it out—a description that fits prospects in the senior market

8-4. When a person dies, property he or she owned will pass to heirs in one or more of the following ways:

- *By operation of law.* A typical example of this method is a home owned jointly by a husband and a wife. At the death of the first spouse, the surviving joint tenet gains full ownership of the jointly held property. Property not passing by contract, will, or operation of law passes under the laws of intestate succession.

- *By right of contract.* The prime example of this is life insurance that is paid directly to a named beneficiary.

- *By will.* If there is a will, the remaining property passes under the terms of the will once it has been admitted to probate. If there is no will, remaining property passes according to the state's laws of intestacy, by operation of law.
- *By trust.* A trust is an arrangement in which assets are administered by a trustee for the benefit of others in a manner specified by the deceased.

8-5. When a person dies without a will (intestate), the courts take control of the estate and, in effect, write a will in accordance with the state's intestate laws. It is unlikely that the state's distribution would match most people's personal wishes. For example, in most states a spouse does not automatically inherit all property when there are children. In the absence of a will, the court must also appoint an administrator of the estate and a guardian for the minor children. Normally, the courts prefer a relative as administrator, but if one is not available or willing to serve, the estate could end up in the hands of a professional administrator. This official generally takes 3 to 5 percent of the estate in fees each year. This arrangement offers little incentive to settle an estate quickly or to minimize the estate for tax purposes. The court would also select a relative as guardian if the children were orphaned, but without any guarantee of the choice the parent might have made. Because the court's appointment does not carry the moral weight of the parent's wishes in a will, children could become the object of a custody battle.

8-6. The will must meet technical and legal requirements. It must be in writing and properly executed according to the state's laws. The will must be signed to indicate intent, and it must be attested to (verified) by the appropriate number of witnesses. Oral wills are generally not valid. No will takes effect until the death of the testator, the person making the will. Therefore it can be changed at any time during life. A new will can be written to revoke prior wills. Because only the original will is valid, it is important to keep it in a safe place that others know. A bank safe-deposit box is not suggested because access to it is limited. Only limited copies of the will should be made and distributed. The original should be left with the estate executor or attorney for safety.

8-7. Definitions:
- *Applicable credit amount.* The credit is an amount that can be applied directly against any gift or estate tax due, and is $1,455,800 in 2009. This means that a person with assets less than $3.5 million dying in 2009 generally will have no federal estate tax payable.
- *Marital deduction.* A deduction of 100 percent of property passing to a spouse either by gift or at death is permitted. To qualify for the deduction, the property generally must pass to the surviving spouse in such a manner that he or she has sole power of control during life or at death. In effect, the estate of one spouse can be passed to the other completely free of taxation, as long as it qualifies for the marital deduction. The marital deduction is merely a postponement of taxation at the death of the first spouse. The property that passes to a surviving spouse will be taxable at his or her subsequent death. Much estate planning is directed toward minimizing this result.
- *Three-year rule.* One strategy for decreasing the value of an estate is to transfer ownership of life insurance. However, the value of any life insurance is included in the estate if the transfer is made within three years prior to the death of the owner.

Ownership includes incidents of ownership that refer to a number of rights of the insured or the insured's estate in the economic benefits of the policy. Examples of contractual rights that reflect incidents of ownership are the rights of surrender and the right to make policy loans, assign the contract, and change the beneficiary. One must relinquish all incidents of ownership to remove the value of life insurance from an estate.

8-8.   The goal of life insurance in estate planning depends upon the client. For most people, life insurance is used to increase the size of an estate to provide for surviving family members. It could be the young family buying insurance as income replacement, to fund college educations for their children, to provide for mortgage redemption, or to build a nest egg for retirement. Life insurance provides the perfect estate enhancement to replace income if the breadwinner of the family should die prematurely.

For older clients and those who have built wealth, life insurance is used to provide estate liquidity. Their children's support and educational expenses are usually things of the past. In addition, these older clients are nearing the end of their income-producing years, and should have less future income to replace. These people can purchase life insurance to provide death proceeds equal to the size of the anticipated shrinkage of the estate due to settlement and taxes.

Life insurance is the most effective way to supply needed dollars to meet federal estate tax obligations. First, the dollars, in the form of death proceeds, are free of federal income taxation. Second, if the life insurance is owned by someone (or some entity) other than the insured, the policy's face amount will not be included as part of the decedent's gross estate. Finally, a sizable death benefit may be purchased for pennies on the dollar in the form of premium payments.

8-9.   Charitable gifts can produce three federal tax benefits:
- Income tax. When the donor itemizes deductions, charitable donations during the donor's lifetime are usually deductible.
- Gift tax. With a few exceptions, qualified charitable gifts or bequests are exempt from gift taxes.
- Estate tax. Charitable gifts that become effective after the donor's death may qualify for an estate tax deduction.

8-10.   Some of the advantages your clients will realize by using life insurance as the vehicle of gifting are:
- leveraging the contribution so it will become a larger gift than otherwise possible with a straight cash contribution. It becomes a gift made on the installment plan through annual premium payments for the life insurance.
- receiving a current income tax deduction for donations made to pay premiums on a policy owned by the charity
- receiving a future estate-tax deduction for life insurance proceeds paid to a charitable organization upon the death of the donor
- creating a new asset and not depending upon other owned assets to make the gift
- avoiding the probate process for the life insurance that would create costs, delays, and publicity connected with the charitable gift to the settlement of the estate

- avoiding possible challenges by potential heirs
- avoiding creditor claims that could be attached to the other assets that pass by will
- creating, through life insurance, a self-completing gift that is fairly simple to arrange

8-11. Distribution planning is a major concern for older adults, who are concerned with maintaining their lifestyle in face of the threats of inflation and taxes. Careful projection of income and expenses, or cash flow analysis, is important in meeting future income needs in retirement. Annuities provide one source of guaranteed income in retirement. Annuities are categorized as immediate or deferred, single premium or flexible premium, or fixed or variable. Life insurance death benefits can be critical for the financial futures of surviving loved ones. The selection of the specific settlement option may be made prior to death by the policyowner or left to the beneficiary's choice. Options include the following:

- *Lump-sum or cash proceeds*. Most payments to beneficiaries are taken as a lump sum cash payment or paid into an interest-bearing checking account. This option offers no protection against the creditors of the beneficiary. Lump-sum distributions allow the beneficiary to manage the money, either reinvesting it at a higher rate, using it to pay estate settlement costs or debts, or using it for whatever purpose they choose.

- *Interest income*. Under this settlement option, the insurance company holds the proceeds and pays interest to the beneficiary based on a rate of return guaranteed in the policy, or a higher rate based on current interest rates. This option preserves the capital for the future, and can allow the beneficiary to make cash withdrawals. This option is designed to distribute the full proceeds at a later date when the beneficiary is ready to receive them, or at the beneficiary's death. The most flexible of all available settlement options, the interest option is also the only one in which income is fully taxable to the recipient. (With the other options, income is made up of principal and interest and only the interest portion is taxed.)

- *Fixed-period income*. Under this option, the company pays out both policy proceeds and interest earned in installments over a specified period. The income received depends on the amount of proceeds, the interest credited, and the time period selected. The fixed period payout for insurance proceeds offers no flexibility to the beneficiary and is not used unless a clearly defined purpose and time frame for need can be established.

- *Specified amount*. Under this option, policy proceeds, plus interest, are used to pay out a specified amount of income at regular intervals for as long as the proceeds last. The larger the payment, the shorter the period of income will be. This option is similar to the fixed-period settlement choice except that excess interest above the return guaranteed by the company extends the length of time for the payout.

- *Life income*. This is a settlement choice unique to the insurance industry. The promise is to pay a stated income as long as the beneficiary lives. At death, the contract ends. This describes a pure no-refund annuity. Whether the beneficiary lives to 101 or dies within the year, the annuity reverts to the company at death. For most, even though it may offer the highest return in income to the beneficiary during life, this option would prove unsatisfactory without a guarantee of return built into the annuity. Because of this, a more popular and commonly used life income settlement builds in a refund or period-certain guarantee.

- *Life income with refund.* The life income with refund option guarantees payments for the life of the annuitant. If the annuitant should die before all the proceeds have been distributed, the balance of payments would be paid, either in a lump sum or installments, to the annuitant's beneficiary or even a third beneficiary, until all proceeds have been depleted. The annuitant is assured through this method that all proceeds will be paid out.

- *Life income with period certain.* Under this payout option, the annuitant receives payments for his or her entire life. In addition, he or she is given a guarantee that if he or she should die within a certain period of time (such as, 10, 15, 20, 25, or 30 years) the payment will be paid to a beneficiary for the balance of the time selected.

- *Joint and survivor life income.* Under this settlement option, income is provided for two people and is most commonly used by married couples for payment of retirement benefits. It can be set up to expire at the second death or to have the refund or period-certain guarantees built into the settlement. The joint income may be set up so that the survivor's income continues at 100 percent of the amount paid when both annuitants were alive, or so that survivor income is reduced to a percentage of the full amount. The common arrangements are joint and two-thirds or joint and one-half. The income varies under the joint arrangements per $1,000 of proceeds depending on the difference in age of the recipients and their sex. The survivor payout percentage can be used to leverage more income during the joint payout if less is taken at the survivor payout.

### *Answers to Self-test Questions*

| | | |
|---|---|---|
| 8-1. | B | pages 8.23–8.24 |
| 8-2. | A | page 8.33 |
| 8-3. | C | pages 8.10–8.11 |
| 8-4. | C | pages 8.6–8.7 |
| 8-5. | A | page 8.15 |
| 8-6. | A | pages 8.8 |
| 8-7. | B | page 8.10 |
| 8-8. | A | pages 8.13–8.15 |
| 8-9. | C | pages 8.3–8.4 |
| 8-10. | A | pages 8.10–8.11 |

# *Glossary*

**ABC Method (client classification)** • a method of prioritizing your book of business prospects and clients into "C" (those who are not interested in developing a relationship with you, or you with them), "B" (potential customers who you wish to turn into clients), and "A" (those with whom you want to do business and who see you as their trusted advisor)

**accelerated death benefit** • a life insurance policy provision that allows death benefits to be paid to the policyowner prior to the insured's death when the insured is terminally ill and has a limited life expectancy

**accumulation phase** • the period of time in a deferred annuity during which the purchase price is deposited with the insurer and accumulated at interest

**accidental death and dismemberment benefit** • a life insurance policy provision that provides an additional amount—usually equal to the policy face value—if the insured is killed in an accident. Also known as double indemnity. The dismemberment benefit, if included, pays a set percentage for the loss of eyesight and/or loss of hands or feet at or above the wrist or ankle.

**activities of daily living (ADLs)** • activities such as eating, bathing, and dressing. The inability to perform a specified number of these triggers eligibility for benefits in a long-term care policy.

**adjustable life insurance** • a variety of whole life insurance allowing the policyowner to change the type of insurance, raise or lower the face amount of the policy, increase or decrease the premium, and lengthen or shorten the protection period of the policy at specified intervals

**administrator** • the person appointed by the court to manage and settle the estate of a deceased person, usually because the deceased person left no will. *See* executor.

**advance directives** • durable power of attorney and living wills

**adverse selection** • a tendency of poorer risks to continue insurance to a greater extent than normal risks, producing an abnormal increase in mortality rates for those less healthy members still in the plan. It also includes the tendency of people who are poorer risks to seek out insurance to a greater extent than those who are normal risks. *See* anti-selection.

**advertising** • the use of persuasive messages communicated through the mass media. The goal of advertising is to create new clients. For the purposes of financial products, advertising is best suited to create awareness of an advisor's personal brand rather than to induce prospects to purchase specific products.

**advisor responsibilities** • an advisor has responsibilities to his or her client, company, the general public, and the industry. These include, but are not limited to, acting ethically, professionally, honestly, and in the best interest of others. Some responsibilities are legal and are regulated by the state and federal departments or imposed by companies, whereas others are promulgated by industry and professional associations.

**agent** • a sales and service representative of an insurance company licensed by the state to solicit the sale of insurance. An agent represents the company and is given powers by the company to act on its behalf. LUTC refers to agents and all producers as advisors.

**amount-at-risk** • the difference between the face amount of a policy and the reserve or policy value at a given time. It is the amount over and above what the policyowner has contributed toward the payment of his claims. Amount-at-risk is the true insurance amount, the amount the company is responsible for paying from the reserve.

**anniversary** • the yearly anniversary of the issue date. Premiums, cash values, dividends, and other policy benefits are determined as of anniversary dates.

**annual business planner** • a booklet used to calculate prospecting and sales effectiveness ratios using the totals from the activity summary section

**annual gift tax exclusion** • a gift tax exclusion of $13,000 for 2009 (adjusted for inflation annually) that a donor is allowed for each donee, provided the gift is one of a present interest

**annual review** • monitoring is the servicing aspect that separates a life insurance policy from a life insurance plan. Meeting with the client on a regular basis helps build the relationship, improve persistency, and provides opportunities for cross selling and referrals.

**annuitant** • the person during whose life an annuity is payable, and usually the person who receives the annuity income

**annuity** • a contract that provides a periodic income at regular intervals for a specific period of time, such as for a number of years, or for life

**annuity certain** • a contract that provides an income for a specified number of years, regardless of life or death. The payments are not linked to the duration of a specified human life.

**anti-selection** • also called adverse selection. It refers to the tendency of people with a greater than average likelihood of loss to apply for or continue insurance to a greater extent than other people.

**any occupation definition** • a strict definition of disability that requires a person to be so severely disabled that he or she cannot engage in any occupation

**applicable credit amount** • a credit to which to estate of every individual is entitled, which can be directly applied against the estate or gift tax

**approach (the prospect)** • the second step of the selling/planning process when the advisor contacts the prospect either on the telephone or face to face for the purpose of obtaining an appointment for an initial interview

**assisted living facility** • a place that provides a supportive living arrangement for residents who, despite some degree of impairment, remain independent to a significant degree, but require continuing supervision and the availability of unscheduled assistance

**automatic premium loan (APL)** • an elective policy feature wherein any premium not paid by the end of the grace period is paid by the insurance company by making a loan equal to the premium from policy cash values

**baby boomers** • the name for the generation born between 1946 and 1964. Their name reflects the sheer size of this group. Boomers are characterized as spenders, inheritors, image-conscious, and youth oriented. This image may change as this group enters retirement.

**behavioristic variables** • group people by their buying and usage behaviors. This type of segmentation categorizes people according to life events (birth of a child, marriage, divorce), type of user (do-it-yourselfer, collaborator, delegator), brand loyalty, benefits sought (convenience, price, quality), and buying motivations (this varies by product. Examples for long-term care insurance could include not burdening loved ones, ensuring choice of care settings and providers, and protecting assets for heirs.).

**beneficiary** • any person, class of people, institution, or trust specifically named in a life or annuity contract to receive the policy benefits at the death of the insured

**benefit period** • the maximum period for which benefits are paid. It begins when the elimination period is satisfied and benefits are payable. When the maximum benefit amount is paid, the policy ends.

**blackout period** • the name of the period of time between a surviving spouse's last child's benefit payment and eligibility for the first retirement income check at age 60 under the rules of Social Security

**bonds** • debt securities issued by corporate or local (federal, state, municipal) government units. A bond is issued when the investor loans money to the issuer of the bond. The bond is essentially an IOU given by the issuer to the investor with a promise to pay a stated interest (coupon rate), and then repay the invested funds (principal) at a specified (maturity) date.

**broker** • a sales and service representative who handles insurance for clients, and represents the client, not the insurance company. They generally sell insurance of various kinds and for several companies.

**budgeting process** • Budgeting and cash flow management are the most basic tools of financial planning. Proper budgeting can help the client obtain adequate insurance protection, savings, or retirement funds. Start by understanding the clients' goals and vision of the future. Each of the family's goals should be prioritized. Once they have listed and prioritized expenses, the family can balance their income and expenses to properly allocate funds among various needs and goals.

**building-block approach** • The financial planning pyramid uses four levels: wealth foundation, wealth accumulation, wealth preservation, and wealth distribution. The individual blocks illustrate how most people feel comfortable building their financial plans—one or a few blocks at a time.

**bundled insurance product** • a life insurance product in which the mortality, investment, and expense factors used to calculate premium rates and cash values are not identified as such (as they are in traditional whole life insurance)

**business life insurance** • life insurance purchased by a business enterprise on the life of a member of the firm. It is often bought by partnerships to protect the surviving partners against loss caused by the death of a partner, or by a corporation to reimburse it for loss caused by the death of a key employee.

**Buyer's Guide** • a publication required by many states to be given to the applicant of life insurance by the insurance company before an application is taken, or at the time of policy delivery. It is designed to help the buyer make a more informed decision.

**buyer's remorse** • the new client may not remember exactly why he or she purchased the product, and may wonder if he or she made the right decision

**care settings** • LTC can be provided in a variety of care settings including skilled-nursing facilities, such as an LTC facility or a nursing home; residential communities, such as an assisted living facility; community-based facilities, such as an adult day care; and the home of the person receiving care

**cash needs** • a part of the needs-based or financial needs analysis approach, cash needs at death represent lump-sum amounts of money that can liquidate expenses that the family will face at the death of an income producer, such as final expenses, debt repayment, mortgage cancellation, or a rent fund, emergency fund, and education fund

**cash surrender value** • the amount available in cash upon voluntary termination of a policy by its owner before it becomes payable by death or maturity

**cash value** • the cash fund within a permanent life insurance policy that is part of the death benefit and is owned by the policyowner for purposes of cash surrender or policy loans

**center of influence** • from the advisor's point of view, an influential person you know, who knows you favorably, and who agrees to introduce or refer you to others

**certificates of deposit** • the customer deposits money with the institution for a specific, limited certain period. Typical CD terms are three month, six month, and one to five years. The institution pays interest on the money at fixed or variable rates from the date of deposit to the CD's maturity date.

**charitable deduction** • An estate tax charitable deduction is allowed for the full value of property transferred to a qualified charity, but only if the property is included in the donor's gross estate. The charitable deduction allows an unlimited deduction for assets passing to a qualified charity.

**charitable giving** • a gift of a present interest to a qualified charity, supported by the federal government by allowing a charitable tax deduction. Life insurance can be used as a vehicle to accomplish a charitable intent and gain estate and income tax advantages.

**claims of creditors** • generally the cash values during lifetime and the death benefits afforded the beneficiary at death are free from the claims of the creditors of the insured and the beneficiary. The only exception to this is that the federal government can exercise tax liens against the cash value.

**client** • a person who has bought from you, but also someone with whom you have developed, or are developing, a strong interpersonal business relationship. Because of this relationship, if the client has any problems in areas relevant to your expertise, he or she will look to you for direction.

**client-focused sales/planning approach** • emphasizes helping clients by providing solutions to their insurance and financial needs and helping them achieve their objectives with a genuine agenda of helping in an open, honest, and forthright manner. The client's satisfaction is central. The advisor's role is helping people recognize and understand their financial needs, providing needed information, removing obstacles to financial success, and assisting in taking positive action to achieve their goals.

**cold canvassing** • a method of prospecting that involves going out and knocking on doors to approach people. It can generate new business that may not have otherwise occurred. It is challenging, time consuming, and rarely as productive as obtaining referred leads.

**commissioner of insurance** • the state official charged with the enforcement of the laws or regulations pertaining to insurance in the respective states. Normally appointed by the governor, but in some states is an elected official.

**Commissioners Standard Ordinary (CSO) Mortality Tables** • mortality tables based on intercompany experience during a particular period. The 1980 CSO table is widely used today, but 2001 CSO tables based on more recent mortality are being introduced and are being considered for approval in the various states.

**community involvement** • If the target market coincides with a social, civic, business, charitable, or religious organization, this is usually the preferred method for creating awareness of who you are and what you do.

**compliance** • following the laws and regulations, including company rules, that apply to the sales of insurance and financial products. These are the minimum standards.

**conservation** • the process of keeping issued business in force, including the reinstatement of lapsed policies, and the efforts by a company and advisor to prevent a replacement of in-force business

**contract** • a binding agreement between two or more parties, legally enforceable to do certain things. An insurance policy is a contract. The Law of Contracts specifies four requirements for the formation of a contract: (1) parties of legal capacity; (2) expression of mutual consent of the parties to a promise, or set of promises; (3) a valid consideration; (4) the absence of any statute or other rule declaring such agreement void (having a legal purpose).

**convertible term insurance** • term insurance that can be exchanged, at the option of the policyowner and without evidence of insurability, for another plan of insurance

**cost basis** • the investment in a contract that determines the amount of the proceeds from the disposition of a contract can be recovered tax-free

**cost-of-living adjustment (COLA) rider** • an increase in an insurance contract to compensate for an increase in the cost of living, such as disability income benefit, long-term care insurance, or a life income benefit

**cost of waiting** • a concept that creates a comparison between a plan started now, and one started three to five years from now. It shows a dramatic difference in face amounts of life insurance protection for a given amount of premium as well as in cash values that can accumulate over the years if a plan is started now rather than later. The same concept applies to investments and retirement planning.

**coverage gap (donut hole)** • under Medicare prescription drug plans, the range in which the beneficiary must pay the full cost of prescription drugs. Under a standard benefit structure, the gap begins after a beneficiary has incurred a specified dollar amount of expenses and continues until the plan begins paying again after total drug costs reach a second specified dollar amount. *Also called* doughnut hole.

**CSO 2001Table** • see Commissioners Standard Ordinary Mortality Table. The new 2001 CSO mortality tables reflect a higher life expectancy and generally lower mortality rates than the previous tables.

**current assumption whole life** • uses current mortality and interest earnings based on current yields rather than overall investment portfolio yields. Current rates reflect today's interest rates. Portfolio rates represent the collective rate being earned on all the funds of the insurer that are invested at different rates at different times with different maturities. In all other respects, it is identical to conventional whole life.

**current retirement gap** • After a prospect decides on a state of well-being retirement income goal, and you identify all income sources, you can apply the current retirement gap formula. This is a simple calculation, which assumes your prospect will retire tomorrow. Calculating takes the following steps: (1) determine their current expenses. (2) calculate existing resources. (3) retirement income need = percentage of current income. (4) retirement income need – existing resources = current retirement gap.

**custodial care** • care services that include assistance with the activities of daily living (ADLs) and instrumental activities of daily living (IADLs). This type of care helps people in the tasks of everyday living, as opposed to medical treatment or supervision.

**customer versus client** • a customer is one who purchases a commodity or service. A client, on the other hand, is one who is a person who engages the professional advice or services of another. It follows then that all clients are customers, but not all customers are clients. Clients are customers who follow your advice consistently, buy from you again, and refer you to others with whom you have developed, or are developing, a mutually beneficial, long-term, business relationship.

**death claim** • when the insured dies, the person(s) entitled to the proceeds must complete certain insurance company death claim forms giving proof of death and establishing a claimant's right to policy proceeds

**deferred annuity** • an annuity contract providing for income payments to begin at some future date

**defined benefit plan** • a pension plan stating either (1) the benefits to be received by employees after retirement or (2) the method of determining such benefits. Employer contributions are actuarially determined.

**defined contribution plan** • a plan in which the contribution rate is fixed and benefits that will be received by employees after retirement depend to some extent upon the contributions and their earnings

**deliverables** • are the ancillary products and service experiences you promise and provide to your prospects and clients. As you carve a position in a target market, look for ways that you can use your skills and background to offer a unique approach to or perspective of the planning process.

**delivery interview** • by delivering the policy in person, the advisor can move a policyowner toward becoming a client. This can be done by reinforcing the sale, establishing monitoring and servicing expectations, and asking for referrals.

**demographic variables** • variables such as gender, education, ethnicity, occupation, income, size of family, marital status, religion, generational cohort, (Silent Generation, Baby Boom, Generation X, and so on), and family situation (single, married with kids and a single income, married with no kids and two incomes, single parent, empty nester, and divorced)

**deposit term insurance** • a form of term insurance in which the first year's premium (the deposit) is larger than subsequent premiums. Typically, a partial endowment is paid at the end of the term period. In many cases, the partial endowment can be applied towards the purchase of a new term or whole life policy.

**direct response** • involves sending letters with reply cards that prospects can return if they are interested in an appointment or more information. Sometimes, the letter will offer a small gift, such as a road atlas or a free booklet, to prospects who respond to the direct mail letter and agree to a free consultation with the advisor.

**disability income insurance** • insurance to partially replace income of persons unable to work because of sickness or accident

**disability waiver of premium** • a policy rider providing for the automatic payment of premium by the company should the insured become totally physically incapacitated. It extends through the period of disability only, and is usually offered to age 60.

**discount brokers** • act as sales representatives only; they merely facilitate the purchase or sale of stock and offer no advice or other extras to the investor. Generally people who use discount brokers are more knowledgeable investors who can plan and execute their own investment strategies. In return for the no-frills treatment, discount brokers usually charge investors commissions much less than full-service brokers.

**dividend** • the return to the policyowner of part of the premium paid for a policy issued on a participating basis by the insurer. It represents an excess of collected premiums over expenses, actual mortality, and investment experience during a period. Dividends may be used by the policyowner: (1) as cash refunds, (2) to reduce the next premium, (3) to be kept at interest by the insurer, (4) to purchase paid-up life insurance, and (5) to purchase one-year term up to the amount of cash value in the policy.

**dividend accumulations** • a policy dividend option representing the amounts of money resulting from the accumulation of dividends, and interest earned on those dividends in the policy when the policyowner leaves the money with the insurer

**dividend addition** • an amount of paid-up insurance purchased with a policy dividend and added to the face amount of the policy

**domestic insurer** • a term used for an insurance company in the state where it is organized or incorporated under state law

**Do-Not-Call laws** • are designed to eliminate unsolicited telemarketing calls without the consumer's prior consent. One of the major provisions of the regulations is the creation of a national Do-Not-Call (DNC) list. Calling a person on the DNC list may result in a fine of $10,000 or more per violation. In addition, the regulations place limitations on telemarketers.

**dual or split option** • a variation of the own-occupation definition of disability, in which benefits are paid during the first 24 months of disability if the insured is unable to perform the duties of his or her own occupation. After 24 months the definition changes to any occupation for which the insured is reasonable suited by reason of education, training, or experience.

**elimination period** • the number of days after a disability occurs before disability income or long-term care policy benefits become payable

**emergency fund** • one of the basic uses of life insurance to protect the family of the insured against sudden large, unbudgeted expenses after the death of the insured

**emerging markets** • are marketing opportunities that develop from legislative, socio-economic, and demographic changes. Examples would be tax law changes, the economic emergence of women, and the increase in minority populations in the United States.

**Employee Retirement Income Security Act (ERISA)** • is a federal law enacted in 1974 that set minimum standards of information disclosure and fiduciary responsibilities in the establishment, operation, and administration of employee benefit plans, including group life, pension, and health plans

**empty nest** • the experience of middle-years parents when their children move out of the home and become independent. This life event requires an emotional adjustment that can be positive or negative. It can mean more disposal income and free time, but can also be sad as the important role of parent is diminished.

**endowment** • cash from a life insurance policy payable to the policyowner if living, at the policy maturity date, normally equal to the face amount. If death occurs prior to the maturity date, the face amount is paid. Some partial endowments will pay some portion of the face amount at maturity.

**equity-indexed annuity (EIA)** • a product introduced in the 1990s that credits interest in an amount that is linked to a stock or other equity index. One of the most commonly used indices is the Standard & Poor's 500 Composite Stock Price Index (the S&P 500®). The return for the EIA will mirror the rate of return for the index to which it is tied. If the index rises by 10 percent over a designated period (for example, monthly, quarterly, or annually) the contract will be credited for a portion of that increase. Most EIAs set a participation rate on the credited interest, which means the annuity may not be credited with the full rate of return of the index.

**escape close** • is a way to end a conversation with a resistant prospect that leaves the door open. One method for keeping the door open is to ask the prospect if he or she would be interested in receiving mail. Remind the prospect to contact you if he or she should have a change of mind.

**estate planning** • a program designed to accumulate, conserve, and distribute the personal assets of an individual at death

**estate tax** • a tax imposed upon the right of a person to transfer property at death. This tax is imposed not only by the federal government but also by a number of states.

**ethics** • behaving according to the principles of right and wrong that are accepted by your profession. Behaving ethically requires putting the prospect's best interest before your own, and maintaining the highest possible standard in all your business dealings.

**ethnic markets** • immigrant populations of racially, geographically, linguistically, nationally, or culturally diverse backgrounds comprise the fastest-growing demographic of the U.S. population. Larger populations can make these groups viable as target markets.

**evidence of insurability** • any statement of proof of a person's physical condition and/or other factual information required for the person's acceptance for insurance

**excess interest** • the difference between the rate of interest the company guarantees to pay and the interest actually credited on such funds by the company

**executor** • the person or corporation appointed by the court to carry into effect (execute) the provisions of a will. The court will normally appoint the person named in the will of the deceased as executor, provided that the person consents and qualifies. *See* administrator.

**executrix** • a female executor

**experience** • a term used to describe the relationship, usually expressed as a percent or ratio of premium to claims for a plan, coverage, or benefits for a stated period

**extended term insurance** • a nonforfeiture value of a permanent life policy providing term insurance equaling the face value for the period of time into the future that the existing cash value of the policy will purchase as a net single premium at the attained age of the insured

**extra frills package** • a different, better, or higher level of service package that includes other ancillary services and frills. The purpose of the extra frills is to make every contact an opportunity to market.

**facility care** • benefits for long-term care provided in a nursing home or other settings such as an assisted-living facility, as opposed to home care

**fact finding** • gathering of all relevant prospect information regarding financial resources and obligations, personal information, needs, concerns and goals, and personal values, attitudes, and expectations in order to determine financial strategies to meet personal and financial goals

**family income policy** • a life insurance policy combining ordinary life and decreasing term insurance. The beneficiary receives income payments to the end of a specified period if the insured dies prior to the end of the stated period plus the face amount of the policy. The face amount is paid at either the beginning or end of the income period.

**family policy** • a life insurance policy providing insurance on all or several family members in one contract, generally whole life insurance on the principal insured and smaller amounts of term insurance on the spouse and children, including those born after the policy is issued

**feature/benefit** • features are characteristics of the product itself, a fact about the product. Features are descriptive, and are not given values. A benefit is what the prospect gets from the feature, what the product does for the prospect, and why he or she wants it. Benefits are value-laden and subjective. They are features that are wanted by that individual.

**federal estate tax** • a tax imposed upon the right of a person to transfer property at death

**feeling-finding** • gathering relevant prospect information regarding the personal values, attitudes, and expectations that are behind a prospect's financial resources and obligations, needs, concerns and goals, and in order to determine financial strategies to meet personal and financial goals

**FICA** • taxes imposed under the Federal Insurance Contributions Act. All the benefits of the Social Security program and Part A of Medicare are financed through a system of payroll and self-employment taxes paid by all workers covered under these programs. The tax for each eligible employee is shared fifty-fifty by the worker and the employer. For self-employed persons, the tax is the combined rate for employers and employees.

**FIFO/LIFO** • First In, First Out and Last In, First Out represent the cost recovery rules, or the methods for determining cost basis that are used to determine gain upon disposing of an asset. First In represents one's investment or cost basis, and Last In represents profit or gains. Life insurance is taxed on a FIFO basis (principal withdrawn first), and annuities are taxed on a LIFO basis (gains withdrawn first).

**final expenses** • the financial costs related to dying. Typically included are funeral expenses, debts, medical expenses, taxes, administrative expenses, and so on.

**financial planning** • must consider all aspects of the client's financial position, which include the client's total financial needs and objectives, and develop strategies for fulfilling those needs and objectives. It is very similar to the total needs analysis view of life insurance planning. This approach sees the personal and financial situation as an integrated whole, with each part potentially having an impact on any other. It encompasses all the personal and financial situations of clients to the extent that they can be uncovered, clarified, and addressed.

**financial planning process** • specifies six steps to the process: (1) establish financial goals, (2) gather relevant data, (3) analyze the data, (4) develop a plan for achieving goals, (5) implement the plan, and (6) monitor the plan

**financial planning pyramid** • uses four levels: wealth foundation, wealth accumulation, wealth preservation, and wealth distribution. The pyramid in its entirety represents an integrated and comprehensive financial plan.

**FINRA** • the Financial Industry Regulatory Authority  formerly called the National Association of Securities Dealers (NASD). Variable products are securities products and require the advisor to have registration with FINRA.

**fixed amount option** • a life insurance settlement option under which the insurer pays the beneficiary the policy proceeds plus interest in a series of installment payments for as long as the money lasts. Also referred to as the fixed payment option.

**fixed annuity** • provide tax-deferred growth. When annuitized, a fixed annuity provides a guaranteed income for life of the annuitant at little risk to the owner. During the accumulation period, the insurer pays interest at a current rate that may fluctuate with changes in the insurer's investment experience. However, the interest rate will not fall below a guaranteed rate specified in the contract. During the payout period, the interest used to calculate annuity payments will be set by the insurer, but it will be no less than a minimum annuitization interest rate stated in the contract.

**fixed period option** • a life insurance settlement option under which the insurer pays the beneficiary the policy proceeds plus interest in a series of installment payments for a specified length of time

**401(k) plan** • a salary reduction qualified retirement plan that allows employees to contribute a portion of their salaries on a pre-tax and tax-deferred basis

**403(b) plan** • tax favored vehicles for deferring compensation exclusively for employees of public schools or nonprofit organizations exempt from taxes under IRC (Internal Revenue Code) sections 501(c)(3) or 403(b). Also called Tax Sheltered Annuities (TSA)

**front-loaded policy** • found in earlier universal life insurance policies where most of the expense charges are deductions from each premium payment that may continue throughout the premium payment period. In a back-loaded policy, the expense charges are usually applied for a stated number of years and will be charged to the policy for a surrender occurring before that time period expires.

**fully insured** • an insured status under Social Security requiring one of the following: (1) 40 quarters of coverage, or (2) credit for at least as many quarters of coverage as there are years since 1950 (or after the year in which age 21 is reached) and before the year in which the person dies, becomes disabled, or reaches age 62, whichever occurs first

**full retirement age** • the age at which a worker can retire under Social Security and receive non-reduced benefits equal to his or her primary insurance amount (PIA)

**future increase option** • a disability insurance rider that provides guaranteed physical insurability without evidence of insurability. The insured must still qualify for benefit increases based on earned income.

**general market** • also called the shotgun approach to marketing, this is an undifferentiated approach, meaning anyone and everyone is a prospect. Boundaries are determined by licensing, geographic, and other practical limitations.

**geographic variables** • segment a market by using political divisions such as states, counties, cities, boroughs, and so on, or by territories delineated by neighborhoods, regions, and miles

**gift tax** • a tax imposed on the donor on transfers of property by gift during the donor's lifetime

**graded premium life** • usually has a series of increasing premium levels over 5, 10, or 20 years. At the end of the period of graded premiums, the policyowner pays the ultimate, level premium amount until age 100.

**group presentations** • a prospecting method in which the advisor educates target market constituents about a topic in which he or she is an expert. It is different than a seminar in that, in most cases, it is not appropriate to give a sales pitch.

**guaranteed insurability option** • a provision or rider to a policy allowing the purchase of additional insurance at specified future dates at attained age without evidence of insurability

**guaranteed renewable** • a life or health policy issued with the promise that it may be continued beyond the current contract period by the insured with the future payment of premiums when due. The premium may be raised on a class basis.

**guardian** • one appointed by the court to administer the estate of a minor. Also a person named to represent the interest of minor children, or disabled or incapacitated individuals.

**health care proxy** • a signed and witnessed legal document that names an individual to make medical decisions about the signee's care. It goes into effect when the person is no longer able to make health care decisions. HIPAA (Health Insurance Portability and Accountability Act) is federal legislation for the primary purpose of making medical insurance more available and protecting privacy rights of patients. HIPAA also spells out the requirements for the tax-preferred status of long-term care insurance policies.

**Health Insurance Portability and Accountability Act (HIPAA)** • federal legislation, passed in 1996, that reforms the health care system through numerous provisions. One of the act's purposes is to make insurance more available, particularly when an employed person changes jobs or becomes unemployed.

**home health care** • care that takes place where the care recipient resides and encompasses virtually any home environment outside of a nursing home

**hospice care** • health care facility providing medical care and support services such as counseling to terminally ill persons and their families

**human life value** • the capitalized value of an individual's earning ability into the future. The present value of that portion of a person's estimated future earnings that will be used to support dependents.

**IMSA** • Insurance Marketplace Standards Association. A voluntary organization of life insurance companies seeking to promote ethical marketplace conduct. Adoption and implementation of IMSA's Principles of Ethical Marketplace Conduct and the Code of Life Insurance Ethical Market Conduct is required for membership.

**incidents of ownership** • elements of ownership or any degree of control over a life insurance policy that would cause it to be included in the estate of the insured

**incontestable clause** • a policy provision preventing the insurance company from declaring the contract invalid after a certain date, usually two years, as established by the individual states.

**increasing term insurance** • a type of term life insurance in which the face amount increases during the term of the coverage

**indemnity basis** • benefits of an insurance contract paid in an amount approximating or equal to the amount lost, no more no less. In long-term care insurance, these policies pay the maximum daily benefit if care is provided, regardless of the actual charges.

**individual retirement account (IRA)** • a popular tax-deferred, individual retirement plan that can be established by anyone with earned income

**inheritance tax** • a tax levied on the right of the heirs to receive property from a deceased person, measured by the share passing to each beneficiary, and typically levied at the state jurisdiction level

**instrumental activities of daily living (IADLs)** • activities that deal with one's ability to function cognitively, such as preparing meals, shopping, cleaning, managing money, and taking medications

**insurable interest** • the condition that must exist at issue of a life insurance policy calling for the person applying for the insurance and the person who is to receive the policy benefits to share a common insurable interest in the potential loss. These are persons who would suffer an emotional or financial loss in the event of the death of the insured.

**insurance** • a contractual arrangement in which a customer pays a specified sum (the insurance premium) in return for which the insurer will pay compensation if specific conditions or events affect the customer. Generally it is a formal social device for reducing the individual's risk of losses by spreading the risk over a group of people.

**insurance planning** • the process of examining all of the client's needs, comparing needs with means, and selling, where appropriate, the types of policies and the amounts of insurance that best suit the client's purposes

**insurance commissioner** • the state official who enforces the state government's regulations and codes governing the operations of both companies and agents licensed to do business in the jurisdiction

**insurance department** • a government department in each state or territory charged with the supervision and licensing of insurance companies and agents and the general administration of insurance laws or codes

**insurance needs** • universal needs for protection from loss exposure to dying too soon, living too long, loss of income from disability, personal property and liability loss, loss of health, and funds to cover unexpected emergencies and to take advantage of opportunities

**insurance trust** • a trust composed partly or wholly of insurance policies. A common type is an ILIT, an irrevocable life insurance trust, designed to keep a life insurance policy out of the estate of the insured.

**insured** • the person whose life is protected by the insurance policy and upon whose life the death benefit is predicated

**insurer** • the party of the insurance contract promising to pay the losses and benefits. It is a term used to refer to the company providing insurance to the public.

**integrated planning approach** • making recommendations for a product within the context of the prospect's overall financial situation and needs.

**interest sensitive whole life** • a policy that has many of the guarantees found in traditional whole life including a guaranteed death benefit and a minimum guaranteed-interest crediting rate. When mortality and expense charges are guaranteed, the policy is often referred to as interest-sensitive whole life because excess interest (credited interest minus guaranteed interest) credited to the cash value becomes the only non-guaranteed element in the contract.

**intermediate care** • medical services that may be available or provided two to four days a week in a nursing home, an intermediate care unit of a nursing home, or at home

**intestacy** • the situation of dying without a will (intestate) in which the state assumes that the deceased had decided to have property disposed of under the laws of dissent and distribution. These are statutory ways of handling real property such as land and buildings (dissent laws) and personal property (distribution laws). The laws of intestacy differ by state.

**irrevocable beneficiary** • the beneficiary designation in a policy that cannot be changed without the beneficiary's permission, or at the death of the beneficiary

**joint life insurance** • insurance on two or more persons, the benefits of which are payable on the first death

**joint and survivor life insurance** • insurance on two or more persons, the benefits of which are payable on the second death

**joint tenancy** • the undivided ownership of property by two or more people in such a manner that upon the death of one the survivor(s) takes the entire property

**juvenile insurance** • insurance on the life of a child applied for and issued to the person(s) having an insurable interest in the child

**Keogh (HR10) Account** • an account to which a self-employed person can make annual tax-deductible contributions of the lesser of 25 percent of income or $30,000

**key person insurance** • insurance designed to protect a business firm against the loss of business income resulting from the death or disability of an employee who is important to the company's operation. The business applies for, owns, pays the premium, and is the beneficiary of the insurance policy. The premium is not a deductible business expense.

**lapse ratio** • the ratio of the number of insurance policies lapsed without value or surrendered for cash during a year to those in force at the beginning of the year

**lapsed policy** • a policy terminated by a company for nonpayment of premiums within the time required. Lapsing is sometimes limited to a termination occurring before the policy has a cash or other surrender value to pay the premium.

**lapse rate** • the probability that a policy in force at the start of a policy year will lapse by the end of the year

**law of large numbers** • the theory of probability that is the basis of insurance. The larger the number of risks or exposure, the more closely will the actual results obtained approach the probable results expected from an infinite number of exposures.

**level premium** • a rating structure designed to keep the premium costs the same throughout the life of the policy

**level term insurance** • term insurance with a constant face value from the date of issue to the date of expiration

**life-cycle marketing** • operates on two generalizations: (1) from birth to death, people experience common life events that affect their insurance and other financial needs, and (2) even in today's modern society, these life events still tend to occur more prominently among people in certain age ranges, or life-cycle market segments

**life-cycle market segments** • organizes life into five different segments of age, which are marked by some common events. This provides a framework to market to people who are generally experiencing similar characteristics, needs, and problems.

**life events** • are important occurrences, such as graduating from college, that often result in substantial changes in people's lives. They are important to marketing financial products and services for two reasons. First, many life events inherently create or increase a prospect's need and/or ability to pay for insurance and/or other financial products. Second, life events serve as a trigger that raises a prospect's awareness of the resulting financial needs or increases his or her interest in meeting them.

**life expectancy** • the average number of years of life remaining for a group of persons of a given age according to a particular mortality table

**life income option** • a life insurance settlement option under which the insurer uses the policy proceeds and interest to pay the beneficiary a series of payments for as long as the beneficiary shall live

**life insurance** • the scientifically calculated pooling, growth, and distribution of money to satisfy two objectives: (1) paying benefits to survivors of someone who dies while covered, and (2) providing distribution of benefits by lump sum or with guaranteed lifetime payments

**life settlement** • is a transaction of selling an existing life insurance policy by its owner to a third party. In exchange for a cash settlement, the policyowner transfers ownership and all other rights of the policy to that third party to obtain a sum of money that exceeds the policy's cash value. The new owner keeps the policy in force by making subsequent premium payments, and collects the proceeds at the policy's maturity.

**limited partnership** • are business ventures that attract investors willing to take some risk, but who do not want to be actively involved in the venture. In other words, the investors want to be limited partners. A general partner is the promoter or sponsor of the organization who manages the partnership and is fully liable for its debts. The limited partners (typically investors) have limited liability to the extent of their investments. The limited partners contribute capital as passive investors, and the general partner provides management talent and assumes liability for the obligations of the partnership.

**limited payment life insurance** • ordinary life insurance having premiums scheduled for a specified number of years or until a specified age. Examples would be 10- or 20-pay life, single premium, or life payable to age 65.

**liquidity** • how easily the investor can liquidate an investment. Investments with surrender penalties, or those such as real estate which may be difficult to sell, are considered illiquid to some degree. If an investment is illiquid, the investor should expect a higher return than returns from a more liquid investment with similar risk.

**living benefits of life insurance** • includes the cash value feature, which can be used during a lifetime to provide funds for income, education, or retirement funds through loans, withdrawals, or surrender

**living trust** • a trust generally established as a way to avoid both the cost and the public nature of probate. By transferring ownership of property to the living trust, one can avoid the costs, time delay, and public record aspects of probate.

**living will** • a legal document that describes the types of medical treatment an individual wishes to receive and chooses not to receive. The purpose of a living will is to let others know of your medical wishes when you are terminally ill and in a vegetative state or unable to communicate.

**loan interest** • the rate of interest that the borrower must pay on the loan as specified in the policy. If the interest is not paid, it will be added to the policy loan.

**loan value** • the largest amount that can be borrowed by the policyowner on the security of the cash value of the policy without surrendering the contract

**long-term care** • the continuum of broad-ranged maintenance and health services to the chronically ill or the mentally or physically disabled. Services may be provided on an inpatient (rehabilitation facility, nursing home, psychiatric hospital), outpatient, or at-home basis.

**long-term care insurance** • the insurance product designed to cover the costs of long-term care expenses, including care at home, adult day-care, assisted-living or nursing home facilities providing custodial, intermediate, or skilled-nursing care

**long-term disability income insurance** • benefit plan that replaces earned income lost through the inability to work because of a disability caused by an accident or illness

**marital deduction** • permits a tax deduction of 100 percent of property passing to a spouse either by gift or at death. To qualify, the spouse must have sole power of control during life or at death. This allows the estate of one spouse to pass to the other completely free of federal estate taxation.

**marketing** • the process of identifying needs that people have, clarifying those needs, and creating and supplying the products and services appropriate to satisfy those needs

**marketing funnel** • A marketing funnel, or marketing pipeline, is used to calculate the activity goals needed to achieve your income goal based on first year compensation

**market segments** • a potential target market. There are generally four types of segmentation variables that marketing experts use to divide a market: geographic, demographic, psychographic, and behavioristic.

**mature-adult market segment** • includes those people ages 59 to 75 who are generally entering or in retirement. They typically seek safety and security in investments, have greater concerns about health care, and have more time to do what they prefer.

**maximum daily benefit (MDB)**—the maximum level of benefits per day that the client purchases, up to the maximum amount the company provides. Typically, benefits are sold in increments of $10 per day up to $200–$300 per day.

**Medicaid** • a government insurance program for persons of any age who have insufficient income and resources to pay for their own health care. It is state administered and financed by both the state and the federal government through the Social Security Administration.

**Medicare** • a federal government insurance plan attached to the Social Security Act in 1965 providing a health insurance program for the aged. It covers hospital benefits under Part A and medical benefits under Part B to persons aged 65 and older. It is designed to cover short-term acute medical conditions rather than long-term chronic conditions that require custodial care.

**Medicare Part A** • part of the Medicare program that provides benefits for expenses incurred in hospitals, skilled-nursing facilities, and hospices

**Medicare Part B** • part of the Medicare program that provides benefits for most medical expenses not covered under Part A

**Medicare Part C** • also known as Medicare Advantage, allows beneficiaries to select HMOs and other alternatives to the traditional Medicare program

**Medicare Part D** • also known as Medicare Prescription Drug Plans, provides for prescription drug coverage

**Medicare SELECT** • a medigap policy that pays benefits for nonemergency services only if care is received from network providers

**Medicare Supplement Insurance (medigap)** • an individual or employer-provided medical expense plan for persons aged 65 or older under which benefits are provided for certain specific expenses not covered under Medicare. These can include a portion of expenses not paid by Medicare because of deductibles, coinsurance, or copayments, and certain expenses excluded by Medicare. It is also referred to as a medigap policy.

**middle–years adult market segment** • includes people ages 38 to 58. They may experience a mid-life type crisis and empty nest as children leave the home. They may have aging parents and dependent children, forming the sandwich generation phenomenon.

**misrepresentation** • presenting an insurance policy as a savings plan, cash accumulation fund, educational savings plan, individual retirement plan, without making it clear that the product is life insurance. Misrepresentation is illegal. Suggesting that a policy has certain features, benefits, values, or guarantees that are not specifically guaranteed in the written contract or failing to reveal limitations or exclusions of the coverage is also misrepresentation.

**modified endowment contract (MEC)** • a life insurance contract that fails to meet the IRC's 7-pay test. Distributions receive less favorable tax treatment than other life insurance contracts. Gains are subject to a premature withdrawal penalty and gains are subject to tax on a LIFO rather than a FIFO basis.

**modified-premium whole life insurance** • with this type of whole life insurance, the policyowner pays a lower than normal premium for a specified initial period of years. After the initial period, the premium increases to a stated amount that is somewhat higher than usual. The higher premium applies to the life of the policy.

**money market certificates** • treasury bills and high-quality corporate debt instruments. Money market funds are high-yield, safe investments, generally paying more than bank savings accounts. Many money market funds are guaranteed by the FDIC up to published maximums.

**monitoring** • the servicing aspect that separates a financial product from a financial plan. A financial plan is monitored and revised to ensure that it is doing what the client intends for it to do. It is the backbone of client-building service activity. Monitoring should be a part of your basic service package offered to everyone who owns a product.

**mortality** • the actuarially expected rate of death of people by age and category. Select mortality reflects mortality of recently selected lives evaluated as good risks. Ultimate mortality reflects the mortality of those lives expected after the effects of underwriting selection has worn off over time.

**mortality, interest, expense** • these factors represent the main variables that determine a life insurance policy premium, and ultimately the performance of the life insurance product over its lifetime. Actuarial assumptions about these factors are made in designing a product. As time passes, actual experience will determine if the product performs as projected.

**mortality table** • a statistical table showing the probable death rate at each age, usually expressed as so many per thousand people. Used to determine longevity and the probability of living or dying at each age, and consequently to determine the premium rate.

**mortgage or debenture bonds** • are secured by a mortgage on property owned by the issuer; debentures are secured only by the credit of the issuing organization. Debentures issued by large, secure organizations carry lower risk (for example, all governmental bonds are debentures).

**mortgage insurance** • insurance purchased to protect the homeowner's family should the breadwinner(s) die before the mortgage is retired. Customarily the benefit is used to pay the outstanding sum owed. When obtaining a mortgage, this insurance refers to insurance for the lender in the event the borrower dies with an outstanding mortgage.

**mortgage redemption insurance** • a type of decreasing term insurance that covers the life of the mortgagee. Should this person die during the loan period, the policy proceeds will pay the approximate balance of the mortgage loan. Some policies are designed to target this through the loan's interest rate and equity increase.

**municipal bonds** • also known as munis, are issued by states, cities, and counties, or their agencies (the municipal issuer) to raise funds. The most attractive feature of municipal bonds is that interest earnings are exempt from federal taxes. If the municipality is located in the same state as the owner, the interest may be exempt from state and local taxes, also. Municipal bond interest rates are normally less than corporate bonds; however, the tax-exempt status of municipal bonds makes their tax-equivalent yield (net yield after taxes) comparable to other bonds the tax advantage.

**mutual fund** • an incorporated investment company whose business is to manage their investors' money. Investors pool their funds as they buy shares, and the fund's managers make investment decisions about what to buy, how much to buy, when to buy, and when to sell securities. Individual investors benefit when the entire portfolio shows a gain, and they share any losses that occur.

**mutual insurance companies** • insurance companies without capital stock, owned by the policyowners. A portion of surplus earnings may be returned to policyowners as dividends.

**National Association of Insurance Commissioners (NAIC)** • state officials charged with regulating insurance. Although the group has no official power, it has tremendous influence. Its mission is to provide national uniformity in insurance regulations.

**NAIC model regulation** • various insurance regulations promoted by the National Association of Insurance Commissioners intended for adoption by the states to create uniform regulation of insurance in all states. The Model Illustration Regulation, for example, establishes guidelines for companies and advisors regarding the content and presentation of sales illustrations.

**NAIFA (National Association of Insurance and Financial Advisors)** • the professional organization designed to support the efforts and interests of insurance and financial advisors. LUTC is jointly sponsored by NAIFA, with whom the American College grants the LUTCF designation.

**natural markets** • groups of people or businesses in which an advisor has easy access for reasons other than just direct personal knowledge or acquaintance

**nests** • groups of prospects to whom you have access and/or affinity, and are therefore easier for you to contact and establish rapport.

**net amount at risk** • the difference between the face amount of the insurance contract and the reserve

**net cash value** • an amount equal to the cash surrender value of a life insurance policy plus any paid-up additions minus any existing indebtedness, including accrued interest

**networking** • the process of ongoing communication and sharing of ideas and prospect names with others whose work does not compete with yours, but whose clients might also be eligible to become your clients. Your clients may need their products, too.

**nominator** • a person who knows you favorably and recommends you. The prospect is more likely to meet with the advisor if the advisor has been recommended by someone the prospect knows and trusts.

**noncancelable guaranteed renewable policy** • an individual policy that the insured person has the right to continue in force until a specified age, such as 65, by the timely payment of premiums. During this period, the insurer has no right to unilaterally make any changes in any provision of the policy while it is in force, including the premium amount.

**nonforfeiture options** • contractual policy provisions that allow the policyowner to receive the policy's cash value in the event that the policy is terminated for any reason other than the death of the insured. The options include lump-sum payment, extended term insurance, and reduced paid-up insurance.

**nonparticipating insurance** • insurance that pays no dividends. Usually associated with the insurance contracts offered by stock insurance companies.

**NOW accounts** • Negotiable Order of Withdrawal accounts with the best features of savings accounts (interest and liquidity), and the best feature of checking accounts (check writing). Funds are deposited in the account and begin to earn interest. When the customer writes a check, funds are automatically transferred to the checking account to cover the check.

**OASHDI** • the old age, survivors, disability and health insurance program of the federal government. This program consists of Social Security and Medicare.

**old-age adult market segment** • includes individuals aged 76 and older. These people must deal increasingly with the death of their loved ones and ultimately themselves. The need for nursing home care becomes a real concern as health issues become more commonplace. They may wish to leave a legacy for the next generations.

**objectives of service** •   monitoring and servicing. This will accomplish four things: facilitate customer retention, invite results in repeat sales to customers, earn ongoing referrals to new prospects, and lower expenses

**operation of law** • one method for property passing at the death of the owner. A typical example is a home owned jointly (with right of survivorship) by a husband and a wife. At the death of the first spouse, the surviving spouse gains full ownership of the jointly held property.

**optional renewable policy** • a health insurance contract that the insurer has the right to terminate at any policy anniversary or, in some instances, at any premium date

**ordinary life insurance** • the most common form of basic permanent life insurance in which coverage and premiums are paid to age 100. The policy is designed to build cash values equaling the face amount at age 100.

**paid-up additions** • units of single premium insurance purchased with dividends of participating policies. One of the customary dividend options

**paid-up insurance** • insurance on which all required premiums have been paid. The term is frequently used to mean the reduced paid-up insurance available as a nonforfeiture option, but can be applied to any policy meeting the requirement.

**partial disability** • the result of an illness or injury which prevents an insured from performing one or more of the functions of his or her regular job

**participating insurance** • Insurance on which dividends may be payable to policyowners as determined by the company's board of directors

**payor benefit** • an optional benefit as a rider offered by most companies and added to juvenile policies for an additional premium providing for the waiving of premiums during total and permanent disability of the premium payor or in the event of the payor's death. The waived period extends to future premiums due between the date of benefit until the covered juvenile reaches a stated age, usually 20 or 25. At that time the juvenile will resume the premium payments.

**payout or annuity phase** • during which the annuity contract is annuitized and the insurer makes periodic annuity payments to the annuitant. The amount of the payments depends on the value of the annuity, the age and gender of the annuitant (used to estimate the mortality experience), and the interest rate used by the insurer. Some annuities guarantee payments for a fixed period (for example, 10 years) while others guarantee payments for the life of the annuitant.

**payroll deduction insurance** • employer authorized deductions from salary earnings of an employee in amounts to cover the premium of individual life or disability income insurance policies. The employer forwards the premium to the company on a billing statement.

**pension plan** • an employer-sponsored system for the payment of annuities or pensions to qualified individuals during retirement, frequently using insurance

**period certain** • the specified time during which the insurer unconditionally guarantees that benefit payments will continue under a settlement option or annuity

**permanent life insurance** • life insurance designed to be in force for the whole of a person's life. Refers to all insurance except term.

**persistency** • the degree to which the life insurance business an advisor writes stays on the books through a specified period of time (usually measured at 13 months, 2 years, and other fixed time periods).

**personal brochure** • is typically a one-page (usually front and back) document or tri-fold that introduces the advisor. Treat it as the prospect's first impression of you. It should impress, inform, and create interest.

**personal interaction** • requires mastering the art of listening and the art of small talk and showing a genuine interest in others. It also marshals your ability to ask meaningful but innocuous questions that help you qualify a prospect. It is subtle and natural and avoids the appearance of shameless personal marketing. This prospecting method works best in gatherings and events attended by a particular target market, especially if the meetings are informal.

**personal observation** • a prospecting method where the advisor pays attention to changes and events in his or her surroundings to observe situations that may call for a solution using a product the advisor offers

**personal recommendations** • are the referrals an advisor receives from clients, friends, and family, and are the dominant prospecting method among most advisors

**pivoting approach** • to transition from one product to another using previously shared information to ask a question relevant to another product.

The pivoting approach can be used with almost any type of financial product sale to pivot to DI products.

**policy date** • the effective date of the policy, which controls the premium due date and contract anniversaries. This may be different than the date of issue.

**policy dividend** • a refund of part of the premium on a participating life insurance policy reflecting the difference between the premium charged and actual experience

**policy loan** • a loan made by a life insurance company from its general funds to a policyowner on the security of the cash value of a policy

**policy reserves** • the measure of the funds that a life insurance company holds specifically for fulfillment of its policy obligations. Reserves are required by law to be so calculated that together with future premium payments and anticipated interest earnings they will enable the company to pay all future claims.

**policyowner** • one who owns an insurance policy. It need not be the insured. Also referred to as policyholder.

**policy summary** • required to be delivered with the policy. It provides the main features of the issued policy such as cash values, (guaranteed and non-guaranteed) premium, the guaranteed death benefit, and the policy's loan interest rate

**pool** • a group of reinsurers or insurers organizing to underwrite a particular risk by sharing premiums, losses, and expenses

**portfolio rate** • the overall rate of return on the insurer's entire portfolio. This rate represents the aggregate rate earned on investments made over many years, and tends to lag behind the changes in current or new money rates.

**positioning statement** • consists of one short paragraph. It is a private declaration of how you want your target market to perceive you, and not necessarily how members do right now. The statement should guide all that you do and is the basis for any value proposition you make to prospects in your target market.

**power of attorney** • is a document legally signed by one person authorizing another person to act on behalf of the signer. There are two types of powers of attorney, a general power and a durable power.

**preapproach** • the first step toward making a sale is to identify the prospect and plan how you will contact him or her for an appointment. If you want a prospect to be receptive to your approach, you must stimulate his or her interest.

**preapproach letter** • is a letter or postcard mailed (or e-mailed) to a prospect with the goal of introducing the advisor and arousing the prospect's interest in meeting with the advisor

**preconditioning** • the process of establishing the interest of the prospect to expect and be receptive to the advisor's request for an appointment

**present value** • the amount of money that must be invested on a certain day in order to accumulate at a specified rate of interest a specified amount at a later date

**prestige building** • is your public relations campaign to position your personal brand favorably in your target markets

**primary beneficiary** • the person(s) who have first rights to receive the policy benefits when the benefits of the insurance policy become payable

**Primary Insurance Amount (PIA)** • the amount a worker will receive under Social Security if he or she retires at full retirement age or becomes disabled. It is the amount on which all other Social Security income benefits are based.

**probate** • the process of proving the validity of a will in court, and carrying out its provisions under the guidance of the court

**proceeds** • the face value of the policy and any increments payable at maturity, on death, or on surrender, less any indebtedness

**profit-sharing plan** • a type of defined-contribution plan wherein the employer agrees to contribute part of the company's profits for the benefit of its employees. Typically, the contributions will be held in a trust fund for distribution at death, disability, or retirement.

**professionalism** • skillful and conscientious engagement in a field that requires (1) specialized knowledge not generally understood by the public, (2) a threshold entrance exam requirement, (3) a sense of altruism, and (4) a code of ethics.

**profit-sharing plan** • a defined-contribution plan with a separate account for each employee that is held in trust for distribution at death, disability, or retirement. The employer may contribute a portion of company profits for benefit of employees. The investment risk rests with the employee.

**prospect** • the potential buyer who has been identified by the advisor

**prospecting** • the continuous activity of exploring for new people to meet and talk to about the products the advisor sells

**prospecting and sales effectiveness ratios** • are quantitative measurements of an advisor's effectiveness in performing the key sequential prospecting and sales activities as they relate to each other and attaining desired production goals

**prospecting methods** • referrals, direct mail, personal observation, networking, tips clubs, centers of influence, social mobility, cold canvassing, public speaking, and seminars

**psychographic variables** • divide a market by lifestyle and attitudes. These variables include things like leisure activities, values, personality, interests, and hobbies.

**pour-over will** • a short will containing provisions specifying which assets are to be transferred to a living trust. It can also state that any property inadvertently left out of the living trust be brought in at death. The property is then distributed as part of the living trust plan.

**public image** • how people—your target market in particular—perceive you. It is composed of all the characteristics that make you recognizable and memorable. As much as you hope it is your financial expertise that causes people to connect with you, more often it is your personal traits and/or the reputation of your character that attracts people to you.

**purpose of delivery** • is an important step in building laying the foundation for future service contacts with a new client. A well-executed policy product policy or contract delivery can create a successful client relationship because it can  (1) reinforce the sale by reemphasizing the objectives of the policy purchase, (2) help the advisor gain the new client's trust and sets expectations for future service and repeat sale, and (3) offer another opportunity to obtain referred leads.

**qualified retirement plans** • retirement plans that are qualified under law to avoid or postpone taxes until the beneficiary retires and begins to take benefits, possibly in a lower tax bracket

**qualified prospect** • a person who has a need for life insurance, an ability to pay, is insurable, and is approachable

**qualifying prospects** • collecting information regarding facts and feelings about key financial issues and situations throughout the entire sales/planning process. We learn what will move the prospect from a possible (and eligible) buyer to a probable buyer and then to an eager buyer, what the prospect is likely to buy, and when and why he or she will buy it.

**readjustment income period** • time period in which a family needs financial support closely equivalent to the family's share of the producer's earnings at the time of his or her death. The length of the readjustment period depends largely on the magnitude of the changes the family will have to make to their living standards.

**rebating** • an insurance sales practice prohibited in most of the United States. In rebating, the advisor offers the prospect a special inducement to purchase a policy, usually as a share of the advisor's commission.

**reduced paid-up insurance** • a form of insurance available as a nonforfeiture option, providing for continuation of the original insurance plan, but for a reduced face amount as determined by the cash value in the policy

**reentry term** • a form of renewable term life insurance under which one rate schedule is used if the insured can prove continued insurability at favorable rates, and a higher schedule if the insured cannot or will not provide continued insurability

**referred lead** • a person who may be interested in the products the advisor sells who has been suggested as a prospect by a present policyowner.

**reimbursement basis** • the method of paying long-term care insurance benefits that reimburses the insured for actual expenses incurred up to a specified policy limit

**renewable term insurance** • term insurance providing the right to renew at the end of the term for another term or terms, without evidence of insurability. The premium rates normally increase at each renewal as the age of the insured increases.

**renewal commissions** • those commissions paid to an advisor for a certain number of years after the first year. It is paid only on policies that stay in force and is usually much lower than the first year commission.

**replacement** • the substitution of one insurance contract for another
**representations** • any statement made before, during, or after a sales interview that materially represents the policy or plan of insurance offered. From the applicant's side, it is any statement made to the best of the knowledge and belief of that person, so it does not have to be true.

**reserve** • the money set aside by a company to fulfill future obligations

**residual disability** • a provision for the replacement of lost earnings due to a less-than-total disability. The benefit is based on the person's loss of earnings (duties) rather than his or her physical condition. This type of provision is often used after a total disability, during a period of recovery.

**respite care** • a form of long-term care provided by an informal or formal caregiver to relieve a primary caregiver from the physical and emotional stress of caring for a family member over a long period of time and/or allowing the primary caregiver to have some personal time

**retention limit** • the net amount of risk retained by an insurance company for its own account, or that of specified others, and not reinsured

**revocable beneficiary** • the named beneficiary whose rights in a policy are subject to the policyowner's right to revoke or change the designation, and surrender or make loans against the cash value

**revocable living trust** • is generally established as a way to avoid both the cost and the public nature of probate. By transferring ownership of all you own to the living trust, you avoid the costs, the time lag, and the public record aspects of probate.

**rider** • an additional provision added to a policy, usually at issue, and for additional premium, to enhance or modify the benefits. These riders include, among others, waiver-of-premium, AD&D, spouse insurance, children's insurance, guaranteed insurability, and so on.

**right of contract** • property passes at death by contract. The prime example of this is life insurance that is paid directly to a named beneficiary. Other examples include annuities, Individual Retirement Accounts (IRA), and qualified retirement plans such as a 401(k).

**risk** • the person insured in the case of life insurance. More generally it is considered the chance of loss.

**risk tolerance** • is the degree of a client's willingness or reluctance to accept the risk that his investment may decline in value and that the premium may increase over time

**risk classification** • the process by which a company decides how its premium rates for life insurance should differ according to the risk characteristics of individuals insured (age, occupation, sex, state of health), and then applies the resulting rules to the individual applications it receives

**Roth IRA** • a type of individual retirement account having the same contribution limits of a traditional IRA, but contributions are made with after-tax dollars in exchange for tax-free withdrawals and the absence of minimum distribution rules at age 70½

**Rule of 72** • a mathematical rule based on the number 72 that will allow the calculation of a variety of factors regarding the value of money over time in a general fashion. For instance, dividing 72 by an assumed rate of inflation will determine the number of years it takes to reduce the value of a fixed amount of money to half its present value. (For example, 72 divided by an assumed inflation rate of 8 percent will halve the value of today's dollar in nine years.) It is also commonly used to estimate the time it takes for a principal sum to double.

**salary continuation** • when an employee's salary is continued at retirement, at death, or at disability, and the employee is not taxed on the income until it is received. Similar to deferred compensation. Also refers to a sick-leave plan, an uninsured arrangement to replace lost income for a limited period of time often starting on the first day of disability.

**salary deduction** • a method of paying individual insurance premiums by the employees of one employer. An agreement between the employee and the employer stipulates the amount deducted each pay period to pay the insurance premiums. The employer in turn signs a master contract with the insurer stating that all such premium payments by these employees will be forwarded to the company.

**sales ratios** • measurements of the relationship between prospecting activity and results. This is a technique for measuring effectiveness and planning to accomplish sales goals. For example, you could measure closing effectiveness by dividing the number of sales appointments by the number of sales.

**sandwich generation** • persons generally in the middle-years segment (ages 38 to 58) who are at the same time caring for children as well as aging parents or relatives

**section 1035 exchange** • exchanging an existing policy for a new one in accordance with the IRC guidelines of Section 1035. No gain is attributed on the exchange. The adjusted basis of the old policy is carried over to the new one. Only the newly added premium will be measured for MEC status. A section 1035 exchange is allowed only when transferring cash values from an annuity to an annuity, life insurance to life insurance, or life insurance to an annuity contract.

**segmentation** • organizing life into five different age groups marked by common events. This provides a framework to market to people who are generally experiencing similar characteristics, needs, and problems.

**self-insurance** • setting aside of funds by an individual or organization to meet his or its losses, and accumulation of a fund to absorb fluctuations in the amount of losses being charged against the funds set aside or accumulated.

**selling** • to give up something (property) to another in exchange for something of value (money). This is a transactional view. Client-focused selling has more to do with helping people get what they want and need through a process of discovery. By developing a relationship the long-term benefits to both parties are served and selling takes a back seat to service.

**selling/planning process** • the 8-step procedure for the advisor to follow from selecting the prospect to completing the sale and servicing the client. It is very similar to the financial planning process.

**seminar** • a prospecting method in which the advisor, alone or as part of a team of advisors, conducts an educational and motivational meeting for a group of people who are interested in a particular topic

**separate account** • an asset account established by a life insurance company separate from other funds, used primarily for pension plans and variable life products. This arrangement permits wider latitude in the choice of investments, particularly in equities.

**service package** • variations in services that can be offered to clients. Some differentiation may take place due to the type of client and the relationship that has developed or is expected to develop with the advisor.

**settlement options** • the several ways outlined in a policy, other than by a lump sum payment in cash, by which a policyowner or beneficiary may choose to have the contract's benefits paid

**settlement options** • ways in which a life insurance proceeds can be taken, typically in cash, under an interest option, under a fixed-period or fixed amount option, or under a life income option

**skilled nursing** • medical care services that may be provided or be available on a 24-hour-per-day basis, including nursing and rehabilitative services that are performed only by or under the supervision of skilled medical personnel and that must be based on doctors' orders

**social insurance offset** • a rider on a disability income policy that pays a fixed benefit in addition to the regular monthly disability benefit if the insured is rejected for Social Security disability benefits

**social mobility** • becoming involved in one's community and becoming known as a person who is willing to work for common community interests. It is a way of building prestige and a good reputation in order to ultimately develop prospects and centers of influence.

**Social Security** • a federal government program, taxed to working citizens, to provide financial security for the general citizenship of the United States

**spousal IRA** • a spouse with earned income contributes to an IRA for a non-employed spouse (or for a spouse earning less than the maximum annual IRA contribution limit)

**standard service package** • the way you handle requests for policy changes and information for anyone in your book of business regardless of their value to your business. Excellent customer service is expected.

**steps of an effective delivery** • involve managing the issuance process, preparing for the delivery, executing the policy or contract review, establishing expectations for an ongoing relationship, and asking for referrals

**stocks** • a way of raising operating capital by selling ownership in a company in the form of stock shares. Investors who buy shares of common stock are owners of the corporation, have voting rights, and may receive dividend payments as shareholders.

**suitability** • is the appropriateness or the proper fit of the characteristics of a product and the needs and goals of a prospect. Fact finding will help determine the client's risk tolerance. Some clients will accept far more risk in their insurance portfolio than others. Determining needs, goals, risk tolerances, and time horizons provide the advisor with information necessary to make a product recommendation.

**supplementary contract** • an agreement between a life insurance company and a policyowner or beneficiary by which the company retains the cash sum payable under an insurance policy and makes payments in accordance with the settlement option chosen

**surplus** • the amount by which an insurance company's assets exceed its liabilities and capital

**surrender charge** • the difference between the cash surrender value of a policy and the reserve held by the company. The charge will be higher in the early years of a policy to cover costs arising from underwriting.

**surrender cost index** • a representation of the annual cost per $1,000 of insurance if the policy is surrendered for its cash value, taking into consideration the sum of the cash value.

**survivorship** • a type of benefit that is contingent upon the survival of one party after the death of another. Joint and survivor benefits in annuities and second-to-die life insurance (survivorship life) policies are examples.

**tangible asset** • include almost anything that has a value in the perception of others, or because the asset is used to produce other goods. As an investment, most tangible assets are highly speculative.

**target market** • an identifiable and accessible group of people or businesses whose members communicate with each other and who have common characteristics and common needs that can be answered by the advisor's products and services

**taxable estate** • is the value of all property or partial interest in property, owned or controlled by the deceased, and reduced by allowable deductions.

These allowable deductions include reasonable funeral expenses, administrative expenses (court costs, attorney/executor fees), claims against the estate, unpaid mortgages, debts, as well as bequests to charities and the surviving spouse.

**taxation of life insurance** • generally any gain received is taxable under FIFO accounting rules. Cash values and dividends grow tax-deferred. Dividends represent return of premium and reduce cost-basis. MEC rules limit premium payments. Excess premiums force LIFO accounting rules. Premiums generally are not tax-deductible for personal insurance; however, some situations allow deductibility of premiums for business purposes.

**tax deferral** • the postponement of the tax that otherwise would have been placed on the investment or its interest earnings. Generally the tax is payable at a future date when the money is constructively received by the owner.

**tax-qualified plan (LTC)** • the type of long-term care insurance contract that meets certain standards of the Health Insurance Portability and Accountability Act for favorable tax treatment

**tax-qualified retirement plan** • retirement plan that qualifies under law to avoid or postpone taxes until such time as the beneficiary retires and begins to take benefits when the taxpayer may be in a lower tax bracket.

**telephone techniques** • methods used to improve your prospecting results, including a pleasant greeting, asking if the prospect has time to speak, creating interest in your call, asking for an appointment, and confirming the appointment

**ten-day free look** • a policy provision notifying purchasers of new insurance that they have ten days after delivery to inspect the policy, and if not satisfied may return it to the agent or company for a full refund of all premiums paid

**term life insurance** • life insurance providing a death benefit for a limited period of time on the life of the insured and expiring without value after the stated period

**time value of money** • the concept that a specific amount of money received or paid at a specific time has a different value, due to interest, than the same amount of money paid or received at a different period of time

**tips club** • one type of networking that meets solely for the regular exchange of information on prospects. Each member of a tips club shares his or her own expertise, business connections, and social contacts with the group.

**total disability** • a health condition that prevents an individual from performing all duties of his or her occupation or any occupation. Definitions differ between companies and social security on what constitutes total disability.

**Traditional IRA** • tax-advantaged retirement plans available to many people with earned income. Under current law, eligible individuals may contribute 100 percent of earned income up to a maximum annual contribution limit.

**transactional selling** • focusing on the immediate sale and fitting the prospect to the product. It is based on the salesperson's power to persuade and closing skills. It creates sales pressure and an adversarial environment.

**transfer of property** • conveyance of property by right of survivorship, right of contract, direct payment, probate, or trust

**trigger** • raises a prospect's awareness of the resulting financial needs or increases his or her interest in meeting them. Sometimes a life event will cause the prospect to begin looking for information and solutions.

**trustee** • the person to whom the legal title to property is conveyed for the benefit of another

**trust** • arrangement by which property is held by a person or corporation (the trustee) for the benefit of others (the beneficiaries). The person who establishes the trust (the grantor) gives the trustee title to the trust assets (the corpus) subject to the terms of the agreement. Trusts can be established during life (inter vivos) or at death by will (testamentary). They can be changeable (revocable) or unchangeable (irrevocable).

**types of investments** • annuities (fixed, variable and equity-indexed), treasury bills and notes, municipal and corporate bonds, a variety of types of stock, mutual funds and unit investment trusts, real estate, and limited partnerships

**twisting** • inducing a policyowner to drop an existing policy (especially one with another company) in order to take a similar policy from the advisor doing the twisting. The act is usually defined as not being in the policyowner's best interests. It may involve fraud and misrepresentation.

**U.S. government bonds** • are considered safe, reasonably attractive long-term investments. As they are viewed as essentially risk-free, government bonds normally yield slightly less interest than high-quality corporate bonds. The interest is taxable at the federal level and exempt from state and local taxes.

**unbundled insurance product** • an insurance product in which the mortality, investment, and expense factors used to calculate premium rates and cash values can be separately identified within the policy. This was first seen with the introduction of the universal life contract.

**universal life insurance (UL)** • a type of permanent life insurance under which the policyowner is allowed to vary the timing and amount of premiums as well as the death benefit. Premiums (less expenses) are credited to the policy account (cash value) from which mortality charges are deducted and to which interest is credited at a varying future rate.

**unrestricted-own-occupation definition** • an individual is unable to perform the substantial and material duties of his or her regular occupation, or the occupation at the time of disability. Even if the insured returns to work in another job while remaining unable to perform his or her own regular occupation at the time the disability occurred, the person is still considered totally disabled for benefit purposes.

**value proposition** • a clear and compelling reason to conduct business with the advisor

**variable annuity** • gives the owner a choice of investment options with the tax-deferred feature all annuities possess. The investment options are very similar to mutual funds but are called subaccounts in the variable annuity.

**variable life insurance (VLI)** • a type of permanent life insurance in which the death benefit and the policy's cash value may vary in relation to the investment experience of the selected fund in which the cash value is invested

**variable universal life (VUL)** • a type of life insurance policy that combines the premium flexibility and design features of universal life insurance and policy-owner-directed investment choices of variable life insurance

**voluntary payroll deduction** • a plan offered to employees under which they may purchase life, health, or property and liability insurance with premiums paid through payroll deduction. The employer does not share in the premium cost. These plans often offer liberalized guaranteed issue, discounts, or liberal simplified underwriting, depending on the size of the group.

**waiver (exclusion endorsement)** • an agreement, attached to the policy and accepted by the insured, to eliminate a specified pre-existing physical condition or specified hazard from coverage under the policy

**waiver of premium provision** • a statement of provision in a life or health insurance policy that the policy will be kept in force by the insurer without payment of further premiums if the insured becomes permanently and totally disabled as defined in the policy

**weblog (blog)** • an online journal that allows for interaction between an advisor and a web audience. Advisors who blog typically will post an article from a financial publication or online news source and give their opinion. Readers can then ask questions and make comments.

**whole life insurance** • another name for ordinary life insurance, referring to premium payment for the whole period of a person's life

**will** • a document prepared by an individual in which instructions are made for the disposition of the property of the estate at death

**women's market** • segment offering significant potential for sales as women gain relative parity with men in the workforce and in financial arenas. Women today are as well-educated, independent, and career-oriented as men, and subsequently are excellent prospects to market to and approach for financial products.

**workers' compensation** • insurance against liability imposed on certain employers to pay benefits and furnish care to injured employees, and to pay benefits to dependents of employees killed in the course of or arising out of their employment

**young-adult market segment** • includes people between the ages of 20 and 37. We examine this segment by grouping them into the following subsegments: singles, dual income with kids, dual income with no kids, and single income with kids.

**zero-day qualification period** • a feature available in some disability polices that allows days of residual (partial) disability to count toward satisfying the elimination period

# *Index*